Pick Up the Pieces

For Luis —

John Corbett

DETROIT

11 April 2019

Pick Up the Pieces

Excursions in Seventies Music

John Corbett

THE UNIVERSITY OF CHICAGO PRESS

Chicago and London

The University of Chicago Press, Chicago 60637
The University of Chicago Press, Ltd., London
Published 2019
Printed in the United States of America

28 27 26 25 24 23 22 21 20 19   1 2 3 4 5

ISBN-13: 978-0-226-60473-2 (cloth)
ISBN-13: 978-0-226-60487-9 (e-book)
DOI: https://doi.org/10.7208/chicago/9780226604879.001.0001

Endpaper art: Jimmy Wright, *Max's Kansas City* (1974), ink on
  paper napkin.

Library of Congress Cataloging-in-Publication Data

Names: Corbett, John, 1963– author.
Title: Pick up the pieces: excursions in Seventies music / John Corbett.
Description: Chicago; London: The University of Chicago Press, 2019. |
    Includes index.
Identifiers: LCCN 2018035642 | ISBN 9780226604732 (cloth: alk. paper) |
    ISBN 9780226604879 (e-book)
Subjects: LCSH: Rock music—1971–1980—History and criticism. |
    Popular music—1971–1980—History and criticism. | LCGFT: Essays.
Classification: LCC ML3534 .C6654 2019 | DDC 781.6409/047—dc23
LC record available at https://lccn.loc.gov/2018035642

♾ This paper meets the requirements of ANSI/NISO Z39.48-1992
(Permanence of Paper).

Contents

Intro 1

1970

The Kinks, "Lola" 15

Edwin Starr, "War" 19

James Brown, "Get Up (I Feel Like Being a) Sex Machine" 25

Black Sabbath, *Paranoid* 33

Captain Beefheart & the Magic Band, *Lick My Decals Off, Baby* 36

The Stooges, *Fun House* 45

The Art Ensemble of Chicago, *Les Stances à Sophie* 50

1971

Joni Mitchell, *Blue* 59

Michael Hurley & Pals, *Armchair Boogie* 64

Harry Nilsson, *Nilsson Schmilsson* 72

Webster Lewis and the Post-Pop Space-Rock Be-Bop Gospel
    Tabernacle Chorus and Orchestra BABY!, *Live at Club 7*;
    Curtis Mayfield, "Move On Up" 75

Genesis, *Nursery Cryme* 78

Derek Bailey, *Solo Guitar* 86

The Rolling Stones, *Sticky Fingers* 91

1972

Lou Reed, *Transformer* 97

Alice Cooper, "School's Out" 108

Yes, *Close to the Edge* 114

The Edgar Winter Group, "Frankenstein";
    Focus, "Hocus Pocus" 121

The O'Jays, *Back Stabbers* 126

Julius Hemphill, *Dogon A.D.* 131

Nick Drake, *Pink Moon* 136

Carla Bley, Paul Haines, *Escalator Over the Hill*;
    Todd Rundgren, *Something/Anything?* 140

1973

Sun Ra, *Space Is the Place* 153

Al Green, *Call Me*;

    Marvin Gaye, *Let's Get It On* 162

Stevie Wonder, "You Are the Sunshine of My Life" 166

Gal Costa, *Índia* 167

Led Zeppelin, *Houses of the Holy* 171

Sly and the Family Stone, *Fresh* 178

1974

Gram Parsons, *Grievous Angels* 187

Average White Band, "Pick Up the Pieces" 193

William DeVaughn, "Be Thankful for What You've Got" 197

The Residents, *Meet the Residents* 200

Brian Eno, *Taking Tiger Mountain (By Strategy)*;

    Dr. Alimantado, "Best Dressed Chicken in Town" 204

Kraftwerk, *Autobahn* 213

Van Morrison, *Veedon Fleece*;

    John Cale, *Paris 1919* 216

Robert Wyatt, *Rock Bottom* 222

Neil Young, *On the Beach* 229

Queen, *Sheer Heart Attack*;

    Sparks, *Kimono My House* 234

1975

Parliament, *Mothership Connection* 245

Van McCoy, "The Hustle" 252

Elton John, "Philadelphia Freedom" 256

Kiss, *Alive!*;

    Electric Light Orchestra, *Face the Music* 263

Bruce Springsteen, *Born to Run* 270

Bob Dylan, *Blood on the Tracks* 273

Patti Smith, *Horses* 279

1976

Boston, "Long Time" 287

Aerosmith, *Rocks* 290

Bootsy Collins, *Stretchin' Out in Bootsy's Rubber Band* 295

Fela and Afrika 70, *Zombie* 300

1977

Richard Hell and the Voidoids, *Blank Generation*;
    Television, *Marquee Moon* 307

Milford Graves, *Bäbi* 313

Fleetwood Mac, *Rumours* 318

Ted Nugent, *Cat Scratch Fever* 325

The Clash, *The Clash* 332

David Bowie, *Low* 340

Suicide, *Suicide* 343

Joe McPhee, *Tenor* 347

Heart, *Little Queen* 350

Pink Floyd, *Animals* 356

1978

Van Halen, *Van Halen* 365

Elvis Costello, *This Year's Model* 373

James "Blood" Ulmer, *Tales of Captain Black* 381

Just What I Needed: A Transatlantic Art-Pop Comedy in Five Acts 391
    Act I: Cheap Trick, *Heaven Tonight*; The Cars, *The Cars* 392
    Act II: Wire, *Chairs Missing* 396
    Act III: *No New York*; Talking Heads, *More Songs about Buildings and Food* 400
    Act IV: XTC, *Go 2* 406
    Act V: Devo, *Q: Are We Not Men? A: We Are Devo!*; Pere Ubu, *The Modern Dance*; MX-80 Sound, *Hard Attack* 411

1979

Forty-One 45s 419

The Fall, *Dragnet* 435

Ramones, "Rock 'n' Roll High School" 441

Ian Dury & the Blockheads, *Do It Yourself* 445

The Police, *Reggatta de Blanc*;
    The Pretenders, *Pretenders* 451

Sugarhill Gang, "Rapper's Delight" 458

The Pop Group, *Y*; The Slits, *Cut* 461

The Raincoats, "Lola" 467

1980

Grace Jones, *Warm Leatherette* 473

Acknowledgments 477

Index 479

Intro

A decade dies a thousand deaths.

For some, the spirit of the nineteen sixties died with Martin Luther King and the Kennedys or Malcolm X, the Munich Olympics or the My Lai Massacre or the Watergate scandal or Nixon's resignation. For those of a less political sensitivity, the end was perhaps signaled sartorially—the exchange of tie-dye for polyester, of miniskirts for hot pants, the rise of the leisure suit and the general widening of collars—or biochemically, in various acts of legislation that outlawed hallucinogenic drugs. There were plenty of gravestones to suggest the passing of a musical era, most obviously the trinity of Jimi Hendrix, Jim Morrison, and Janis Joplin, but also Brian Jones, Duane Allman, Don Drummond, Baby Huey, Tammi Terrell, John Coltrane, and Albert Ayler. Depending on who you were and what you were into, the sixties might have hung in there, baby, or died with four students in Ohio. Wherever you place the skull and crossbones, passage into the seventies is most often framed as a departure from idealism, a loss of innocence, and, for better or worse, the encroachment of corporate enterprise into every pore of human endeavor—including music.

For my family, the nineteen sixties died in the summer of 1969. We were decamped in a rustic house in the hills on the other side of the bay from San Francisco, a place called Orinda Heights, having made an epic two-week cross-country drive. Our station wagon was without an air conditioner as we dipped from Cleveland all the way south and then back up to northern California. My one-year-old sister, Jill, screamed nonstop with an ear infection. The backs of my legs stuck to the vinyl upholstery, and the seat belt buckle burned my thigh. The journey seemed to take forever. And it was glorious.

I only remember one song from the trip, Bob Dylan's "Lay Lady Lay," which issued continuously from the car's AM radio. It couldn't play enough times for my parents, who nudged each other every time it came on. I had no idea why. But there were snake pits in Arizona and reptile parks in Texas and the awesomeness of the Grand Canyon and a squad of moles decimating the front lawn of our rental in Orinda, so I was more than amply distracted.

We experienced the end of the sixties one day on Telegraph Avenue, in Oakland. I remember it as if it were a dream—hazy, impressionistic, more of a general vibe than a specific sequence of events. But a single occurrence, the decade's death rattle, stands out sharply. We were window-shopping, having visited Upstart Crow Bookstore. I was six and done up in dapper duds. My youngest sister, Jennifer, was but a glimmer in Bob Dylan's eye, and Jill, just able to walk, lay asleep in the stroller. Out of nowhere, a woman jumped into our path. At one point she must have been a classic hippie, but now she was a witch, the Hollywood variety. She was terrifying. Greasy clumps of hair held back by a beaded headband, which framed remote eyes, her dress torn and stained, some sort of scabrous deal on her arm, wilted flowers pinned to her shirt. She professed interest in me—such a cute little boy, so sweet—and peered into the pram, but really she wanted money, which she let my mother know, quickly and forcefully. A tall dude who had sidled up next to her outstretched a gaunt arm and poked a finger in my face. "*You* belong in London!"

One smacked-out couple, that's all it took. My parents experienced this confrontation with great heaviness, compounded by the stunning news of the Manson Family killings down in Benedict Canyon. Several more times during our stay, my folks faced off with the disillusioned dregs of the Summer of Love. A host of desperate dropouts congregated in the ravine behind our house, cavorting late into the night, gently menacing the neighborhood from their wooded lair. Mom and Dad interpreted it all as evidence of a spiritual dead end; these unfortunate young people, they reasoned, had tried it all—from sex, drugs, and rock 'n' roll to Zen, the Children of God, crystals, and anything that seemed even slightly redemptive—and had come up empty. It scared my parents senseless. Generally open-minded, proffering a free-to-be-you-and-me attitude, they then and there decided that their children would grow up Episcopal, thinking that at least this would give us an anchor we could fasten ourselves to or discard. I'm not sure that is how it worked. They were afraid I would turn into a biker or join a cult, but that was as likely as me becoming a day trader and spending nights at the strip club. I understand their impulse. All they wanted was a clean slate for the new decade.

...

A decade doesn't mean anything in itself. It's an arbitrary threshold. Nothing magical happened at 12:01 AM, January 1, 1970. A decade is just a way to hold back the rush of time, to keep ourselves from experiencing history as a continuous, nonstop flow, instead parsing it into segments, manageable and distinct, with enough duration to allow for meaningful change. For such a sweeping task as viewing history, ten years is sufficient. You can say *it was like that then—it's like this now*, and, following the pace of contemporary life, after ten years your observation will ring loud and true. A decade sets a place marker so we can compare then and now not just as moments whirling past but as distinctive chunks of our collective story. And there's really no *the* nineteen seventies. There's *our* nineteen seventies, *their* nineteen seventies, and then there's *my* nineteen seventies.

Someone seeing the decade from another perspective, with different input and experience, will have another point of view and will draw other generalizations. In this book you'll find my generalizations. (*Talkin' 'bout my generalizations.*) My observations. (*My observations, baby!*) My nineteen seventies.

How can we account for change over time? For the mutations of culture? How do you get from B. J. Thomas, "Raindrops Keep Falling on My Head" (*Billboard* Hot 100's first number-one song in 1970) to Michael Jackson, "Rock with You" (same chart, same month, ten years later)? If you draw a line from one to the other, surely it will not be a straight one. Maybe it's not a line at all. Could be lines. Or a knot. A frayed wire. An earthworm wiggling on the lawn after a soaking shower. Braids. Cornrows. A weave. Yes, maybe it's a carpet, a Malian mud cloth, some intricate textile. That's it, let's say you get from one moment in musical history to another by moving across a swath of fabric, the threads hugging and slackening and reconvening and intertwining, thousands of interdependent lines crisscrossing their way from Point B.J. to Point M.J. How do you get from one song to the other? It's not a line, honey, it's a loom.

The second half of the twentieth century is too complex a fabric to completely map where all the different lines go, especially with something as subtle and multiform as popular music. Apart from the natural cultural ebb and flow, there are industrial forces at work. Since the dawn of recording, in the early part of the century, music has vacillated between periods of consolidation, in which there's a more concentrated set of gatekeepers and less diversity, and moments in which musicians kick against centralization and resist homogeneity. The seventies saw a full cycle of those changes, the rise and fall, centralization and dissipation, as well as a rather new kind of DIY resurrection. Somehow, against all likelihood, "Raindrops" and "Rock with You" were both meaningful to me in about the same measure. So were two distinct versions of "Lola" by the Kinks and the Raincoats, recorded on the outer edges of that decade. Even if it's futile, I'm interested in trying to trace out the nonlinear path that leads from one to the other, undoing all that weaving, knowing full well it might end up a heap of filaments on the floor.

This, then, is a look at that heap, the sound of the seventies as I made sense of it at the time, from the sublime to the pathetic, and also as I pieced it together after the fact, from later points in life, when I uncovered compelling music I had missed and parsed things about my music that I'd failed to grasp. The things we don't notice about the music we like could fill a book. Some of it was admittedly obscure, but much of it I see now was painfully obvious. Lyrics I couldn't understand, references I missed, implications lost on me. I experienced plenty of personal changes in that span, living in three different cities—Virginia Beach then Philadelphia then Iowa City—and passing from age seven to seventeen. It was a time to dance and a time to rock. Certain listeners chose sides: dance or rock. By nature I'm a lover not a fighter, so I did it all, danced and rocked and everything else. I did things I shouldn't have been doing given that I was doing the other things. But I don't think I was special. I think plenty of my peers were listening across those limina. The rockers were dancing and the dancers were rocking.

Reggae singer Joe Higgs's memorable phrase "life of contradiction" applies here. Our enthusiasms were those of just such a contradictory nature. I held a lighter aloft at stadium rock at the same time as I whispered conspiratorially at Unabomber punk; I remained secretly true to Fleetwood Mac while snickering through the Rotters' snarky seven-inch "Sit on My Face Stevie Nicks." The contradictions were more than just ones of aesthetics or trade-magazine gossip. My friends and I loved all sorts of music that was at odds with the prevailing phobias of our tribe—mostly those based on misunderstandings of race, class, sexuality, and gender. We idolized people we were supposed to fear or despise. I think we looked for them to show us a way out.

Contradiction was also at the heart of music production back then. The seventies are sometimes depicted as the big sellout. Stacks of money were made. Piles of cocaine were snorted. Even punk's DIY revolution at the end of the era, if looked at critically, was seized upon as a get-rich scheme: Malcolm McLaren's "The Great Rock 'n' Roll Swindle." Souls were sold, stars were made, and hedonism was on parade. But in all the decadent partying, there was immense fecundity. Le freak was chic, and it was a rhythmic peak. It was the best of times and it was messed-up times. We were dazed and confused, also amazed and amused.

There were separatist exceptions immune from the lure of inter-mixing, artists who were purposefully myopic in their outlook, but in general the period was marked by a special curiosity, a fasci-nation amongst musicians and audiences alike with what other people were doing, across town or over the ocean, leading to a won-derment about what it would be like to be them, to wear their sequined shirts or platform shoes, to drive their cars and drink their drinks, love their loves, even live their lives. And sing their songs. Sometimes, in the position of a fan, that fascination was felt subconsciously, distantly, as an appreciation for the unfamiliar doings of strangers, and other times it resulted in something more transformative, calling for the reevaluation of deeply held beliefs. Either way, rampant curiosity presents a rallying point where *my* nineteen seventies—the generalizations culled from personal expe-riences, which in turn led to a set of impressions—perhaps bridge with other people's nineteen seventies. In other words, maybe my generalizations are more generalizable than I think. I don't know, can't say. To the best of my recollection and with my closest anal-ysis, the excursions herein represent a working understanding of the soundtrack of my youth, seventy-some reflections on the music that raised me. There's the music itself, its sound and meanings, and there's the way it fits into a life, a childhood, an adolescence, a developing perspective, a range of contradictory understandings—the music and the world and the dark alley where the music and the world meet to fight or get it on.

...

If you live in this world | You're feeling the change of the guard.
STEELY DAN, "Change of the Guard" (1972)

Let's say the decade starts with the Beatles' fractious demise and ends with the birth chirp of rap. In between, the music industry changes and it stays the same, listening habits change and they stay the same, the soundtrack changes and the song remains the same. Some embers of the previous decade take a long time to die down. Indeed, the first half of the seventies, in certain spheres of music, clings tenaciously to significant developments of the sixties. Psychedelia had a long half-life, and its implications were not immediately digested. You could easily think of this period as a hangover of—and from—the earlier era's extravagant utopian thinking. Consider David Crosby's 1971 unsung classic *If Only I Could Remember My Name*. According to the exhausted view insinuated by the record's title, the new decade began in a stupor. Get high, get off, and get away.

And then, as the story goes, the seventies got worse, growing more and more cynical until they ended in a shambles after an increasingly bloated star system weaned on excessive input in every open orifice led to the implosion of the record industry. Continuing the oft-told tale, out of this train wreck emerged an independent network, a DIY EMT that declined to perform CPR on the corpse of popular music, instead sawing it up and using its body for Frankenstein parts.

OK, lots of colorful narratives are possible. Were the seventies actually a continuation of the sixties, the next passage in their death-driven joy ride into glassy-eyed oblivion? Let's see what we find by decade's end. In any case, an overall tonal shift is apparent in the seventies with the emergence of fresh adaptations of country and bluegrass music by rock musicians, the influence of reggae and funk on disparate unrelated genres, the proliferation of exciting new approaches to arrangement in soul and folk rock, whole new paradigms of creative jazz, unheard-of experimentalism penetrating the mainstream, versions of irony and sarcasm that had rarely been sounded, album-oriented radio and concept records, face paint and fade-outs, cowbell and slap bass, barre chords and Rocksichords, safety pins and iron crosses, and lots and lots of hair, a more prolific and varied outpouring than anything imagined in the musical *Hair*: Afroing out, Mohawking up, ponytailing back, buzz-cut off, and dangling down. In one quick decade, you have Springsteen's go-kart Mozarts, the wizards of progressive rock, composing with all the complexity they can muster, alongside three-chord reductive rockers and pneumatic punks all hailing rock 'n' roll, and vamping funk-meisters splishing around in rhythmic subtlety and modal jams.

Lest we forget, the middle of the road was newly paved, yacht rock's course recently charted, and light rock a fresh whisper in the ear of sensitive listeners. An atmosphere of musical intermingling that grew out of the aforementioned sense of mutual wonder characterizes the whole period. That heterogeneity is one of the themes of this book. The world was growing smaller, united by mass mediation and global capital and jumbo jet planes and better communication, some of which were in turn inspired by raw curiosity, a veritable you-show-me-yours-and-I'll-show-you-mine kind of cultural production.

Styles have been mixing more or less forever. Polymorphous cross-pollination is an underlying feature of many trends in twentieth-century popular music, exacerbated by the spread of records, which allowed people to listen in on what other people far away were up to. And to form an opinion based on that eavesdropping. Or even to become an admirer. During the British Invasion of the sixties, London rockers were wildly popular in the US, while in the UK record connoisseurs were digging northern soul, a simultaneous boom of British interest in black American music, another turn of the revolving door of transatlantic exchange. The term "fusion" was coined to describe the collision of jazz with funk and/or rock, but it was by no means confined to those genres. Popular music was almost inherently fusion music in the seventies.

When I interviewed bluegrass guitarist Doc Watson, he told me that in his North Carolina holler in the forties they were listening to, among other things, Memphis Minnie 78s; deep woods hillbillies listened admiringly to the guitar playing of a black woman. John Miller Chernoff, in his beautiful book *African Rhythm and African Sensibility*, says that he found the most popular singer in West Africa to be Jimmie Rodgers; traditional African tribes venerated the yodeling brakeman of early country music. This groundwork for cultural recombination made all variety of mix-and-match possible in the fifties and sixties, from Elvis Presley to Caetano Veloso. By the seventies it had all come to a head and was forced into an extroverted position, made public, so that suddenly it was perfectly logical, for instance, for Wild Cherry to play that funky music.

Many dynamics were at play in all this musical interbreeding, not just aesthetic ones. Politics played a role, as the civil and human rights struggles called for pride of place on the national and global stage. Already in 1964, Sam Cooke, once a warbler of dulcet ballads, had forecasted: *A change is gonna come.* In the process of becoming more visible, African American urban life was being dramatized and rendered marketable. The time to cull what Motown and Stax had produced in terms of crossover had arrived at record labels. Everything was up for grabs, anyone was a possible consumer, narrow target audiences were a thing of the past, and the new idea was to throw the pasta at the wall and see what stuck and who would eat it.

If there was a sense of political reality at stake in the seventies, there was a concomitant investment in make-believe, in constructed versions of culture. Some of this was trumped up to appeal to the preconceptions—prejudices even—of an existing audience, in the manner of blaxploitation films and their attendant soundtracks. George Clinton took that tactic straight to the people, a racially mixed crowd of Parliamentarians, by presenting a superfly stage show featuring a low-rider spaceship and a cast of street-preaching singers, some in diapers and some with hoodlum hats, crooning: *Fantasy is reality in the world today.* Meanwhile, Clinton's other jam, Funkadelic, posed the inter-generic question of putting fantasy into practice: *Who says a funk band can't play rock?* For Clinton, everything was a serious joke—make-believe was a cover for actionable philosophy; costumes and props, invitations to cross over and see what was happening on the low-down side of town. Meanwhile, on the other shore of the Atlantic, Ian Anderson had fabricated a completely different fantasy with Jethro Tull that involved a rock mythology based on a largely invented image of the folk music of the British Isles mixed with tropes from Shakespeare and Dickens, replete with flute and lutes and leotards. And codpieces. Have I mentioned the Renaissance Faires? Whole bands seemed to arrive on the scene having wandered away from one with a coach full of wardrobe.

The tricky flip side of hybridity and cross-cultural borrowing was that sometimes it counted on the ignorance of its audience. I am part of that irreputable clan. I thought the members of Led Zeppelin were certifiable geniuses because I had never heard any of the country and early electric blues to which their songwriting referred. And seeing him cited didn't send me on a hunt for Joe McCoy's records, to pick one instance out of many. Jimmy Page and Robert Plant didn't hide their passion for that music, but I had no idea that the rhythmic and melodic ideas weren't all theirs. I'd never heard the Kinks' "You Really Got Me," so I thought Eddie Van Halen had composed it, and as a hard-hitting pop metal song, it impressed me greatly, hungry little moron that I was. We weren't much for fine print in those days. Incidentally, I still love Van Halen's version and I still think Page and Plant are geniuses, but that opinion is now better informed. At least I like to think so. Cover versions and adaptations involve their own hoodoo, nothing to cast aspersions at—Mark E. Smith of the Fall once said that a successful cover version is "half not knowing and half mutilation"—and now we understand the politics of cultural appropriation a bit more fully for the complex, though not unexploitative, process that it is.

...

George Carlin had a routine in the seventies that goes something like this: What sets American entrepreneurs apart from those of other lands is the idea of combining stuff. If you can find two things that have never been put together before, they figure, get a hammer, nail them to one another, and, as Carlin put it: "Some schmuck will buy it!" I remember listening to that bit on his record, thinking he was on to something. It's what we might call "your chocolate in my peanut butter syndrome."

An awful lot of music in the seventies, American or not, embraced this chocolate-in-peanut-butter syndrome, finding its way by mixing unlike sounds—ones originating in different countries or classes or periods or genres—and engaging listeners in the act of paying attention to something hidden or distant from them, giving them a chance to test out a new identity—racial, ethnic, gender, sexual preference—or just a flamboyant outfit. In this, the music achieved something special, more than just the chocolate or the peanut butter alone. A true fusion that was so incredibly delicious some schmucks eagerly plunked their money down. Me included.

The intersections were not always literal. And they were not necessarily as obvious then as they seem now. Maybe some can only be understood in retrospect. I thought about that when I saw a music video mash-up of the Bee Gees' "Stayin' Alive" and AC/DC's "Back in Black." It's nothing short of miraculous how these songs fit together. Despite all differences, they turn out to be structured almost identically, so that with a little fancy editing, the disco dancer's anthem maps directly onto the headbanger's hallelujah. Dirty guitar riff meets chorus of hysterical angels, the Gibb brothers, who turn out to sound uncannily like "Back in Black" singer Brian Johnson. Disco and heavy metal: uncomfortable bedfellows of the nineteen seventies, together again, unnaturally.

Matter of factoid, the album *Back in Black*, from whence the single, is dedicated to AC/DC's erstwhile singer Bon Scott, who drank himself to death in February 1980, leaving Johnson at the mike. So long, Aussie rocker. That's a suitable place to plant our headstone for the decade. In loving memory of my nineteen seventies. Rest in pieces.

1970

"Lola"

It began with bewilderment. That and a genuine respect for things I couldn't understand.

I remember being impressed by a T-shirt I saw on an older kid. It repurposed a famous W. C. Fields quotation: "If you can't dazzle them with diamonds, baffle them with bullshit." A teenager with a curse word on his chest was already an attention grabber, but the motto made me think. Its proposed dichotomy was between being rich and being smart, or between having sophisticated taste and using convoluted language, or being successful and being a hustler, or having superficial friends and having gullible ones. You could interpret it different ways. However you read it, I could relate to the sense of bafflement. Being baffled was a constant condition.

In a big house at the corner where our street curved and went up a hill, my friend Gary had access to a stash of records left behind when his older brother went to college. Now and then, we would go up to his room for a listening session. Our first order of business was memorizing all the Monty Python LPs. The real meanings of the troupe's routines and the motives of their makers were inscrutable to two young boys in a distant suburb of Philadelphia. But the actors were strange and likable, with an assortment of odd accents and what appeared to be passages in which men pretended to be women, which we thought was hilarious. We did not know what surrealism was or the Spanish Inquisition or a budgie. Neither did we understand the Elizabethan prehistory of cross-dressing in Britain.

At this point in time, the American suburbs were an unremitting hotbed of homophobia. So as not to be utterly ostracized, outcast, and publicly decried, little boys on playgrounds nationwide— I mean nubile children without their first pubic hair or any sexual experience—were basically required by unwritten law to publicly affirm their straightness and denounce anyone otherwise inclined. I think of my friend Peter, with whom I went to the Poconos a few winter weekends on visits to his family's cabin. He was soft, quiet, and sensitive, prone to read and draw on his own. I always thought: *He isn't an aggressive dipstick like most of the other knuckleheads*— which is why I liked him. In hindsight I expect he was gay, and he probably knew it even then. I can't imagine how painful it would have been to sit through all the insufferable macho mouthing off with such a secret held inside.

I had no bad feelings about homosexuality. In truth, I had few feelings about it at all at that point. It was little but a faraway abstraction. I was equally perplexed about heterosexual how-tos. Nevertheless, like my idiot classmates, I knew all the declensions of the words "fag" and "queer," and I hurled them without second thought at anyone doing something I deemed strange or out of the ordinary. I might call someone "light in the loafers" or "limp wristed" just to get a rise. For little peckers with such an undeveloped knowledge base, we sure had an arsenal of insults.

...

One rainy summer day, Gary told me he'd found a single that I needed to hear. We went into his house through the back door, by way of the kitchen, grifting bottles of Royal Crown Cola Lemon from the fridge, and tiptoed upstairs. For some reason, it seemed necessary to sneak. Like he was sharing a cache of *Playboy*s or something.

The song "Lola" starts off with nine emphatic chords and a jangle of National Steel resonator guitar, arpeggiated. Then Ray Davies speak-sings the story of his liaison in North Soho, somewhere we'd never heard of, in a place where champagne tastes like . . . *C-O-L-A cola.* Gary and I looked at our RCs and listened on. Drums added a relaxed backbeat, then a loose bass line slipped in, all of it sort of misregistered, disheveled, until a distorted guitar snapped it together a half minute in, transforming the mess into an action-packed pub-chant classic replete with maracas, piano, and harmony vocals. I noticed that Davies didn't try to sound American, left his accent intact. But the lyrics seemed to be a basic love song, sort of boring, and I wondered why we were paying such detailed attention.

"Just wait," said Gary, sensing my restlessness. "It gets better."

I liked the line about her nearly breaking his spine, and then it got even more interesting. *Well, I'm not dumb but I can't understand / Why she walk like a woman and talk like a man.* This was taking a different turn and fast. Not only was an uncommonly strong woman assuming control over a docile, naive protagonist, she was saying she's going to take him home and make him a man. *Well, I'm not the world's most passionate guy,* he says, but the lyrics say one thing and the song says something else. The music was getting inflamed, fervent, and the singer was clearly in love. What kind of alternate universe was this? Then the punch line, confirming our suspicions: *Well, I'm not the world's most masculine man / But I know what I am and I'm glad I'm a man / And so is Lola.*

The Kinks built momentum, rocked the song to its anthemic climax, and finished.

We sat motionless. Time stopped. Gingerly, I lifted my hand and placed it on top of Gary's, cradling it while instinctively waiting for it to recoil. It didn't. Hesitating, my pulse quickening, I enjoyed the softness of his skin, a gentle flush stinging my cheeks.

No, wait, sorry! That's not what happened.

The record player returned the automatic tonearm to its holster, and we sat dumbstruck. We didn't move, not knowing what to do.

Question marks ricocheted around the tiny room. Light rain salted the window. Nothing changed, but something had been pried open. Something I was ill equipped to understand. *Girls will be boys, and boys will be girls.* From now on, even in suburbia, it's going to be a mixed-up, muddled-up, shook-up world. The only one not confused, as the Kinks would have it, is the ambiguous one: *L-O-L-A Lola.* But this is not a crying game. The revealed isn't reviled. She is revered.

Finally I snapped out of it and broke the silence: "Wait, Lola's a *guy*! Your brother's not light in the loafers, is he?"

Gary punched my arm: "Shut up, creep."

"Man, oh man," I said. "That was funnier than Monty Python! Let's play it again."

"War"

I caught the opening salvo of the seventies in Virginia Beach. Dad had enlisted in the navy after experiencing pangs of guilt for having not been conscripted. He was finishing medical studies when he might have otherwise been headed into the jungle, and he opted to do a few years at the Portsmouth naval hospital to make up for his absence.

I was seven when we hit Virginia, and my collecting habits at that time were confined to frogs, toads, turtles, lizards, and the occasional salamander. Owning records was not in my repertoire. These years were mostly spent with my parents' collection. They had a small selection, some good things to choose from: the Moody Blues, the Mamas & the Papas, Simon & Garfunkel. I had an early portable cassette tape machine, on which I listened to the Partridge Family, whose TV show I loved to watch, and the 5th Dimension, who had recorded my favorite song, "Up, Up and Away," back in 1967. I especially loved *The Beatles*, playing that album's four sides end to end. Songs about monkeys, piggies, blackbirds, honey pie, glass onions, warm guns, weeping guitars, and doing it in the road— whatever "it" was. The lyrics were word salad to me, as opaque as the record's cover was white.

I attended Virginia Beach Friends School. This made for an interesting contrast with everything else around us, which was exclusively oriented toward Vietnam. My seven-year-old classmates wore POW or MIA bracelets; the father of one kid in my year was shot down during Nixon's Christmas bombing of Hanoi; the same kid nearly immolated our entire class and their families on a field trip by pouring cooking oil into a tube feeding oxygen into the common tent; my father took me to the airfield to sit in a F-4 Phantom jet cockpit; another Phantom crashed in a field a mile from our house, the huge mushroom cloud drawing my attention away from a new show called *Sesame Street*; I found the boot of one of the airmen killed in the crash, foot included, while hunting for salamanders.

It was a complicated time in American history and a fascinating period to attend a pacifist school near a military base. The sixties were still hanging in the air, including radical politics and alternative pedagogy. We called all our instructors by their first names, preceded by the appellation "Teacher." (Except for Mrs. Anderson, our stellar English instructor, an older woman who would have none of that.) Social studies was taught by Teacher George. He wore a dashiki and sported a huge Afro that he teased out as far as it would go. Teacher George was so white, he was almost a ghost. He built a gigantic tepee in which we all sat cross-legged, learning very little about history or anthropology but playing touchy-feely games. Our studies with him were all social. A few years after I left, Teacher George was fired for smoking pot on campus. He was rolling doobs with his eight-year-old students.

Somehow I managed to acquire my first seven-inch single during this period, Edwin Starr's "War." I wonder now how I heard the song in the first place, probably on the radio; my parents bought me the little disc of vinyl, and I played it to death on our home stereo. Something about it seemed more stirring than "Up, Up and Away" and my other favorite, the Carpenters' "(They Long to Be) Close to You." Those songs were dreamy, uplifting, and lyrical. Starr grunted, shouted, and called out: *Good god, y'all!* A song built on interjections verging on interruptions—it was visceral. I was just discovering my viscera.

"War" also introduced me to some important African American musical techniques. Call-and-response, a staple of the black church, was an integral structural part of the song. *War, huh, yeah / what is it good for?* asked Starr, answering his own question: *Absolutely NOTHING!* And then, for emphasis, he added: *Say it again, y'all.* His deep voice was ragged, almost torn, which fit the words. He effectively performed an internal dialogue of frustration and resistance. But it wasn't Starr's urging alone; there were his singers, who would alternate with the front man. The singers worked as a unit, baritone sax croaking bass notes, skilled tambourine shakes stirring the upper frequency register, while Starr ad-libbed his part alone, a reverend preaching to the congregation. The choir declares *War!*, after which Starr replies, *Good god, y'all*, slipping it as a syncopation, then the singers lay down, *What is it good for?* and Starr sets them up with a heavy *Absolutely* as they hammer down the final word, *NOTHING!* I was magnetized to this unknown way of singing. It was joint, communal, ecstatic. To a seven-year-old white kid whose experience with church service had been, as my father put it, all smells and bells, the music was pure excitement.

And the song's message, which was emphatic, aligned nicely with my placental antiwar sentiments. These were, I admit, highly inconsistent. I played with GI Joe and set up dramatic war scenarios with toy soldiers. An expert on WWII, I recognized all the aircraft by nickname and number, had visited an aircraft carrier, and read anything I could find about the Battle of the Bulge, blitzkriegs, and Pearl Harbor. Somehow, WWII was distant enough not to seem real; I found it fascinating in a History Channel sort of way, any pathos buried in newsreel and narration. Fascinating, that is, until I saw the 1971 movie *The Snow Goose*, which sent me into a hysterical fit of self-loathing, renouncing war play completely, albeit temporarily.

But "War" was mighty convincing. The opening: a little press roll on the snare like at a military burial. Then, over a chugging verse reminiscent of James Brown's "Money Won't Change You,"

Starr importunes the listener against armed conflict, detesting it, or as he says despising it: *(War) It ain't nothing but a heartbreaker / (War) Friend only to the undertaker*. Near the song's end, it reaches a fever pitch, more agitated and funkier than most other singles associated with the usually smooth and cosmopolitan Berry Gordy and Motown. The original version of "War," recorded by the Temptations for Motown just a few months earlier, provides a perfect example, lacking Starr's explosive power, even if it does have a cute "hut-two-three-four" march chant, which Starr wisely chose to jettison. Motown held back from releasing the Temptations' version as a single, and Starr's "War" was issued on the subsidiary Gordy label, probably to refrain from offending Motown's crossover audience, which included plenty of conservative whites. *Induction then destruction / Who wants to die?!* Starr nearly blows a gasket, moving back into the chorus as it reaches ultimate entreaty. *Peace, love and understanding / Tell me, is there no place for them today?* the singer intones as the song fades out.

"War" was a huge hit, Starr's biggest. It was number one in the US pop music charts and earned Starr a Grammy nomination. Where other antiwar songs were peaceful, this one was rough-and-tumble. And it was black. Urban black, gritty black, funky black. Not folk-friendly Richie Havens extrapolating on "(Sometimes I Feel Like a) Motherless Child" at Woodstock ("Freedom," 1969), not pop-reggae Jimmy Cliff singing about his friend dying in Vietnam ("Vietnam," 1970), not the pastel-jacketed Jackson 5, employing many of the same gospel tropes, dancing in tandem about the joyous return of brothers from the war ("Hallelujah Day," 1973). In two minutes, Starr went head-to-head with the idea of war, its insanity and inanity, furiously berating it and anyone associated with it.

The level of African American involvement in Vietnam was the highest in the history of US combat. Martin Luther King Jr. called it "a white man's war, a black man's fight." Conscripted black soldiers died in disproportionate numbers. Meanwhile, at Virginia Beach Friends, working through my Wordly Wise exercises, digging for sarsaparilla root, finding black widow spiders, or back at home searching for snapping turtles and hunting for my stolen bicycle, all I knew was that I saw more black people on television now. A few of them were actors; most of them were deployed to Indochina. And I had a single by Edwin Starr, whose demands and delivery made me curious to hear more black music.

...

One day I saw a bumper sticker on a car: SEND THEM BACK TO AFRICA. I asked my father what it meant.

"It's racist," he told me. "It's saying that black people should be sent to Africa. It's very ugly."

"Do they want to go back to Africa? Are they from Africa?"

"Well, no, not them exactly. Not black Americans. Their ancestors were brought from Africa as slaves."

"Can they go back if they want to?"

"Well, son, there was a movement led by a man named Marcus Garvey. He was a black man and he advocated returning to the place where the ancestors came from. But I imagine most American black people have lives here that they wouldn't want to leave. They're free to go, I suppose."

"Would they have relatives there?"

"I doubt that they would know where in Africa they were from. Their ancestors might be from several different countries."

Virginia Beach was, in my experience, lily-white. I don't remember knowing that there were black people there. This is weird, given that, even just in the musical sphere, it's a stronghold of African American culture. Rappers Clipse and producer Pharrell Williams came along decades later, and became favorites of mine long before I knew they were from Virginia Beach. In the nineteen sixties, however, the city was almost completely segregated, a fact that didn't change until the early seventies, a few years after the Fair Housing Act outlawed redlining and other discriminatory practices.

I had two friends who didn't have a color. They were transparent. They were imaginary. Judgie and Juba were my imaginary playmates' names—a little African sounding, no? I mean, Juba is a West African dance that was popular with slaves on plantations. Don't ask me. Judgie and Juba came to me, told me what they were called, not the other way 'round. But I was interested in Africa, mostly because of the animals. I dreamed of living somewhere with exotic fauna. One morning my parents informed me that we'd be moving to Guam. At school, I located the island in an encyclopedia, which evoked fantasies of a perfect existence in Micronesia spent capturing unusual sea creatures on the coral reef and amphibians in the tropical forest. My excitement was short-lived; a few days later they informed me that instead we'd be relocating to Philadelphia.

My paternal grandparents went on safari every couple of years and brought back images of birds, oryx, lions, and water buffalo. I would sit in their dark basement in River Forest, outside Chicago, watching carousel after carousel of slides, dreaming of going to Africa. On the walls of the stairwell up to the second floor, they displayed an array of items they'd bought on these trips, tribal masks that were awe inspiring and a little frightening. When I was eight, my grandparents invited me to go on safari with them. My parents were upset that they had not been consulted, but I was elated. In the end, Mom and Dad decided not to let me go, saying that I wasn't old enough to travel like that. I'm not sure exactly whether they thought my grandparents wouldn't be responsible (possible) or that they would try to turn me against my mom, whom my grandmother didn't much like. Anyway, they presented a unified front, and I was effectively grounded in Virginia.

Sometime that same year, I think I realized that at my age the time limit on imaginary friends was up. One morning, I told my parents that our beloved Judgie and Juba had made a special announcement: they would be traveling to Africa and might not come back.

It sounds strange, but I never put these things together until now—the bumper sticker, my grandparents, my imaginary friends. Unwittingly I had my invisible buddies doing what I wanted to be doing, going where I wanted to go. Up, up, and away, they went back to Africa.

James Brown

"Get Up (I Feel Like Being a) Sex Machine"

I've considered compiling the definitive list of great songs with squeaky drum pedals.

The tiny sounds are barely there, chirping microscopic songbirds whose cheeps and tweets are usually all but cloaked by whatever din they're helping provoke. The hi-hat or more often the kick drum would need a little WD-40 to shush the sound, which has an indirect relationship to whatever rhythmic activity is going on in the song, since it's part of the process rather than the intended product of the music-making effort. Contained to a frequency range up above pop music's norms, it's made by a foot only vaguely aware of the song's trajectory; like someone mindlessly whistling, not thinking about the words or melody or harmony, the squeaky pedal is part of pop's covert sonorities, its unofficial profile.

I first noticed John "Jabo" Starks's squeaky pedal on the cassette machine in my blue VW Beetle in 1984. I remember that I was driving on Chicago's Eisenhower Expressway, the music blasting as loud as possible to be heard over the rush of air. I had the convertible top down. Suddenly I heard a little peeping noise. Something must be wrong with the car, I thought. I lowered the volume and the sound disappeared, so I knew it was something related to the music. It took me pulling over to the curb, idling awhile, and concentrating with my eyes closed to identify the source. When I did, it filled me with mirth. And then I went hunting and found plenty more examples. Once you start to notice them, they seem to proliferate.

But that was a long time ago, and high-frequency exploits are a young person's game. Nowadays I have a harder time finding the squeaks. I fear for my ears.   …

There's something extra appropriate about equipment needing lubrication on a song called "Get Up (I Feel Like Being a) Sex Machine."

> *Fellas, I'm ready to get up and do my thing!*
> *(Yeah! Yeah! Do it!)*
> *I wanna get into it, man, you know?*
> *(Go ahead! Yeah!)*
> *Like a, like a sex machine, man . . .*
> *(Yeah!)*
> *. . . movin', doin' it, y'know?*
> *(Yeah!)*
> *Can I count it off?*
> *(OK! Alright!)*
> *One, two, three, four!*

Let's simplify that exchange in the way a lover might describe what they were going to do before doing it, a little game of heighten the anticipation:

> *Hey, baby!*
> *(Yeah, honey!)*
> *I'm just gonna touch you here, OK?*
> *(Touch me, baby!)*
> *I'm moving my hand to touch you now.*
> *(Move your hand!)*
> *Can I touch you now?*
> *(Touch me, goddammit!)*
> *OK, here I go, I'm touching you on the count of four!*

It's more than just a great song. As I hear it, James Brown's "Sex Machine" is a kind of manifesto. It lays out one of the central tenets of his work: the synthesis of the organic and the mechanical. Brown was so far ahead of his time that much of the musical development of the decade had to do with other folks figuring out how to catch up to him and eventually, in hip-hop and rap, to apply the logic he'd uncovered.

Of course by then there were actual machines doing much of the work.

Jabo, young bassist Bootsy Collins, and Bootsy's brother, guitarist Catfish Collins, had to get into it manually, movin' and doin' it with fingers and hands and arms all coordinated in a repetitive rhythmic engine that was absolutely precise and also so funky it had a proper stink. Repetition was essential. Brown wrote and produced a song for Lyn Collins called "Rock Me Again & Again & Again & Again & Again & Again." It needed to be convincing, like a loop, almost inhumanly exact. The play of that machine-like replication and beautiful human grit gives it a libidinal drive unlike anything else.

Musically, JB is a teaser. He makes you wait, makes you want it, tells you about the upcoming change, but then he holds back. The apparatus keeps churning. Keep it right there. It stays in one key, basically on one note or cycling the same motif, vamping and vamping and vamping. Brown moves his *get up* around, calling out different notes, while Bobby Byrd sings the same responsive *get up* every time. Contrast and insistence, call-and-response—the James Brown special sauce comes in a brand-new bag with TENSION and RELEASE written on it in indelible marker. Not all the ingredients in the bag were so new. Calling and responding is a venerable old church routine. The play of contrast and consistency as a formal device links the funk bass line to the so-called "obstinate bass" of baroque's theme-and-variations methods. What was spanking new, though, was each iteration sounding like a magnetic recording. So tight it's like a loop.

Against the machine regularity of the band, Brown plays a

simple, almost fumbling low-down piano trill—the organic versus the mechanical. Then he asks Byrd "permission" to go to the bridge; again, it's like a lover asking if it's cool to do something insanely pleasurable to their partner: "Can I stroke that thing? Is that OK? Would you like that?" After getting the thumbs-up, Brown instigates the bridge's harmonic change, the song is into its plateau phase, and James asks the band if he can take it back to the top, counting it off in eight sure hits. The singer actually turns the beat around as he reenters, but he recovers so miraculously you'd think he planned it that way. In fact, he might have—live versions recorded subsequently are arranged the same way. At the tail end, delaying not only satisfaction but conclusion, Brown asks six times if it's OK to stop before the band plays a five-hit tag and the song is over.

If you want to hear Jabo's squeaky pedal plain and clear, just listen to the band hit it and quit it on those five notes.

...

Around the same time as the episode in my Volkswagen, I saw James Brown and the J.B.'s in concert. The gig took place at the Lone Star Café, a small venue in Manhattan. The club was wall-to-wall with people. My girlfriend Donna was short enough that she could barely see, so we fought our way to the lip of the stage. There I learned about Brown's pleading and demanding dominance-and-submission techniques firsthand. With his corner man and emcee Danny Ray, Brown did his famous cape routine, falling to the floor during "Please, Please, Please," Ray draping him with the red garment and escorting him to the side of the small stage while the crowd went apeshit and bellowed for him to return. Not only was he a ruthless tease, Brown was a ham. With the powder keg tamped, the tiny room exploded as he threw off the cape and jumped back to the microphone, flinging it dangerously toward the crowd, only to tip it back to his mouth with a flick of his foot on the stand's base. This trademark move was timed to the moment that the band kicked into "Papa Don't Take No Mess," and the jammed house went absolutely berserk. I've never been at another concert where the crowd became such a single organism—sweaty ladies and dripping dudes mashed together in a huge group grope that bounced up and down as one to the tight, insistent funk.

The glow from that gig still warming my grill, I went to see Brown at Brown, the university where I was in school, in Providence, Rhode Island, about three weeks later. I rounded up a bunch of friends and we arrived early, but the band's bus had been waylaid and they didn't arrive until an hour after the appointed start time. Much to my disappointment, during the first set Brown didn't sing at all. He played organ and a little piano, neither of them with what you'd call gusto, clearly out of joint from the travel hiccup. I considered the concert a wash, and Donna and I headed home to study.

The next day, some of the people in our party told me what I'd missed. JB came onstage for the second set dressed in a skintight, pale pink spandex jumpsuit and gave the people what they'd longed for in the first half, and then some. Three songs in, obviously inspired by his own performance, he got a raging erection. Hearing this, I imagined myself in that pickle, recalling similar situations at the swim club or a friend's pool, where I'd explored myriad creative ways of masking hard-ons, such as pointing at a passing airplane, walking bent all the way over like a hunchback, or crouching, tucking, and flinging myself into the pool in an unprovoked cannonball.

James Brown didn't hide his pride, he flaunted it, calling attention to the encased wand by pointing at it and shouting out: "Hey, hey, hey, hey!" His penis became, as it were, another member of the band. In a brilliant act of improvised theater, JB turned around between songs, instructing the J.B.'s to play the only thing right for the occasion, a piece of his own that started with an imperative: *Mama, come here quick, bring me that lickin' stick.*

...

In his personal life, the licking stick was not theater. Neither was it funny. Brown was a serial domestic abuser. He beat his wives, at times with terrible violence, as his daughter Yamma detailed in her 2014 book *Cold Sweat: My Father James Brown and Me*. Sometimes this ugliness was perversely reenacted in his stage show. The last time I saw him, in Memphis in 1996, he pantomimed knocking down his wife Tomi Rae Hynie, who was also a dancer in his ensemble, a tasteless stage antic that nearly everyone knew mirrored actuality.

I don't know how we can reconcile such evil shit with the undeniable genius of someone like James Brown. If I'm honest, much as I wish it weren't true, I think the two are tangled up together. Brown was a narcissistic weirdo, sometimes in a fascinating way, always in a manner that put him at the center of his concerns. In "Super Bad" he's so cranked up about how much soul he's got that it makes him want to kiss himself and maybe *try myself with you*. That's sex proffered as an act of beneficence. Conversely, in "I Can't Stand Myself," Brown is flipped out about being touched, and the line *can't stand your love* remains ambivalent: is the touch noxious to him, does he feel guilty about it, or it just so intense that it can't be withstood? Whichever, you can sense the radioactive aura it evokes.

On Marva Whitney's "You Got to Have a Job (You Don't Work, You Don't Eat)," she and Brown harmonize on the subtitle and alternate singing the lyrics. Brown repeatedly directs her to *call Maceo* (the saxophonist Maceo Parker), which she does. On the one hand, this could be a normal interjection of spirit, like "sing it for me" or "hit me"—you know, "Call Maceo!" But it has another edge, one of complete control. That kind of bullying is how Brown worked, with contemptuous misogyny flamboyantly staged against utter musical originality. The Brown-Whitney exchange involves a relay that Brown played out in many songs, as he (Brown) tells her (Whitney) to tell him (Maceo) to play:

JB *Call Maceo!*
MW *Maceo!*
JB *Call him!*
MW *Maceo!*

JB *Call him!*
MW *Maceo!*
JB *Holler a little! Call him!*
MW *Maceo! Blow your horn!*

This banter's got a military vibe, a martial quality, the sergeant demanding something of his private—on your belly and give me fifty push-ups—just to flex, to show hierarchy, submission, the power of brute patriarchy. Sir, yes, sir.

Brown's authority trip was not confined to women. His exchanges with Bobby Byrd often took the same dictatorial turn. To the listener, his dominion over time and energy and other folks can be thrilling—he always ups the ante, taking an already massive groove like Byrd's "Never Get Enough" and urgently adding a scream and compelling the singer: *Come on, Byrd, do it!* The terrifying discipline that Brown required of his band is well documented. Their compliance—which included paying fines for missed cues and enduring verbal or physical attacks for minor errors—made it possible for him to impose inhuman demands on them. He required their absolute devotion, essentially turning them into funk machines. Young and unruly ones like Bootsy didn't last very long, even if they were exceptionally gifted.

If you've never heard it, listen to the first few tracks of the live concert from 1971, recorded in Paris and released later as *Love Power Peace.* You can find it as a video, which is even more astonishing. The band plays three minutes of "Brother Rapp," Brown's moonwalk laying fresh pavement for Michael Jackson, and then with nothing but an imperceptible visual prompt, the large band switches midstep to "Ain't It Funky Now." New key, new tempo, started at an unexpected place. This isn't stopping on a dime—a dime's too damn big. This is stopping on a speck of dust, a grain of sand, an atom. It is impossible. And James Brown made the J.B.'s do it.

The seventies would have sounded very different, and much less wonderful, without his contribution. He made badness supergood, equated blackness with pride, put a glide in your stride and a dip in your hip. Brown was an expert at whipping a band into shape, sometimes literally. Five years before the start of the decade, he'd already changed cultural history, and he'd do it again once or twice along the way. Picked up and built upon, Brown's music would lead George Clinton and Miles Davis and the Bomb Squad and countless others to extirpate the unfunky and inaugurate electric jazz and hip-hop revolutions. I know deejays who refuse to play his music at a dance party. They say it's like cheating.

Black Sabbath

Paranoid

Count to ten and say "heavy metal."

1) It's a thin line between dumb and great.
2) We are required by blood pact to love this album for its first rhyme, answering *masses* with *masses*. Consistency is the hobgoblin of little minds—and goblins of all sorts, along with witches and faeries, are welcome here.
3) Sustain—the love of sound that could go on indefinitely without decay, though not having anything against decay, because it's dark and nasty, and we want to be dark and nasty and will do whatever it takes. Especially in the living room of our suburban house.
4) A thin film of distortion covering everything like dust in an abandoned mansion.
5) Lack of historical specificity—this antiwar album, to which conflict does it refer? Presumably Vietnam, au courant in 1970, or a post-apocalyptic robot war. But the opening strains of air raid sirens evoke bombardment during WWII, and other references could place it in any British military scenario, particularly some-

thing medieval or Victorian, or a more modern engagement, say the Great Northern War, the War of the Quadruple Alliance, the First Opium War, the Anglo-Sikh Wars, the Taiping Rebellion, the Anglo-Burmese Wars, the Second Opium War, the Indian Mutiny, the Bombardment of Kagoshima, the British Expedition to Abyssinia, the Anglo-Zulu War, the 9th Xhosa War, the 'Urabi Revolt, the Boer War (part 1 or part 2), the Boxer Rebellion, the Mahdist War, or the Turkish War of Independence. Lots to sing about. The empire's War Pigs were busy for centuries. From 1722 to 1725, there was even the Drummer's War.

6) Speaking of combative drummers, Bill Ward's drumming here takes us on a prehistoric, atavistic trip, thud-like enough to make Troggs drummer Ronnie Bond feel like Roy Haynes. At this point during concerts, heavy rock drum solos begin to seem a convenient time for a bathroom break.

7) Riffage. Everything revolves around the power of a guitar riff, an ostinato featuring a few notes or several chords in an easy-to-memorize pattern, compelling the listener's head into a downward motion and upward retort like a dipping bird.

8) Seriousness can be ridiculous. *People think I'm insane because I am frowning all the time* ("Paranoid"). The gloom that hangs over Black Sabbath is an adolescent malaise, the kind that drives kids to draw iron crosses and swastikas on their notebooks without thinking about what they mean. It's a comic book omen, each idea outlined in black pen, a caricatured misanthrope in a dystopian strip.

9) Ozzy Osbourne's voice sets the tone for the rest of metal history. We spent days mimicking the opening invocation to "Iron Man" by singing through a fan, though Oz apparently used a ring modulator for the ripple effect, same device through which Tony Iommi sometimes fed his guitar. Osbourne has since become such a celebrity goof, but it's important to recall that he was a really inventive vocalist.

10) Heavy metal, heavy drugs? Not so much. Check "Hand of Doom,"
with its terrifying narrative of death by skag in Vietnam; compare with the Velvet Underground's euphoric pro-smack "Heroin." Our masters of reality kill narcotic romance like a cock-
roach.

Lick My Decals Off, Baby

Knock out Mama Heartbeat. That was Don Van Vliet's main mission as a mature musician. She'd kept time simple, 2/4 or 4/4, until he complicated the rhythm with a dope smack for rock's allegiance to steady duple meter. By 1970 Don had Mama H. on the ropes.

Trout Mask Replica was the perfect party killer in 1969. Or so I'm told by people who were young adults in that year. When the revelry got long in the tooth, they'd put on Beefheart's double LP. It was sure to clear out late-night stragglers.

Many Beefheart aficionados consider *Trout Mask Replica* to be his unconditional masterwork. I do not number myself among them. *Trout Mask Replica* is a brilliant record. *The Spotlight Kid* is a brilliant record. *Clear Spot* is a brilliant record. Beefheart's last three efforts, *Shiny Beast (Bat Chain Puller)*, *Doc at the Radar Station*, and *Ice Cream for Crow*, which I regard as a closing triptych even though I know that's not how they were conceived, are all brilliant records. But the Captain's ultimate contribution to humankind is *Lick My Decals Off, Baby*. Inspired by the success of *Trout Mask Replica*, next time out he and his Magic Band cut the LP of a lifetime.

To boil it down, one simple sound lifts *Decals* over the top: xylophone. Tuned percussion—malleted, wooden, and many-barred. Marimba, to be precise, played by Ed Marimba, known outside the confines of Beefheart's circle as Art Tripp. It's an instrument common to Latin American folk and popular music, particularly in Guatemala and Mexico, and widely known to US audiences due to the mainstream popularity of the Baja Marimba Band, Julius Wechter's faux Mexican exotica ensemble. You could say that Beefheart wrestled the marimba back from Wechter and Herb Alpert, whose A&M label had cashed in with a sluice box full of Baja Marimba Band LPs.

Marimba is *Decals'* secret ingredient, but there's not one note of it until track five, "Bellerin' Plain," locked in mellifluous counterpoint with Zoot Horn Rollo's guitar. Even then it doesn't appear until halfway through the song. Delay gratification; intensify satisfaction.

...

Decals is frequently described as "experimental." It's not. That word tends to be deployed loosely in reference to things that are noisy or are unconventionally put together. *Decals* is both of those. But such characteristics don't make something experimental. This LP is a coherent set of songs, not a series of sonic experiments. There is some caterwauling saxophone, true, and there are electric guitar features—electric guitars played without accompaniment ("One Rose That I Mean") or in a mind-meld duet with electric bass ("Peon")—and rhythms you'll have trouble counting. But this is a pop record. An outrageously inventive pop record so audacious that it can barely contain itself, pushing lyrical and musical complexity to a breaking point. Nevertheless, a pop record. A selection of words set to music, some verse/chorus architecture, love songs and protest songs, all put together by someone with at least a little sense of how what he's doing fits into the bigger popular music picture. The first line of the first song, which lends the LP its title, plots *Decals* relative to the Beatles' first US hit:

Rather than I want to hold your hand
I wanna swallow you whole
And I wanna lick you everywhere it's pink
And everywhere you think
Whole kit and caboodle and the kitchen sink

Which brings us to five interrelated leitmotifs on *Lick My Decals Off, Baby*:

1) Sex
2) Prehistoric times
3) Ecology
4) Housecleaning
5) Feet

The most prominent of these is the first, appearing right out of the gate in a song dedicated to fellatio and cunnilingus. *She stuck out her tongue and the fun begun*, he sings, bursting out of a bustle of wood block and cowbell, courtesy of Drumbo, the drummer. In the first of several songs about themselves—meta-songs we might call them, where Beefheart observes the song as it goes along*—he intones:

This song ain't no sing-song
It's all about the birds and the bees
And where it all went wrong
And where it all belongs
And the earth all go down on their knees
Looking for a little ease

A little head, he means. The birds and the bees, otherwise known as intercourse, are replaced with a thorough licking *everywhere that's*

---

* These include "The Clouds Are Full of Wine (Not Whiskey or Rye)," with its self-referential line: *Melodies that go on, go on, go on / Go off, go off, go off*, and "Circumstances" on *Clear Spot*, where he invites guitarist Zoot Horn Rollo to *hit that long lunar note and let it float*. I think this is related to the meta-commentary on some early blues, where a guitarist like Tommy McClennan might say to himself just before adding an ingenious fill: *Take your time because it's the only shot you got.*

pink, all the way to *the kitchen sink*—a delightful plumbing allusion. His lyric has been transcribed as: *Heaven's sexy as hell / . . . Goes together so well / And so on*, but I'd always heard: *Havin' sex is hell*, which carries a very different meaning. Either way, it ends up as an order from a man on the verge of getting blown: *I want you to lick my decals off, baby / And I don't want you to be lazy / 'Cause it's driving me crazy.*

In "Space Age Couple," Beefheart chides futuristic humans, urging his protagonists to *Flex your magic muscle* and *Shed your nasty jewelry . . . Why don't you cultivate the grounds / They're the only ones around.* Sex also subtends "I Wanna Find a Woman That'll Hold My Big Toe Till I Have to Go," a surreal stream about doing the do with sweet potatoes that have *eyes that yawn and yearn down yonder below the ground and their golden hair is a dirty brown.* Beefheart planted feet in this song, too, as he goes in search of the song's titular toe fetishist. "The Buggy Boogie Woogie" is a darkly gentle piece that begins with the poignant, far-seeing line: *What this world needs is a good retreat.* A little ecological prescription for cleaning up—Beefheart takes a broom and sweeps and sweeps, but there are just too many feet. He's committed to housekeeping. At the end of the title track, he returns a wagging tongue, rejecting advances in favor of doing chores: *She stuck it out at me and I just thumbed my nose / And went on washing my clothes.* On "The Smithsonian Institute Blues," he predicts human extinction, memorably permuting *a new dinosaur t'be in an old dinosaur's shoes* into *Dinah Shore's shoes*, staging *Homo sapiens'* final days at the La Brea Tar Pits, adding: *All you new dinosaurs / Now it's up to you to choose / Before your feet hit the tar / You better kick off them old shoes.* He laments the world as a worn-out rug on "Petrified Forest," singing: *Soon it will fray and we'll drop dead into yesterday.*

. . .

A digression on Beefheart's singing. It is often said that he had a five-octave range. This urban myth has been perpetuated by scriveners as esteemed as Robert Christgau, but it must have been formulated by someone who had never investigated such an interval on an actual physical instrument. Five octaves = sixty notes. If you started at the bottom of the piano, you would have to make your way three-quarters of the way to the top note. A male singer's range is normally about two octaves, three if you include falsetto. Five is preposterous. Beefheart does have an extremely malleable voice; he can tickle the low yo-yo like nobody's business, and he can screech like an excited chimpanzee. But Beefheart's vocal endowment is passed around among critics as common knowledge, an adolescent kid cutting contest: "Have you seen how big Beefheart's . . . *voice* is? He may be a weirdo, but boy is he hung!"

The key to Beefheart's singing is not range; it's flexibility. He took cues from Howlin' Wolf, who knew how to move his voice from the depths of his chest into his throat and out onto the forward part of his mouth. Listen to the way Wolf sings the word "evil" in the song of the same name, like he's wringing out a wet shirt. Beefheart switches from Dock Boggs nasal to profundo baritone, sometimes in the course of one line. You can hear him drop into a natural speaking voice in the middle of "Bellerin' Plain" and on the dreamlike "The Clouds Are Full of Wine (Not Whiskey or Rye)," his vocal chords unclenched; he almost sounds pedestrian, like an actor momentarily stepping out of character. You hear the bottom of his range on "Woe-Is-Uh-Me-Bop," one of the LP's greatest moments, on which Ed Marimba works his miraculous sonorities kaleidoscopically, swapping riffs with Mr. Rollo, joining forces in dazzling xylo-guitar fusion.

. . .

The late sixties had totally flummoxed people in the music industry. Psychedelic rock convinced some record companies that up was down and weird music might be the next big thing. Major labels issued free jazz and European improvised music just to see what would happen, and big-time outfits threw up their hands and took chances on the wildest shit they could find, looking for something with traction. To wit, in 1968 Warner Bros. signed a distribution deal with Frank Zappa's Bizarre label. *Trout Mask Replica* was issued on Bizarre, under Zappa's watchful eye, and six months later the guitarist founded Straight, which was distributed by Reprise, a Warner subsidiary. Straight in turn put out *Decals*. Retrospectively, it's important to remember how confused the mainstream music business was: the generation gap made manifest.

Warner/Reprise produced a minute-long television advertisement for the release of *Decals*. Conceived by Beefheart, it contained a surreal set of images, the names of the band members and the corresponding place they lived verbally listed by a narrator over a shot of a hand flicking a cigarette at the wall interspersed with an image of TV static. This sequence was followed by a short, angular dance by the Captain, then a segment of bass guitarist Rockette Morton walking across the screen with an egg beater, and an enigmatic final shot of Beefheart's foot kicking over a bowl of white paint, visually conjuring a lyric from "Doctor Dark": *The moon a pail of milk spilled down black in the night*. Straight tacked on an image of the record cover, which is the first Beefheart LP to sport a Van Vliet painting, with a Don Pardo–like voice-over introducing it, to lend the ridiculous stab at PR that professional touch. The ad was banned first in Los Angeles, where it was called "obscene," and then nationwide by the National Association of Broadcasters. And they hadn't even heard the record.

Beefheart plays a lot of saxophone on *Decals*. Or perhaps it's better to say he plays saxophone for a long time. It's not his surest tool. An Ornette Coleman admirer, Beefheart's emulation is the sincerest form of flatulence. I would say he is an enthusiastic beginner, serviceable at best, although he's very musical in general, so the playing does have a sense of shape and dynamic. But facility-wise, his constant finger wiggling and overblowing can wear out its welcome. There might be a tad too much saxophone here, matter of fact, my only beef (excuse me, it had to be said) with the record, especially during "Flash Gordon's Ape," on which his extended multitrack soprano soloing obscures fascinating lyrics. "Japan in a Dishpan" is more successful, a heavy instrumental closing the first half of the program with squalls of free-blown horn all the way through. It might have been a better choice for him to concentrate on harmonica, an instrument he played quite well, and not too often, and a good device for stirring up energy in the upper end of the frequency spectrum.

He chose mouth harp on "I Love You, You Big Dummy," the most influential song on the LP. It is a certifiable proto-punk classic. If you listen, you can detect the rough, irony-steeped attitude that Johnny Rotten sharpened into a fierce spike, the same needle that Greil Marcus threads in *Lipstick Traces*. (I disagree with Marcus's statement that Beefheart sounds plotted and planned in comparison with *Never Mind the Bollocks*—Rotten is terrifying, yes, but his band plays routine heavy rock and power pop.) A song that both embraces (I love you) and rejects (you big dummy), it features one of the weirdest fake laughs and most convincing banshee calls in popular music. The song's punch line twists the knife, taking the two opposing sentiments and turning them back on their object: *I love you, you big dummy / Quit asking why.*

...

Back to Mama Heartbeat, onetime lone pulse of popular music.

The Beefheart approach to undoing Mama H.'s iron grip is unrelated to the slick numerology of King Crimson or Mahavishnu Orchestra, displaying none of prog rock's showy pretension or jazz funk's odd-meter vamps. The Magic Band adopted ragged complexity. Their vibe is more connected to the blues—down-home guitar evangelists and early urban electrics, where the asymmetrical rhythmic concept was based on feel more than trigonometry. Those musicians played solo or in very small groups, where they could add or subtract a bar at will and not send the entire train careening off the rails. Beefheart's rhythms are spastic. They sputter and jump, lurch and bump. He incorporates oblique references to Latin music (timbale-like accents so numerous it's hard to tell what the meter is), marching rhythms with a humid New Orleans swamp-rock quality, some deranged Bo Diddleying, abrupt time changes, and a now-and-then nod to the flagrant delinquency of the garage band. Two tempi share one space; one rushing, the other lagging. In "Flash Gordon's Ape," I hear him lampooning number-crunching progressives:

It makes me laugh to hear you say how far you've come
When you barely know how to use your thumb
So you know how t' count t' one

The unique rhythmic quality of Beefheart's music in this era is in part the result of the perverse process used to compose it. Sometimes working out a piece on the piano and recording it on a cassette machine, he then shared the parts with the band in a labor intensive act of oral transmission, an idea passed between an utterer and a learner and reproduced by means of rote memorization. This has led to much debate in the Beefheart world about how much of the music should be attributed to Van Vliet and how much was his band's. It seems obvious to me that it's some of both. He would never have achieved the miraculous "One Rose That I Mean" without Bill Harkleroad—Zoot Horn Rollo acknowledged by his unmasked name—who was the Magic Band's musical director on *Decals*, taking over for John French—Drumbo unmasked—who had served the function for *Trout Mask*. And French's contribution is spectacular. He runs the toms and chokes the hi-hat, sometimes in tight tandem with Harkleroad's lightly amplified guitar, along the way sneaking in cowbell for a change of texture. Mark Boston— Rockette Morton's alter identity—is an active part of the plan, his bass never just laying down the beat or showing harmonic direction; he plays double and triple stops, tangling with guitar, adding layers of action. Aside from the saxophone, very little is improvised, but it's not mapped out in the way a written chart would be, it's sweated and squeezed into existence.

Van Vliet may have been a tyrant, even violent and unpredictable, but he was the sun zoom spark. If you want confirmation, try Mallard, the band that the Magic Band formed after they abandoned their Cap'n. Here are the same personalities, all brilliant musicians, and the music's OK. Just OK. It's not brilliant. It isn't extreme or insistent enough. It lacks the lumpy commitment. Everything makes sense and nothing is left over. Nothing minor is fought over. Those little things, like the timing on "Peon," which gets a lesser repeat performance on Mallard's debut LP, are what make *Decals* so peculiarly luminous. A charismatic figure like Van Vliet may well be unpleasant to work under. But what made the music magnificent is the combination of his X-ray vision, the band's improbable loyalty, and the brute force way that they machete themselves into one of his songs. With all that against her, Mama H. didn't stand a chance.

Fun House

Let's talk about danger.

One of the defining characteristics of rock: it's dangerous. But what exactly does that mean? It's just music, someone making sounds, singing a song, moving around on a stage—what could be so boot-quaking about that? Is the notion of danger just a rhetorical conceit, part of an elaborate mythology designed to endow the music with raw power through mystification? Sure, that's part of it. And that's some of the fun: the mythmaking and the myth belief. Why not? Let us have our myths . . . and eat them too.

Rock danger is not typically physical or material. It's different, say, from lighting a cigarette while gassing up your car, free-form bungee jumping, or running with scissors. Deviance, sedition, and subversion are its agents; as George Carlin once said of his own comedy, executed properly rock will "curve your spine, warp your mind, and win the war for the Axis."

Iggy Pop tasted material peril early. His band the Iguanas played their high school prom with Iggy's drum kit set up on a seven-foot pedestal above the rest of the group. As a mature Stooge, he was fearless when it came to his own personal safety. Jim Morrison and members of the Rolling Stones had jumped into the audience, but

Pop was the original stage diver, putting his mesomorphic physique into direct contact with the crowd. After nearly fifty years of singers and players flinging themselves headlong into the audience, it's necessary to recall just what a radical step it was when Iggy did it. It was an Artaud move—total dedication without thought of consequence.

Iggy Pop's pact with the masses was that they would hold him aloft, while he stood like Jesus on their outstretched hands, slathering himself with peanut butter or euphorically covering his pectorals with ground beef, like Carolee Schneeman had in her 1964 performance *Meat Joy*. On the cover image for the first Stooges LP, stitches on Iggy's chin had to be airbrushed out. I remember seeing him lounging post-song on *The Late, Late Show* in 1980, hipping Tom Snyder to the difference between Dionysian and Apollonian art, a missing tooth evidence of some hazardous stunt, verbal eloquence offset by a demented *Beverly Hillbillies* smile.

...

What kind of danger are we talking about?

· Unpredictability
· Lawlessness
· Perversity
· Boundary confusion
· Personality disorder
· Criminality
· Anarchy
· Madness
· Glee
· Delight
· Vertigo
· Ecstasy

This is not Elvis Presley scandalizing a TV audience with some pelvic shake work. No prissy sniggering, gush of first suburban arousal, protective parenting, or vague waft of juvenile delinquency. Mick Jagger, John Lennon, Pete Townshend, Steppenwolf, the Monks, the Sonics—begone ye Pharisees of faux rebellion. Iggy's is debauchery and debasement on a cosmic level, a yawping spiritual chasm, sensible reason ripped and torn asunder and tossed into the sewer. He's a somatotonic sociopath with a continental schwanz; he's a prizefighter buffeted by blows but still zombie-walking toward his opponent, punch after punch, backing the poor sap up against the ropes, beaming, *That all you got?*

There's a glint in Iggy's eye, something in his voice, a psycho menace that slips out every time he yelps like a rabid dog or emits an unholy moan, a lurking, barely contained maleficent presence. He would productively bottle up and hold inside the implicit threat when he made records like *The Idiot*, *Lust for Life*, and *New Values*, but the singer uncorks all the way on *Fun House*, drizzling hot liquid threat all over his glistening, brickwork torso, breaking off the bottleneck, shards of glass piercing his chest, rivulets of blood a-skein on his skin, TV eyes above a wide wily midwestern grin.

In 1970 Iggy's routine is some Viennese Actionist shit. Eat-your-own-shit shit.

Taking a line from Günter Brus, Otto Muehl, and Hermann Nitsch, there's no dope he won't do, no hole he won't fuck, no line he won't cross. Complete the trajectory and we end up at GG Allin, where all the allure has vanished, the power of implication withers, and our subject turns into a pathetic puked-up lump. That might have happened to Iggy right after recording *Fun House*, when he and his comrades had their first taste of heroin. Total entropy is a fate he narrowly avoided. But this side of complete identity dissolution, Iggy retained his potency and mystique, fearlessness and unpredictability maintained as potential energy, insinuation building tension, the singer holding on to the shreds of a ransacked persona like a baby blanket in a bomb shelter.

A jolt of Iggy is the same 'lectro shock as Jerry Lee Lewis, Hasil Adkins, Wanda Jackson, Johnny Rotten, Ted Milton, and James

Chance, the power cord that would zap Mark E. Smith, PJ Harvey, Chrissie Hynde, and Birthday Party–era Nick Cave. Beefheart gave rock 'n' roll palpitations, *Poprockus arrhythmia* in its full Latin designation; Iggy attempted mouth-to-mouth resuscitation, or butt-to-butt resuscitation, to invoke Funkadelic's perverse-reverse formulation. Is Iggy the godfather of punk? This is more death-defying than punk. It's punker than punk. Where punk is an affect, the Stooges have no time for affect. To be affected means holding on to something, whether it's a haircut or an outfit or a riff. Those fetishes are up for grabs on *Fun House*. Throw them overboard into the drink, cut ties, head out into the gale.

Your challenge, Mr. Pop, was to make a nuclear-powered record with a fifty-year half-life. With brothers Ron and Scott Asheton and Dave Alexander, he accomplished just that over the course of two weeks in May 1970, at Elektra Sound Recorders on La Cienega Boulevard in Los Angeles. Iggy could look back from the couch on Dinah Shore's talk show in 1977 and with reason claim to have helped wipe out the sixties. It's like the suitcase scene in *Kiss Me Deadly*: buy a copy of *Fun House*, open the gatefold, and you'll understand— careful when you unwrap it because it's warm to the touch, glows in the dark, and might take out the civilized world.

...

In less capable hands, *Fun House* danger might be definitively gendered. There's enough macho about it for that to be the case, sufficient testosterone to fuel a cock-rock fandango. But part of the boundary confusion in Iggy's persona is gender related. Look at the way he arches his back, his occasional bleach blond hair, his eyeliner, the lubed-up rippedness of his body, his overextension of the tropes of glam and glitter. He's not a dude, he's a freak. When Iggy ominously sings, *Stick it deep inside*, on "Loose," I don't hear it as a patriarchal poke. He's too strenuously neutral in any gender assignations, referring rather to a polymorphous looseness—could be his dick in any hole, a foreign object probing his nethers, a needle in the arm, or an emotion he needs to bury.

Fun House was the record the Stooges had been intending to make all along, more precise but also more reckless than the band's slickly produced debut. Recorded live, without overdubbing, using a vocal setup meant to emulate the way that electric bluesmen worked when they would sing into a harmonica microphone, it's a spontaneous rock record, brutal and marvelous in equal measure.

As powerful and unprecedented as *Fun House* is, it contains one big missed opportunity. The band was conversant in free jazz, and in some ways this record is the first genuine free jazz/rock fusion. The Stooges tapped tenor saxophonist Steve Mackay, a record store clerk who played in some progressive local Ann Arbor jazz bands. He acquits himself adequately on his three tracks, but he also quickly reaches the limitations of his capacity, and he sounds out of his depth next to Iggy's voice, a little more closing-credits-on-*SNL* than creator-has-a-master-plan.

What would it have been like for them to draft a major league action jazz saxophonist for this musical summit? Imagine Pharoah Sanders or Frank Lowe wailing glossolalic over the pummeling drum part on "Fun House" or through the broken time on "L.A. Blues," where Mackay sounds the most ineffectual. Why not? Ornette Coleman, perchance? For that matter, the MC5 had already joined forces at least once with Sun Ra's Arkestra, performing together live in concert, so how about borrowing Marshall Allen and John Gilmore for "1970"? Let's think big—why not Albert Ayler? Imagine Iggy and Albert cajoling love cries out of each other, conjuring a new kind of spiritual unity, garage jazz built for speed, asking no questions and telling no lies, prying the lid off the new decade's sky with their sonic can-opener.

Les Stances à Sophie

When Lester Bowie died in 1999, *DownBeat* magazine asked me to collect comments from his friends and colleagues for a memorial. The Art Ensemble of Chicago's trumpeter was just fifty-eight years old. A master of shouts and slurs, normally decked out in a white lab coat, stylish pointy beard, and horn-rim glasses, Bowie had been a force in creative music since moving to Chicago from St. Louis in 1965 with his wife, a promising soul singer named Fontella Bass. That year, he served as her musical director as she took to the studios of Chess Records. The band Bowie assembled included future Earth, Wind & Fire leader Maurice White on drums and Louis Satterfield on bass—both members of Phil Cohran's Artistic Heritage Ensemble—with pre–Rotary Connection Minnie Riperton on backing vocals. The session resulted in "Rescue Me," a million-selling soul classic.

Bass was one of the first people I interviewed for the story. Though they eventually divorced, she and Bowie had raised their four children together and remained friends. At the end of our conversation, I was compelled to thank her for singing "Theme de Yoyo," which she had recorded as a guest with Bowie and the Art Ensemble during their Parisian sojourn in 1970.

"Oh, that's so sweet of you. You remember that?" she said.

The song had not yet had its renaissance, which happened a few years later, but it had been a stone-cold hit in my head since I had acquired the LP *Les Stances à Sophie* in high school.

"That was a good one," she added, followed by a reflective silence.

Then something magical happened. Fontella dropped her voice, hummed a few bars of Malachi Favors's bass line, and sang the song. All of it, quietly, like a purr, in a voice that had lowered an octave in the intervening three decades.

Your head is like a yoyo
Your neck is like a string
Your body's like a camembert
Oozing from its skin

Your fanny's like two sperm whales
Floating down the Seine
Your voice is like a long fuck
That's music to your brain

Your eyes are two blind eagles
That kill what they can't see
Your hands are like two shovels
Digging in me

And your love is like an oil well
Dig dig dig dig it
On the Champs-Elysées

My wife, Terri, who had been walking past my office, caught sight of my expression and stepped in, her face asking what was up. I put my hand over the transmitter.

"She's singing 'Theme de Yoyo,'" I explained, holding up the receiver for both of us to hear.

When Bass finished, I composed myself and said: "That was incredible. I have to admit, I am totally blushing." She laughed and we said good-bye. When we heard of Bass's passing the day after Christmas 2012, Terri and I toasted her and relived that call for a few friends.

...

The Art Ensemble crossed the Atlantic Ocean in 1969. They lived in Paris and traveled widely, performing, recording, releasing LPs, and garnering an international reputation that would have been nearly impossible where they'd come from back in the midwestern United States. In Europe, they encountered Don Moye, the drummer who would become the fifth member of the band, replacing Phillip Wilson, who had left to play with the Paul Butterfield Blues Band. While they were temporary Parisians, "de Chicago" was added to their marquee name, and it stuck. When they left the States, they were regional phenoms. By the time they returned to the Windy City three years later, they were famous jazz musicians, greeted with a warm homecoming at the University of Chicago, in a concert that would be released as *Live at Mandel Hall*, their return an integral part of their legend. Back on the South Side, they wouldn't have needed to be "of Chicago," but the suffix was like cheering for the home team by wearing their T-shirt. I think it made Chicagoans feel recognized.

In the sixties, Chicago was an especially diverse place for black music. There were soul, gospel, and R&B musicians, and a very active jazz infrastructure. Rock 'n' roll's early history is lodged in the city, particularly around Chess Records, so there were also rock and even country outposts, and all sorts of what is often referred to locally as "white ethnic" music, meaning music that comes from the many neighborhoods—Polish, Ukrainian, Czech, Bosnian, Lithuanian, Serbian, Italian, Irish, German, and Greek—as well as that of Latino and Arabic immigrants. In other cities with such diversity, one often found less intermixing between worlds, but in Chicago a Venn diagram would show huge common areas.

I was once speaking with filmmaker and composer Ed Bland, who, with Sun Ra's assistance, made *The Cry of Jazz* in 1959, and he mentioned having heard that I'd issued some music by Hal Russell, the erstwhile jazz drummer and later vanguard saxophonist and bandleader whose original name was Harold Luttenbacher. "I worked with Hal back in the fifties," Bland told me. "Last time I saw him, he was picking up arrangements for a polka band I dealt with. He drove the charts to the far Southwest Side and played the gig."

The Art Ensemble of Chicago made stylistic diversity one of their hallmarks. Saxophonist Joseph Jarman explained:

> If you're a writer, it's your responsibility to read everything you possibly can so that you can find out what words are about . . . up until the late 60s we were always categorized, and it was only possible for you to self-realize certain situations. But then we discovered that if you begin to self-realize, then you became a universal property, and then you must use the whole spectrum of conscious reality. You must make it your responsibility even to understand what Muzak is about and how it's constructed. All these sounds and silences, and all these instruments, are just tools.*

. . .

Les Stances à Sophie was recorded in July 1970, just as the Art Ensemble's working visas were up and they were preparing to leave Paris. The session took place on a commission for a soundtrack to be used in a feminist film by Moshé Mizrahi. Don Moye makes his debut with the group, and if you want an example of the polyglot "universal property" approach to style that Jarman describes, it's an ideal place to start. The band explores improvisations on a Baroque melody for flute and flugelhorn ("Variations Sur un Theme de Monteverdi [I, II]"), swarming notes based on South Indian nadaswaram music ("Theme Amour Universal"), a skewed bebop composition presaging Roscoe Mitchell's later composition "The Key" ("Theme de Celine"), a luscious Bowie-led spiritual with Bass joining on voice

* Joseph Jarman, interviewed by Peter Kostakis, *Coda*, December 1977, 2–4.

("Proverbes I, II"), and some hard-driving free jazz featuring AEC's patented little-instruments—tables of percussion instruments and other whizbangs—as well as a crashing crescendo of gongs ("Theme Libre").

In contrast to the stylistic bricolage of *Les Stances à Sophie*, perhaps an artifact of its function as a film soundtrack, the Art Ensemble's *People in Sorrow* stretches a spacious, meditative blanket over both sides of an LP, its restraint and constancy a testament to the band's investigative intrepidness. Recorded a year earlier, without Moye, in Boulogne-sur-Mer in northern France, it remains one of the most luminous albums of creative music ever made. Even when the playing gets more agitated near the end, a nasal drone on a double reed lends it an unbroken quality. Both records were first released on the French Pathé-Marconi label and later reissued on Nessa, which has linked them discographically together. Taken as a pair, they cover the two ends of the spectrum of Art Ensemble interests, from the quick-change proto-postmodernism of *Les Stances à Sophie* to the introspective airiness and contemplative quality of *People in Sorrow*.

...

Jazz has been an integrative art form since its invention. In its infancy in New Orleans, it served as an intersection for different musical narratives, incorporating African, European, and Latin American elements, sometimes recursively revisiting existing African American musical styles, drawing them into conversation with one another. In the nineteen seventies, creative musicians took hybridization to a new level, resulting in a profusion of hyphenates such as jazz-rock, jazz-funk, jazz-gospel, and punk-jazz. On "Theme de Yoyo," the Art Ensemble refers to R&B and funk, but through the same distorting eyeglass that Archie Shepp did on "Mama Too Tight" (1966) and Albert Ayler did on "Heart Love" (1968).

What was uncovered in those precedents was the way that a steady foundation, like the Famous Flames–like groove on Shepp's tune, would set off a bracing free solo. Contrast was key. The sturdier the funk, the more fucked up the solo could be—listen to Ayler overblowing massive chambers of air against Bernard "Pretty" Purdie's drums. Purdie played with James Brown on formative records; worked with Steely Dan, Joe Cocker, and Hall & Oates; was musical director for Aretha Franklin; and claims almost credibly to be the most recorded drummer in history. His appearance on Ayler's record, along with the saxophonist's open appeal to a more popular audience, ticked off some of his more doctrinaire fans, but the music has lasting power. With a deliberately shaggier rhythm section, Shepp's hilarious funk has more of a marching band feel, the interlocking horn parts zigzagging across a football field in my imagination. Shepp's garrulous tenor is an expression of joyful riot, the cheerleader and her pompoms erupting in kinetic glee.

"Theme de Yoyo" starts with Malachi Favors's wobbly bass line—fat, funky, and fine. The horns almost sneak in, Jarman, Bowie, and Roscoe Mitchell roll together on a backbeat-heavy unison part, the ghost of Louis Jordan or Roy Brown adding a swing-blues sass. It's in the midst of this R&B ruckus that AEC introduces one of its signature moves—the 4/4 rhythm suddenly gives way, opening up a swirling hole in the rhythm, like the song's been hit by a tornado, grown unstable, collapsed. Just as abruptly, the beat resumes control with a single snap, and this aphasic moment is over.

The first time I heard "Theme de Yoyo," the vertigo-inducing rhythmic destabilization was one of the most exciting things I'd ever experienced, and it's lost none of its original impact on repeat play since then. Over the course of a few seconds, mid-horn-line, a drama unfolds, tension is introduced, a system undermined, the grid eroded, and then all of a sudden the tension is relieved, order restored, and the melody continues. It's an intensely thrilling kind of musical breakdown. Unlike the Shepp and Ayler examples, where coordination and chaos occur together—one the organized backdrop for the wildness of the other—on "Theme de Yoyo," funk and free alternate to build a storyline of the birth and death and rebirth of a sort of musical order. (In the film, the female protagonist teaches her husband's American client how to do "the fight dance" during "Theme de Yoyo," punching him rhythmically to the beat.) Roscoe Mitchell in particular would go on to use this device in future music, as on pieces like "Snurdy McGurdy and Her Dancin' Shoes" and "JoJar." And there's a lot more to "Theme de Yoyo," including Fontella Bass's seductive singing and ecstatic tambourine, Mitchell's and Jarman's incendiary solos, Bowie's soaring trumpet, and the satisfaction that one can clearly detect in a band that has finally found its drummer.

1971

Joni Mitchell

Blue

What makes a perfect record perfect?

Start with quality ingredients; there can't be a weak moment, all the songs must have a gravity of their own, and they need to work together as a unit. Flow is incredibly important, how tracks progress, pacing, contrast between songs, continuities and breaks, the program's sequence, the crucial flip between sides—which needs to feel urgent, not optional—the way that in the end the whole exceeds the sum of its parts. If it is indeed a perfect record, when the second side is over the listener should feel compelled without hesitation to go back to the beginning and start over.

The first half of the seventies brought the apex of the album as a medium. A decade prior, labels had still seen albums as receptacles for already popular songs: take a couple of those, add filler, put them together, throw them in the oven, and bake. Or half bake, anyway. With watershed LPs like the Beach Boys' *Pet Sounds*, the Beatles' *Rubber Soul* and *Revolver*, the Kinks' *Face to Face*, and the Mothers of Invention's *Freak Out!*, albums were being treated seriously by the mid-sixties, and by the time Joni Mitchell recorded *Blue*, the long-playing record album was fully asserted as the true musician's palette, rather than a clearinghouse for unrelated tracks.

Once a collection of family snapshots, an album could now be a major motion picture; once a set of little windows, now it could be a wide-open door. By 1971, a record album was a drawbridge, opened and extended into a span from our fortresses of solitude to the other side of the moat, whatever mental waterway might encircle us.

For a sense of how to construct an ideal seventies LP, consider just the economy of main instrument choices on *Blue*. In order of appearance: dulcimer, piano, guitar, dulcimer and guitar, piano, dulcimer, guitar, piano, dulcimer, piano. So symmetrically balanced it's almost a palindrome. Mitchell's perfect record is dedicated mostly to songs about leaving and journeying, about returning or being homesick. Seen from the fairly conservative folk enclave that it crawled out of, *Blue* is a joyful, rambunctious, even shocking outing—take the lines from the title track: *Acid, booze, and ass / Needles, guns, and grass / Lots of laughs, lots of laughs*—even as it is also gut-wrenchingly melancholic and plainly romantic. I hear it as a full-force embrace of mobility and independence—the former domain of guys, now a right to be enjoyed and cherished and protected by women. Move over Roger Miller, Mr. "King of the Road," and Steppenwolf, with your road anthem "Born to Be Wild," and all you ambling, one-night-standing, commitment-averse, uprooting, circumambulating, papa-was-a-rolling-stoning fellas, there's a new captain at the helm: she's a hard-drinking free spirit, and she's got some lost time to make up for.

Mitchell starts the record right off with wanderlust, her first words: *I am on a lonely road and I am traveling, traveling, traveling, traveling*, amplifying the feeling later: *I am on a lonely road and I am traveling / Looking for the key to set me free*. By boat, plane, foot, and ice skate, her whims and fancies take her to a Greek island, Paris (she doesn't like it there), Spain, Las Vegas, maybe Amsterdam and Rome, and return home to her Ithaca, which is California. You hear Mitchell's original Canadian-ness when she lands on the word "sorrow" as "soe-row" on "Little Green," a poignant 1967 song, revived for this recording, from the perspective of a young single mother, also in the reverent way she intones the Canadian national anthem, "O Canada," in the middle of "A Case of You." With its stunning use of dulcimer—an otherwise out-of-step Appalachian hill instrument unhip like the banjo was when the Monks chose it as their replacement for rhythm guitar—*Blue* is as eloquent a setting of poems to music as you'll find, a call to live life where you find it, loving the one you're with, departing from them eventually in an inevitable moving along, no matter how hard or sad. Cameo appearances by Stephen Stills and James Taylor are supporting rather than soloistic, as are subtle hand percussion and two little pedal steel interjections. *Songs are like tattoos*, Mitchell sings, her pure-toned voice channeling jazz torch into painful memory. She's brought her flash art book here to select the proper tattoo for your travels and travails. A song lives with you. You carry it around forever—a mother, sweet Marie, mermaid, anchor, skull—even after you've moved on. *Ink on a pin / Underneath the skin / An empty space to fill in.*

On "The Last Time I Saw Richard," the album's tremulous closer, Mitchell recounts her friend's capitulation to a straight domestic life, drinking in front of the TV, having warned her two years earlier: *All romantics meet the same fate someday / Cynical and drunk and boring someone in some dark café*. She's a romantic, for sure (note that at one point she fondly recounts being told that *love is touching souls*), but not above reproach, at song's end she admits her own *hidin' behind bottles in dark cafés*. So Richard's right. But she insists: *Only a phase, these dark café days.*

...

I once had a girlfriend who liked to put on *Blue* without anyone around because she wanted to make herself cry. She felt more human when it was over, she said. Matter of fact, I have never been with a woman who didn't love the record. I have met a few who don't, mostly gals who think it's too mushy or syrupy or girlie. On the other side, I'm also familiar with a man or two who has used it as a way to play their inamorata's heartstrings, guys who would spread display feathers in a false dance of sensitivity. It's a strong emotional tincture, *Blue*, pulling in different directions, embracing recklessness, lamenting the state of the world, feeling an inner existential longing, and it can be used in several contrasting ways.

The point at which I realized it was a perfect record was my first year in college. I had heard it before, casually, but a friend of mine urged me to put it on, and we sat listening to it all the way through in silence. She had just come from the campus women's center, where she'd been grilled about her sexual preference. Finding out that she was a virgin, the women leading the discussion informed her that she could not possibly know her own orientation, which she had confidently asserted was heterosexual. After the meeting, my friend was pissed off and wanted only to do one thing, which was to listen to *Blue*. I think seeing the depth of its resonance for her made it ring that much more loudly for me, and I put it on repeatedly that semester, finding it delicious in a way I was unaccustomed to, over and over, until my water-polo-playing roommate asked me if something was wrong.

"Only a phase," I assured him, adding under my breath: "These dark café days."

...

A quick memory as a sort of male chauvinist counterpart to *Blue*: about a year later, with my girlfriend—relatively soon my first wife—and our friend Barbara, I drove to Boston to see Loudon Wainwright III. I was almost a groupie of Wainwright in those years, saw him many times, each one of them memorable. This was the most special, easily so, though as usual it started with just the singer and his acoustic guitar onstage, a one-man guy through and through. Loudon sang our favorites, including the devastating "Lullaby" (*Shut up and shut your eyes / No more histrionics, no more college tries*) and "Whatever Happened to Us," a song of the insurmountable gap of gender, with lines like: *We used to be in love / But now we are in hate / You used to say I came too early / But it was you who came too late.* We loved "Rufus Is a Tit Man," the ode he composed to his son long before he could recognize its impending irony. *So put Rufus on the left one and me right on the right / And like Romulus and Remus we'll suck all night,* he sang to Kate McGarrigle. *Come on, mama / Come on and lactate awhile / Yeah, look down on us, mama / And flash us your Madonna smile.* Loudon's spectacular agility with language was not always so blunt, but even in more poetic and oblique songs, he recounted his womanizing and philanderings with excruciating honesty, which is ultimately what earned him our respect and adulation. He was a cad, but at least he copped to it.

At gig's end, the three of us hung out, contemplating a late meal. I went up to the stage to thank Loudon as he packed up, and he joined us at our table for a beer. The food idea broached, we found ourselves hiking from Central Square to Harvard Square, in search of Chinese, me toting the singer's instrument. Half an hour later, bathed in the orange glow of a neon sign, true to loutish form, Loudon set his sights on my gal.

"Where are you staying?" he asked her.

"Back in Providence," she said. "In my apartment."

"Well, if you were tired and didn't want to make the drive, I've got a nice hotel room." He smiled, cocked his head into an inquiring position, and poked at his plate flirtatiously with his chopsticks. "I could sleep on the floor."

"I don't think *John* would be very happy about that!" shouted Barbara, sweetly attempting to defend something that didn't need defending.

"Thanks, no. But I appreciate the offer," said my girlfriend. "I'm not quite that tired."

Armchair Boogie

On occasion, otherwise loner musicians will pal up, meshing their productions, tying their fortunes together, for one reason or another. Like twin stars, the partnered performers end up caught in one another's rotation, sharing an orbital axis. One is perhaps better known or has resources unavailable to the other, but the other always has something else, some street cred or singularity of vision, that feeds its twin.

For better and for worse, Captain Beefheart and Frank Zappa maintained this kind of interdependency on and off through the first decade of Beefheart's music. Zappa also colluded with bona fide wild man Wild Man Fischer before the two split over a monetary dispute. Brian Eno and David Bowie partnered for a time, as did Bowie and Iggy Pop, and a string of exceptional records were born—the Bowie-Eno Berlin trilogy (*Low*, *Heroes*, *Lodger*) and the Pop-Bowie Berlin twosome (*Lust for Life*, *The Idiot*). These kinds of relationships can involve an intimate exchange of musical ideas, or they can simply be career support, an alley-oop or leg up.

On the basis of a big hit with his band the Youngbloods, Jesse Colin Young signed a deal with Warner Brothers in 1971, awarding him his own label, Raccoon Records, to be distributed—much the way Zappa's Straight/Bizarre deal worked—by the parent company. This made Young a de facto curator, not only putting out Young-bloods LPs and his own solo recordings, but also selecting a roster of acts to record and release, which included singer Jeffrey Cain, Youngbloods drummer Joe Bauer, Banana and the Bunch (all the Youngbloods except Jesse), a jazz record by Kenny Gill, the blue-grass group High Country, and an ultra-weird outing titled *Crab Tunes* by a one-off group called Noggins. Raccoon was short-lived but resulted in at least two of the most unusual and rewarding releases of the decade, *Armchair Boogie* and *Hi-Fi Snock Uptown* by Michael Hurley.

A hippie holdover from the uncommonly rich folk music scene in Bucks County, Pennsylvania, Hurley was a childhood friend of Steve Weber, who went on to form the Holy Modal Rounders with Peter Stampfel. Hurley was "discovered"—as the hagiographical terminol-ogy would have it—by folklorist Frederic Ramsey Jr., who recorded his debut LP in 1965 for the Folkways label. This might have classed him in a more mainstream way, alongside label-mates Pete See-ger and Ella Jenkins, but Hurley was a certifiable looney tune, not a wholesome folkie, cut more from the cloth of the Fugs than the Weavers. Like many of the down-home bluesmen he loved, he was a rambler, an itinerant singer with a wobbly voice, a gorgeous old Gibson with Woody Woodpecker painted between the f-holes, and a mile-deep wellspring of songs gathered from others or invented by him.

Hurley was also, as my father likes to say, hornier than a three-headed cow. Later on he would release a record innocently enough called *Weatherhole*, which turns into a randy innuendo when you remove the first letter and read what follows as three words. One of his anthems, the inimitable "Open Up," kicking off the second side of *Armchair Boogie*, pays tribute to the cosmic vulva:

Open up, eternal lips
And swallow me

Free-falling through the abyss
That's where I want to be . . .
Well, it's just a little bit
But I'm feeling kinda naughty
Take me to the tip
Of the heavenly body
Open wide, let me slide
To sweet bye and bye.

Elsewhere he gives a grandmother masturbation lessons: *Use your left hand / Feels like someone else.* Hurley sometimes referred to himself as a hobo; I think you could say he was a hobosexual.

Armchair Boogie was recorded at Hurley's then home in Brookline, Massachusetts. It's credited to Michael Hurley & Pals, which in itself shows the casual nature of the session: dogs bark; people laugh and talk after songs; the sound is sweet and homey with the feel of a sitting room, people encircling a coffee table, singing and listening to one another, passing instruments around. Hurley plays the lovely solo guitar "Red Ravagers Reel," waits a beat, and then says to someone in the room: "You play one!" Jesse Colin Young is the nominal producer, plays electric bass on one track and electric guitar on another, and provides a handsome photograph of Hurley for the back jacket. The front cover features a painting of Boone, half of the two-dog team Boone & Jocko, protagonists in one of Hurley's comic strips; an example of these is reproduced as "Boone & Jocko in The Barren, Choking Land," an accompanying booklet with the LP.

Side one opens with "Werewolf," Hurley's signature piece, one he'd already recorded on his first album and would wax again numerous times. In a haunting minor key, with Robin Remaily's ad libitum violin, the song's basic conceit is strange and uncannily powerful—a portrait of the title character, it asks the listener to think compassionately upon a monster, even as it has killed a young woman, to understand the werewolf's inner torment over its own violent nature.

For the werewolf, for the werewolf
Have sympathy
'Cause the werewolf he's somebody like you and me
Once I saw him in the moonlight
When the bats were flying
All alone I saw the werewolf
And the werewolf was crying
Crying, "Nobody, nobody, nobody knows
How much I love the maid as I tear off her clothes
Crying, "Nobody, nobody knows my pain
When I see that it's risen that full moon again"

Hurley wrote a sort of sister song for "Werewolf" titled "Light Green Fellow," given a similar treatment with Remaily on fiddle, dedicated to a frustrated peeping tom: *Looking in the window but it's so dark I don't see you / Why don't you light a candle? / Your curtains are drawn but I'd see through.* Why is he light green? *Your sheets are green and your light is yellow . . . I'm a light green fellow.*

On "Get the Best of Me," a talking blues, Hurley laments the pace of a dizzying world, recalling the snoozing pooch on the LP cover:

You know something right here and I'll tell you for a fact
A man can't let easy ease
'Cause soon as he get a little bit of slack
He starts reeling it in until he's in a tight squeeze . . .
Well, if I could only take my easy ease
And see another woman walking in her BVD's
Then I believe I'd dive in and swim the sea
If I could let you, baby
Get the best of me.

The record's tonal range covers a spectrum, from ridiculous to tender. Sung in a very approximate British accent, "English Nobleman" depicts an aristocrat in a mental institution who has chosen instead of sword fights to throw pies. The gorgeous Gene Autry cover "When the Swallows Come Back to Capistrano" is picked and sung with passion and optimism, while "Troubled Waters" undulates darkly. The record's closer, "Penguins"—a gentle, light instrumental—features Hurley's mouth trumpet in harmony with Michael Kane on cornet. The other timeless Hurley classic on *Armchair Boogie* is "Sweedeedee," a song, like "Troubled Waters," later recast by Cat Power. Also a talking blues, it paints a retrospective picture of a relationship, a bohemian couple in New York, two turbulent soul mates ambling through Washington Square, the "fleabag apartment" and the "scumbag coffee shop," all remembered with bittersweet fondness:

> *Wash the clothes, Sweedeedee, and hang 'em on the line*
> *And I can see by the way you wash the clothes*
> *Your cookin' must be fine*
> *I'm with you in the mornin', baby*
> *Till the break of day*
> *I know you don't want my heart*
> *Tryin' to make me go away*
> *Seem like everybody got a little hard luck sometime*
> *And I know one thing for sure*
> *I been having mine*

On the two-minute-long "Jocko's Lament," Hurley sings: *I think I'll get a girl / 'Cause then when I ain't got nothin' / Still got my girl / And you know what she's got.* Like so many of Hurley's songs, it's a lyric that manages somehow to be at once uncomfortably sexist—is there another oblique pussy reference quite like this in popular music?—and genuinely loving, a secret bridge from childlike curiosity to old man filth. Plumbing those ambiguous, shady emotions is his specialty, in songs that are honest and poignant and almost too weird to sit comfortably in your mind.

...

In 1985 I was living alone in a little house in Providence, Rhode Island. Having taken a year off between sophomore and junior year in college, I found myself in the alien position of being around school but not in school, which made me feel a bit like a townie. An enthusiastic townie, that is, because I could do any of the fun things—see movies, attend lectures, go drinking with my classmates—without having tests or papers. And although I had to work, I was otherwise completely free. I attended an unprecedented number of concerts. And I bought too many records.

One of them was Michael Hurley's *Blue Navigator*, an LP on the ill-fated Rooster label. The record's master tapes were lost a few years later in the fire that consumed the company's offices and shut the label down. I was attracted by the comic drawings on the cover, all by Hurley, and strange song titles with a tone unfamiliar in any excursions I'd made into folk music. I took a chance, brought it home, and found it even more unorthodox and magical than I'd imagined. *Blue Navigator* kicked off with "Werewolf," Hurley's cult hit, and proceeded to move from one oddball place to another, singing into existence a skewed, hermetic little universe of vagabonds, wayward barflies, and woodland creatures.

On the back of the record jacket, Hurley provided contact information, which I assumed to be for the label. Wanting more music, but never having seen another release of his, I dialed the phone number and was surprised to be greeted by Hurley himself. I expressed enjoyment of his music and wondered if there was a way to sample more of it. He gave me his address and said to send a check for ten dollars and he'd make sure I got some. Before hanging up, I asked if he had plans to play in New England anytime. He said yes, he'd be performing at a place called the Blue Plate, outside Boston, in Massachusetts. About two weeks later, a package arrived containing a hand-decorated cassette with the two Raccoon LPs, instantly the only thing spinning on my car stereo. His letter gave me specifics on the upcoming gig, ending: "See you in Mess-of-two-shits."

The Blue Plate was situated on a curvy, unlit rural route in the middle of nowhere, something like two hours from Providence. A genuine hole-in-the-wall, albeit a classy one, it had wooden booths, a few scattered tables, a long bar, and a cozy feeling, not at all unlike the joints in Hurley's songs. It would be a stretch to call it a performance venue. By the time we got inside, Hurley was set up, a stool and his woodpecker-bedecked guitar staking out some territory in one corner of the room. The singer himself was seated in one of the booths, surrounded by about a dozen of his paintings. Aside from Hurley, me, my friend Rob, the bartender, an electric bassist, and a percussionist named Bones, there wasn't another person in the place. I waited to say hi until after the concert, which was delivered to these listeners as well as two or three regulars who assumed the position at the bar. Two sets like this, paintings occupying spots like they were audience members. It was as strikingly personal and unusual a performance as I'd hoped, his improvised sense of form and dropped beats sometimes throwing bassist and percussionist off, but the whole wobbly-wheeled wagon hauling such depth of feeling that it confirmed his growing status in my pantheon. When I went to introduce myself, Hurley had joined his artworks at a booth and invited Rob and me to pull up chairs.

"How much are the paintings?" I asked.

"Well, this one here is nine hundred dollars," he answered, indicating a large group scene with several monsters gathered around a swamp, a thin flock of bats overhead. "And I've got one that's six hundred dollars." He pulled forward a medium-sized canvas featuring a naked woman sitting on the hood of a car, her tongue wagging and a foamy beer in her left hand.

"Wow, those are just wonderful," I told him. He sensed that I didn't have that kind of money.

"This one is about half that," Hurley continued, showing me a small painting in which musical notes were circling a phonograph like flies. "Those are some Cool-Ass-Grooves," he noted. "I'd give it to you for two hundred dollars."

After a few minutes of mutual silence, scratching his chin, he said: "Hold on, let me look for something." Hurley produced a portfolio and extracted a small watercolor featuring Boone and Jocko in a bar, with plates of beans, an illustration of the first verse from "Jocko's Lament." In a speech bubble, the dog's song was written: *When I was a puppy dog / I never had the blues / Fell asleep every night / And woke up feeling new.*

"How much?" I wondered, instigating the first art purchase of my life.

Hurley was an old-school haggler, a seal-the-deal man, and he wasn't going to let me go home empty-handed.

"Forty dollars," he told me.

"Sold!" I shouted, slapping my hand into Hurley's and shaking on the sale.

I turned to Rob: "Hey, man, can I borrow forty dollars?"

Nilsson Schmilsson

What is weirdness? Where does it come from? The peculiar some-times originates within the nearly normal, a pip of sand rendered into perverse pearlescence right there in the belly of Joe Oyster.

Between Captain & Tennille's "Muskrat Love" and Zolar X's "Space Age Love," there lies an immense expanse of strange-music-gone-straight and straight-music-gone-strange. Just for a minute let's take a trip to our imagination station and fantasize about John Denver singing Kevin Coyne's "Marjory Razorblade" or Seals and Crofts singing selections from the Shaggs' songbook. Or perhaps Bread's main man, David Gates, covering the Residents' "Santa Dog"—the oversensitive guy who warbled "Make It with You," "If," and "Baby I'm-a Want You" tackling the immortal holiday lines: *Santa's dog's a Jesus fetus / Santa's dog's a Jesus fetus / Santa's dog's a Jesus fetus / Has no presents / Has no presence in the future*. The super fruitcake of soft-rockness sings the masters of wack. If only.

Now rotate 180 degrees, take a veritable nutcase, and watch him sing some massive hits. Presto, you've got Harry Nilsson.

This is a matter of context. A song that advertises itself as being weird instantly feels more normal, just as one that claims to be sad is almost automatically less so than a happy one that slips a little line of *saudade* into the mix. Same goes for the erotic. A flash of something sexy is worth more than an endless loop of hard-core porn. So comes Nilsson with *Nilsson Schmilsson*, the self-negating title suggesting something different afoot. It's a bright, poppy record, generally speaking, that produced three successful singles, including "Without You," a song borrowed from Badfinger, which went to the top of the charts. If you listen to it carefully, Nilsson's take on "Without You" is quite a strange song; it's elegantly arranged, as is the whole record, showcasing his powerful and pure voice, trembling in sappiness, building into a doleful crescendo, *I can't live, if living is without you*—basically, he's singing a suicide note. "Jump into the Fire," a minor hit, takes overwrought emotion the other direction, using slap-back reverb, Herbie Flowers's down-tuned bass, and a ridiculous tom-tom break to echo the assertion: *We can make each other happy!* Even the novelty hit "Coconut" is bona fide bonkers: a one-chord calypso wonder that features Nilsson singing in three registers, playing different characters over spare hand percussion and a goofy vocal canon. Almost buried in the fade-out, Paul McCartney joins for some sweet harmony vocals—classic Nilsson to hide the superstar cameo.

The wiener and all-time champ on this record, though, is a little winsome ditty called "The Moonbeam Song." With a poky saunter, strummed acoustic guitar, and double-stopped little cowboy bass line, Nilsson starts the song as if it's a soft-rock contemplation: *Have you ever watched a moonbeam / As it slid across your windowpane?* It's gentle and ambling and toothless and the singer continues: *Or struggled with a bit of rain / Or danced about the weather vane / Or settled on a moving train / And wondered where the train has been.* We're on a railway, and then the train jumps the track: *Or on a fence with bits of crap around its bottom / Blown there by a windbeam / Who searches for the moonbeam / Who was last seen . . .* and here Mr. Nilsson's line of thought becomes one with the convoluted trail he's narrating, a tangle of string and paper and other debris gathered at the base of a fence, a weird tone creeping into his easy-going voice: . . . *looking at the tracks of the careless windbeam / Or moving to the clacks of the tireless freight train / And lighting up the sides of the weather vane / And the bits of rain and the window-pane / And the eyes of those who think they saw what happened.*

First time into it, "The Moonbeam Song" is an exemplary case of where-the-fuck-are-we-and-how-did-we-get-here? Nilsson sets it up perfectly, with an innocent, innocuous introduction, transformed by overanalysis into a paranoid-schizo freak-out burrowing into the scenario in slow motion. And that final image is a killer, the moonbeam a glint in the eyes of bystanders who may or may not have really observed the miraculous confluence of quotidian events. Probably not, he suggests. They think they did, but they didn't. Don't overlook the submerged drug reference: windowpane is LSD delivered in a thin transparent sheet of gelatin. That's what Nilsson's done: in a single turn of phrase, he slipped a tab of acid into our soft drink. Call it the clause that refreshes.

**Webster Lewis
and the Post-Pop Space-Rock
Be-Bop Gospel Tabernacle
Chorus and Orchestra BABY!**

Live at Club 7

Curtis Mayfield

"Move On Up"

I made it through the nineties without learning the name Webster Lewis. Across three decades I had never heard of him. Lewis wasn't invisible to everyone, however. He started out as a keyboardist, arranging for and playing with some genuine jazz heavyweights like Herbie Hancock and George Russell, also with soul seductor Barry White, and he eventually waxed modestly popular disco records including "Saturday Night Steppin' Out." In between, Lewis made a concert recording in Norway, at a venue called Club 7. His debut as a leader, issued by the tiny Counterpoint outfit, was incredible. But hardly anyone heard it.

I finally caught up with *Live at Club 7* at the Hideout in Chicago. It was 2007 and drummer Paal Nilssen-Love was manning the turntables between sets. He'd said he had something special for me, indicating with a thumbs-up from the booth that this was it. A scavenger for lost sounds and a connoisseur of the highest order, Nilssen-Love was trustworthy, and I knew, in the words of Stevie Wonder, by way of Rufus and Chaka Khan, he'd tell me something good—sure enough set my soul on fire, yes sir, maybe even make me wish there were forty-eight hours to a day.

The track "Do You Believe" starts with almost a minute of drums alone: loose limbed, funky, halting empty spaces inserted into a hard-pocket groove that begins to roll along and shake it off, like a long-distance runner in the first leg of a marathon. When Lewis adjoins his keyboards to Jimmy Hopps's cymbals and snare, there's already a spritz of good energy released into the atmosphere— charged ions, happy mojo. It's a spirit-raising night in Oslo, courtesy of a band with a freight train of a name and an all-cap caboose tailed by an exclamation point. The keyboard vamp, a few chords with a three-note turnaround, is a perpetual-motion machine. I picture M. C. Escher's ever-ascending stairwells or Tommy Roe's upward modulating bubblegum hit "Dizzy"—Lewis's organ works that way, as two saxophones pick up the chords, thickening the arrangement, doubling the organ notes, gathering steam, but using the same materials, an insistent gospel repetition that looks way ahead to certain instances in techno where a simple repetition is built and broken down and built again, moving upward, always upward, to a top that's constantly deferred.

Judd Watkins's beautiful vocals combine old-fashioned baritone jazz crooning with the fervency of a gospel solo, floating over the harmonies, cool and imploring. Dry, punchy staccato rhythm gives way at one point to an even looser swing feel, not changing the form but releasing the hand brake a bit, charging up the gospel goodness, until finally the whole song culminates and concludes.

Or so it would seem.

A hovering emptiness, the field after the cavalry has left, dust kicked up by horse hooves, slowly settling, then . . . a solitary drummer emerges from the cloud, starting back up, da capo, a little darker at first, Lewis unleashing an acid-green keyboard interval before the whole showboat revives with yet more force, vamp returning with even more verve. The effect is the same as a single with a song split over two sides, "Mashed Potatoes (Part 1)/Mashed Potatoes (Part 2)." The revisitation. The reprise. Come again. One more time. Restated, the music's gravitational pull is irresistible. Once we've been through it a first time, its sound is fresh in the memory, and the return brings a special thrill. It's a fake-out. And it's for our own good.

So it is, too, on Curtis Mayfield's upbeat "Move On Up," one of the most uplifting songs of the early seventies. (Note the pileup of "ups" here—this is the era of 7 Up, which is, lest we forget, in George Clinton's invented etymology an abbreviation of the question: "Is heaven up?"). A beaming ray of light of a song with bubbling congas, a shuffling snare with snap and pop, and a funky string section, "Move On Up" is so full of optimism it's easy to get carried away writing about it. Mayfield's paean to forward social movement is at once calming and stirring, from the gentle massage of *Hush now, child*, to the lilting falsetto of *Move on up!*, the singer's banner-like message set against congas and drum kit, hotly pursued by a tightly voiced horn arrangement. Like George McCrae's "I Get Lifted," it siphons gospel spirit into a secular soundtrack, and like Chicago's "Beginnings," it extends the era of modal jazz, incorporates Latin soul, and predicts an age of extended versions and disco twelve-inch singles, stretching out beyond itself—in the process never losing its ability to flush endorphins. Ironic, in Chicago's case, that a song with its title is nearly all ending.

Almost too abruptly, Mayfield's horns break tempo to perform an Amen cadence, brass at a funeral formally announcing track's untimely end. Full stop. The casket is lowered. But no, wait, it's a ruse: he is risen! Another fake-out. From still air the drummer hits it, and we're off to the races again. Here's the conga, Mayfield's rhythm guitar chords, tenor saxophone, the sweep of strings, ebullient horns diving into a vocal-less coda that lasts the length of the song. And, yes, it emanates from a Christian source, the mystery of the stone rolled away and the revelation of a Second Coming.

Both these songs stage their own death and resurrection.

Nursery Cryme

Mr. Gedekes shifted weight on his tall stool, directing attention to the next student's project, which was hanging on the wall. He ran his high school art class casually, diverging from technical instruction and philosophical musings—the virtues of observational drawing and cut-and-paste collage; the vice of tracing and copying—to the introduction of his junior-year students to the music of Thelonious Monk; he played us *Criss-Cross* and extolled its many attributes. When end-of-class critiques came around, he was all business, and the sessions could turn ugly if he didn't think appropriate effort had been expended.

"Tad, why don't you show us your artwork," he said, exasperation evident on his whiskered face.

Tad Kleinhoffer was an enormous, thick-necked tree trunk of a boy. His family ran a farm in the rolling fields to the west of Iowa City West. Kleinhoffer played center on the football team and had never said or done anything to make anyone in his art class think he was even aware of his surroundings. He had neglected the other assignments, so when the final instruction was issued—compose an original drawing—none of us thought we'd see anything at all. Gedekes had repeatedly tried to engage the fellow, gently feeling around for any sort of light he could turn on, a topic or image to revive the lunk, but without result. Normally a dogged optimist, the teacher had given up and resigned himself to issue a failing grade. Thus it was with no sense of expectation that he asked Kleinhoffer to pony up.

Tad removed a cover sheet tacked to the wall, and a gasp ran around the room. Gedekes's face changed abruptly, a quizzical smile moving to replace despair. His take was not ours, however. What he saw was an elaborate pencil drawing, a cartoonish image of a beast, something we could see by his face that he imagined Kleinhoffer thinking up, a sign of life where there had been zilch. The teacher stood up, pulled his glasses down from the crown of his head, rolled up the cuffs of his white button-down shirt, put his hands into his jeans, and walked over to the drawing, examining the page closely. Kleinhoffer squirmed.

"This is a beautiful drawing, Tad," he said.

"Uh, thanks," Tad replied, looking past his giant thighs at the paint-splotched linoleum floor.

"Tell us a little about it."

"It's a dog. I call it 'Hair of the Dog.'"

Mr. Gedekes pondered his student's sudden awakening, wondering if he could have played any part in it. Meanwhile, the other kids and I glanced around the room at each other furtively. Sensing something in the atmosphere, Gedekes turned from the wall to face me. I looked away, ashamed but on the verge of busting up.

"Corbett, what's going on?"

I couldn't hold the laugh any longer and so stood, excused myself, and ran into the hallway, breaking into an uncontrollable fit of hysterics so raucous that the adjacent journalism class came to check it out. After a few minutes, I regained my composure and went back into the class, where they had left Tad's traced copy of the cover of Nazareth's *Hair of the Dog* to critique the next student's piece.

Gedekes shot me a mean look. Later he confronted me, but I didn't rat on Tad. Instead I told my teacher that it was an inside

joke I'd been sharing with someone else in the class. He never sus-
pected Tad's transgression. I think he was proud of the progress
they had made together.

...

All the students in that room knew the Nazareth drawing had been
copied because record covers were our lingua franca. They were a
secret language, a cache of coded messages, our own version of gang
graffiti—marking turf, showing allegiance, throwing signs. Some
kids identified with the monochrome of AC/DC's *Back in Black*,
others with the droll visual pun of REO Speedwagon's *You Can
Tune a Piano but You Can't Tuna Fish*, or the bright orange fantasy
novel imagery of Meat Loaf's *Bat Out of Hell*. With whichever crew
you cast your lot, their visuals were as personally meaningful as
a heraldic emblem. We decorated our notebooks with hand-drawn
band logos, copying them verbatim from our favorite LPs. I went
so far as to work out new designs for various band names, taking
artist Roger Dean as my model. All the lettering intertwined with
itself like a dumber version of Dean's classic logos for Yes, Osibisa,
and Budgie. I illustrated Earth, Wind & Fire's name with matching
icons for each of the elements—trees growing on the word "Earth,"
"Wind" spelled out in billowing curtains, and a flamed "Fire."

We communicated on our own bandwidth via record covers, and
they in turn communicated their own arcane messages to us. Perhaps more than any of my classmates, I was in thrall to their designs.
In Gedekes's class the next semester, I made a composite of Elvis
Costello images, compiling maybe five of them into one silkscreened
composition that I titled "Rigid, Not Stiff." The Kleinhoffer episode
made me especially upfront about my sources, which were drawn
freehand, never traced.

...

In 1971 Genesis was gothic. Not goth, à la Bauhaus; gothic, à la
Edward Gorey. Abandoned dance halls, bleak rooms, dust on crystal candelabras, creepy balustrades, a solitary organist playing a
toccata, the kind of landscape that Be-Bop Deluxe labeled "surreal

estate." If you follow Genesis's development, you hear them crawling out of a nebulous folksy origin into a highly original, if overwrought, early middle period, before singer Peter Gabriel's eventual split and the Phil Collins glossification (*A Trick of the Tail* is a cute, shiny version of these extremely edgy, misshapen records) and eventual pop overhaul and world domination. I've long left behind the pretense and mannerism of their early middle records, finding them too theatrical and inbred, but they're worth revisiting, unlike, say, most of the Van der Graaf Generator records, which are equally pretentious and mannered but not as deliciously peculiar.

I bought the Genesis LP *Nursery Cryme* and its partner, *Foxtrot*, out of the cutout bins at Discount Records. They had already been in print for six and seven years, respectively, and Charisma had reissued them in cheap editions without their original gatefold sleeves. In fact, the ones that I bought didn't even have paper inner sleeves, leaving the vinyl exposed directly to the raw cardboard interior, something that instinctively makes my skin crawl. But the exterior cover images were reproduced intact and they effectively caught my attention. Owning *A Trick of the Tail* gave me the false impression that I had a sense of Genesis, but I quickly realized that on these earlier efforts, *Nursery Cryme* and *Foxtrot*, there was a different singer—Gabriel rather than Collins, the latter confined to the drum kit, save on "For Absent Friends," where he sings lead—and that the whole concept was really something different, a progressive rock sound with an aesthetic that was weird and grandiose and baroque and incredibly British and exotic enough to be very desirable.

My childhood was steeped in what you might call young adult literary proto-surrealism. My father read Lewis Carroll's *The Hunting of the Snark*—the inspiration for *A Trick of the Tail*—to me when I was young, and he challenged me at age eight to memorize "Jabberwocky," which I did. I can still recite it. I latched on to words like "frumious Bandersnatch," "uffish," and "frabjous," recalling them later when I first encountered Dada poetry by Kurt Schwitters and Hugo Ball. My family delved into other parts of Lewis Carroll's oeuvre, we devoured Dr. Seuss, and together we read Tove Jansson's Moomin series. I was not and am still not much of a science fiction enthusiast, nor did *The Hobbit* hold my interest, but C. S. Lewis was absolutely captivating and some of my earliest book memories are of Dad reading me Roald Dahl's *James and the Giant Peach* when I was five and my sister Jill was a newborn. I can smell the fruit's flesh, feel its fuzzy exterior, and imagine myself climbing inside to set off on global adventures. Out of these recitations and readings came a taste for the absurd, for juxtapositions of unrelated things, disjunction, non sequitur, dreamlike imaginings, fantastic narratives set in unfamiliar places—in short, the elements of the uncanny in surrealism.

In ways sometimes obscure to us, as adolescents and then as adults, we find methods to extend our childhood, looking for legitimate grown-up interests that prolong playtime. *Nursery Cryme* was a natural for a guy like me. Start with the fonts, which are Victorian, as British as could be. They set things in a distant place, geographically and psychologically, with their bifurcated serifs, hyper-ornamentation, circus-banner-like decoration, filigreed and multicolored letter interiors, and drop shadows. The backdrop onto which these letters were laid was a painting, evidenced by craquelure, fine networks of dry cracks that overtook patches of the cover, clearly designed to provide a patina of age. The image that was cracking was that of a bright yellow-green pasture or lawn, a field of stripes converging on a distant vanishing point, a vast croquet court. In retrospect, I'm sure that subconsciously I related this green tableau to the cornfields that engulfed our little city in Iowa, but I didn't make that association at the time. Instead I responded to the figure of a deranged little girl in a frilly cap and lace dress looking straight at the viewer, arms cocked and ready to swing her croquet mallet at a severed head bleeding on the grass at her feet. A nurse or nanny whizzed toward her on wheel-shoes, while other shenanigans quietly unfolded at the estate depicted on the back cover, off to the side of the field of play. This place, it turns out, was based on an actual manor in Coxhill, near the village of Chobham, where Gabriel grew up. And the content of the scene is loosely adapted from *Alice in Wonderland*, the eighth chapter, titled "The Queen's Croquet Ground," in which Alice uses a live flamingo as a mallet and the Queen first utters the line "Off with his head!"

The cover was painted by a British artist named Paul White-head. He'd already designed the band's sophomore release, *Tres-pass*, and would go on to create a counterpart for *Nursery Cryme* in its follow-up, *Foxtrot*, which sported a reworked version of *Nursery Cryme*'s imagery as a tiny detail on its back cover, a titillating self-reference that furthered the impression that these two releases made up a hermetic universe. To make *Nursery Cryme*'s cover look older, the painter varnished his finished work with honey, which dried yellow, giving it a distinctive glow.

Whitehead is an extension of the unique variety of surrealism that arose in Britain, initially in the nineteen thirties, with artists like Roland Penrose, Conroy Maddox, Leonora Carrington, Emmy Bridgwater, Eileen Agar, Grace Pailthorpe, Reuben Mednikoff, and Desmond Morris, the latter a zoologist best known for his book *The Naked Ape*. Even earlier, there was an existing history of fantasia in British lit and art—think of *Alice*, of course, but also *Gulliver's Travels* and William Blake's poems and paintings—and such non-aligned grassroots surrealists as Mervyn Peake, whose 1939 book *Captain Slaughterboard Drops Anchor* visually presaged so much about American underground comics, and Ivor Cutler's uncatego-rizable poetry and stories, the droll Life in a Scottish Sitting Room series in particular. (I've always thought it was a wonderful co-incidence that Charisma, the label that issued these Genesis LPs, had a logo sporting the Mad Hatter, the White Rabbit, and the Cheshire Cat.)

I brought the Genesis records home because of their covers, but I fell for the music, which was of a piece with the visual imagery. Indeed, Whitehead based the *Nursery Cryme* cover on the opening song, "The Musical Box," which plotted the band's modus: eccentric

characters in narrative songs unfolding according to multipart, epi-
sodic forms, lots of timbral variety from an evidently large arsenal
of instruments, musical materials indebted to classical composers
of different eras—Bach's counterpoint, the chromatic mists of the
impressionists, and the dramatic dynamic shifts of the Romantics.
What I recall most, though, was not being able to parse the instruments. I couldn't pick apart the keyboard from the guitar or the
organ from the bass, and it probably didn't help that bassist Mike
Rutherford was using bass pedals as well as a conventional strung
axe, with strings, neck, and headstock. Also, Tony Banks used a
mellotron, a keyboard that actually plays back taped tones of other
instruments, making identification additionally perilous.

In these songs, the players often merged their sounds. Lines are
played in unison by strings and keys, the orchestral colors resisting
dissection. Normally, analyzing instrumentation would be a first
step toward understanding how the parts fit together. But in the
case of these cheapo American reissues, the absence of a gatefold
cover to study meant there were no accompanying credits or lineup
information (even song titles were only to be found on the records'
inner label). The players and instrumentation remained a question
mark.

If I'd been able to pull the music into its composite parts, I might
have noticed the way guitarist Steve Hackett taps the instrument
with both hands, a technique I'd fetishize when Eddie Van Halen
used it on his band's debut and something I always associated with
metal, but a sound that I would come to despise when it was repurposed for lighter jazzy purposes by Stanley Jordan. Hackett introduces the concept, which was being explored in different contexts
already by Hans Reichel and Fred Frith (see Reichel's *Wichling-
hauser Blues*, from 1973, and Frith's *Guitar Solos*, from 1974), on
the song "The Return of the Giant Hogweed." I loved this saga's
loopy idea, extrapolating the voracious invasion of a non-native
plant, *Heracleum mantegazzianum*, which was in actuality introduced to British shores by a Victorian explorer, into a paranoid

sci-fi fantasy in which humans need to fight back the out-of-control vegetation at night because *they need the sun to photosensitize their venom.*

Fleeting mentions of Genesis in musical press at the time that I bought these records mostly attended to the band's post-Gabriel incarnation. Gabriel's eponymous solo LP was just hitting stores, only to become an instant hit on my turntable. I do remember a tantalizing image of Gabriel in the bat costume from "Watcher of the Skies" (on *Foxtrot*) popping up in *NME*, and later I'd discover that the surrealist imagery of the songs and covers extended into the band's extravagant live performances, Gabriel donning costumes for specific songs, including "the old man" from "The Musical Box," and other guises of fox, flower, reverend, and invented characters named Magog and Rael. But it took me years of listening to figure out who was doing what on songs like "The Fountain of Salmacis," drawn from Ovid's telling of the classical story of the attempted rape of Hermaphroditus by Salmacis, and "Harold the Barrel," a comic romp with instrumentation that confuses even contemporary Genesis specialists and contains the overtly *Through-the-Looking Glass* line: *Harold the Barrel cut off his toes and he served them all for tea.*

...

All this in mind, I contemplate the irony of sitting in London at Frieze Masters Art Fair, almost four decades after acquiring my first Genesis LPs, which I bought for $3.99 each in 1977. With my gallery, I am exhibiting a painting by Desmond Morris in a booth dedicated to the surrealist legacies in London and Chicago. We might not have a Tad Kleinhoffer drawing on offer, although I'd kill to see "Hair of the Dog" again; Whitehead's canvas for *Nursery Cryme*, on the other hand, would be perfectly at home.

Derek Bailey

Solo Guitar

There are few musicians who actively shun the commercial angle. When it comes down to it, most performers want to be liked, or at least heard. Folk, with its populist agenda, and punk, with its antagonistic stance, both courted an audience, publicizing their efforts, releasing records, and adopting marketing campaigns and advertising budgets. Project Mersh, as the Minutemen would later call it, was a necessary evil.

I recall stumbling upon British guitarist Derek Bailey for the first time. It was 1980 and I found his music desperately confounding. A devotee of post-punk and power pop, and a newbie to classical music, I was beginning to toy with the jazz section of the record store. My dad had given me ruthless shit for listening to Janáček before thoroughly having explored Mozart, but I'd already started to feel an urge accurately described by François Caradec when he wrote: "There's a pile of books that have to be read, that everybody's read, that I've not read, probably because I thought that they'd been read sufficiently without needing me to read them as well; meanwhile I read other books."* I applied that same impulse to the acqui-

* Quoted in Paul Fournel, *Dear Reader* (London: Pushkin Press, 2012), 7.

sition of records. The ECM label had released records I particularly enjoyed by Codona, Ralph Towner, Egberto Gismonti, Jan Garbarek, Keith Jarrett, and the Art Ensemble of Chicago. Soon I was buying every ECM LP that I could find.

I'd learned from the independent DIY music scene in London to network new acquisitions by label, searching for anything on Small Wonder or Step Forward or Postcard, so it was logical that I treat jazz the same way, and I turned my attention to ECM, who had a consistent graphic design, easy to ID. Their pretentious motto—"the most beautiful sound next to silence"—suited my neo-hippie experiments in identity, indulged tentatively in tandem with my crunchy-granola girlfriend. That ECM's catchphrase was gratingly precious never occurred to me, nor did the idea pop into my head relative to the music—that it, too, could be gratingly precious—until I heard about Jarrett's concert hall tantrums, in which he huffed offstage when people made any noise at all, and then at once the delicacy and fragility of it began to seem awfully contrived. A couple of years later, my sophomore roommate in college accused me of walling myself off in an escapist ECM echo chamber. After honest evaluation, I couldn't say he was totally off the mark.

But when I was indiscriminately buying ECM vinyl, I managed to dig up a copy of the Music Improvisation Company's eponymous LP, recorded in 1970. I have kept the shrink-wrap on it with a series of slashed-price stickers that ended up at one cent. The members of the group were mostly unknown to me, but I recognized one of them, the wonderful Scottish-born percussionist Jamie Muir, who had added so much to King Crimson's *Larks' Tongues in Aspic*, an album that he named. A painter by inclination, Muir was a brilliant colorist, known to bloody himself with chains and sheet metal, blowing birdcalls, shaking rattles, and other noisemakers. In MIC, Muir had plenty of tone color to bounce off of, with Evan Parker on saxophone, Hugh Davies on electronics, Christine Jeffrey singing, and Derek Bailey on guitar. I knew that it was freely improvised music, a general concept that I thought I understood.

First time round the turntable, *The Music Improvisation Company* stumped me. Like an itch you can't scratch, something in this particular record stood out, a little annoyance you can't immediately locate but you can't ignore. Specifically, as a wannabe guitarist myself, I couldn't make heads or tails of what Derek Bailey was doing. It was spiky and kind of nasty, didn't try to blend with the others at all, and generally seemed rebarbative. I'd long admired the surprising sounds that Jimmy Page coaxed from his guitar using a violin bow; trying it out left me with a rosiny mess on my strings and pickguard. To my untrained ear, Bailey's playing more closely resembled the sounds I made when I was mindlessly fumbling around on the frets, unsystematically looking for a system.

The ECM guitarists I'd been listening to—Towner, Gismonti, Terje Rypdal, John Abercrombie, and an up-and-comer named Pat Metheny—all treated their instruments as melodic vehicles, resonant boxes that could pump out harmonic progressions. They were technicians of radiance. Extrapolate on ECM a little bit, take the wrong turn, and you end up at New Age's doorstep—Windham Hill's William Ackerman, Michael Hedges, and Alex De Grassi. The ECMists and their progeny were generally inclined toward a beautiful sonority. Relaxing, even sentimental sounds. Vibratory string things stimulating peaceful feelings.

That's not Derek Bailey's modus operandi.

Bailey ignored conventional standards of beauty. His music could be beautiful in its own way, but it was rigorously made on his terms alone. Already a presence on the young progressive jazz scene in London during the mid-nineteen sixties, he carried himself as if he were an elder statesman, even though he was only in his thirties. He was forty when MIC recorded its ECM record, but you might have thought he was ten years older from the grizzled authority with which he launches his little electric guitar ambushes. Like a musical Samuel Beckett, Bailey's about as unsentimental as you could ask for.

...

Solo Guitar was Bailey's second release on Incus Records. With Parker (and briefly drummer Tony Oxley), he formed Incus as an outlet for their music, joining a small list of self-producers with musician-run labels. For a taste of the many pleasures and punishments made available by the guitarist, this first lone outing is a good place to start. There's plenty of the unamplified or lightly amplified semi-acoustic plucking he's best known for, which combines harmonics with open strings and fretted notes. To someone not listening carefully, it could seem like a mouse had gotten loose on the fingerboard and was scritching around, making a funny little bothersome racket. But if you do pay close attention, another kind of logic appears, with a maximum of tone-color juxtaposition, enharmonic shifts in the sound of a single note facilitated by a personalized volume-pedal setup, by means of which he could throw a sound from one timbre to another or turn a magnifying glass on one particular microscopic clank. In his solo improvisations, Bailey also sometimes messed with feedback, allowing it to spin almost out of control, playing other sounds in front of it, swallowing them up in a throbbing drone, and then killing the speaker dead like he'd shot it through the heart.

In addition to three archetypical free improvisations, *Solo Guitar* contains rare forays into composed music. For the neophyte, this offers a delicious opportunity to listen to Bailey's thought process from two angles, contrasting his complex extemporaneous free play with his perverse approach to Dutch pianist Misha Mengelberg's "Where Is the Police?," Dutch saxophonist Willem Breuker's "Christiani Eddy," and British composer and bassist Gavin Bryars's "The Squirrel and the Ricketty-Racketty Bridge." After a quirky little melody, the Mengelberg track turns into an eight-minute meditation on envelope variation, one note played continuously with slight changes to the articulation, until a brief high-pitched synthesizer interruption ends it. Bailey shuffles charts at the opening of the Breuker track, almost ostentatiously reminding the listener that he's reading the linear piece from sheet music. Bryars, who was an erstwhile improviser and played with Bailey in early formations, wrote his minimal piece as an exercise in hammer-on—rather than plucking or strumming the strings, fingers tap the fretboard to produce tones. Working on two instruments at once, Bailey moves up and down the neck of one, back and forth across the bridge, punctuating with single chords on the other guitar.

The compositions do nothing to soften the improvisations on *Solo Guitar*. In a decade that is full of experimentation and provocation, it remains one of the most resolutely thorny statements on record, as thoroughly unpopular as music could dare to be. Bailey once told me: "Most music rides in on a tidal wave of hyperbole and bullshit." Though it didn't cure me of my interest in a range of popular genres, including some that were blithely compromised, his craggy Sheffield soundtrack put a question mark to them, asking for an honest reassessment.

All that to the tune of one slim penny.

Sticky Fingers

First day in English class, 1977, having moved from Philadelphia to Iowa City, the teacher asked us to give an example of a simple declarative sentence. She called on Dwayne, seated at the back of the room, in overalls, white tee, and red scarf, who rose to his full six feet eight inches, took off his cap to reveal a tangle of greasy blond hair, and said: "Maah tractor's on faaar."

In our high school, the students were either professors' progeny or farm kids. It was a stark divide. Most of the male children from farms hung out down smokers' hallway, barely acknowledging anyone else. The cluster of classrooms down there were conveniently the same ones they attended—shop, where they'd fabricate personalized gun racks or chicken coops to take home; journalism, where some of them took photos for the school newspaper, for which they got full English credit; and home economics, which was stocked with gals. I was always intimidated by the hulking presence of these hallway boys, whose manual labor schlepping soybeans, slopping pigs, or planting corn on their family farms made them stronger and harder than the relatively delicate sports enthusiasts, though some of the farm fellas crossed over onto the football or wrestling team. We always had dynamite wrestlers.

We referred to these guys as shit-kickers. I knew a few of them personally, but I don't think I got what made them tick, what the music they listened to meant to them, what made their tunes kick shit. I incorrectly thought that boogie bands like Foghat or ZZ Top would be tough enough for their taste, and I expected to hear those groups as I walked down the hallway that came in from the rear parking lot, where all the smokers and potheads hung out. But I never did. I heard the Rolling Stones.

At the end of sophomore year, I developed a crush on a classmate named Deanna Olson. Not raised in Iowa, and generally thick when it came to social signals, I didn't realize she was a farm girl. Somehow I managed to arrange for us to get together one Saturday at her home. My parents drove me there. We hit the driveway, which was dirt and about a quarter mile long, stretching back from the rural highway to a little white farmhouse in a clearing, surrounded by cornfields. I'm sure my folks wondered what was up, but I blithely waved them off and trundled over to my sweetheart's door. She greeted me and told me to meet her out at the barn, where we mounted her mini-bike and spent the afternoon zipping all around her property, her dusty dog nipping at our heels as she held her hands around my torso and I slalomed crusted-over potholes. I revved the motor, jerking forward, so she'd squeeze a little tighter. Deanna's long blond hair, blue eyes, and flushed cheeks were all I saw when I looked at her, and to me her innocent voice just seemed demure. Day's end, I was further smitten.

The following weekend, we arranged to go out to the reservoir for a night swim. An older girlfriend of hers drove us, and a friend of mine came along to even it out. The driver was a lead-foot. We made the ten-mile trip in breakneck time, boys in back, gals up front. Along the way, the driver put a tape of the Rolling Stones' *Sticky Fingers* in the deck, and she corked that mother up to full sandblasting volume. We all nodded along as Mick sashayed his way through "Brown Sugar" and "Sway," and then felt the hush of "Wild Horses." Once at the swimming hole, the four of us sat in the car polishing off

a six-pack, then another. A joint was passed around. Her face illumi-
nated by spliff tip, Deanna seemed less angelic, but to my buzzing
brain, only in a way that made her more desirable. Her friend took
a drag, then on the exhale asked: "You guys ever tried angel dust?"
I said no, that I wasn't into hard drugs. "Ah, shit, it's not that hard.
You put a little in your dope and smoke it." She chuckled at her own
joke. "I don't have any right now or we would have been working on
it." Deanna was looking at the ground, smirking.

We stripped down to our suits and took a dip, the water in the
quarry reflecting light blue against a harvest moon. Each of us
swam separately, savoring the silkiness of the night, the quiet of
the chiseled rocks. It was like taking a bath when the electricity
goes out. I remained chaste in spite of howling hormones. After
we'd dried off and dressed, the girls wanted to smoke some more.
I was very high already, but I continued apace. By the time we hit
the road, we were beyond toasted.

People are lucky to make it through high school alive. Several
kids in my class didn't, and those who died on the road did so under
identical circumstances to ours that night. The weed and beer
seemed to make our driver want to drive ever faster. She resumed
the cassette, the dark road rising and falling, my friend and me
just smiling and laughing and exchanging "wow" glances as the
car flew past the black of fields and groves of trees down the unlit
rural route. I remember looking forward to see that we were about
to cross a bridge at spectacular velocity, that we were in the middle
of the road, and that there were headlights in the opposite direction. As fast as the crisis arose, we reached the other side before
the other car did, and it was as if nothing happened, even though I
could see plainly that disaster had been narrowly averted. The girls
were singing along with Mick, hollering "bitch!" with him, Deanna's
friend periodically asking her to take the wheel so that she could
feign Keith's guitar parts. This might be the first time I'd ever seen
a girl play air guitar.

When I got home, I thought to myself that there might be more to Deanna than I'd realized. Something was strange about the contrast of our two dates, the pure joy of one and the demonic intensity of the other. I wasn't sure how I felt about it, but I knew then that Deanna was a shit-kicker. The Stones had only confirmed it.

My final experience with Ms. Olson: even though I sensed it was fated to fail, I asked her to a movie. She agreed, told me to choose, so I selected one that I'd wanted to see, Woody Allen's *Interiors*. Again, I was oblivious to the subtleties and monstrosities of our local form of class dislocation. Midway through, around the point that the Ingmar Bergman–like plot had reached the apex of its New York upper-crust stuffiness and I was thinking to myself, "This is the least funny Woody Allen film I've ever seen," I put my arm around her shoulder. I reversed the gesture a minute and twelve seconds later, counted painstakingly in silence as it elapsed, when her iciness grew acute and stung my palm.

Making small talk on the walking mall outside afterward, I asked Deanna what she thought. "I liked the costumes," she said.

1972

Transformer

Swoop swoop, oh baby, rock rock.

I learned what a simile was when I was eleven. My teacher was a folksy pop singer named Melanie. Her song "Brand New Key" had a lingering radio presence from when it first rocketed to the top of the charts a couple years earlier. Growing up in a family of punsters, I knew that one word could have multiple meanings. But sexual innuendo was a brave new world to my cohort and me, and we gingerly shared our experience of this song, which, in my case, had inexplicably made my trousers tight. *Well, I got a brand new pair of roller skates / You got a brand new key*, sang Melanie in a sexy-sweet schoolgirl voice. *I think that we should get together and try them out to see / I been looking around awhile, you got something for me.* "I might have something for her," I thought to myself, not knowing much but knowing that much.

It might have been later that year that, having discovered another layer of meaning to the word "come," and harboring the deeply held assurance that it was such a contraband double meaning that adults—at least the adults we all knew, mainly our parents, naive and sexless in our minds—couldn't possibly fathom it, my friends and I set about terrorizing the neighborhood with nudge-nudge wink-wink and bold emphasis every time the word appeared. I remember one softball game in particular, out on the street in front of our houses, in which we hammered the dopey joke into the pavement. Imagine a roundabout with four makeshift bases, each covered by some little dipstick hollering out "*Cum* on, batter, batter, batter, let's go!" or "Here *cums* another strike!" Rather quickly, one of our folks sniffed out this ruse and collared us, amusedly, warning that our secret wasn't so secret.

If one word could stand in for another, one image for another, if a roller-skate key could be a penis and a beckoning phrase could mean jizz, then it stood to reason that one person could secretly stand in for another. Wasn't identity as malleable as language? Wasn't it just a mask or costume? Aptly, Halloween was our chosen holiday. I remember stuffing a pillow into my shirt one year and borrowing a blond wig and a skirt from my mom, going door-to-door asking for candy dressed up as a secretary. (No off switch on the genius machine, in those days.) We played around with our identities like they were made of Silly Putty. As many kids did in the era of self-recording, my buddy Scooter and I used my cassette recorder to create customized programs, mostly based on existing television formats—quiz shows, late night variety shows, serial sitcoms. These were populated with a range of colorful characters, some recurrent, others offensively stereotyped, a little theatrical cast of alter egos. Saying things that only we could understand and trying on new identities were two sides of the same coin, a means of setting ourselves apart in a world of our own making, as entities we alone could invent, suburban kids never straying too far but gently teasing the boundaries of our parents' routinized bourgeois lives and mainstream values.

Though, to be fair, our parents had their own fantasy lives to cultivate. Inspired by a Richard Schickel review in *Time*, which she didn't read very closely, my mother suggested a movie to several local couple friends looking for something to do on a night out. They drove to an unfamiliar theater, where they attended *Deep Throat*. I'm told my mom was mortified. Not only did they manage to stay for the whole movie, however, they decided unanimously to stay for the second feature, *The Devil in Miss Jones*. In church the next morning, my mom was confronted by several women who had already heard about the prior evening, as had people up and down our street. Mom expected a harangue, but the women wanted her to choose movies for their film club. My parents certainly weren't swingers, but it wasn't out of the question that people like them might be. Trying out other lives, others' wives, and others' husbands was within a reasonable framework in polite society.

...

The visual artist Jimmy Wright came up under circumstances a universe apart from mine. Born and raised in a fundamentalist Christian community in rural Kentucky, he settled in New York in 1974 at age thirty. Once there he dove headlong into the city's edgy gay nightlife, documenting clubs, bathhouses, and street scenes in graphite, gouache, ink, and watercolor, observing the heavy action, always feeling a bit like an outsider to the city's underground. I've been friends with Wright for the last fifteen years. I'm also his art dealer. Most of the time when I visit New York, I stay with him. He's a night owl, so we sit around the huge marble table in the main room of his loft in the Bowery, talking into the wee hours, flanked by large sunflower canvases he started painting in the early nineties when his partner Ken died of AIDS. Dead flowers, sad and beautiful. Wright has helped me understand the New York scene as it was before I began to know it firsthand, in the early seventies when it was the jumping-off point for so many cultural movements, its garbage-strewn sidewalks proving as fertile as they were toxic.

One night during the first year he lived in Manhattan, Wright made a drawing at Max's Kansas City on one of the club's four-ply napkins. He sketched a sequence of five figures nestled shoulder to shoulder at a bar in the back room. The ink outline of the profiles bled through from the top layer to the bottom. Once back at home, Wright separated them, shading each of the four sets of personages, applying colored ink with brushes. On one row, a lipstick dyke stirs her drink, while on another sheet the same outline is filled in as a boy with an arm tattoo and blue eye shadow. One figure is transformed from a dark sunglassed fellow in a striped suit to a southern belle with bare shoulders and huge boobs. In the course of twenty faces, a panoply of seventies ideals is on parade, a hip New York typology from glam to glitter to proto-punk to disco to drag queen to sexpot to straight. Well, nearly straight. Straight as a role to play. Wright's napkin drawing is the perfect expression of the Lou Reed mentality.

...

I remember seeing Lou Reed's *Transformer* LP for the first time in Scooter's living room. The copy was his older sister's. Its cover portrait reminded me of nothing so much as Peter Boyle in *Young Frankenstein*, our favorite new movie. The hulking singer appeared face forward, his expression serene, almost beatific, dark eye shadow set against a pure white face, which had been made up and then overexposed, eliminating any shading, his hair vanishing into a cloud above him like a massive Afro or a puff of smoke. In stark white silhouette, Reed's ears poked out like bolts from the sides of his head. The edge of his guitar was rimmed in fluorescent orange and green, adding electric charge to the corpse. The emptiness of his visage was impressive.

Images on the rear cover also caught our attention, two glossy photos, side by side, one of a scantily clad dark-haired woman with bright lipstick, high cheekbones, and five-inch heels, posed with a hand covering her crotch in front of some slinky reflective material bunched into a sort of peacock tail; the other photo depicting a fifties-style greaser with a military cap, cigarettes rolled into the sleeve of his white T-shirt, a wedge of hairy midriff, his back arched theatrically, a gigantic semi-hard cock sculpted by his snug jeans.

"I hear they're the same person," Scooter whispered, even though there was nobody around but us.

We studied the images in microscopic detail, determined that it was true, and let this fresh data scamper around our heads, upsetting all sorts of preconceptions. The first song was already confusing, its narrator flouncily describing its subject as vicious for having lashed out with a flower; any sadomasochistic implications, like the fact that this flower-wielding bully wanted to be hit with a stick (Lou only had a guitar pick) were too subtle for our untrained ears. But then Reed sang the words *When I watch you come / Baby, I just want to run . . . far away*, and I glanced knowingly at Scooter.

There was childishness in some songs. Certain passages sounded daffy. Such disarmingly surreal moments appealed to us because kids are natural-born surrealists. With the words *If I could be anything in the world that flew / I would be a bat and come swooping after you*, for instance, Reed set up a series of absurd and menacing scenes in "Andy's Chest," all of them predicated on the idea of self-transformation. It's a singsong ditty full of ham-handed jokes and drippy puns. *Are all the mountains boulder after you?* asks Reed, before describing a woman whose proboscis grew so long that *When people say her feet smell, they mean her nose.*

We found these gags mildly funny and extremely weird and like nothing else in rock music that we'd heard. We could detect an infusion of irony, but this was a sensibility we'd not explored—we were just getting acquainted with sarcasm. "Oh, *suuuure!*" we'd proclaim, indicating disbelief. Jokey moments on *Transformer*, where Reed feigned innocence, made us more comfortable in the unfamiliar world of songs like "Walk on the Wild Side," a graphic novel version of true-life stories from Warhol's Factory, the coming-to-town tales of Candy Darling and Holly Woodlawn as well as hustlers and junkies and drug dealers and other denizens of the dark. Over Herbie Flowers's ingenious bi-directional bass line, Woodlawn's journey from Miami concluded with the terse capper: *Shaved her legs and then he was a she.* On the LP, we heard Reed depict Darling as someone who *Never lost her head / Even when she was giving head*, and then were astonished not to hear the same line when the song played on the radio. Another track described the application of makeup with exacting precision, enough so that at album's end, when Reed sang, *Good night, ladies / Ladies, good night,* somehow we knew he didn't mean women, he meant something closer to what a gym coach might say when ushering reluctant runners into taking a final lap. "Giddy up, ladies," I remember one such sadist instructing us as we pulled up our tube socks, adjusted our jock straps, and dashed off once more to the math building and back.

...

In the early seventies, many of us cautiously experimented with new identities. It was a time to upset preconceptions from the comfort of our bedrooms. For some middle-class white suburban kids, imagining gender fluidity and alternative sexualities were attractive pastimes, though they contradicted the generally prescribed mainstream attitude about queerness, which we understood was negative. Even today, conventional wisdom about glam and glitter, both London and New York versions, all too often comes with a kind of heteronormative undertone. Gender elasticity in rock, it seems to me, tends to be viewed from a straight standpoint, as an option for straight guys. Decked out in fur boas, flowing locks, lipstick, and mascara, the glam man offers a titillating alternative to humdrum suburbia, a campy, sardonic, in-the-know option that engaged us straight kids in thinking about another way to move through life, sexually, sensually, and socially. It permitted temporary escape from the rigidity of regimented behavior. But it was always aimed at straights. In his lightning bolt makeup, Bowie's Aladdin Sane, we understood, was a lad insane. We secretly longed for the frisson of that madness, a metallic drop of blood on the tongue, a taste at least of the unconventional.

Which is all fine and good as a fantasy for hetero boyhood. But how did it work for kids who were not straight or didn't see themselves as fitting into a strict gender binary, maybe some of whom were not from the suburbs or the city? What did it mean for someone whose visit to the wild side would be more than a stroll, more committed than the casual amble of the flâneur? Jimmy Wright was a farm kid who had immersed himself in the cosmopolis, and he was confident and frank and open about his gayness. Talk with him about his memories of music from the period, and they include the same insane heroes, perhaps most centrally Bowie. But as a self-identified queer person rather than someone experimenting with queerness from the safety of straight life, did he experience that sense of alternative identity in glam and glitter?

Wright already knew about Lou Reed when *Transformer* came out. "Wild Side," the album's single, was a surprise radio success. Wright had been hip to glam quite early, already as a grad student a couple of years before moving to New York. His immersion in the music commenced back then with a T. Rex concert to which he was brought by two gay men, both of them glam fans. He was the driver when this threesome made excursions from school in Carbondale, Illinois, to St. Louis to hear not only T. Rex, but Bowie on his first American tour, and also Iggy Pop, with bare-chested, stage-diving antics. "These two friends were tall and skinny with long hair, one very curly, one straight and wavy," he says. "Theirs was the sexuality of a rock star, which was the opposite of looking like a repressed, straight middle-class boy. It was the tail end of the sixties, in the middle of the sexual revolution, so we were still surrounded by hippies. Being a hippie wasn't so appealing. But being a glam rock star was very appealing. It gave the two men, who were a couple of years younger than me, a way of dressing and adopting mannerisms that was in a sense beyond gay."

In Bowie, Reed, Pop, and T. Rex, Wright says that certain gay men recognized something different, a way to go undetected by mainstream society, to veil their gayness in glitter. In other words, they saw a possible way to pass for glam. "You could be masculine but feminine," he says. "In a university town, once glam and glitter hit, nobody questioned or challenged that."

Seen retrospectively from the present, when there's a long-standing perceived antipathy between gayness and rock, this introduces an interesting twist. In its day, it suggests, glam appealed across sexual orientations. I have a good sense of what the music meant to straight kids. Of them, the only ones interested in passing were those who were actually gay and pretending not to be, of which there were no doubt plenty. Straight kids dealt with their own complicated feelings about their sexuality, including homosexual feelings, even if they were basically straight or were going to choose to live a straight life. Glam gave these boys the opportunity to explore those feelings. But that is different from glam enabling gay kids to have a normalized place within a certain part of society and popular culture by means of passing. Maybe most provocative is that this means both uses of the music were available at the same time. These musicians and their work could be understood and loved for divergent reasons—on the one hand, because they made queer erotics visible for straight guys; on the other, because they made queer identity invisible for gay men.

"Glam gave gay men a vocabulary that had not been available before," says Wright. "It was theatrical, it was sexual, and it came from rock 'n' roll. That legitimized everything." By moving from a rural southern town to New York City, he was able to embody the new rock star identity, not just observe it. He cheered for Bowie at Madison Square Garden. He saw scenester Taylor Mead drop drunkenly to the floor at Max's Kansas City, rise, and proclaim: "I'm going to sue this place for every penny I owe it!" At Club 82, quite high, Wright heard sexpot rocker Cherry Vanilla sing her song "Shake Your Ashes," and at CBGB he watched transsexual punk Wayne County take out a heckler's teeth with his microphone stand. He saw stage shows by the Cockettes, attended Charles Ludlam's Ridiculous Theatrical Company, went to productions by Robert Wilson, and sought out performances by Lindsay Kemp, the British pantomime master with whom Bowie had studied.

Another lad gone insane: Wright dyed his hair red and shaved off his eyebrows.

"Some of these rock 'n' roll dudes are really ugly, and yet they're so sexy," he says. "With Lou Reed, you add a sense of sexual fluidness. This is a straight man, but he's not—this is a sexy man who's available." For Reed, it had been a time of extensive experimentation with drugs and especially with sexual and personal identity. On *Transformer*, produced by Bowie and bearing tribute to Warhol, you can detect a cabaret aura. Cabaret is there in the arrangements, for instance, the unusual choice of tuba on two tracks—again, Herbie Flowers gives the record its most distinctive musical character—and the stage show vibe of Reed's lyrical scenarios. It's no coincidence that Bob Fosse's movie *Cabaret* came out the same year, spotlighting Joel Grey's special presence as a queer persona. It was one of my father's favorite movies. We sang the title song and the campy "Money" around the dinner table—*A mark, a yen, a buck, or a pound / Is all that makes the world go 'round*, and please pass the peas. Popular culture experienced a sudden upswell of interest in the kind of decadence represented by Weimar Germany. Reed's next record would be called *Berlin*.

At the end of the *Transformer* period, as a matter of fact, Reed married a woman, quietly outing himself as straight or bisexual and ending the most extensive of his forays into the wild. I wonder whether this biographical morsel is meaningful. Does it lessen the subversive impact, for instance, of an eerily soft song like "Perfect Day," with its ominous line *Just a perfect day / You made me forget myself / I thought I was someone else / Someone good*? Does it deflate the omnivorous claim of "I'm So Free," when Reed sings, *I do what I want and I want what I see*? If *Transformer* was all tinsel and eyeliner, and the message was that every person is mutable, that anyone can be anything by shaving their legs and plucking their eyebrows, who cares if its mouthpiece was queer forever? Maybe that made it even more powerful, the simple fact that an aspirant middle-class, straight, white rock 'n' roll poet with street cred could fashion himself into a thuggish glamour puss, cop a line from Nelson Algren, invite the *colored girls* to step up to the microphone, cue a baritone saxophone solo by Ronnie Ross, and intone an anthem to alterity.

...

Soon enough, glam itself would transform. It was set up to meld with a nascent version of punk to form another kind of decadent, gender-bendy image in bands like the New York Dolls and the Mumps. And a kind of Balkanization had been percolating with all the experimentation, so that a few years later gay identification with rock would be less available, the significations of groups like Sweet and Queen being conveniently cordoned off primarily for hetero use. As fabulously expressive and flamboyantly fey as it once seemed, seventies rock was reclaimed by heteronormativity and gender binaries. (At least that was the plan, though I think seventies rock never lost its illicit appeal to homoerotics, even in its most manly, brutally straight passages.) And by the middle of the decade, disco had overtaken gay subculture, which by then had its own well-developed scene at underground clubs, as well as the better-known spots like Danceteria and Studio 54. "For gay men, disco was a tribal experience," says Wright. "I was not interested in cluster-fucking five hundred half-naked men on a dance floor, so I never got into it."

...

Flipping through an old sketchbook, Jimmy locates a sketch of Iggy Pop he drew in 1973, after watching the muscular young man mesmerize an audience with X-ray nipples and a Froot Loop gaze. He views such souvenirs wistfully, but these days Wright finds more fulfillment painting supercharged still lifes at home alone and defending his loft against rapacious developers than going to concerts or throwing down at all-night parties. His opposition to the binaries of sex and gender remains sensitive, delicate—he's so vicious, he'd hit you with a flower. Having walked awhile where the wild things were, passing for glam, and drawing from life, he has now internalized alterity, moving beyond gender androgyny and its accoutrements, keeping a sprinkle of glitter a-glint in his heart.

On a bookshelf in his office, a single platform shoe six inches tall would have its own seventies stories to tell, if only a heel could speak. "Good night, ladies," it might say, lamenting its lost mate. "Ladies, good night."

And me? I still like dumb puns and laugh involuntarily at cum jokes. And when I hear that song by Melanie, it always rings desire's doorbell.

"School's Out"

I was just within Mr. Cooper's target demographic.

Not in the case of "I'm Eighteen." I was seven. That song made me feel like a baby, like there was a secret society of adults concerned with a universe of problems that were a complete unknown to a poppy seed like me. And there was. I refer to Alice Cooper's logical follow-up, "School's Out," an anthem with a militant riff and lyrics that served as fantasy fodder for future vagrants, a rock version of Jean Vigo's 1933 film *Zéro de conduite*. By the time it hit the airwaves in July 1972, to coincide with the end of the school year, I was turning nine and the prospect of a life without teachers and classmates, however fleeting, was increasingly urgent.

The LP on which Cooper's song appeared—his fifth, which bore the same name as the single, his biggest to date, peaking at number seven on *Billboard*'s Hot 100—depicted the state of things in this young boy's head with startling accuracy. The design sported a wooden desktop that was hinged at the top and flapped upward to reveal the desk's interior, just like ours at school did. On the desk's surface were carved initials and a tattoo-like image of a heart pierced by a knife. In the upper-right corner, routed-out text spelled the artist's name and the title of the LP. And the desk's insides were more or less spot-on—notebooks, pencil, eraser, crayons, marbles, slingshot, comic book, orange, switchblade, and a pop quiz that contained all the album credits. Best of all, on the first edition the clever design wrapped each vinyl record in a pair of lace panties.

I think I was born with a libido. My earliest sexual memories start when I was four, and although their intensity spiked when I hit puberty, the raw curiosity and drive were there all along. I played doctor with neighbor girls, getting caught at age five one rather terrifying time by a pissed-off mother in Barrington, Rhode Island. When I was seven and we lived in Cleveland, I showed mine as I was shown hers with an older girl up the street. That year a friend and I discovered the stash of *Playboy* and *Penthouse* magazines that my father inherited from the Corbett Clinic, the industrial medical outfit started by my great-grandfather in Chicago, where they had once provided reading material in the waiting room. The cache of soft-core porn followed us to Philadelphia and Iowa City, and through my adolescence I unearthed and secretly combed it for tidbits of carnal knowledge that may have escaped my attention.

Music has always been linked to sex, but in the seventies the association was inescapable—consider that when the Electro-Harmonix company introduced its bold new guitar pedal in 1970, nothing about naming it Big Muff seemed out of line. I've always thought it appropriate that this device appeared at a time when women proudly preserved their pubic patches rather than buzzing them down to crew cuts or waxing them off altogether. But what did panties signify to a nine-year-old? What could I have gleaned from their use in a record cover design? As sexual as my imagination was, my drives were basic. Probing and examining were the name of the game. Objects of clothing had none of the fetishistic flicker they would gain, and panties were just something I wanted to take off. I did understand one thing about this aspect of the *School's Out* package, which was that it meant to suggest that the goodies beneath the underwear—the grooves, the music—were highly desirable. It probably dawned on designer Craig Braun, as it did me, that the LP has a little hole. I salute you, Mr. Braun.

Ultimately, the panty-clad version of the record was banned by the Federal Trade Commission not for being indecent, but because the undies were flammable. Alice Cooper's response: "Who would be lighting a cigarette or a match down there anyway?"

...

Alice Cooper was part of a whole cadre of artists that my friends and I admired as much for their persona as for their music. Perhaps, in his case, even more. His stage show, which I never experienced first-hand, was the subject of endless speculation and rumor among my peers. As a progenitor of shock rock, Cooper's concerts were trailed by a litany of urban myths. He ripped the head off a live chicken and drank its blood. He'd blown up a sheep with dynamite. He let a boa constrictor slither up his butt. He was planning to electrocute himself onstage. He'd accidentally chopped up a live baby, thinking it was a doll. Someone had slipped a real guillotine in place of the rigged one and it cut off Cooper's head.

My interest in ridiculous spectacle comes naturally. Mitchell Corbett, my great-grandfather, was an orthopedic surgeon and an aficionado of the circus, professional wrestling, and boxing. He was friends with Roy Rogers, Gorgeous George, Joe Louis, and Jack Dempsey, and would torment my great-grandmother by sponta-neously inviting a troupe of midget wrestlers over to the house for dinner. A circus gave him a lion cub as a present, and he kept it at the Corbett Clinic, allowing patients in the waiting room to take Duke for a walk. The same circus gifted the family two young chim-panzees, Sally and Susie. My dad's first tricycle was a hand-me-down from Susie. When these animals grew too large to be viable domestic pets, they were donated to the Brookfield Zoo. In 1940 the newly founded Ice Capades invited Mitchell to be a partner, which would have meant that Dorothy Hamill might have later dazzled visitors with her moves and hairdo at the Corbett Ice Capades. My great-grandfather declined the offer, but in 1969 my first doe-eyed crush was on Peggy Fleming, whom I eagerly saw when the Ice Capades came through Cleveland.

We squared shock rock—and its relatives in glam and metal—with similar preoccupations of the era, most obviously horror movies and professional wrestling. Like those endless founts of entertainment, Cooper depended on faux scandal and moral outrage to generate publicity. And we were after cheap thrills and simpleminded titillation—I recall a fifth-grade science class in which the teacher was called away for a spell, and we dimmed the lights, encircled the black marble chemistry table, and held a séance around one of our own who lay still while we all chanted, "Light as a feather, stiff as a board," and miraculously lifted him using but one finger each. Predisposed to love shlock as we were, we ate up Cooper's shtick like a tag team match, say the Sheik and Abdullah the Butcher versus Terry and Dory Funk, or a hokcy terror like *The Texas Chainsaw Massacre*. Was it provocative? In a lascivious way, it was. Did it provoke us in any deeper way? That might be a hard case to make.

But in some sense I think this devil's triangle of suspended disbelief set the conditions for some of the most influential musical culture of the seventies, from Kiss to the New York Dolls to Devo. It's now more fashionable to look to David Bowie as the prototypic character chameleon, but Cooper's version of adopted identity was equally meaningful, appealing not as a deep exotic intellectual mystery—Bowie's department—but as something near and dear and stupid as hell. Cooper was a comic book anti-hero who celebrated the unthinkable and took our beloved dead-baby jokes to the main stage. His name was Alice. He dressed in women's clothes. He wore makeup. This alone was the source of endless moronic conversation. Anything androgynous was innately fascinating and fueled the speculation. Is he gay or is he just a cross-dresser? I hear he sleeps in a coffin. Maybe he fucks corpses?

As put on as we knew his stage persona to be, Alice Cooper scared us. Not all the campy monstrousness. You could see through the running mascara that he was a down-to-earth Detroit boy—later in life, a Republican and a professional golfer—whose dabbling in the darkness was all smoke and mirrors. When the smoke cleared, we could see ourselves in the mirrors. Broken shards. Shattered little half-wits staring back at ourselves, unsure what was made up and what was actual, what was shallow and what had lasting depth. We thought we were ready to break loose from the shackles of miseducation, to celebrate school's ultimate termination, to blithely spend an endless summer exploring our inner idiocy, but at the sound of the recess bell, we were only running from ourselves, repulsed by the cretins we saw in the busted mirror's reflection.

...

A related story obliquely intertwined with this one.

My cousin Tim visited me once in Iowa City. Seven years younger than me, he was the same age as my little sister Jennifer, who had just turned nine. Tim idolized me, for whatever conceivable reason, and I adored him back, enough to torture him like the younger brother I didn't have. On my wall, among various posters and flyers, was one from *Blues for Allah*, the only record I've ever owned by the Grateful Dead.

"What's the Grateful Dead?" asked Tim.

"It's a band," I told him. "A band whose members kill their fans. They select some of their die-hard followers and put garbage bags over their heads and then bury them alive by the side of the road. The fans love the band so much that they're thrilled to be killed. And that's why the band is called the Grateful Dead."

Tim gasped. But he believed me wholeheartedly for a few years, treating the story as a simple music fact, commonly known, just as Jennifer believed our sister Jill when she explained that Elton John wore those outlandish glasses because he was blind—a belief only dispelled by attending an Elton John concert together, years later, long after Jill had forgotten the deceit. The opening moments in which Elton jumped all over the piano and flung himself around the stage tested the bounds of credulity. Indeed, it was literally incredible—that is, not credible.

A few months after I'd blown Tim's mind, on a lark with a red-headed girl named Anne, I went to a Grateful Dead concert. I watched as Deadheads formed a daisy chain around the center seats at the auditorium and the drummers performed a thoroughly tedious twenty-minute jam. We left before it was over. In the parking lot on the way to walk Anne home, we encountered a kid selling incense.

"I'm just trying to get to Des Moines tomorrow night," he said. There was something ghoulish about his skinny arms and deep-set eyes.

"I've been at every gig for the last month, but I'm just about out of cash. Can you help me out?"

I handed him a couple of bucks and accepted some of the noxious sticks.

"It's that last concert of the tour, man. If I don't make it, I'm just gonna curl up and die."

Close to the Edge

The band performed on a circular stage that turned continuously while they played, rotating them 360 degrees like slices of pie in a diner display. With my friends Doug Cannon and John Corrigan, I went to hear Yes at the Five Seasons Center in Cedar Rapids, Iowa. This unexpected quirk of their *Tormato* tour set the British group back the princely sum of 50,000 pounds, and we wondered why we needed to see a band from all sides. What would be interesting about periodically observing Jon Anderson, Chris Squire, Steve Howe, Rick Wakeman, and Alan White from the rear, except perhaps to experience the music as if we were onstage with them? Then maybe that was exactly the point—to prove that their magic was real, that they were actually playing everything, there was no prerecorded tape or synthesizer shortcutting, that Wakeman really could play two keyboards at once, arms crossed, Howe letting rip a skittering solo, his twisty guitar cord cascading behind him into his pulsing amplifier.

"With all this spinning, and them having to move around so much, how do they keep from getting their wires tangled?" I whispered to Corrigan. "Seems like a disaster waiting to happen, like when a dog gets its leash wrapped around a tree."

"I wonder if they get dizzy," he replied. "I mean, it's not going too fast but it might mess up your head. There must be some kind of centrifugal force up there pulling them toward the edge of the stage."

"Speaking of which, I sure hope they play 'Close to the Edge.'"

My buddy Scooter Johns and I had already had a spinning-stage experience two years prior in Philadelphia. This involved an even stranger premise, as it was a stand-up comedy gig by George Carlin, our hero and the reigning philosopher-king and chief linguistic anthropologist in our adolescent empire. An expert at pointing out undetected details of life, like the fact that on escalators the hand-rail never travels the same speed as the stairs, it was almost too ripe a situation for him to work with, preoccupying him and clearly making him uneasy. He was brilliant, but on the lazy Susan it was uncomfortable watching him struggle to figure out who to look at as the crowd inched by him, and it was equally weird to have him pirouetted in slow motion before us, sometimes delivering a punch line in the opposite direction from where it was set up. I'd never considered the spatial specificity of comedic or rock music practice before, but in both cases it seemed to confuse rather than enhance the experience.

Yes was my first retrospective concert, by which I mean a band I'd previously been deep into but one that had slightly faded from my primary pantheon, providing a more distanced perspective. I bought *Fragile* and *Close to the Edge* in 1975, added *Tales from Topographic Oceans* a year later. The four years between those enthusiastic purchases and the concert seemed an eternity. And in Yesland, there had been important changes, none graver than the loss of Bill Bruford, the drummer who left to join forces with King Crimson. From my vantage, that was like a sports superstar going free agent and leaving for another world-class team in a different city. There was also a string of solo albums by the independent members of Yes. Wakeman alone released five: *The Six Wives of Henry VIII*, *Journey to the Centre of the Earth*, *Myths and Legends of King Arthur*, *No Earthly Connection*, and *Criminal Record*. These records are kind of amazing in a hilariously puffed-up way. Howe issued *Beginnings*, on which he made the disastrous choice to sing himself, and *The Steve Howe Album*, which came out around the time of the concert. Squire made *Fish Out of Water*, maybe the best of the batch, a real sleeper, while drummer Alan White recorded the eclectic and unsuccessful *Ramshackled*.

And then there's Anderson's *Olias of Sunhillow*, which was simply excruciating and served to push me all the way out of the fold. The cover riffed on Roger Dean's classic design for *Fragile*, but a short graphic novel was inserted into the LP, illustrated by the cover designer David Fairbrother-Roe, the artist who also crafted a memorable image for Nazareth's *Hair of the Dog*. Anderson's concept album presented the portentous New Age story of an alien race with ridiculous names, ornamented with lots of harps, flutes, and other heavenly instruments, the singer's Bee Gees–register choral flourishes, and none of the musical substance of records made with the other Yesmen, rocking about as hard as the jubilant last song in *The Grinch Who Stole Christmas*—you know, all the Whos down in Whoville. For Yes fans, it was a richness of embarrassments.

The seventies were the era of errant solo forays. As bands gained stature, their members often sought to express themselves outside the confines of the group, releasing LPs—usually eminently forgettable ones—under their own names. It seemed a sort of rite of passage upon entering stardom, and nearly everyone tried it, from the Who to Kiss, from the Rolling Stones to the Eagles, from the Revolutionaries to Parliament. Stepping out was just the thing to do for musicians with means and a manager. The members of Led Zeppelin had the good sense to wait until the band broke up in 1980 to start recording solo LPs, but they were in the minority, and when they went for it, Jimmy Page and Robert Plant each made surprisingly good records under their own auspices.

...

As it turned out, "Close to the Edge" was one piece that Yes did not perform that night, though they did play the album's two other songs, "Siberian Khatru" and "And You and I." But the great concert reminded me how much I adored *Close to the Edge*, in particular what an unusual and powerful bassist they had in Chris Squire. He's much more active than most of his species were in the seventies—rather than pinning down the beat and anchoring the harmonic progressions, Squire played melodies, serving as Yes's Jaco Pastorius or Larry Graham. His instrument was engineered at greater volume and was more articulate in the overall mix than was customary. He turns it into a hard-driving motor when needed, keeping pace with the quicksilver guitarist and keyboardist, joining forces with Bruford's pneumatic percussion. Listen to the way Squire's gargantuan presence alters everything when he hits town on "And You and I" or the galvanizing instant in "Close to the Edge" when Anderson sings, *Now that it's all over and done / Now that you find, now that you're whole*, and the bassist gooses the end of the phrase with a walloping line that boomerangs out into the next verse. The album offers a bountiful set of arrangements, sometimes odd and engaging, like a segment pairing electric sitar with harpsichord or Wakeman's organ feature on the title track's slow movement "I Get Up, I Get Down," on which he fingers the pipe organ at St. Giles-without-Cripplegate in London, as well as resplendent passages including the ascending melody of "Siberian Khatru" or Howe's spectacular Paganini-oid picking, which livens many a part of the program.

Yes is what happens to psychedelia when it hits the seventies. It goes corporate—not prog rock strictly speaking, with its analytic and experimental embrace of avant-gardism, but a kind of uplifting prog pop. This music is free of hippiedom's lifestyle implications. It's meant for solitary epiphany rather than communal enlightenment, emphasizing synergetics rather than group gropage, deploying ambiguous themes that are overwhelmingly positive—hey, man, they are called Yes after all—and *Dianetics*-like in their mix of light-of-the-world quasi-biblical message and schnazzy new-tech gleam. Wakeman's use of Moog synthesizer verges on a computer-game gloss. *Achieve it all with music that came quickly from afar* goes the first verse of the title cut, suggesting something mystical or techno-logical, a psychic or radiophonic transmission from another plane. Anderson has explained that the lyrics to *Close to the Edge* were inspired by Hermann Hesse's *Siddhartha*, and they have an oblique poetics that was, to us, impossible to understand with any specificity but suggested something profound: the abstruse universal.

What captivated us most was something more banal. These musicians made no bones about their virtuosity. In fact, the music was designed to showcase prowess. Difficult time signatures indebted to fusion groups like Mahavishnu Orchestra, for instance, played in terrifying tempi with grace and subtlety. Yes was a band that we listened to on the sidelines, as bystanders, never thinking we could aspire to their accomplishments. When, as all fumbling young guitarists do (and any healthy orangutan could), I accidentally discovered the beginning notes to "Roundabout," I felt I'd turned the key in the lock of some ancient portal. But it was too easy, those open-tuned harmonics, plucked from the most obvious place on the instrument. And it was only a few notes, the rest of the song was an ornamental flourish out of reach for mortal teenagers.

My friends and I had developed a mythology around the fetish of prowess, segregating all other musicians from those who, in our parlance, had "classical training." This erroneous and misguided label was thrown at many players, most of whom had nothing of the sort. Anyone in truth who could do something that we couldn't figure out. "I've heard he was classically trained," someone would say, and that was that. It was absolute and irrefutable—like installing an MD after their name, it meant they were authoritative and had gone through an official hazing process, out of which they emerged with all the arcane information about frequency and pitch and form and rhythm that a classical musician would need. It so happened they were rockers. That was their choice—but clearly they could have done anything. Classical training was our simpleminded way of explaining how a musician could become a doctor of sound.

...

We loved *Close to the Edge* for its combination of songs and extrapolations. The title track lasted eighteen minutes, which was impressive and immersive, and the gatefold cover proved useful for neophyte dope fiends. Nine months prior to seeing Yes in concert, I returned to Philadelphia from Iowa City to visit Scooter, the only time I would come back. Before I'd left for the Midwest, I was not smoking pot, but in the interim I'd sampled a little, and while spending time with my pal, I expanded my involvement with the drug. Toward the end of my stay, basing our actions on our normal insatiable drinking regimen, Scooter and I decided to try to smoke as much as we possibly could in one sitting. He procured a dime bag, and one night we began rolling joints, separating leaves from stems and seeds in the crotch of the gatefold of *Close to the Edge*. We toked on them one after another until we were about halfway through the dope. Sensing that we would soon reach the point of incapacitation, I suggested we put on some music, and for the occasion nothing seemed more appropriate than the very record we were using to clean our weed.

A few words on Scooter's room. I was sleeping on a slat bed next to his bunk. He had long shag carpet, on which sat a big box fan that was cooling us off in the July evening heat. His turntable was on a dresser about four feet behind the fan, and beside it was a taller dresser with his combs, powders, colognes, and deodorant— the essentials in his daily grooming routine—arranged thoughtfully on top of it. Outside his locked door and across the hall, when they came back from their dinner party, would be his sleeping parents. His dad was an imposing ex-military doctor with a George Jones flattop who once declared the twelve-year-old Scooter a pussy after he had smashed his arm over the head of our friend Scotty. Dr. Johns told his son his freshly fractured arm was nothing but a scrape. A week later it had to be rebroken and set.

Back on the scene of the ganja extravaganza, I placed the needle in the groove, stumbled my way back to take another few hits before falling over onto my bed, five slats of which promptly broke, leaving me with my butt wedged in a mattress pothole. I was incapable of adjusting myself, let alone getting upright, so I lay there listening to Steve Howe, my mind propelled along by his guitar solos, a mix of ecstasy and fright filling my THC-addled noggin. After what seemed a long time but was only a few minutes, I choked out: "Scooter?" He grunted back at me, and I said: "I'm flying! I mean really, in my head I can fly!"

And then I fell fast asleep. In the still of the night, Scooter woke up and registered that the record had finished—hours earlier— and was thumping in the run-off groove. As he got out of bed, he wakened me. I watched him move toward the stereo, but when he got to the fan, still stoned, he misjudged the distance past it to the tonearm. I could see his silhouetted figure vainly reaching over the fan, as if, like Plastic Man, he could stretch the four feet to turn off the record. I was already consumed with tittering by the time he fell forward onto the fan, pulling all his toiletries down onto the floor with an apocalyptic crash, in the process bumping the record back into monstrous loudness, followed by the tortured noise of the fan caught in the shag rug. It was one of the most extreme soundscapes I've ever heard, and I was absolutely paroxystic with laughter until a heavy knocking befell the door and Dr. Johns shouted: "Scooter, what in Sam Hell is going on in there?!"

Sobering fast, Scoots jumped up and stammered incoherently: "Uh, the rug, the fan, the record, my cologne. You know, we're *really tired*!" His dad told us to keep it down or we'd be in for it, as Scooter turned the fan and record off and hobbled back to his bed.

We spent a protracted time listening to nothing but the night sounds out the window. I broke the silence: "Hey, you all right?" Scooter said yes. We listened to a little more quiet, and I added: "Holy crap, that's a great record."

"Frankenstein"

"Hocus Pocus"

A bumper sticker built for me might read: "I Heart Gonzo Rock."

Like the over-the-top journalist Hunter S. Thompson, gonzo rock exaggerates everything, amps it up, and slays it. Think of "Farm Film Report" on the Canadian comedy show *SCTV*: Big Jim McBob and Billy Sol Hurok talk briefly with guests like Freddy Fender, Randy Newman, Neil Sedaka, Helen Reddy, and the Village People, and then "blow them up real good." Exploding musicians. That's muy gonzo.

Gonzo makes a space for twin guitar solos. More on that, but first: Edgar Winter, Focus, instrumental rock, and the special sauce of virtuosity ladled thick like maple syrup over eggs and sausage with a side of ridiculously overdramatic gestures and an order of albino keyboards or yodeling flautist served extra crispy. Hellfire, this here is gonzo too!

Edgar Winter had already played the piece that would later be reanimated as "Frankenstein" with his brother, guitarist Johnny Winter, a few years earlier. Johnny's best known for his proto-gonzo hardball "Rock and Roll, Hoochie Koo," written by Rick Derringer, appearing along with RD on *Johnny Winter And*, after Edgar had split to form his own band, Edgar Winter's White Trash. You gotta love a guy what jokes about his own albinism. But maybe the Texas-born keyboardist's humor cut too close to the bone, because he toned the band's name down to the Edgar Winter Group by the time of *They Only Come Out at Night*, an album not originally meant to contain "Frankenstein." That track, thought of as best suited for extended live jams, was first deemed suitable for the B-side of a single. By popular demand, literally after radio fans made a nuisance of themselves by requesting said B-side, Epic Records flipped it to an A-side, and it instantly shot up to the top slot on the American charts, where it hung out for a week, menacing the airwaves like the monster it was. Epic included it on the LP, too, bless their greedy little hearts.

I loved the hyperbole of "Frankenstein." I mean that in the science fair sense of the word—hyperbolic geometry, paraboloids, hyperboloids, all the -oids of wavy-shaped and quickly ascending or descending variety, anything to suggest the sort of screen-saver undulations that tease the common mind, seduce Op artists, educate topographers, and form a major swath of the architecture of psychedelia. And of course, there's nothing better for all that sonic saltwater taffy than a synthesizer, gonzo crankshaft par excellence. Winter moves around between instruments, playing alto saxophone adeptly in a swift jazzy segment; he takes a thunderous timbale break, trading very un-Latin flourishes with his percussionist, and dons a strap-on keyboard—the first popular musician to do this, using an instrument of his own design—equipped with a pitch-shifting knob, the synth version of a whammy bar. Whole lotta gonzo going down. None of it would matter if not for the brazen riff, a big, bulbous, ripsnorter with boot-clomping bass and a bunch of boogie. The ultimate moment comes at 3:20 into the song, when an alien space tentacle descends from the sky in the form of a squishy synthesizer noise, eclipsing everything else, sweeping guitar, bass, drums, sax, and keyboard to the side, then engaging in a quick shoot-out with the drums before the Heffalump riff rejoinder hits and the song peaks, climaxes, and is finished.

Gonzo rock is based on excess, but if there's an excess of excess, things can switch from giddy to farcical. It takes a refined ear to locate the threshold. On "Hocus Pocus," the Dutch prog rock quartet Focus walks a razor's edge between razzle-dazzle roller coaster and weird novelty gewgaw, pushing the gonzo *mas* gonzo, landing way out past gonzo's condo. It was just heavy enough and foolish enough to appeal to me, at nine, on both fronts. After a ragged, distortion-saturated, hard-rocking riff and strip-club drum break, Hammond organist Thijs van Leer takes the lead by yodeling variations on the main riff motif in a couple of descending vocal arpeggios over swelling organ, ending back up in the ionosphere with strained high notes. A third round of these weird breaks goes even further into the outback, with a hiccuping hillbilly vocal display reminiscent of the DeZurik Sisters, Grand Ole Opry stars who had a tandem chicken-clucking routine; another romp lands the flutist on his main axe, and on the penultimate one he does a zany one-man-band routine, whistling and playing harmonium, before returning to the by then normal-seeming yodels. Between each of the breaks, guitarist Jan Akkerman counters with hot and heavy solos that, by comparison with the chimp-like antics of his bandmate, seem nearly academic. When I first heard it, it was an experience unlike any I'd had before, maybe one I never needed to have in the first place, like pole vaulting into a pile of rice pudding.

This is hard rock by way of Spike Jones and His City Slickers.

Bigger, faster, louder: essential mid-seventies buzzwords. In concert, Winter stretched his song out, jamming Coltrane length on sax and bashing around on drums, giving his band members some as well. Focus, on the other hand, sped their ditty up, challenging themselves to make it sound something like a song as it blazed past. Akkerman, in particular, is impressive in the few TV versions preserved for posterity, like one on the NBC show *Midnight Special*, where his punkish slashing and shred-like picking help amplify the song's energy, and van Leer's tomfoolery is even more unhinged. By strapping on his keyboard, Winter suggested that guitar could be displaced from its throne as reigning king of gonzo performance. The portable piano and synth add-ons allowed him to bounce around the stage, grimacing and waving his long white hair like a sun-bleached rancher wielding his rifle at a rodeo. If "Frankenstein" momentarily nudged guitar out of the spotlight in favor of keys and synth, "Hocus Pocus" adopted an all-means-necessary mentality, imagining that anything, even the most unlikely material—folkloric vocals, flute, pursed lips, squeeze box—could replace hard rock's mainstay, much the way that saxophones overtook trumpets as the icons of jazz. Time has proven them wrong, however. Nobody thinks of heavy metal and imagines a goofball Dutchman playing flute or a titanium dioxide Texan with a strap-on synth.

What will be remembered eternally, however, are twin guitar solos. These represent the royal legacy of Bigger, Faster, Louder, extending the oscilloscope-destroying outrageousness of gonzo rock into more stable domains, infiltrating some that are tepid and decidedly non-gonzo. It was a thing. The Eagles' "Hotel California" is perhaps the best-known example of the gratuitous harmonized doubling of plectra. Guitarists joined forces, swaying as one while they played the same notes or intertwined, mock-Bach, sometimes on double-necked guitars. If one guitar line was good, two were automatically better. Derek and the Dominos did it on "Layla," so did Dickey Betts and Duane Allman on many Allman Brothers songs. And Boston, and Queen, and Thin Lizzy, and Steely Dan.

Here we are in goo-gobs of gonzo. On all those solos, the volume knob should be turned up high. A hot pot, as the saying goes—the potentiometer turned clockwise, like lighting a burner. We're beyond the era of the transistor radio into that of Marshall stacks, where loudspeakers earn their name and they serve as gangplanks for the band almost as much as they fulfill their other rightful purpose: to kick out the jams at maximum amplitude. Conjure the photograph by Steven Steigman, used for a widely circulated advertisement by Maxell audiotape: a guy sits in a Le Corbusier chair, a tall speaker placed at his feet and pointed his direction, his hair and tie blown back, martini glass tumbling from the side table, lampshade above him thrust back by the implied musical blast. As musical subjects of the nineteen seventies, we existed to be blown away.

...

A short coda on Lester Bangs, top columnist on gonzo rock:

What made Bangs the quintessential music writer of the seventies was the way he spinal-tapped them for their gonzo. He could be as harsh as he was adulating. There was little in the middle. Discovering his writing in the pages of *Creem*, I read his legendary Lou Reed piece "Let Us Now Praise Famous Death Dwarves" and his essays on metal and punk and glam, which gave me a context and unpacked meanings; but more importantly the essays were gonzo too, showing an empathy with the music, resonating at the same frequency as the most deranged and self-indulgent of its makers. Through his words I got a feeling that was like listening to what he was writing about. His was a paraliterature of rock's excesses; he massaged the most bodaciously hyperbolic among them for anything he could extract, his language as soloistic and balls-out as any johnson-flapping hophead with an electrified git-fiddle wired into an ample o' fire. Only Richard Meltzer gave him a run for his money. Anything but square, Bangs remains, in my mind, square one.

Back Stabbers

One fistfight. That's the sum total of my pugilistic experience. There was nothing impressive or graceful about it. After I'd successfully out-rebounded him at the hoop, Wayne Schick gave me a round-house elbow to the nose from a crouching position, a fully leveraged sucker punch that sent blood geysering onto my white shirt and the gymnasium floor. Without a boxer's bone in my body, I nevertheless had pride enough to shake off the stun, put up my dukes, and say: "You jagoff, you want to fight? C'mon, you fucking coward, let's do this!" At which he clocked me two or three more times before people intervened. He was prancing around like a white Muhammad Ali, bellowing: "I'm the champ! Want some more?" But even his buddies, popular kids at Abington Friends School Jon Braverman and Chad Ewing, held him back and castigated him. "What's your fucking problem?" said Braverman. "Are you crazy? He didn't do anything but beat you to the ball!"

Thus ended my career in the ring.

What can I say? I'm a lover, not a fighter.

The thing that distressed me was that Wayne and I had never been adversaries. I always thought he had an attitude, acting mean and cool beyond his scrawny exterior, but I didn't hold it against him. We were all adolescents looking for our way, and braggadocio just seemed to be his. I didn't know much about him, except that we came from different worlds—him from working-class South Philly, me from an upper-middle-class suburb. But we were both of Eastern European stock, and we both took long bus rides to our private school; his gruffness just struck me as defensive.

What was more evident than the class disjuncture, though, was his adoption of what we interpreted as black mannerisms. He liked to swagger around and talk tough, clipping words in apostrophe endings—killin', trippin', bitchin'—and deploying unfamiliar slang, making crude comments about girls, puffing himself up, and looking for trouble. At our insulated school, there were no actual black students or teachers, so we were basing our interpretation of his actions on a bunch of stereotypes gleaned from movies and television. I think he actually picked these things up from the street, but I have no way to really say. What I know for sure is that he didn't like being out-jumped by a soft nerd like me. And though he might have been able to give me a humiliating thrashing, I could have gone ten-for-ten on the boards against his punk ass any day of the week.

...

I have a specific memory of Wayne from before the fight. We were on a bus, one of the classic snub-tailed orange jobs, shorter than a normal school bus, not much more than an overgrown van. Our class was on a field trip downtown in a caravan of several vehicles, and there were no chaperones on ours, so of course we had music blaring in the rear of the bus, and all the boys had congregated in a little moronic cluster, heaped atop the green tall-backed seats. Wayne was standing above everyone else, lip-syncing, while a scrum of fellows egged him on. The portable radio played the O'Jays' three-year-old smash hit, "Back Stabbers."

Blades are long, clenched tight in their fist
Aimin' straight at your back

And I don't think they'll miss
(What they do!)
They smile in your face
All the time they want to take your place
The back stabbers

Our school was Quaker. The majority of the students were Jewish. Everyone on the bus was white, except the driver, who might have found the scene amusing or distressing, depending on her state of mind. None of us knew anything about popular music or the music industry; I had only just bought my first vinyl LP that year, and my interest was still gestating. I recall classmates using vulgar terms for African Americans, and those same kids were the ones who loved black music the most. Like Wayne. On the radio, for a time it was what we all listened to. Nobody seemed to think of it as black music. We thought it was American music. Hip music. Popular music. Music.

We were from the city where Philly soul was born, home of the Delfonics and Philly Groove Records and Kenneth Gamble and Leon Huff's Philadelphia International Records and Sigma Sound Studios, the facility where the O'Jays recorded "Back Stabbers" and their other gigantic hit "Love Train," produced and arranged by the Jamaican-born Thom Bell in the same year Bell co-wrote "I'm Stone in Love with You" for another Philadelphia act, the Stylistics. The sound was a global inspiration. We heard our city's music reflected back at us in singles by Hall & Oates ("Sara Smile," "Rich Girl"), David Bowie ("Young Americans"), and Elton John ("Philadelphia Freedom"). It transcended geography and ethnicity. At the time it was so ubiquitous that we didn't even think of it as local. It was what music on the radio sounded like, anywhere and everywhere.

The music on the back of the bus, that day and most others, definitely sounded like Philly soul. My sister Jill and I rode forty-five minutes every morning from our house to school. Whenever we were allowed, we entertained ourselves with that music, our dancing inspired by weekly viewings of *Soul Train*, where we admired the studio dancers' moves and Don Cornelius's great catchphrases like: "We got another sound comin' outta Philly, and that's sure 'nuff dilly." Majestic, sophisticated, orchestral, even symphonic, Philly soul made use of Sigma's pioneering twenty-four-track board, layering instruments and turning voices into choruses, transforming stripped-down soul compositions into complex scores with highly chromatic arrangements that evinced ever more nuanced emotions. Philly soul was about hues, shades, breaking down the heart's response to sound into fractions, apportioning those out like pigment to a painter. On LPs like the O'Jays' *Back Stabbers*, the program was pushed from being a collection of radio songs to something more elaborate, neither a fleshed-out concept tightly composed as an album nor an aggregation of singles, instead toggling between gritty stories of double-dealing like the title track or "Shiftless, Shady, Jealous Kind of People," and celebratory anthems like "Love Train," "Time to Get Down," or "When the World's at Peace."

...

The violence of the fight, the ugliness of the epithets, the glee in our dancing, the radiance of the song, its resonant lyrical twist, the magnitude of our appreciation, the depth of our ignorance, Wayne's knuckles and smirk—all of these things converge in my memory. It's remarkable how we tended to our contradictions. We pretended they were just songs, anybody's ditties, but we knew better. The underlying disparity was too plain.

We loved black music; we feared black people.

It was more complicated than that, though. The fear got mixed up together with the love, and jealousy slipped in, even with those exuberant babies bopping naively at the back of the bus, expressing their adoration in the most palpable manner possible, shaking a tail feather, joyful embodiment undercut by shit their parents and playmates had said, nasty clichés and hateful lies floating around in their little underdeveloped crania. Expressed one way or another, white folks were basically jealous of black culture, certainly of the music, also the sports and comedy, and what came out was that fucked-up fear-love, the explosive combination of admiration and resentment. The nature of that jealousy came as a projection of romantic fantasies, some perception of freedom and natural aptitude, of a relaxed way of moving through the world, forthright sexuality, rhythmic inventiveness, the possession of cool, and a general lack of constipation. We saw those things in the Jackson 5 and Minnie Riperton, in Eddie Kendricks and Rufus, in B.T. Express and Donny Hathaway. Man, oh man, did we envy it.

My parents tried to shelter my two sisters and me from racism. I didn't encounter it in my family until I was at the end of college, when I brought my girlfriend to meet my grandparents and they made anti-Semitic comments, only realizing she was Jewish by the shocked look on our faces. That would have been around the time that the same grandparents tried to convince me that black people were congenitally lazy and dirty. I argued bitterly with them, but inside my head what I kept thinking was that this misshapen attitude had been there all along, I'd just missed or ignored it. Secretly I was afraid that it had subliminally deformed my own views. I felt pity for my progenitors that day, and I don't think I ever trusted them again.

...

Meanwhile, just outside our mid-seventies suburban Philadelphia bubble, a dirty rotten police commissioner named Frank Rizzo—who had rounded up the Black Panthers and subjected them to a strip search in front of newspaper reporters and who promoted police brutality against African Americans—was elected mayor and boasted that if successful in his bid for a second term, he would "make Attila the Hun look like a faggot." The devil wiggles his way into many different bodies—fat crusty old torturers and openhearted dancing children alike.

A friend has just betrayed you—Brutus, Judas, Wayne—and now your nose is broken. This was our everyday duplicity, set to a perky beat: smile in their face, all the time want to take their place.

Dogon A.D.

In certain circles, it has become commonplace to declare the seventies a terrible time for jazz. In *The Jazz Scene*, Eric Hobsbawm writes, "The best that could be said about jazz in the early nineteen-seventies, even in New York—as usual it was said by Whitney Balliett—was that it had stopped collapsing." Speaking of the period in the short segment dedicated to it in his jazz documentary, Ken Burns said: "The question was whether jazz, the most American of art forms, would survive at all."

Do not listen to them. This is utter bunk, a smear campaign, a revisionist conspiracy, the wrongheaded perspective of musical museologists insensitive to the potential for an art form to change. You want proof positive? Just listen to the new music that was being made by South African expats in London, bands as beautiful and original as the Blue Notes and Brotherhood of Breath. As a matter of fact, the seventies were a new golden age for jazz, not only the electric path paved by Miles Davis but all species of creativity that spawned in New York's lofts, Europe's festivals and concert halls, funky spaces in Los Angeles, a row house in Germantown, Pennsylvania, and especially in the cities of the Midwest.

Down in St. Louis, the Black Artists Group (BAG) was founded in

1968, much along the lines of Chicago's Association for the Advancement of Creative Musicians (AACM), which had been founded three years earlier, banding together the most progressive African American players, in BAG's case with dancers, actors, poets, and visual artists as well, in an atmosphere of collective action and self-presentation. Alto saxophonist Julius Hemphill was one of the cofounders and primary movers-and-shakers of BAG, which continued into the new decade and launched Oliver Lake, Hamiet Bluiett, J. D. Parran, Joseph Bowie, Charles "Bobo" Shaw, and Luther Thomas. Hemphill had come up from Texas, where his pedigree couldn't be more pure: attended the same high school in Fort Worth as Ornette Coleman, check; studied clarinet with the great John Carter, double check. He went on to be one of the great composers of his generation, his works often featured by the World Saxophone Quartet (W.S.Q.), an ensemble he co-founded in 1976 and through which he reached the widest audience.

Hemphill's first record, *Dogon A.D.*, was self-produced for his Mbari label, and it was issued with a beautiful black-and-white cover, very DIY, the label's name writ large along the bottom edge, like it was the band's name. *Dogon A.D.* is a quartet record featuring Hemphill on alto and flute, with Baikida Carroll on trumpet, Abdul Wadud on cello, and Phillip Wilson on drums—classic jazz front line/rhythm section format but nothing conventional about the way the music sounds. A local release in its first incarnation, known only to folks in St. Louis, it made a bigger splash when it was reissued in 1977 on Arista's Freedom series, a crucial imprint on a big label that helped disseminate some of the best recordings of creative music in the seventies. Two of the decade's visionary producers were involved, Michael Cuscuna and Steve Backer, both smugglers of essential contraband into mainstream venues.

The long track from whence the LP takes its title is one of the key epic statements of new jazz in the era. Among its remarkable distinctions, it manages to draw on Wilson's schizoid experience having been a member of the Paul Butterfield Blues Band and the first drummer for the Art Ensemble of Chicago, in making an 11/8 rhythm into a staggeringly funky thing of joy. Over the course of fourteen and a half minutes, Hemphill builds a nearly continuous solo, his spiritual blood brother Wadud sawing the cello with a deep blues soulfulness that is raw and mantra-like in its repetitive incantation. It feels right and wrong in equal measure, the theme carrying its own piquancy with honked barnyard dissonances and some contrary motion between the horns and string. Most of all, it takes its own sweet time, in no hurry to get anywhere in particular, but out for a righteous stroll.

Knowing a little about the session's producer casts the music in an alternative light. Oliver Sain was a polymath musical persona who worked along a corridor from his birthplace in the Mississippi Delta up through St. Louis to Chicago. Descended from a musical family, his grandfather a noteworthy blues musician and member of the Beale Street Sheiks, Sain played drums with Sonny Boy Williamson and Howlin' Wolf and saxophone with Little Milton, before forming the Oliver Sain Soul Revue in the early sixties. Fontella Bass began her singing career in Sain's band, and it was with him that she had her first taste of success on Chess in 1964, a year before her smash single "Rescue Me."

In 1965 Sain settled in St. Louis and opened his own recording facility, Archway Studios. A year later, Hemphill moved up from Texas, having played R&B with Ike Turner, a friend and occasional colleague of Sain. At that time, the jazz, soul, and rhythm-and-blues worlds often overlapped. Jazz players appeared on blues and soul recordings and gigged around readily, looking for a little scratch or a long stretch—recall Wilson's steady job with Butterfield—and sometimes the genres mingled in other ways. Hemphill and his band entered Archway in February 1972, working with Sain to produce *Dogon A.D.* The bluesiness of the title track is a logical point of connection, although Sain's main orders of business that year had been recording his first LP, *Main Man*, and reuniting with Bass to produce her new, quite liberated-sounding record *Free* for Chicago's Chess label, where she'd had her big break.

Now, it's not like *Dogon A.D.* is an Oliver Sain record. The music he made under his own steam was light instrumental funk with crunchy, sometimes quirky arrangements, often using familiar pop and R&B songs as starters, and later he'd have low-boil hits with disco-friendly cuts like "Booty Bumpin' (The Double Bump)" and "Party Hearty." Hemphill was clearly in charge of his recording, which was serious in tone and weight, and when it was issued, it also had two other beautiful, more abstract and diffuse tracks, "Rites" and "The Painter," aside from the ragged funk of "Dogon A.D." But it's interesting to imagine the session, with the highly experienced producer of popular music and the firebrand creative music saxophonist, six years his junior, recording more than enough music for a debut album that would percolate for five years before captivating adventurous jazz fans worldwide.

In fact, they recorded another track that was left off the LP. One can immediately understand why they excluded "The Hard Blues," which was even longer than "Dogon A.D.," meaning that it would have fully occupied the other side of the vinyl; it is as stated a grinding blues, so in a way might have seemed a redundancy. "The Hard Blues" is a little different, though, in that it adds baritone saxophonist Bluiett, which thickens the soup, and it has quite a different structure, with its chugging blues offset by a lithe little bebop-like section, bright and surprising. This cut would be repurposed as the centerpiece of a different Arista Freedom release, *'Coon Bid'ness*, which beat its counterpart to the shelves, finding release in 1975, two years ahead of *Dogon A.D.* And "The Hard Blues" really set the table for the blues component of protean Hemphill's W.S.Q. contributions, reappearing frequently in concert and on the 1991 saxophone sextet, recorded after leaving W.S.Q., *Fat Man and the Hard Blues*. The first time I saw Hemphill, in Boston in 1985 with his JAH Band, which included a twenty-something guitarist named

Nels Cline, he played "The Hard Blues." It was, in many ways, his signature song.

To return to Archway Studios for a moment, if you listen carefully to the way "The Hard Blues" is mixed, you'll notice a present from Mr. Sain. On the heaviest part of the main theme, Sain hardpanned the horns back and forth in time to the beat. On headphones, it's almost unlistenable, but played on a good stereo, you get a funny sense of the producer hatching an idea, gestated in his soul experiences, of sweeping the sound of two saxophones and trumpet back and forth, like windshield wipers, adding another percussive element into the very fabric of the recording. It's a remarkable, if ungainly, moment in the history of jazz-pop relations, drawn from an extremely fertile passage in the saga of creative music.

Pink Moon

Let's get paranoid. Not just two-tokes-look-over-your-shoulder, I mean science-fiction-plot paranoid. They're-out-to-get-you paranoid. "*They* who?" you say. Fair enough. Could be a secretive government agency seeking to program your thoughts or a subversive group out to sabotage that government or counterinsurgent cyborgs pretending to be subversives but actually working for the Chinese government. Or maybe it's just a company trying to sell cars. Yeah, that's it. Let's go with corporate paranoia.

Earth date: 1999. Our setting feels much like the present, but, even though very few humans can see it, this is in truth the dawn of a new age. A quarter century earlier, in 1972, seeds were planted in the form of a song, the title track to a record by a British singer named Nick Drake, which had been quietly inserted into the memory banks of a select group of people: a folk rock sleeper cell. In its era, the song and its album were not widely known, sold modestly, garnered a mixed critical response, and the song was still obscure when the singer killed himself in 1974 at age twenty-six. Drake's death further buried the trail of secret memory implantation, as he was not personally present to cultivate his reputation or identify the implant technicians. Nevertheless, his admirers slowly grew in number as the song and its memory wound up helping to spawn a dreamy new genre known as shoegaze, and by the time of the memory retrieval, his three LPs had acquired a cult status.

In the year before the new millennium, an expert team of sentiment snatchers led by Jonathan Dayton and Valerie Faris was dispatched to retrieve the memories that had been implanted decades earlier and to create a vehicle for the extraction of emotional content in those memories. That vehicle was literally a vehicle: a Volkswagen Cabrio. A year earlier, in 1998, a test memory had been successfully extracted by a different technician, Wes Anderson, who used a film called *Rushmore* to wrest a similar memory titled "The Wind" by Cat Stevens. Anderson would continue to utilize cinema for memory extraction, innovating a technique in *The Life Aquatic with Steve Zissou* (2004), in which memories of David Bowie's songs were indirectly retrieved by being sung in Portuguese by Seu Jorge.

The Nick Drake extraction involves a VW television ad. The spot starts with a swooping overhead shot along a river at night, the camera joining a car as it crosses a bridge on an unlit country road. In the silent black car, a multiracial group of four beautiful, beaming young people enjoy the night air and full moon, as a melancholy acoustic guitar song called "Pink Moon" with minimal lyrics and finger-picked minor chords occupies the soundtrack, perhaps on the car radio or just in the minds of the kids. Gravel under the car's wheels momentarily calls attention to the sound of the real world, as the quartet pulls up to a little country house, where a group of carousers are partying. The carload of introspects exchange knowing glances; quick shot of reverse lights coming on, the car's logo shining above them; the foursome is off down the dark road again, preferring their intimacy to the bustle of social interaction.

This extraction was so complete and successful that, with the exception of a few devoted sleepers who decried its premature removal, it silenced its critics. The ad was universally praised, having withdrawn the painfully shy memory—which for each of its fortunate original listeners seemed exquisitely personal, fragile—

and transferred it into a new context in which it could be widely exchanged and appreciated. And where it could identify a new demographic—the millennial hipster—to whom they might sell cars, a poignant little message humbly trailing the ad's montage: "Drivers Wanted."

The Cabrio was hip by association, a car for thoughtful people who shrink from big crowds and prefer melancholic intensity to roughneck horseplay. Unfrozen and re-released, Drake's music underwent its own metamorphosis; what was an underground specialty was catapulted to superstar status, as *Pink Moon*, the LP, was reassessed and canonized. Hence, a seventies music memory was co-opted and redeployed. The heartstrings that Drake so sensitively struck in a session conducted over just two nights in 1971, unedited recordings with his guitar and voice and a single piano overdub, were called back into active service, and other songs, like "Parasite," "Horn," "Things Behind the Sun," and "From the Morning," ranging from painfully confidential to bossa gauzy, were likewise raised from their slumber. On his tombstone, a line from the last of these is uncannily close to foreseeing what happened: *Now we rise / And we are everywhere.*

One listener who had been implanted with the song in the seventies was sitting at his computer, where he was very surprised to see the ad, both because TV ads on the internet were unfamiliar and because he regretted the fact that the song was being used this way, that its network of associations, dark and mysterious and in the domain of his private thoughts, would now include something as ordinary as hustling automobiles. Also, the song had been previously unknown to others. It was his to introduce to them; he'd discovered Nick Drake—or it almost seemed like that since nobody else seemed to know the singer. Now Drake would be public property. Although it wasn't the first time he said, "I knew about so-and-so before they were famous," it might be the saddest.

Two years later, Wes Anderson, now the Godfather of a new film genre, the playlist movie, set out to perform another extraction, a project titled *The Royal Tenenbaums*, this time with a song called "Fly" from an earlier Drake record, *Bryter Layter*. AT&T used "From the Morning" for yet another corporate extraction in 2010. That sentiment snatch was successful, but seemed less miraculous. By then, using Drake for memory retrieval seemed like old hat, as common as extracting emotion from a Motown song after *The Big Chill*.

Carla Bley, Paul Haines

Escalator Over the Hill

Todd Rundgren

Something/Anything?

The words synergy (syn-ergy) and energy (en-ergy) are companions. Energy studies are familiar. Energy relates to differentiating out sub-functions of nature, studying objects isolated out of the whole complex of Universe—for instance, studying soil minerals without consideration of hydraulics or of plant genetics. But synergy represents the integrated behaviors instead of all the differentiated behaviors of nature's galaxy systems and galaxy of galaxies.

R. BUCKMINSTER FULLER

Synergetics: Explorations in the Geometry of Thinking (1975)

Until all creative thought is extinguished, curiosity will be the yeast in our bread and the seeds in our mulch, the oar in our pond and the little motor on our model plane. Raw curiosity helps things grow and makes things go. Being curious expanded my musical horizons and drove me to listen to things unfamiliar, not just out of concern for the music itself, but as an act of putting myself in someone else's shoes. My attention could be focused on another person and their enthusiasm. "How," I sometimes thought to myself in genuine wonder, "could anybody like *that*?" This question led me to observe those likers of alien things as they listened, to attempt listening as they did, and as often as not to discover something enlightening in the process. I remember once seeing an older friend dancing like a possessed person to a group opening for Tom Petty and the Heart-breakers and thinking: "Look at him love the shit out of that very ordinary music; there must be something I'm missing." And because the J. Geils Band hadn't yet soiled themselves with "Love Stinks," I discovered that there was indeed much there to love.

How to adopt alien ears?

It's not a matter of being undiscerning. It's learning to discern differently.

First, adopt what Zen Buddhists call Beginner's Mind.

Suspend judgments, especially ones based in aesthetics.

Accept that you will make the mistakes of a novice, because you know no better.

Try to understand how the system of discernment native to this unfamiliar music relates to other systems of discernment you under-stand better.

Hold fast to a relativistic attitude, all the while establishing likes and dislikes within the newfound music.

Become a neophyte connoisseur.

Discern differently.

Curiosity leads us out of the tribe. Gingerly, under cover of night, we sneak into someone else's closet, try on their clothes, steal the ones we like, shock everybody back home by appearing one day in a green forage cap and dark blue monkey jacket, like our head is bound for the woods and our body for the sea.

We are curious; we embrace eclecticism.

...

The seventies embraced eclecticism wholeheartedly. Even boutique labels, those offspring of major labels that were bestowed upon powerful artists both as playthings and as farm teams for new tal-ent, were rarely homogeneous in their output. The Beatles promoted acts as different as Ravi Shankar and Badfinger on Apple, their imprint of EMI, while Led Zeppelin's Swan Song, whose parent company was Atlantic, issued records by Bad Company and Dave Edmunds, neither of whom come automatically to mind when thinking of "Stairway to Heaven."

The decade also saw the rise of compilation records, many of them miniature studies in eclectic programming. K-tel and Ronco produced roundups of disparate artists that promised scintillation beyond compare with titles like *Superhits*, *Dynamic Hits*, *Hit Action*, *20 Blockbuster Hits*, *High Energy*, *Reflections*, *British Gold*, *Souled Out*, *Right On*, *Disco Nights*, and *Southern Fried Rock*, this exaggerated overreach perfectly lampooned by SCTV, who mock-advertised a comp titled *Gordon Lightfoot Sings Every Song Ever Written*. There were also *Nuggets* and *Pebbles*, the comps that aided in the rediscovery of American garage rock, and Warner Bros.' so-called Loss Leaders series of two-LP sets compiled by Dr. Demento, including *Appetizers*, *Deep Ear*, *All Meat*, and *Collectus Interruptus*, the last promising "Twenty-Six Songs of Unique Delight, Derring Do, Heartbreak, Scandal, and Lurid Sensation." Coupled with the heterodox offerings of free-form and progressive radio, a concurrent phenomenon, these various-artist albums, even the most genre-specific of them, helped hatch the concept of the mix tape and instilled amongst those of us who treasured them an abiding respect for the ability to craft a continuous idea out of diverse parts.

From the time I started devoting myself to music, I lived by the code of conduct of eclecticism, actively seeking out new experiences, fanning out from rock and pop and experimenting with all sorts of other sounds, but I don't think I fully understood what I was up to until the start of the next decade, when I first heard *Amarcord Nino Rota*. On his first record, producer Hal Willner showed me what I'd already been doing.

...

From an adjacent mixing studio waft the familiar strains of seventies Queen. I knock on the door, and the engineer looks up from his console, anticipating my question: "Willner? He's down the hall." As

I leave, they resume, another guy in the room saying: "Can I just have the drums?" One punch and a button strips away everything else, leaving Roger Taylor's kit stark naked. I stop outside the door, listening as they isolate various parts: Freddie Mercury's vocals, one by one, dissected, a cappella, Brian May unaccompanied. Some remastering project, I think, and then I feel the fourteen-year-old in me holding its sides in glee. "Holy cow," Little Me thinks, "right inside that room they're rejiggering the motherboard of my youth."

Willner invites me into his tight studio/office. It's the Museum of Cool Shit. His desk is surrounded by bits and pieces of cultural history, some effluvial, much of it invaluable. "Everything's got a story," he says, inviting me to ask about whatever interests me. "Do you recognize that lion?" I don't. "It's Pookie, the puppet from *Lunch with Soupy Sales*." He picks up a metal blade. "Feel how heavy this is." I do. It's an iron sword with the word "Gonzo" in relief on the handle. "Ralph Steadman designed it for Hunter S. Thompson's funeral. He was just gonna leave it there." Willner points at a black-and-white photograph on the wall: "That's the original of Kitty and Lenny. I got it when I did the box set." A reclining Lenny Bruce looks up at his daughter in an iconic shot. Willner produced a six-CD box of Bruce's comedy, *Let the Buyer Beware*, in 2004. He flips through a heterogeneous array of albums, including one titled *Pronouncing the Classics*, designed to aid classical music radio announcers. Willner locates a copy *Whoops, I'm an Indian*, the only LP under his own name, which he constructed out of samples from 78 rpm records.

Suffice it to say that Willner is one of the most influential figures behind the scenes in contemporary music. As a record producer, he came up under the wing of Joel Dorn, who in turn came up under Ahmet Ertegun, the man whose marvelously catholic interests and impeccable judgment made Atlantic Records a tastemaker and trendsetter in a stunningly wide range of musical arenas spanning jazz, soul, pop, and rock. Along with producing musical segments for *Saturday Night Live*—which have been some of the key introductions of new music, including very unusual and offbeat stuff, to the general public—Willner was musical director for most of *Night Music*, the short-lived but perfectly realized network television show that brought together great music of all varieties, known and unknown, historical and cutting edge, beautiful and obnoxious. I watched every single episode, at the time silently thanking Willner for his generosity. He is a heroic figure in my mind.

I realize that the table of contents to this book reads like one of his productions.

In a series of tribute records that started with *Amarcord Nino Rota*, his dedication to the composer who wrote for Federico Fellini's films, Willner produced homages to Thelonious Monk, Charles Mingus, Kurt Weill, and Walt Disney's soundtracks, among others. These utterly transformative cultural mix-and-match patchworks are his pride and joy. They bring Leonard Cohen, Tom Waits, Marianne Faithfull, and Debbie Harry into proximity with John Zorn, Eugene Chadbourne, Elvin Jones, and Muhal Richard Abrams. No wall is too tall: genre, style, geography, and renown are all surmounted in the name of synergy.

Willner is one of this art form's high priests. I heard his productions as they came out, and this made me feel that I'd been granted retroactive permission to approach unlike music with equanimity, assessing tracks on their own terms but relishing them together, treating juxtaposition as a generative force. Willner helped me better understand the mix tapes I'd already been making, gave me further license to explore and combine. Quintessential postmodern genre clashes—his brilliant tribute compilations are very much the template for a new musical collage mind-set.

"I was just doing what I had been taught to do," he says, pulling up tracks for a T. Rex tribute he's working on to play me versions of the glam rocker's songs as recast by Macy Gray, Nick Cave, Lucinda Williams, Beth Orton, and Joan Jett. "I remember Bill Graham's concert lineups, which would include very eclectic mixes of artists. I worked with Joel Dorn, who was passionate about many things and saw how they could be brought together. I was there for Rah-

saan Roland Kirk's *The Case of the 3 Sided Dream in Audio Color*"—
the saxophonist's unusual record that had many different kinds of
people on it, from Sun Ra baritone Pat Patrick to Afro-Cuban pianist Hilton Ruiz to jazz-rock drummer Steve Gadd—"and we got
crucified in the press for that. But think of Tom Dowd, Tom Wilson.
These producers all had good ideas. They weren't blindered; they
were curious and they brought things together. They were also characters. Some of them were very fucking wild people, even completely
crazy. But they did incredible things. We were listening to all sorts
of music. I remember Carla Bley's *Escalator Over the Hill*—that
made perfect sense to me."

...

Bley's ambitious triple LP is an excellent skeleton key to unlock
Willner's way of thinking, a sensibility that started earlier but
crystallized at the beginning of the seventies. With a libretto by
Canadian poet Paul Haines, pianist and composer Bley and her
then-husband, trumpeter Michael Mantler, invited a spectacularly
mottled group of participants into their jazz opera, or as they called
it their "chronotransduction," a lineup wide-ranging enough to pull
in a promising young singer named Linda Ronstadt; the superstar
bassist and vocalist from Cream, Jack Bruce, whose own *Songs
for a Tailor* presages much of the genre intermingling; free jazz
luminaries Don Cherry, Jimmy Lyons, Enrico Rava, Roswell Rudd,
and Charlie Haden; figures from other parts of the jazz continuum
including drummer Paul Motian, Jimmy Knepper, and Sheila Jordan; and Karen Mantler, Bley and Mantler's four-year-old daughter.
The Warhol actress Viva makes a cameo as herself. The music's span
is equal to its makers—five different ensembles perform at different
intervals, including a nineteen-piece version of the Jazz Composer's Orchestra, a quartet spotlighting Miles Davis guitarist John
McLaughlin, an "Original Hotel Amateur Band" with filmmaker and
artist Michael Snow on trumpet, an octet with trumpeter Cherry
and violinist Leroy Jenkins in the foreground, and an atmospheric
incidental music trio called Phantom Music, with Bley on organ,

celeste, chimes, and calliope, Mantler on altered piano, and Frank Zappa keyboardist Don Preston on Moog.

Bley's music is droll and beautiful, comical and heartbreaking. An overall air of cabaret incorporates Kurt Weill, tango, experimental music, electronic music, Tibetan drone, jet-propelled free jazz, prog rock, and country music. But her approach is not pastiche, really; she locates a common humanity in all these different musics, a core root perhaps, or just an opportunity for mutual fascination. Juxtapositions are not attempted for cheap effect. They take a dramatic conceit, even a jokey one, and make it the grounds for elaborate musical theater, still hard to pin down forty-five years after the sessions, which spanned from 1968 to 1971, and then took a year to be released.

In addition to her own catalog, much of it plotted and executed with Mantler until their split in 1992, Bley's compositions gave shape to spectacularly wonderful records that explored some of the same terrain, including Gary Burton's *A Genuine Tong Funeral* (1968) and Haden's *Liberation Music Orchestra* (1970). And she contributed to Willner's first tribute, *Amarcord Nino Rota*, with a suite of arrangements of Rota in much the same vein, bringing things full circle. Listening to Willner's choice of go-to tenor saxophonists, the late Gary Windo and now Mars Williams, you can hear continuity with Bley's tenor on *Escalator Over the Hill*, Gato Barbieri, who reached his widest audience via his work on *Last Tango in Paris*. All of them have a penetrating, hard tone, a joyous sound, and a penchant for going apeshit crazy in the midst of a beautiful melody.

Escalator remains a peak achievement in Bley's career. With its death reference title, it winds in and out of lucidity, landing in different scenes like one in which the character Ginger, played by Ronstadt, and her friends, played by Haden and Steve Ferguson, sing a little cowboy song, eerily recalling Haden's own history as a child performer warbling like so. Though Haines's text is suffused with a dose of absurdity, the opera's opening line, sung by Preston, rings with a political clarity that periodically has uncanny resonance, perhaps none louder than the present day: *It's in the lobby of Cecil Clark's / That people raised for one thing / Like cows for milk / And chickens for legs / Vote for something weak and to the point.*

...

"I was in a hotel lobby the other day," Willner says as I prepare to take my leave, reluctantly, from his museum. "Nobody was under forty, but there in the background was Lady Gaga. I mean, there's always been pop music, but Lady Gaga wasn't tailor-made for any of those people. There's no diversity. Now it's one world, one music." He shakes his head somberly. "One world, one music."

That such a slide into monoculture would get Willner's goat is obvious. It's the repudiation of all he's stood for, his crusade for cool shit of any stripe, hence his maintenance of the Museum of Cool Shit. "I've been buying Zappa stuff at auction; the family is selling it off. It's crazy. Some going for big bucks, but then I got this"—he holds open a wooden object—"the music box that Stockhausen made for him." Willner opens the lid, and little discordant plucked metallic sounds sneak out. "With everything I've bought, they send me some weird little extra. Look at this." A child's ceramic ashtray mono-grammed MUZ and another, this one a snowman, with DZ etched in the bottom. "Moon Unit and Dweezil," he sniffs. "What the heck do I want with these?"

...

Two weeks later, at Willner's invitation, I am in a Brooklyn studio watching Todd Rundgren sing T. Rex's "Planet Queen." Rundgren's sipping a hot beverage in the vocal booth, his bicolor hair still parted at center to reveal a long, friendly face, cracking jokes as the engineer and crew work to get the session set up and airborne. They only finalized booking the studio time a few hours earlier, and everything's about as on the fly as can be. This sort of improvised configuration is how it rolls on Willner's variety records, which are assembled with the producer's vision of a totality as the balance of parts—hence, calculating who will go together, what style or genre or tempo or arrangement would be interesting for the piece, and for its place in the program. An ensemble that had been planned to record earlier in the day, with Debbie Harry singing over a Salvation Army band, is postponed. Debbie is having a good run with her new Blondie record and the timing didn't pan out. But a couple of days later, they'll be in a different studio with former New York Doll David Johansen and actress-chanteuse Charlotte Gainsbourg.

Once everything is in place, there's only an hour left to lay tape. The band has used the time to rehearse, deciding on a form and tempo, allocating solos, how the cues will work. Directed by trumpeter Steven Bernstein, who chooses to play slide trumpet, it's a sweet combo, with an ace creative-jazz rhythm section of bassist Tony Sherr and drummer Kenny Wollesen, a top-notch old-school session organist named Brian Mitchell playing Jack McDuff's Hammond B-3, which the studio had acquired, and a pianist I seem to recognize but can't quite make out through the control room glass. He sounds fantastic. I ask Hal. "That's Donald Fagen," he says, nonchalantly.

Rundgren is brilliant, his voice in stellar shape even when he jumps an octave in the third verse. He's funny, too, with a good sense of swing, tapping some inner Sinatra, and extrapolating in a lascivious beat poetry *Sprechstimme* interlude that he narrates extemporaneously, conjuring entirely different scenarios on each take. This shouldn't surprise me: he's been touring a recent bossa-nova record. *Flying saucer take me away / Give me your daughter*, he belts out the original T. Rex lyrics. *I've come for your daughter / Give me your daughter / Give me your daughter*, he sings, morphing ad lib vocalese, then speaking: *But I'm not picky / I'll take your son / Give me your offspring / I've come for your offspring*. Fagen helps the singer push this approach to the song beyond novelty, adding such depth of musicianship that it shifts the vibe into some Mingus-like rave-up. Listening to the playback, Bernstein turns to the pianist and says: "In that one spot, you go to the five and then you could play, you know, something else, like that Steely Dan chord." Fagen nods with the casual cool of a jazz musician: "Sure, I know what you mean, I could do that."

After four times through the tune, Rundgren's car is waiting out front. They've got at least two viable versions, more than enough. It seemed impossible in such a tight frame, but this is what decades in the business teaches you. We sit in the control room, Rundgren already suited up in a hoodie and black sunglasses, listening to the last take. Fagen is reclining on a big comfy couch, his wife, singer Libby Titus, tucked in and snuggling, bobbing her head to the music.

It's a small world. Titus had a daughter with drummer Levon Helm, singer Amy Helm; Bernstein worked extensively with the Helms in upstate New York, near Woodstock; Rundgren and Fagen both still live up there, the latter in Bob Dylan's home in the hills above town, a onetime arts colony known as Byrdcliffe. In 1970 manager Albert Grossman founded his Bearsville label just outside of Woodstock, on which Rundgren released classic LPs including *Hermit of Mink Hollow* and *Something / Anything?*

In the context of rock record making, *Something / Anything?* suggests comparison to *Escalator Over the Hill*. (It's worth noting that Bley also lives in Woodstock.) Of course, the one major difference is that Bley recruited a small army of collaborators, while Rundgren made the first three sides of the double LP on his own, playing almost all the instruments himself. But the music forsakes no diversity for its having been made by a single musician. On the record's culminating fourth side, titled "Baby Needs a New Pair of Snakeskin Boots (A Pop Operetta)," Rundgren engages in a little bout of reverie, his own chronotransduction, incorporating two snippets from his fetal foray into garage rock, dredged from the archives of 1966. And it's in the same set of grooves that he reintroduces "Hello It's Me," a song he'd recorded with his band Nazz on their eponymous 1968 debut. If you're looking for one cut you can call the earworm of the decade, I think this poignant love song is a perfect candidate, but it's only part of the fabric of this brilliant bicoastal double album, a studio concoction in which the studio is a central character, with false starts and talk-back breaking the fourth wall and exposing a partially improvised songwriting and arranging process. It gave me insight into how records are made, enticingly depicting their mise-en-scène; I'm thinking about *Something / Anything?* the whole time as I watch the singer wave his dulcet wand over a song T. Rex originally recorded a year prior, in 1971.

In the intervening decades since I first heard Rundgren's masterpiece, I've spent lots of time in studios, observing sessions, serving as a producer or writing liner notes, sometimes remastering historic music from old tapes. It's a familiar ambience—the dead air of downtime between takes, the seen-it-all drollness of engineers, the dramatic neutrality of mixing boards, the live room and isolation booths and baffles, nowadays the inevitable tangle of analog and digital gear. All the stuff that's ritually disavowed on records, the same stuff that has been gradually revealed to listeners, a million pictures of musicians slumped on sofas in studios, the curtain pulled back to reveal, as Rundgren's next record would have it, *A Wizard, a True Star.*

...

Tendering his opinion on the best take, Rundgren is off to meet his ride, as are Fagen and Titus. Bernstein and studio owner Andy Taub and I wade deep into a Sun Ra geek-out. Bernstein has made hand-collaged books of the Ra songbook that archivist James Wolff had dug out of the Library of Congress archives twenty years ago, a nerdily loving gesture; he gave copies to Taub, who's a thoroughgoing Ra fanatic, and Willner, and kept one for himself. Via Ra, we are brought back around to Willner's omnivorousness—he booked Ra on *Night Music* and had angled to get Ra and Al Green to play together. Maybe the Reverend would sing "Space Is the Place." Green wasn't having any of it: "He's from Saturn, eh?" And that was all.

In the great synergetic galaxy of galaxies where all things are interpolated into one mutually respectful arrangement, some alluring combinations will just have to haunt our imaginations.

1973

Space Is the Place

Some artists have a fraught relationship to their time. Sun Ra's position was more extreme: he was an outright enemy of time. Ra resisted the human imperative to expire—"Choose Life, Not Death," he once titled an essay—and he memorably titled a piece "It's After the End of the World, Don't You Know That Yet?" At the beginning of the semi-autobiographical film *Space Is the Place*, he eagerly anticipated a moment when people would "consider time officially *ended.*" He was, quite literally, looking forward to the end of time. A musician like this, as you can imagine, might have a complicated feeling about his own place in history.

...

The last time I spoke with Sun Ra, I asked him for his take on the enduring legacy of the great American songbook.

It was 1993. Ra had returned to Birmingham, Alabama, where he'd been born nearly eighty years prior. He would die there, from complications associated with pneumonia, a few weeks later. The pianist, composer, and bandleader's first published composition, "Alone with Just a Memory of You," written in 1936 together with one Henry McCellons, conveyed a tender, awkward Tin Pan Alley tone that betrayed his love of sentimental song craft. This passion is driven home repeatedly in a survey of Ra's magnificently gigantic discography. He employed anachronistic singers like Clyde Williams and Hattie Randolph. He played familiar compositions with double-entendre titles meaningful to him, such as "East of the Sun," "Keep Your Sunny Side Up," "I Dream Too Much," "Out of Nowhere," "This Is Always," "Second Star to the Right," and "Over the Rainbow." Never mind that Ra is known to many as one of the most adventurous and innovative figures in the history of the twentieth century. That he brought synthesizers to jazz. That his costumes and light shows paved the way for psychedelic rock. That he wrote apocalyptic and deeply philosophical poetry. That he identified as extraterrestrial. That outer space and the unknown featured as prominently as ancient Egypt in his unique proto-Afrofuturist *Weltanschauung*, which often manifested as a circus-like performance troupe called the Arkestra.

Ra couldn't resist a good song.

His reply to my question was typically elliptical, asking me to consider his interest in comic books. The reason he read comics, especially when he was a young musician, he said, was that the artists that made them worked within a set format and had crazy deadlines, which meant they had to be creative under pressure. They didn't have the luxury of time. The great ones rose out of a homogenizing environment, and the individual spark ignited by their work happened in such a strict context that its genius was undeniable. Like Jerome Kern, the Gershwins, and Cole Porter, comic book artists had expressed their ingenuity in an especially claustrophobic and constraining genre: the popular Broadway show tune.

...

It's after midnight at the Zig Zag Tavern, so named for its staggered stage shows and the way its leering clientele darts between them. The year is 1951. The town is Calumet City, Illinois. Sun Ra is at the piano, right hand playing a bluesy ostinato, left hand leaving the keyboard for a moment to flip the page of Schopenhauer's *On the Freedom of the Will*, propped up on the piano lid. There's a chorus of whoops and hollers from the other side of the white sheet behind which he and his bandmates are hidden. Ra recognizes the cue and begins a volume swell. One by one, articles of women's clothing are tossed into the air, appearing for a flash above the white curtain. Ra nods at drummer Tommy "Bugs" Hunter, who winds up and begins to deliver a bump-and-grind beat, tenor saxophonist Red Holloway ladling on some extra groove juice. They have been back there since six o'clock and will be there until the other six o'clock. His accomplices have been relieved at intervals by other musicians, but not Ra. He will play behind the strippers, various emcees, an occasional comedian, through the night. The piece is finished, panties finally flung high, accompanied by wolfish sounds, and now the pianist is up adjusting his tape recorder, changing the reel, and waiting for the next girl to hit the stage. He's closed Schopenhauer and opened the latest edition of *John Carter of Mars*, a comic book modeled on *Buck Rogers*. For the rest of the night, when he's not eating a sandwich from the bar or running back and forth to the toilet, Ra will read and record and perform, an automatic multitasker.

…

Ra played at strip clubs and speakeasies in Calumet City in the forties and early fifties. With hundreds of bars and dozens of clubs, all controlled by the mafia, Calumet City's State Street was known nationwide as "Sin Strip," a simmering destination with a semi-legit façade (fancy ballrooms and floor shows from Sally Rand to Dizzy Gillespie) and a bad reputation that attracted visitors from Chicago, twenty miles north, and beyond. It was also a popular spot for musicians from the Windy City, like Ra, who went there looking for work outside the union and for payment under the table. The labor was not lucrative, but if you wanted it, with so many clubs it was plentiful. And as Ra told Dave Hoekstra in 1987: "All they wanted you to do was swing." He added: "Some of the best drummers played the Street. The strippers always had to have a good drummer—for their bumps, you know."*

In her book *Striptease: The Untold Story of the Girlie Show*, Rachel Shteir describes a couple of scenes: "In Cal City, the cheap and tawdry strip acts verged on sex shows. In 'The Devil and the Virgin,' the virgin undressed, coerced by a devil in white tie and tails. Cal City's most decadent act was a stripper named Roszina's 'Beauty and the Beast' number. She began wearing a gorilla costume on one side of her body and a strip outfit on the other. As the music got wilder, the 'gorilla' would rip the strip costume from the stripper's body. The lights faded with the 'gorilla' on top of the 'stripper.'"

Alton Abraham, who was Ra's manager and closest adviser through the Chicago years and into the nineteen sixties, told me that the Calumet City gigs were incredibly rough, especially for black musicians. Robert Barry, who drummed with Ra in many of those strip clubs, confirmed this, saying that along with the dangers of gambling misunderstandings and drunken fights, there were other perils: the club owners were mob connected; some of the understaffed police department were on the take; and there was a sense of self-rule to the nightlife. Barry saw two men beaten to death with metal pipes for not paying their bar tab, and he watched as a fellow musician was thrown through a plate-glass window for messing with the strippers. Knives were common. Guns were not unfamiliar. It was a classic wide-open town.

...

Ra told Hoekstra about one of the colorful emcees:

> He was "The Man With the Glass Head." . . . [T]he club's other pianist always played for him. One night the other pianist had to go across the street and play for Charlie Ventura, and it came that I had to play for the Man With the Glass Head. So the Man With the

---

* Dave Hoekstra, "Sun Ra's Calumet City,"
http://www.davehoekstra.com/travel/sun_ras_calumet_city/.

Glass Head got up and said he couldn't do his usual bit because
he had a different pianist. I got mad, so suddenly I hit a chord on
the piano and everything on the piano—the music, the flowers—all
jumped to the floor. He turned around and looked at me, and said,
"On second thought, uh, I think I will do that—just play whatever
you want to." When I got through playing for him, he said it was the
best music he ever heard.

...

William "Bugs" Cochran lived at Fifty-Fourth Street and Prairie
Avenue, on Chicago's South Side. As a youngster, he played in the
alley, where he often heard the Freeman Brothers—saxophonist
Von, guitarist George, and drummer Bruz—rehearsing in their
garage. From his front door, any way you went there were musicians. Drummers Robert Barry and Walter Perkins lived around the
corner. Saxophonist John Gilmore lived across the street. Von lived
a block down Prairie. And Sun Ra lived right next door.

Cochran started playing jazz drums. Before long he was part
of the Ra coterie. "I didn't see it as such an experience at the time,
but later it stood out," he says. It was the early nineteen fifties.
The band, which was not yet called the Arkestra, sometimes used
two bassists and two drummers plus tympani, creating a thicket of
rhythm, including odd time signatures. Ra's music had a different
sensibility from the soul jazz and ballads that Cochran would play in
his trio with organist Clarence "Sleepy" Anderson and guitarist Leo
Blevins, sometimes adding Gene Ammons (when he wasn't in jail)
on tenor sax. Not only would Ra's band play adventurous modern
music, but he'd transform corny tunes into something fresh. "We
had a jazz thing on 'Take Me Out to the Ball Game,' little twists,
you know, not what you'd normally hear."

On off nights, Cochran might pick up work at Minsky's Rialto
burlesque house at State and Van Buren or the Admiral Theatre up
on Lawrence Avenue, backing strippers, picking up a few bucks. One
night, Ra invited him to play in Calumet City. The trio consisted
of Ra on the club's upright piano, a trumpeter named Arthur, and

Cochran, barely twenty-one, on drums. Cochran picked the others up in his gray Oldsmobile 88, his Slingerland kit hiding in the car's giant trunk. They drove straight down Halsted Street, as there was no expressway yet, eventually turning east, arriving while the sun was going down and leaving when it was coming up.

The band took no breaks, but each musician periodically sat out, running down the block for a hot dog, while the others kept the action hopping. "They had some rough characters out there," says Cochran. "Musicians worked behind a cloth sheet. You did what you needed to do and then left, otherwise they'd bring the heat down on you. I was just in, age-wise, so I kept it cool. We played standard tunes, something the girls could dance to, kept in a danceable tempo. If you didn't get involved, didn't mess with the girls, just got to business, everything was all right."

...

When Ra moved to New York in 1961, there wasn't much work to support him and his small band. These were lean years in the Village. Abraham would wire small amounts of money via Western Union, a couple of dollars at a time, maybe lunch money for the guys or funds for blank tape. In spite of those challenges, Ra didn't choose to play mainstream jazz as a way of making the bills, as he might have. Rehearsing and recording at the Choreographer's Workshop and then at his home, which he called Sun Studios, he not only persisted in advancing his music, he also built the Arkestra back up in size, adding key new players and issuing numerous LPs on his own Saturn label, many featuring the music he had recorded while in Chicago.

Ra's sidemen were dedicated. Extremely so. Still, in this money vacuum, even his featured tenor saxophonist, John Gilmore, took more than a year's hiatus to join Art Blakey's Jazz Messengers and record with McCoy Tyner, Paul Bley, Andrew Hill, Freddie Hubbard, and Elmo Hope. What did the leader and mentor Ra take on as support work? Instead of joining the jazz mainstream, which might have meant playing hard bop, he took commercial jobs making kitschy, lowbrow recordings like *It's Limbo Time* (with Roz Croney, Queen of the Limbo) and *Batman and Robin* (with the Sensational Guitars of Dan & Dale).

There is reason to believe that Ra didn't take this work strictly for dough. Parallel to his interest in the great American songbook, which he said he grew to know in depth playing in Calumet City, he was also fascinated with exotica, then an increasingly popular genre of recording. Ra's 1959 LP *Jazz in Silhouette* has shades of the slinky adaptations of Latin music typical of exotica artists like Esquivel and Martin Denny, as well as "Hours After," a blues track lascivious enough to have been at home in a burlesque parlor. For Ra, these were seductive alien universes. In the terminology he would adopt later, exotica offered an "alter destiny," a compound and wholly constructed alternative reality in which otherness is embraced, disparate bits of jazz, experimental music, and tropical make-believe patched together by means of "myth-science," meant to be enjoyed through the ears as a journey out of one's own limited biosphere.

...

Back in Calumet City: Why the sheet? Ra told his biographer John Szwed that he had called it "the iron curtain." It was there, Abraham explained to me, with a dual purpose. First, it kept the customers, who were almost always white, from seeing the band. But more importantly, it kept the band, mainly African Americans, from seeing the girls. The racist assumption was that they would not be able to control themselves. Beauty and the beast. Gorilla and the stripper. Today it boggles the mind.

...

In the early seventies, Ra spent time on and off in Oakland, teaching his course "The Black Man in the Cosmos" at Berkeley and working with producer Jim Newman and director John Coney on the film *Space Is the Place*. The movie's narrative opens in a Chicago nightclub set in 1943, based on those in Calumet City. It is here that Ra and his arch adversary, the Overseer, first square off. The release of the Blue Thumb album, also titled *Space Is the Place*, is likewise depicted in the film. The story time-travels forward to a racially charged early seventies Oakland, and we see the Overseer cast doubt on Ra's authenticity as an underground black hero. As evidence of Ra having conspired with "the man," the Overseer points at this briskly selling new LP. Ra's young acolytes are momentarily turned against him, convinced that Ra has sold out and wants to cash in with a million-seller.

To know Ra is to know this is a patently ridiculous idea. Even the shard of squealing music that plays on the acolytes' radio, confirming their worst suspicions, is so dissonant, abrasive, and noncommercial that imagining it as a capitulation to capitalism is nonsensical. Nonetheless, I think this passage is in the film because, as far-fetched as it seems, Ra thought it was possible. Back to the earliest days of his record company, El Saturn, he and his colleagues aspired to influence the whole world through music, which first meant gaining mass popularity. And in his mind, the way you gained the world's ear was by writing a catchy song.

Start with a few words that flow together, and then inject them into a melody that invades the mind, a hook, an earworm—let's call it an ear-hookworm. Emphasize repetition and variation, pull out some clever rhymes, a pattern that sticks. We prefer not to think of it this way, but songwriting involves masterful psychological control. Leave the concert humming the tune, the words ricocheting around in your head. Ra's entry in the great American songbook— his signature tune that takes its place alongside Porter and the Gershwins and Kern and Howard Arlen and Hoagy Carmichael and Johnny Mercer and Rodgers & Hammerstein—might just be a jingle that does all that, a song with the same title as the film and the LP, the very title that Szwed took for his portrait of Ra. Saxophonist Pat Patrick's baritone ostinato weaves together with June Tyson's voice:

Space is the place
Space is the place
Space is the place
Yeah space is the place
Outer space is a pleasant place
A place's that's really free
There's no limit to the things that you can do
There's no limit to the things that you can be
Your thought is free
And your life is worthwhile
Space is the place . . .

Al Green

Call Me

Marvin Gaye

Let's Get It On

Our family attended one of the Episcopal churches in Iowa City. Major features of each Sunday's service, for me, included: staving off sleep by trying to avoid repeating or reading aloud anything that I didn't really believe, which meant being silent most of the time; scoping the scene for hot adolescent churchgoing girls—then grappling with an onset of seething lust, not from a conflicted moral standpoint, but pragmatically strategizing how to navigate moving from a kneeling position, in which I was staring at the back of naked thighs beneath a cotton dress, to a full upright and locked position without revealing the crotch tent that had formed in my dress pants. Reading from the hymnal seemed to help. That was the extent of Bible study in my world. I was not religiously persuaded.

Coming from an uptighty whitey Anglican atmosphere, I have long admired the way that soul music negotiates the corporeal and spiritual, Saturday night and Sunday morning, the imminence of temptation in the midst of living an upright life. Part of what I so relish is its acceptance of uncertainty, doubt, or at least fallibility, and the recognition that no sin is original. A blend of African American sacred sounds and secular themes, soul started from a position of rhythm-and-blues embodiment and ingested gospel intangibles, audible in the effortless blend of lead and background singers, the mix of down-to-earth blues harmonies and more indefinite ethereal intervals. These have kept Ray Charles, Aretha Franklin, and other harbingers of soul among the most powerful Sta-Fresh sounds in American music.

With Willie Mitchell's magnificent production, lumbar support from the Memphis Strings, Charles Chalmers' gritty horn arrangements, and Al Jackson Jr.'s piecrust-crisp drumming, Al Green's *Call Me* is an immaculate embodiment of soul, in particular its delectably ambivalent articulation of the notion of devotion. At any given time, Reverend Green sings both to God and to his paramour. Sometimes God *is* his lover; other times his lover is inhabited by dizzy divinity. Green's passion exceeds its target, spilling over onto things around it. Love is everything; everything is love. In his personal and professional lives, he's walked the line, moving between sexy abandon and Christian discipline; he's taken tragic and psychotic events—like the terrible girlfriend freak-out that led to Green being scalded by boiling grits and left her dead—as ominous portents, drawing him back onto the path of righteousness, but judging by the way he sings, he's by nature a sensualist, so delicate and caressing and intimate is his delivery. He preaches at his own church, the Full Gospel Tabernacle. I went down to Memphis once hoping to see him in action; Bishop Green wasn't there, but his painting of Armageddon guarded the rear wall, a remarkably un-church-like panorama of a city under siege featuring Jesus hovering in the parted clouds like a traffic copter, reminding us all of the wages of evil.

Green covers two country songs, the Hank Williams classic "I'm So Lonesome I Could Cry" and Willie Nelson's "Funny How Time Slips Away." Country music has traditionally articulated a similar kinship between religious and secular strains—consider the George Jones discography, for instance, which hopscotches back and forth between songs like "The Window Up Above" and "White Lightning." There's no contradiction felt in those switch-ups, and you sense the affinity in the way Green sings these words, his deep emotional commitment, the love that's divine and human at the same time. On many of *Call Me*'s songs, multitracked vocals pair Green with himself. He's a great improviser, dovetailing the voices, harmonizing alone, so intimate and powerful that it requires two or three of him to accomplish the telling of the tale. He's both present and in abeyance, awaiting a call from his lover, ready to be taken, but also aware that when earthly affairs are over, Jesus is waiting for him. The beautiful, cooling organ, courtesy of Charles Hodges, adds a church connotation, but when Green sings, he heats everything back up, a translucency in his voice on "Have You Been Making Out O.K." that turns the simple, caring question into a simmering skillet of emotion.

...

My wife, Terri, and I saw Nusrat Fateh Ali Khan once in concert. Rather than appearing at any of the logical downtown venues, we were surprised to see that the legendary Qawwali singer was performing in a high school gymnasium on the West Side of Chicago, where his audience was almost exclusively Indian and Pakistani. At several points during the breathtaking music—long pieces, drone instruments making a bed for the singer, not unlike the giant pillow that supported his massive body, from which an otherworldly voice projected into fettuccini-like lines of melisma—the entire audience would collectively gasp, then burst into cheers and applause. After this happened a few times, I turned to the man next to me and asked what it was all about. "Oh, you see, this music is religious music, devotional music, but the poetry expresses divine love in metaphors of physical love. So those times when we all applaud, those lines are especially sexy!"

With this in mind, I want to draw attention to a single such moment on Marvin Gaye's *Let's Get It On*, a moment on that self-same song, toward the beginning, when he's just about to sing the chorus, the four-word chorus, as forthright and unmetaphorical a statement of physical desire as has ever been sung. Let's. Get. It. On. It's the converse of Nusrat's method; Gaye transforms the secular into the spiritual, sexy into devotional. The event I mean is not even made of words. It's a musical moment. And by moment, I really mean something momentary, fleeting, there and gone in a blink lasting less than a second. I have repeated it thousands of times trying to catch it, but it's like a beautiful little creek, flow of water just moving along, ain't it funny how it slips away.

Drummer Uriel Jones of the Funk Brothers is sensationally buoyant on the whole song, but he introduces a little fill just shy of the "Ooooh" that consists of a shuffle and shake punctuated by a big cymbal splash. Nothing super flashy but miraculously timed. More than any of Gaye's explicit yearnings, this minuscule flick of the drums is the place where I hear the flash of flesh as it disappears into thin air. I'll use a phrase I almost never do: it makes time stand still. Maybe it's no coincidence that this happens on a record that praises sexual liberation. It is aphasic in the ancient Greek sense, meaning that it induces speechlessness. A moment in which time is lost, unaccounted for, maybe a sort of orgasmic snare, *le petit mort* of drums. Just for that instant, that suspended breath, the spirit enters my body, filling me, flushing me, transporting me from the realm of a bored kid in church into what passes in my adult world for rapture.

"You Are the Sunshine of My Life"

For once, pay no attention to anything else in this song.

Not the beautiful singing.

Not the shimmering Rhodes.

Not the ride cymbal, so capacious and intoxicating.

Listen to the bass drum. Stevie's on the kit. He sets up a continuous *thump-thump*, subliminally urging the song along, nothing to draw attention, constancy in motion.

Now hear what happens.

At its close, the song is transmogrified. Not much changes on its surface. No chorus of angels. No swell of strings. The music continues, but for some reason it seems to explode with emotion.

Are you still listening to the bass drum?

Just before the last iteration of the chorus, concentrate and you will hear a seizure hit Stevie's right leg. His kick drum doubles down. It begins to twitch with improbable speed.

What a limber ankle.

The bass drum is jubilant.

Low-frequency convulsions.

Shin-splint oscillations.

Stevie Wonder's foot speaks in tongues.

Gal Costa

Índia

Count to ten and say "tropicália."

1) I am fortunate that I didn't know about this record when I was a teenager, lest I had left for Brazil in quest of Costa, whatever the cost.

2) My friend Rick Wojcik turned me on to tropicália in the early nineties. Encountering it was like finding a parallel universe that had existed all along, a distorted alter reflection of my childhood, inhabited by singers and players who knew and loved some of the same things that the musicians in our world did, like the Beatles and psychedelia and African ethnographic recordings. But these singers and players were equipped with a whole trick bag unfamiliar to us, including the native musics of Latin America (samba, bossa nova, fado, baião, candomblé, frevo, capoeira), Brazil's folk-protest music tradition, their avant-garde classical music and contemporaneous art, and a palette of original ideas fomented in the rich cultural petri dish of Bahia.

3) I don't understand more than a few words, but Brazilian Portuguese is the most sensual language on earth, especially when sung.

4) Especially when sung by Gal Costa.

5) The cover of *India* does not beat around the bush. It *presents* the bush, covered only by a bright red bikini bottom that puts the brief in briefs, a disrobing in the jungle, bush in the bush. Above: midriff, navel, black and red beads, braceleted hands; below: Costa's mons pubis, revealed as her grass skirt is undone, contemporary beach culture squaring off with the Indian within. This is a special kind of direct address, objectified genitals staring back, not satisfied to be stared at, an assertion of positive sexuality, veldt sexuality, indigenous sexuality, sex as nexus.

6) I have always assumed, perhaps incorrectly, that *India*'s design was a response to Caetano Veloso's *Araçá Azul*, the cover of which features Veloso in a similarly skimpy red bottom, belly button jutting over the right margin, face obscured by shadow, the singer's svelte torso reflected in an oval mirror that might have come in handy for a testicular self-exam. Speaking of which, the title means "blue fruit," depicted graphically on the verso, leaving precious little to the imagination. *Araçá Azul* is the most adventurous of Veloso's records, truly astonishing in its willful disdain for pop norms—long stretches of sound poetry met with psych-rock, evanescent bossa, and the incredibly strange Ping-Pong game of "Gilberto Misterioso." Or the epic "Sugar Cane Fields Forever," which includes an episode of Afro-Brazilian traditional drumming and chanting (with trombone choir) and recitation of words written by the Brazilian poet Sousândrade, whose extraordinary long poem *O Guesa Errante* (1884) concerns a Musíca Indian teenager who starts in the Colombian Andes, travels through the Amazon en route to the United States, finally arriving at Wall Street.

7) The Indian was a central figure in Brazilian modernism. Tropicálists like Veloso and Costa adopted and adapted modernist ideas, including those of Sousândrade and Oswald de Andrade, who coined the term *antropofagia*, invoking cannibalism—specifically an anti-colonialist form of humans eating humans—in

a description of the syncretic-omnivorous approach to artistic production. Brazil is a synthesizer of so many diverse cultures— African, indigenous, European—and in turn has long consumed and reworked art, literature, and music from exogenous locales, very actively in the nineteen seventies, be they Fluxus, flower power, or the Flamin' Groovies. Though the tropicália movement technically ended with the military dictatorship in 1969, its musicians' taste for mixing things up and broaching expected boundaries, and the relevance of indigenous people for them as exemplary of resistance, never ceased. Hence, beyond the blatant sexuality comes a deeper significance for *Índia*, looking back through Brazilian modernism and the brutal history of colonialism to an idealized utopian place outside of authoritarian politics, a naive image, but beautifully and purposefully so.

8) *Índia* itself is a magnificent LP, subtler in its subversiveness than *Araçá Azul*, Gilberto Gil's luminous arrangements merging impeccably with Costa's emotionally precise, knife-like vocals. It is surely a summit of one line of tropicálist thought, a Brazilian masterpiece that should be on any list of the seventies' most important.

9) Hopelessly infatuated with Caetano Veloso's music, I became familiar with his son Moreno's work—Papa V had dedicated a track to the boy and his sister on *Araçá Azul*, "Julia/Moreno," but I first heard the CD by Moreno + 2 called *Music Typewriter*. Inspired by the way his music updated tropicália, I invited Moreno + 2 to play at the JazzFest Berlin, when I was its artistic director in 2002. Just before he went onstage, Moreno spoke to his father, who was about to go on a trip into the desert. "What crazy person booked you at a jazz festival?" Caetano asked. A year later, when he performed in Chicago, Caetano had his publicist contact me, saying he wanted to meet the guy who had Moreno play on a jazz stage. Standing behind the scenes at the opulent Chicago Theater with Caetano Veloso was a once-in-a-lifetime moment, but earlier that day there had been another

one. We happened to be in our car right next to Veloso's limousine, waiting at a red light at one of the city's busiest intersections. Suddenly a woman in the car in front of us recognized Caetano, put her car in neutral, swung open her door, leaving it ajar, and ran to his limo, screaming his name and banging on the window in awestruck hysteria. When the light turned green, the limo driver took off and she trailed after on foot, leaving us waiting for her to return to her car and slip away.

10) I booked Moreno for a second gig, this time at the Art Institute of Chicago in 2015. He, his wife, and his manager spent a few days in town, enjoying several good meals with us and treating us to a Bob Dylan concert, which was somehow a perfect delta of all the creative interpersonal waterways. While we were driving around showing them the city, I mentioned my affection for Gal Costa's *Índia*. "Yes, of course, that's a classic," said Moreno. Looking plaintively out the car window, a half-smile on his lips, he added: "There's a funny picture of me naked in her hands." "I'm assuming you were quite young," I said, the simple pleasures of the record's cover quickly evaporating in a cloud of confusing new imagery. "Of course, I was a baby! She's my godmother."

Houses of the Holy

Scooter slugged his beer and put the can on the side table. Fanning out his fingers, he threaded the aluminum pull tab on to his pinkie like a ring. I gazed out the side of the curved windshield onto his front lawn, which was quilted white. In the distance I could see the low wooden fence that bounded the house next door, where I lived.

We were holed up in a Winnebago that Scooter's folks kept parked in the driveway, which they used for an annual family vacation, serving the rest of the months as a bat cave for us. Both Scooter's public school and my private school had called a snow day. The adults were at work, so nobody was in charge, and even though it was brittle cold outside, we had the heat cranked in the camper and could be assured of privacy from his sister and brother.

I pressed stop on the cassette player while he ran inside to steal a few more cans from his father's stash. His dad drank them so fast that he never noticed their absence. When Scooter returned, I hit play. He'd filled a bucket from his garage with snow, a makeshift cooler for the beers. The atmosphere felt positive, a little impromptu party. We were unperturbed, like we preferred; this was a celebration of being left to our own devices.

"I don't understand how they do this," I said.

"What?"

"Like that guitar riff, where did that come from? How did they think of that? Did you ever stop to ask, where does it come from? Do they just think it up on the spot?"

"Yeah, it rocks so hard."

"But why is it so much better than the riffs other bands use?"

Scooter sipped and pondered and sipped again. "I don't know. But it is."

We would both turn fourteen that summer. For three years we'd been best friends, ever since a night at Valley Forge on a Boy Scout camping trip, when, as assigned bunkmates and mutually faltering members of the troop, we'd exchanged all sorts of confidences and thereby sealed an airtight bond, which included the pricking of fingers, some vows, and unearthing the stakes on another tent.

"I mean, how do they compose something like that? Does it come into their mind and then they just play it?" I asked, flicking my pull tab at Scooter's feet.

"I hear Jimmy Page is some sort of musical whiz kid. Like a savant or something."

"Is he classically trained?"

"Nah. That's fine for someone like Rick Wakeman or Keith Emerson. But I guess if you're classically trained, it drains some of the rock out of you and you can't be as nasty as Zeppelin."

Led Zeppelin vacillated between histrionics and preternatural cool. Briefly known as the New Yardbirds, they had the pedigree of a first-generation British Invasion band but had managed to shake off the trappings of that earlier movement, the suits and skinny ties, the jerky rhythms and trebly guitars, the harmony vocals applied to garaged-up R&B. That was our parents' music, not ours. The Kinks and the Rolling Stones never completely lost the British Invasion connotation—even after they'd matured, we always heard in them a bit of the Dave Clark Five.

Not Led Zeppelin. With a fresh new name containing a deliberate misspelling, they flipped convention a righteous bird, replacing those old-fashioned attributes with a contemporary sound, longer songs, compositional experimentation, carnal insinuation, and coarse-grained distortion where the tin-toned treble had been. Zeppelin weren't pop; they were solid rock. They were tough and monumental. In the music of other bands, their mineral content would harden into metal. But Zeppelin themselves were loose-limbed and feral, naughty, occasionally evil. Page spewed riffs like they were going out of style. They were going *into* style. His guitar parts were our definition of vogue. *Let the music be your master*, Led Zeppelin told us. *Will you heed the master's call?* Oh yes, we heeded.

In the camper there was no stereo system, just the built-in AM/FM radio. I had brought my portable cassette player so we'd have control of the music. A few weeks earlier, I'd manually recorded *Houses of the Holy* in its entirety from the stereo in my bedroom, starting over a couple of times when my mother had made noise in the hallway outside. Scooter lent me his copy, as I didn't have it, and I brought the LP back so we could peruse the gatefold while we listened.

"I fucking hate the color orange," I said. "But somehow with these weird naked kids on rocks, I love the way orange looks on this record."

"*Oh*-range," Scooter said, chiding my midwestern accent. "What are you, Canadian? Dork."

"Sorry, I should have said *ah*-range. Asswipe. You sound like you're from Jersey. Next you'll tell me we should wait 'on line' instead of 'in line.' Like that makes any sense at all. Where's the line? What line am I standing on?"

"Fuck off back to Canada."

We sat smiling and sipping. The little Sony speaker did its best but was unable to reproduce John Bonham's drums as anything more than what a wind-up monkey would hit.

"No, but really, how do they make this stuff up? I mean . . ." We paused to listen to "The Ocean." ". . . I can't even fricking clap to this rhythm, I keep missing a beat. What are they doing? It's such a bitch."

"But it's wicked raw, too. They don't lose the rawness. They're the precision raw bad boys of rock."

"You said it."

...

After a while we bundled up and headed out into the snow. Behind our houses was Wissahickon Valley Park, which led through tall trees to an open-air pavilion down by the Wissahickon Creek. More stream than creek, it was in places quite deep and fast, and in its shallows it widened to fifty feet across. The sustained cold snap had frozen it over, which was rare. When we were together, Scooter and I were daredevils. He nearly fell to his death once when we were rock climbing in another park. Invincible little numbskulls, we pissed ourselves laughing. The iced stream was irresistible, so we took turns walking as far as we could toward the middle of the waterway, where the crust got thinnest, once there gingerly hopping up and down until the surface gave way, plunging one of us hip deep into freezing water. Convulsing in laughter, the soggy guy was fished out of the drink, and the routine started up again, finding another spot and tempting fate. Neither of us ever got pulled under the ice, though that could have easily happened. After a couple of hours, chilled to the bone, our pants frozen to the point that walking was arduous, we trundled back to his house, changed into dry clothes, and thawed out in the camper. En route, it had started snowing again, heavily, the air hushed with its dampening effect.

"Let's listen to 'D'yer Maker,' pretend it's 'Dryer Maker,'" I said.

"Ooh, that's a hot one," he retaliated. "That joke makes me want to listen to 'The Crunge' and pretend it's 'The Cringe.'"

"This line of conversation is making me want to be 'Over the Hills and Far Away.'"

"But really, my bet's on 'No Quarter.'"

Flakes fluttered down on the Winnebago. Scooter shuttled backward through the other songs until he found the beginning of "No

Quarter," with its eerie keyboard intro and opening lyrics: *Close the door, put out the light / No, they won't be home tonight / The snow falls hard and don't you know? / The winds of Thor are blowing cold.* It seemed to pair perfectly with the day.

"I mean listen to that bad-ass distorted guitar part," he said, as Jimmy Page's definitive melody imposed order on the nebulous tune. "It's so simple, but it's just so cherry. And they put it in the middle of this other slow, weird stuff, with piano—who's playing piano, anyway? And Bonham's monster drums."

"He's the best drummer in music. There's Keith Moon, but he's almost too wild, so there's Bonham. Fattest gun in the West."

The drummer's inimitable pocket and sloshy ride cymbal were icebreakers in the song's frozen tundra as the band took it on home. I pressed fast-forward and found the beginning of "The Crunge." Its broke-back funk stretched the capacity of our little imaginations, Page's acidic jazz chords and the song's timing gently pointing at some references we didn't know. We thought John Paul Jones was just a bassist, but he played keyboards too—that was him on piano. *Houses of the Holy* utilized more overdubbing than their first four records had, and Jones's bass and piano could be heard simultaneously in some places.

"Pluck a duck, where does that rhythm come from? And the bridge, what's the story with the 'confounded bridge' they're looking for?"

The dry Brit humor and nod to funk both flew over our heads. Neither of us recognized their reference to James Brown. Anyway, this was a heavy rock band. When we listened to "D'yer Maker," we didn't know that the title was a play on the word Jamaica, twisted up the way a Cockney might. For that matter, we didn't recognize the opening drum thwacks and the jerky rhythm as having anything to do with reggae because, like many Americans in 1976, we didn't know what reggae was.

We let the tape roll on into "The Ocean," listened to the final track on the record another time.

"Don't forget Plant," said Scooter. "Without him, it wouldn't work. He can sing better and higher than lots of girls. Take the screaming ones that mob him, his groupies. He sounds like them when he pleads, *Oh baby, I still love you so*, at the end of 'D'yer Maker.' He whines like a girl and still gets the girls. How does that work?"

I returned my attention to "The Ocean."

"Zeppelin saves the most bitchin' song for the end. I still don't understand how they think up these riffs. They're so serious it's hilarious. I keep losing track of this one. What kind of beat is that, anyway? It's not 4/4 or 2/4."

It's in fifteen.

...

A day after my fourteenth birthday, I bought an electric guitar. It was my way of going in search of those riffs, though I was not successful in finding many of my own. I purchased the instrument from Susie and Beth Miller's stepfather, who worked at a guitar shop. Rather than buy a Gibson or Fender, in a typical move I went for something more obscure than was advisable, a solid body electric made by Martin, a company known almost exclusively for its superb acoustic instruments. Beautifully tooled, it was extremely heavy, which gave it excellent sustain but made it awkward to move around with, like carting a barbell with frets, and it behaved most like a Les Paul, without the distinctive double humbucker pickup sound.

Most of Jimmy Page's recordings were made on a Les Paul. Later, after I'd left town and slowly lost touch with Scooter, I would hear bits and pieces of the rhythms and riffs I knew from Zeppelin records on down-home and electric blues records. When I finally heard James Brown take it to the bridge, I knew something about what he was up to from having memorized Zeppelin's "The Crunge." It was a strange de-evolutionary feeling, learning about those essential African American genres through the iconic hard rock band. But that's the way it went then, and Zeppelin transformed those influences into something undeniably their own, which is more than you can say for some white rockers with blues roots.

...

"You ever notice we skip over the songs without riffs most of the time?"

Scooter nodded and took charge of the Sony, looking for the beginning of our favorite song. When he located the start of "Dancing Days," he spun the little dial to the loudest position, hitting play. The song's boomeranging slide guitar mystified us further. We had never heard Indian music, so once again Zeppelin seemed like magicians pulling a new sound out of their hat every time. A few months down the turnpike, when we heard "Kashmir," with its bowed guitar part, and the delayed issue of the title track from *Houses*, which also appeared on *Physical Graffiti*, the same applied. Led Zeppelin was apparently able to invent whole new genres with each track.

Thirty-eight years later, under very different circumstances, I attended a press conference at a legendary studio in Berlin, where the newly remastered first three Zeppelin LPs were being unveiled. I met Mr. Page and asked him to sign a *Zeppelin III* beer coaster for my cousin, who is an accomplished jazz musician; Page obliged, inscribing it: "For Tim—good luck with the guitar." Listening to the refurbished music in Germany, I felt a little pang in my heart remembering those dancing days with Scoots, wishing they were here again, also happy they're not.

...

The beer and ice escapade had drained us. We sat in twilight, nodding, eyes closed, mouthing the words: *As the evening starts to glow / You know it's all right / I said it's all right / You know it's all in my heart.*

"Hey, Corbs, you think we could come up with riffs this cool?"

"Yeah, man. I know we could. Those riffs would rule."

Fresh

There he is, the same guy who once sang the praises of simple songs and everyday people, the seraphic center of a new flower-powered universe, offering his third meditation on thankfulness in as many records, each of which had a different tone, warning everyone in his circle: *Remember all yours coulda been all mine.* It's a jealous, hubristic lyric, redolent of drug-fiend paranoia, on a record that flashes between being a suicide note and a comeback, a celebration of vanquishing dependencies and an admission of submitting to them, a slip of paper that reads "thank you" and another that says "gone fishin'." Mixed messages couched in some of the most inventive pop music ever put to tape.

Fresh is more Sly than Family Stone. It continues a gradual slide toward solipsism that started with its predecessor, *There's a Riot Goin' On*, an ominous and complex outing that was a cipher of the zeitgeist, with molten funk and nervous pop bearing witness to a poetic vision that drew negative energy in equal proportion to all the upbeat positivity of the early Family Stone's music. They'd once represented the ideal end-of-era outcome, a multicultural, mixed-gender troupe, drawing together different musical styles without regard for their supposed audience, casting demography aside, as a result calling forth a whole new crowd, one that appreciated the anti-segregationist egalitarian medley of psychedelic, soul, funk, doo-wop, rock, electronic music, and jazz.

Parliament-Funkadelic would certainly not have been the enterprise they became without Stone's nudge, nor would the Temptations have expanded their erstwhile conservative horizons. Even Miles Davis turned an electrified ear toward Sly's musical omnibus. But now Sly and what was left of the Family were something else, another kind of sign of the times, and as times were changing, so was Sly's outlook. He had answered Marvin Gaye's question *What's Going On*, with *There's a Riot Goin' On*, his own version of the Stooges' "No Fun," which was in fact pretty fucking fun. Anyway, riot has a dual meaning, no doubt Sly's point.

Bay Area counterculture had turned on itself. Altamont provided terrifying evidence of the fact, most vividly in the person of one Meredith Hunter, the mystery man who was stabbed to death by the Hell's Angels. With his black shirt, brown skin, and mint green suit, he stood out against the hippie-biker crowd, a fly dude in the ointment, exactly the kind of fan that the Rolling Stones wanted, the prancing Huggy Bear that Mick Jagger emulated lying limp at the foot of the stage along with the optimism and good faith that had brought everyone together. Who was Meredith Hunter but a Sly stand-in? The enigma, the sporty rags, the killer instinct, even the pistol he'd waved that brought on his brutal demise—they're all Sly. *Looking at the devil*, Sly sang on *Riot*, as all hope slipped away, oozing into the parched earth like blood out of a wound. *Grinning at his gun / Fingers start shaking, I begin to run.* And a little later: *Thank you for the party, I could never stay.* Show's over, folks. A cop on the scene, or maybe just an Angel. Move along, people. Nothing to see here.

...

For Sly, there was a break. He had been pressured to deliver a new record, his label finally issuing a premature greatest hits anthology to keep him—yes, I think the word would be "fresh"—in people's minds, after the runaway success of *Stand!* With ambivalence and opacity, *Riot* hadn't fit the bill. The suits were impatient for a new one. *Two years, long wait / Two words: get straight*, echoes the outro on "In Time." They wanted 1973's version of "Dance to the Music" or "I Want to Take You Higher." But the happiness machine wouldn't function. A sinister vacancy showed up when their smiley-go-lucky got busted. Catching Sly smiling had once seemed plausible, but to sing such a gleeful ditty now would be an outright lie. *I don't know what to do / No more selling me to you*, he says, indicting the prior joys.

The mother's milk had curdled. The drugs got dark, the lifestyle mean, splits within the Family pitted member against member. By the time bassist Larry Graham acrimoniously left the band, the lyrics to their *Riot*-era hit "Family Affair" began to sound prophetic: *You can't leave 'cause your heart is there / But sure you can't stay 'cause you been somewhere else.* Blood may be thicker than mud, but dope and money, it turns out, are thicker still. I remember hearing that song on the radio, thinking it sounded positive, about solidarity and sticking up for one another. I didn't feel the undercurrent.

With the Family retreating into the background, *Fresh* is a lonely record. It's the sound of a brilliant man alone in his room. Sly is Gene Hackman in his apartment at the end of *The Conversation*, with his stereo and saxophone, tearing out the walls in search of the bug. So isolated the floor throbs. Even the sex is solitary. *Put a little tickle on the Jones's head*, sings Sly, introducing a magnificent masturbation metaphor. *Turn off the lights and go to bed.* On "Everyday People," he'd insisted that there were *different strokes for different folks*, but here he laughs that he had to change his stroke. Wacked on whatever, Sly fiddled with the tapes endlessly, guarding them from others, making multiple versions of the record. *There's a reeling when you don't know what you're doing*, he sings on "In Time." Maybe he was indeed so blitzed that he didn't know what he was doing, judging by the ingenuity of the rhythms. More likely he knew exactly what he was up to. There had never been another record like it, especially in terms of time—and not just the drums, both the flesh-and-blood kind and the electronic Maestro Rhythm King that gurgles below like a balafon or log drum, but also the horns and voices and guitar and organ and bass. It's the first genuinely harmolodic funk record. *Fresh* predates Ornette Coleman's electric groups and later outgrowths like Ronald Shannon Jackson's Decoding Society. There's the sour note at the end of the main guitar line on "In Time": the interlocking horn parts—fragmentary, hocketing, assuming a rhythmic function—or, on "Frisky," sustaining a dissonant chord that reappears where you'd think it would change.

So *Fresh* is lonely, but it's not morose, not wigged out in Quaalude Butoh like parts of *Riot* were; it's sped up, time-lapsed, sometimes even more manic than Sly's favored drug. *I switched from coke to pep and I'm a connoisseur,* he explains. The fidgeting brilliance of the drums across the record—a perpetual tap dance on the snare—perhaps shows the impact of this new friendship with amphetamines. He's reflective, not necessarily regretful. *If I could start all over again / I'd be in the same skin I'm in.* But anything optimistic cloaks a hidden cloud. "Que, Sera, Sera," which is as close as the record comes to changing tone, turns out to be equally devastating, heartbreaking even, Sly and sister Rose preaching the gospel of fatalism in a duet for the ages. Sly, it appears, is the real man who knew too much. On "I Don't Know (Satisfaction)," which on the surface sounds like a black pride song, he takes ennui even further: *Nothing in the way, but another day / And we're gonna push it on out the way.* Pushing days out of the way, that's the sound of resignation, a maverick anticipating the bleakness of his destiny. Sadly, there's not much in the rest of his subsequent biography to date to contradict this forecast.

...

Rerun the *all yours coulda been all mine* line. Imagine for a moment Sly looking back at his mid-sixties hope from the vantage of its having been dashed on the reef of the seventies. He witnesses himself, the child prodigy, happily sharing his vision of a new, improved society, inventing the Family, inviting its members to take joint credit for what is, in fact, a vision of his, in effect giving away his talent. Once the Family adage might have been "from each according to ability to each according to need"; now it just seemed like taking advantage, siphoning off someone's charisma. Add a dash of junkie jealousy, and Sly might even think of doing something criminal in retaliation. It gets that crazy. On *Riot* and *Fresh*, Sly pulls everything back, takes his toys, and goes home. *Let me have it all*, he wails, and he might as well be saying, "Let me have it all back." Playing many of the instruments himself, it's as if he's saying that the other musicians were superfluous all along, to show he could have done it alone.

...

Only one song from *Fresh* made it into my ears back when it was released. Whenever "If You Want Me to Stay" came on the radio, I turned it up. It was my favorite song that year. Most of the lyrics were impenetrable to me—what does "death wish" mean to a ten-year-old?—but I loved the bass, the rhythm, Sly's cool, slightly jive-talking delivery. Now, in the context of the other songs, I hear him conceding to sticking around, as he put it, *available for you to see*, as if he were on display, and also as if he might well enough have left for good, even though elsewhere he sings about doing dangerous things (read: dangerous substances) and almost dying, but hanging around anyway. *Something coulda come and taken me away / But the main man felt Syl should be here another day.*

The line I liked the most on "If You Want Me to Stay" was a little outburst made twice, after Sly has complained about being taken for granted and warned that he might be hard to reach by phone (read: on a weeks-long drug binge), singing that he wishes he could *get this message over to you now*. First time it's part of the song; second iteration it's something else. Even at ten, I thought it was unusual. He blurts the words, as if he's trying to reach out of the radio and grab the listener, shaking them and saying: *I'll be so good, I wish I could* / *GET THE MESSAGE OVER TO YOU NOW*. I think it's a kind of existential desire to be heard, really heard, over the din and through the woods of words and music, to communicate purely and directly, to send a message of loneliness and insecurity straight to our brainstem.

...

There's a mickey in the tasting of disaster. The first line of *Fresh* is portentous enough to infer what follows. In those prophetic words, we catch a glimpse, for instance, of a world of cinema in which it's possible to turn a profit on *Towering Inferno* and *The Poseidon Adventure*, and also the new blaxploitation model, pimping out the ghetto as a suburban fantasy of grit and grime and mean streets; maybe even turn a profit on *Mean Streets* and other more emotionally layered movies by Martin Scorsese or Nicolas Roeg, ones that chart the interior life of disaster, emotional breakdown, psychic disintegration—*Taxi Driver*, *Raging Bull*, *Bad Timing*, *Don't Look Now*. The morsel of catastrophe that Sly offers up is even more personal. He's talking about the fact that people will pay to watch his life explode, same way we would eagerly buy a ticket to hear Richard Pryor tell us about setting himself aflame. The gruesome gain of others' pain. "If you want me," Sylvester Stone seems to say, "here I am, coming atcha, big brilliant fireball of confusion. Watch the combustion as the cars collide. I'll let you in as long as you pay for the view." So there's a lie to the idea of no more selling me to you: he's still for sale, it's just a different Sly that's on the market.

One song stands out on *Fresh*, for its sanguinity. *Had it been left up to you* / *Would you try?* / *Would you try?* / *If it were left up to me* / *I would try*, sing Little Sister, the vocal trio that defined an earlier Family vibe. But it's a sham. Sly has given up trying. And lo, that song turns out to be an outtake from five years earlier. Even Larry Graham is there, thumbed bass popping, though his name is absent from the credits. "If It Were Left Up to Me" is a bright spot that just reminds us how desolate things really are, how despairing this spectacularly original new music is, and in that way it's the saddest song on the record. As if to rub it in, the next track, "Babies Makin' Babies," maps life as a short trip sketched in six words: *From the womb / To the tomb* . . .

...

The cover of *Fresh* says it all. It is the first in the discography to depict Sly without the Fam. In Richard Avedon's photograph, Sly seems to be kicking his heels, maybe implying he'd kicked the habit, which is of course not true. Is he jumping for joy? Keeping on dancing? Kung-fu fighting? Or is he in free fall?

1974

Grievous Angels

In September 1973, after a booze and drug bender inspired by an impending divorce, Gram Parsons took a lethal overdose of morphine. The singer died in the desert a few hours from Los Angeles, in a room at the Joshua Tree Inn, out among the rock formations and monumental cacti. He'd bought a tainted batch from an unknown woman. As directed by his well-to-do family, Parsons's body was embalmed and readied for burial, a fate for his physical remains that he loathed; he had expressly told friends he didn't want a funeral. Two of those friends—his manager Phil Kaufman and his assistant Michael Martin—intervened by impersonating employees of a funeral home and swiped his corpse from the airport. They enlisted a policeman to help place it in the back of Martin's personally owned hearse, and then they drove it back into the Joshua Tree National Park. There they doused the body with gasoline and set it aflame. Their cremation was only partially successful. Authorities eventually nabbed Kaufman and Martin, and Parsons was professionally incinerated. A rumor originating with Manuel Cuevas, the costume designer who made the Nudie suit that Parsons famously wore on the cover of the Flying Burrito Brothers' *The Gilded Palace of Sin*, suggests that the singer had mapped out and foretold his death in the symbols on the suit—pot plants, naked girls, poppies, and a flaming cross. To defray the costs associated with his capture and prosecution, the manager pitched a benefit party he called "Kaufman's Koffin Kaper Koncert."

A couple of law-breaking renegades raise hell and steal their amigo's dead body to dispose of it in the manner he would have wanted. If you substitute a horse-drawn carriage for the Cadillac hearse, the story of Gram Parsons's final ride could easily be a scene in an early seventies revisionist Western, or what Pauline Kael called the "acid Western." This strange new subgenre of movie mapped the outlaw figure and pioneer spirit of the traditional Western onto a hardened, existential version of post-hippie counterculture. You could think of the movies as high plains Zen noir. Saturated with dark humor, fatalism, and double entendre, acid Westerns are more Richard Brautigan than Louis L'Amour, more Peter Fonda than John Wayne, more Byrds than Ray Price, more Robert Altman than John Huston.

Altman, in fact, made one of the best of them, *McCabe and Mrs. Miller* (1971). It's couched in a haunting soundtrack by Leonard Cohen, with Julie Christie as a British opium-smoking madam. Warren Beatty plays self-made businessman John McCabe, a gambler and habitual mumbler who at one point murmurs: "I've got poetry in me." There's certainly poetry in *Pat Garrett and Billy the Kid* (1973), Sam Peckinpah's adaptation of Rudolph Wurlitzer's incredible screenplay; Wurlitzer is known as the architect of the acid Western. Singer Kris Kristofferson stars as Billy, and Dylan composed the soundtrack music, which included the song "Knockin' on Heaven's Door." Dylan has a small but important role as the Kid's ethereal, almost sprite-like sidekick. Asked his name by a group of bad men, the Dylan character identifies himself as Alias. "What's your last name?" "Alias whatever you like." What do we call you, they press. "Just Alias." It's as clever a feint as when Odysseus tells Polyphemus the Cyclops his name is "Nobody." Wurlitzer has recounted the story of introducing Dylan to Peckinpah at the director's hacienda in Mexico. Peckinpah's only words in the bizarre encounter were: "I'm more of a Roger Miller man."

There are precursors, like Peckinpah's own *The Wild Bunch* (1969) and George Roy Hill's *Butch Cassidy and the Sundance Kid* (1969), for which Hal David and Burt Bacharach wrote "Raindrops Keep Falling on My Head," a huge hit for B. J. Thomas. A goofier take on the subgenre, written by members of the comedy troupe Firesign Theatre, *Zachariah* (1971) is a gay Western based on Hermann Hesse's *Siddhartha*. The film includes performances by the James Gang and Country Joe and the Fish, as well as a memorable scene in which former John Coltrane Quartet drummer Elvin Jones takes a gun-slinging solo in a saloon. Remarkably, when the filmmakers lost the segment's soundtrack, they asked session drummer Earl Palmer to overdub Jones's playing, which the legendary New Orleans musician did with amazing likeness. Think about it: you have the drummer who played on "You Send Me" with Sam Cooke, "La Bamba" with Ritchie Valens, "The Old Laughing Lady" with Neil Young, "I Hate My Generation" with Cracker, and the theme music for *The Flintstones*, *The Brady Bunch*, and *The Partridge Family* reconstructing a solo by the groaning triplet king who helped break up jazz rhythm and played on Trane's initial forays into free jazz, including the incendiary *Live in Seattle*. And he nails it. Talk about versatility.

...

I bumped into the key philosophical cornerstone of the countercultural Western in a line by Dylan. On "Absolutely Sweet Marie" from *Blonde on Blonde*, Dylan sings: *To live outside the law, you must be honest.* I first read it as an epigraph in Tom Robbins's novel *Even Cowgirls Get the Blues*, and the idea gave me pause. "Right," I thought, "the law doesn't define honesty. Honesty is beyond the legal system, it's an ethical code, and it starts by being true to oneself, by looking in the mirror, Grasshopper, and being truthful about what you see."

Parsons's work with the Flying Burrito Brothers, a brief two-year stint, had a poignant, yearning, evil twinkle with a streak of profundity that put it at a meeting point like the one Dylan evokes, a crossroads between lawlessness and honesty, also a juncture between two genres: rock and country music. The Burritos added other influences to their intoxicating home brew, like Norteño, R&B, and soul. Hear, for example, their cover of James Carr's "The Dark End of the Street" or their gender switch on Aretha Franklin's "Do Right Woman." Other acts combined similar influences with exciting results—the Band, Doug Sahm and his Sir Douglas Quintet, Creedence Clearwater Revival, Ry Cooder, Mickey Newbury, Linda Ronstadt—though eventually the country rock genre would lead to some much blander bands like the Eagles and Poco. The acid Western version of country rock had enough cachet among musicians to take it to the main stage with the Rolling Stones, starting with "Honky Tonk Women" in 1969, directly influenced by Keith Richards's friendship with Parsons, and continuing with "Wild Horses," released by Parsons prior to the Stones' version (there is evidence that Parsons actually wrote the song), and on songs like "Torn and Frayed" from *Exile on Main Street*, which bore Parsons's unmistakable imprint.

By the time Parsons recorded two solo records, he had taken country rock to another place. The music on *GP* and *Grievous Angel*, the latter recorded just before his death and issued in memoriam, locates a vanishing point on the horizon where the references disappear and something else is revealed. It's a kind of cultural sublation, a deep fusion of disparate parts and a partial reinvention of American music. Those signposts of country and rock and other roots are still there—old-time fiddle, pedal steel, rock backbeat, close harmony—but they're transformed, much the way Richard and Linda Thompson did with traditional music of the British Isles when they left Fairport Convention.

Parsons, too, had a partner in crime on these LPs, singer Emmylou Harris, whose role shifted from background to near partnership on the second one. (Parsons had reputedly wanted to credit these sessions to the two of them together, but his widow, Gretchen, jealous of Harris, refused to let this happen, and the record was issued exclusively under his name.) Their voices overlap magnificently on smoky slow songs like the Roy Orbison hit "Love Hurts," Tom Guidera and Walter Egan's "Hearts on Fire" (with its knife-twisting xylophone part), and the evangelical "In My Hour of Darkness," written jointly by Parsons and Harris, a tear-jerking closer: *In my hour of darkness / In my time of need / Oh, Lord grant me vision / Oh, Lord grant me speed.* The song's second verse, ostensibly about guitarist and vocalist Clarence White, could also be Parsons singing about himself.

> *Another young man safely strummed his silver-stringed guitar*
> *And he played to people everywhere*
> *Some say he was a star*
> *But he was just a country boy, his simple songs confess*
> *And the music he had in him, so very few possess*

On a lighter note, Parsons and Harris romp their way through Tom T. Hall's "I Can't Dance" and the Louvin Brothers' "Cash on the Barrelhead." Parsons sings one of his early songs alone, "Brass Buttons," and they spin a drinking/gambling story on "Las Vegas," with the ominous line: *Well, I spent all night with the dealer / Tryin' to get ahead / Spend all day at the Holiday Inn / Tryin' to get out of bed.* And on "$1000 Wedding," a mutation of the murder ballad, the singer's bride is either no-show or dead, and he laments:

> *And where are all the flowers for the girl?*
> *She only knew she loved the world*
> *And why ain't there one lonely horn and one sad note to play?*
> *Supposed to be a funeral*
> *It's been a bad, bad day*
> *Oh, supposed to be a funeral*
> *It's been a bad, bad day.*

On his visionary "Return of the Grievous Angel," Parsons sings, almost retrospectively: *'Cause I headed West to grow up with the country / Across those prairies with those waves of grain / And I saw my devil / And I saw my deep blue sea / And I thought about a calico bonnet from Cheyenne to Tennessee.*

...

Four years after Parsons's death, I heard Emmylou Harris open for Jackson Brown. Her performance did nothing for me, failed to move me in the slightest. It's hard for me to square with the way I felt later—the way I feel now, loving as I do Dolly Parton and Patsy Cline and the Carter Family women—but at the time I thought her singing was stiff, unsoulful, old-fashioned, corny even. I detected a little hillbilly in her delivery. That was an immediate turnoff. It was an instinctive response for me, an impulse to flee, perhaps like the distaste that many African Americans felt in the seventies for the blues, which they heard as backward and unsophisticated in the face of funk and soul. Class trumps race, in a case like that. I heard Harris sing and all my coal-mining town heritage and Polish immigrant-class aspiration welled up against it like white blood cells fighting a virus. It didn't take consideration; I just didn't dig the way it sounded—whiny and woodsy, a hick from the sticks. Little Feat were about as country rock as I got. At that point, I hadn't heard Parsons yet; I discovered him later. And ironically, I wouldn't have liked him either. He would have sounded like a hillbilly, too. That's what he wanted, the Nudie suit part of a class mask he'd donned, even though he had a trust fund and he'd studied at Harvard before devoting the rest of his short life to music.

I hear the posthumous album, *Grievous Angels*, as the high point of his music on a trail leading nowhere. Its joyful vibe is brutal irony, like the tail end of an acid Western: as the credits roll, an elegiac song keeps a stiff upper lip and our protagonist is dead, frozen in the snow, like John McCabe, or on the losing end of a bullet. Or just flat out in the sun, wasted on bad morph doled out by a mysterious femme fatale. Supposed to be a funeral, it's been a bad, bad day.

Average White Band

"Pick Up the Pieces"

A telescoping short list of pickup lines and things that needed picking up or straightening midway through the seventies:

- Sticks
- My room
- "Haven't we met?"
- Patty Hearst's life
- Leaves in the yard
- Barrel of Monkeys
- Dad's dry cleaning
- "Hey, sailor, got a light?"
- Drive-thru from McDonald's
- The horse in *Blazing Saddles*
- Mitchell, Haldeman, Ehrlichman
- The glass building in *Towering Inferno*
- "If I said you had a beautiful body, would you hold it against me?"
- 1,353,000 dead bodies in Vietnam since 1965, 587,000 of them civilian

Don Cornelius introduced the Average White Band on *Soul Train*: "Five super-talented young men from Scotland and one from England who all play and sing like they were raised on corn bread and black-eyed peas is something that has to be seen to be believed."

Seeing AWB was the point. Confirming they were white. That they'd grown up across the Atlantic, where Caucasian was no occasion, where it meant a whiter shade of pale, stay-out-of-the-sun-pasty-white-dude white. Seeing them and hearing them at the same time was useful, too, because you could also testify to the Celts' funkiness. They were funkier than Tower of Power, but too slick to be compared with the more odiferous side of funk, say Sly or Lyn Collins or the Meters or Betty Davis. To them, funk meant tight and slick, where to others it signaled loose and raw. AWB played up their whiteness, making it a novelty, the little disingenuous humility in their use of the word "average" in the moniker not fooling most of their listeners, especially the black ones, who dug them with ferocity in spite of their race and country of origin. And at least in part *because* they were white. It was a role reversal, having the white guys do the dance, make the party atmosphere, be the entertainment. (Ethnicity was indeed onstage as the seventies scaled their midpoint—recall Redbone's performances in full Native American costume, belting out their soul hit "Come and Get Your Love," and War's Afro-Latin hits "Why Can't We Be Friends" and "Low Rider.") Two years later, basing a lyric on what black fans had been shouting at them at gigs, an Ohio band called Wild Cherry would capitalize on the role-reversal with their chart topper "Play That Funky Music White Boy."

James Brown didn't take kindly to AWB's name or fame. In protest, he gave his band the pseudonym AABB for the Above Average Black Band. AABB issued only one single: "Pick Up the Pieces One by One." But the territoriality also tells you that AWB really had something. With tight saxophone arrangements on sweet chord changes executed by the Dundee Horns, "Pick Up the Pieces" effectively floated between funk, disco, and jazz-rock. A nine-note pop-

corn guitar line repeated precisely against syncopated chordal guitar, judicious organ smears, solid and undemonstrative bass, and a
super snappy drum part made it an ideal dance-hall smash, particularly when the music momentarily stood in place—an organ swell
drones, the horns repeat, organ and bass cease, and in the clearing
the band chants: *Pick up the pieces, uh-huh, pick up the pieces.* It's
a new twist on the classic musical release, and for dancers it was
red meat, inviting breakaway moves amid the snapback when the
band dives back into alignment.

AWB didn't need to be specific about what pieces they meant. It
was the middle of the seventies. Things were going haywire. The
American president was resigning. The United States was pulling
out of Cambodia. Inflation in Britain was spiraling out of control. Ali
beat Frazier in Manila. There were pieces everywhere. All around
the world, there were plenty of broken things to keep us dancing
and picking up, dancing and picking up.

But AWB had its own picking up to do. By the time they appeared
on *Soul Train* in 1975, their original drummer Robbie McIntosh was
dead. McIntosh and guitarist/vocalist Alan Gorrie both overdosed
on heroin at the very party in L.A. thrown for them to celebrate the
success of their album *AWB* (often referred to as the white album)
and its massive hit single, "Pick Up the Pieces." Gorrie survived,
but not McIntosh. His replacement was the lone English guy mentioned by Cornelius, Steve Ferrone, an agile session player who'd
played in the groups Bloodstone and Brian Auger's Oblivion Express
and would go on to work with Chaka Khan and Tom Petty and the
Heartbreakers. On *Soul Train*, he doesn't get much camera time.
Maybe seeing him dampened the AWB race punch line.

You see, Ferrone is black.

· The surviving astronauts on the TV version of *Planet of
  the Apes*
· Darwin, Australia, after being flattened by Cyclone Tracy
· Litter, encouraged by the Clean Community System

- New York's finances after bankruptcy
- 15,000 smallpox victims in India
- A brain in *Young Frankenstein*
- Lucy's skeleton in Ethiopia
- Bodies in *The Godfather II*
- George Foreman in Zaire
- Vomit in *The Exorcist*
- The U.S. government
- "What's your sign?"
- IRA bomb sites
- My grades
- 52 cards

William DeVaughn

"Be Thankful for What You've Got"

Solo conga sets a smooth groove, cuing Afro-conscious listeners hip to the Latin and Caribbean diaspora. The driver of the song assumes a leisurely speed, perfect tempo for a lowrider. At the first corner, they stop to pick up electric bass, organ, kick drum and quiet hi-hat, then two guitars—one with a porno wah, one clean-toned, adding sparse Wes Montgomery soul-jazz octaves.

Just as the singing starts, the organ flames up like a grill hit with a squirt of lighter fluid. *Though you may not drive a great big Cadillac / Gangster whitewalls / TV antennas in the back,* DeVaughn croons in a buttery alto, reaching up into his falsetto range for the next line: *You may not have a car at all / But remember, brothers and sisters / You can still stand tall / Just be thankful for what you got.*

Offsetting the angelic ease of DeVaughn's voice, the drummer pounds a thunderous backbeat on a low tom-tom, now and then throwing in a little syncopation. Somewhere, surreptitiously, a xylophone has slipped on board, adding sumptuously warm arpeggios to the cool organ tones. *Be thankful for what you got / Though you may not drive a great big Cadillac,* he repeats, but he interjects: *Diamond in the back / Sunroof top / Diggin' the scene with a gangster lean / Gangster whitewalls / TV antennas in the back.*

...

This is such an undeniably beautiful and tender song. It paints a particular picture: a guy out for a cruise on a beautiful day, seeing and being seen, his luxury mobile giving him pause to reflect on his privilege, his place in the world, all the others who might not be as lucky as him. But there's a little set of contradictory impulses here, if you get down to it, an internal conflict between thankfulness and yearning, acceptance and dissatisfaction, community and selfishness, generosity and avarice.

On the one hand, this fellow says, you should be thankful for what (meager possessions) you've got, which presumably include your spirit and intelligence and friends and other non-material things, the meaningful stuff in life, all the gifts we rejoice in on Thanksgiving Day. On the other hand, our mack daddy taunts us from the comfort of his front seat, we poor folk who might not have a car at all, with the lavishness of his description of this, perhaps the most desirable mack-mobile ever made. To his "brothers and sisters," he advises that a car doesn't matter in the bigger picture, then he turns each term of illustration over in his mouth, delectating over them like they're so wonderful that even the words taste good. Hey, brothers, you don't require this wicked sunroof or the Caddy's diamond-shaped rear window. Now, sisters, you're OK without these out-of-sight whitewalls. And the gangster lean: a posture reserved for badass motherfuckers.

Is this a social consciousness message or a blaxploitation song?

Paradoxically, those were two intertwined paradigms in 1974—the call for solidarity in poverty and an abiding respect for the nobility of upward mobility. Think *Sanford and Son* (debuted 1972) versus *The Jeffersons* (debuted 1975). And that play between gratitude and materialism was not just a framework of self-understanding within the African American realm, but constituted a dominant dualism in the white construction of blackness, too, conjuring caricatures of blackness, archetypes of settling and ambition. If you want to understand something about crossover, the search for a way to sell music to black and white audiences simultaneously, "Be Thankful for What You've Got" is the place to look.

Upon its release, with its Curtis Mayfield–like sound capitalizing on the crazy success of Curtom's soundtrack to *Super Fly*, the song shot to the top of the R&B charts and to the fourth position in the overall *Billboard* ratings, showing that it was almost equally popular with black and white audiences. It was appealingly realistic, on the one hand, but it also indulged a fantasy about black culture, a kind of romance about the virtue hidden in destitution, and a humorous and captivating image of our mack daddy, driving into your white suburb, much the way George Clinton and his crew would later, to serve up an imaginary view of the ghetto, observed from a safe distance, like animals in a petting zoo, in which the righteous vies with the flamboyant for the hearts and minds of people who want the same thing as any red-blooded American consumer—a sweet ride.

Meet the Residents

About halfway through the seventies, the weirdo nerds were roused from their slumber. Like the zombies in George Romero's *Dawn of the Dead*, they gradually came to life, stretching and shaking off their mortification, only to realize how powerful was their hunger. The first portion of the decade was under the control of the popular kids, the football players and cheerleaders, but somewhere along the way it was time for the revenge of the weirdo nerds. They were flesh-eaters. And they were famished.

Of course, weirdo nerds had been there all along, keeping to themselves, reading *Mad* magazine, underground comics, and *Heavy Metal*, letting their greasy hair grow out, obsessing over *Star Trek*, making plastic explosives in their friend's barn, and trying to get high on dried banana peels. They—we—constituted all hybrid variations of freak and geek, drawn from stoners and druggies, outcasts, intellectuals, queers and gender dysmorphs, introverts and exhibitionists, sarcastics, spastics, and flaming fantastics. Future math geniuses, artists, and sociopaths united in their mutant coup d'état, displacing the proverbial hard-rocking homecoming king and queen.

The division between straight music and strange music grew more pronounced. Think of Journey, Supertramp, Kansas, and Styx, and wonder aloud how they could exist in a world of Devo, Henry Cow, Pere Ubu, and the Residents.

...

If a weirdo nerd was starting a band with other weirdo nerds, what would be the natural thing to do? Keep it secret. That's the ticket: do it but don't let anyone know. Record it in your basement, come up with a bunch of in-jokes and biting critiques of mainstream culture, write screenplays and make films, but do it all privately. Or just let a few people in on the fact, but don't actively try to spread it around. Create a mythology around the mysterious band, an origin story with quizzical names and false information. If and when the ensemble performs, they should do it in masks and costumes, never revealing their actual identities. Shroud the band in uncertainty. Retain control of productions. Make up collaborators. Cultivate a cult-like following.

The Residents did all of this. We know they were working in a suburb of San Francisco by the early nineteen seventies, though they claimed to have been from Shreveport, Louisiana, and to have made hundreds of hours of home recordings before the start of the new decade. They formed a company appropriately titled the Cryptic Corporation, they forged allegiances with guitarist Snakefinger (aka Phil Lithman) and invented a mentor in the form of a Bavarian avant-garde composer named N. Senada—possibly so-named in homage to the road on which Captain Beefheart recorded *Trout Mask Replica*, Ensenada Drive, or a pseudonym for the renegade composer Harry Partch—who they claimed had elaborated a Theory of Obscurity, a script that the Residents put into action by relishing their relative unknown-ness for the first years of their career, even while running a record label, Ralph Records. They shared a name with packages addressed to unknown recipients. Who were these goofballs? Residents, that's all. From their first production, a double seven-inch called *Santa Dog*, in 1972, to the end of the seventies, they issued a string of extremely strange records, seven singles and seven LPs, displaying all the inbred strategies cataloged above and never for a moment letting down their super-nerd guard.

The mystery propagated by the Residents wasn't romantic. It wasn't like J. D. Salinger, Thomas Pynchon, or William Faulkner; it didn't lead to suppositions of grandeur or beg for the work to stand on its own. Instead, theirs was the kind of privacy sought by people involved in something subversive, illicit, perhaps illegal—the active undermining of pop music's prevailing mythos. And mystery was just part of its nerd-ball theatricality. The first edition of their debut LP, *Meet the Residents*, which reputedly sold only forty copies in the first year—bear in mind, though, that much information about them is self-reported, and therefore not entirely reliable—had a cover based on the Beatles' first album, same font and layout, each of the Fab Four's familiar faces juvenilely vandalized. They would take aim at the Beatles repeatedly, though ironically their lumpy brand of tape music exploration might best be cast as the logical descendent of "Revolution 9," from the White Album.

Using willfully bizarre, put-on voices, sometimes altered by singing or talking into a vessel, the Residents were not above being crude or ludicrous, their particular version of cultural subterfuge as much rooted in the power of humor as in the necessity of noise. You could try to understand them in relation to other aggressively nonconformist musical acts, say Beefheart and Partch or the Bonzo Dog Doo-Dah Band or Destroy All Monsters or Moondog or Sun Ra. This will take you part way there.

At least as helpful will be a comparison with funk art, a visual arts movement also based around San Francisco whose ranks included Robert Arneson, Joan Brown, Jess, Clayton Bailey, Roy De Forest, William T. Wiley, and David Gilhooly. And factor in some of the imagist artists from Chicago who spent time in the Bay Area: Jim Nutt, Gladys Nilsson, and Karl Wirsum. In the sixties and seventies, these artists also used humor and crudeness in their work, which had links to surrealism and Dada. They were open to stupid puns and psychosexual references. Gary Panter, an artist who is a big fan of funk and imagist art, worked on graphic design for some

Ralph Records; Panter also designed the set of the eighties TV program *Pee-wee's Playhouse*, in part inspired by these artists. The Residents contributed occasionally to the show's soundtrack.

There is a childlike quality to the Residents. But it's an attitude more like the behavior of actual children than the adult idealization of child's play, which is to say that it can be mean, even cruel, is generally snotty, and likes to repeat a joke many times, beating it into the ground until it stops being funny and turns into something else. One of their basic methods is making music by making fun of music. But there's a difference between satire and subversion, parody and prank. A comparison with the Rutles, the mock Beatles group formed by Eric Idle and Neil Innes also in the mid-seventies, is informative. In one, a genuine affection for the object of ridicule holds sway; in the other, an air of contemptuousness reigns.

Listen to "Boots," on *Meet The Residents*, their disinterring and defilement of Nancy Sinatra and Lee Hazlewood's 1966 hit "These Boots Are Made for Walkin'." Contorted, Muppet-like lead vocal, perhaps maintaining the singer's anonymity, hard-panned left and right, like the early Beatles' records, with a magnificently dissonant horn section, the singer devolving into a minute of *walk all over you* repetitions. On the wistful melody of "Rest Aria," an out-of-tune piano is joined by various colorful instruments, building like a deviant elementary school exercise in orchestration, Carl Orff gone awry—xylophone, whistling, electric keyboard, trumpet. "Infant Tango" features Snakefinger's hilarious guitar stylings, which alternate with the horns in lampooning wah-wah funk, while the ten-minute-long "N-Er-Gee (Crisis Blues)" is more abrasive, including a short snippet of garage band the Human Beinz's "Nobody but Me," sampled and then mauled by the Residents. It also includes some dopey marching band charts with illogical halts, an absurd anti-oil-corporation protest song that ends with the line: *Go home, America, 55'll do.*

Do double nickels and slow down, they suggest, and not only to save gas. Dare to be stupid. It's your birthright as an American. As a member of the new weirdo nerd army.

Brian Eno

Taking Tiger Mountain (By Strategy)

Dr. Alimantado

"Best Dressed Chicken in Town"

In 1979 I worked at a record store. One day, examining the packing list for some new arrivals, I spied the entry "Brian Eno/Peter Schmidt, *Oblique Strategies*." Not having read any advance press on a fresh Eno collaboration, I riffled through the box looking for the vinyl. I came up empty-handed, though a strange little object, smaller than the LPs and singles, fell out onto the ground. A black box of cards, it measured roughly three by four inches, with the Eno/Schmidt title embossed in silver on its long edge. First published in 1975, this was the third edition, fresh off the press. I opened it up and randomly drew one of the cards, which read: "Water." I drew another: "Turn it upside down." Another: "Don't be frightened of clichés." And again: "The tape is now the music."

There are moments in our lives that can be thought of as gateways. We stand in front of something unfamiliar. Our brains are at that instant perfectly disposed to see in it a glimpse of our future, to sense ways the unfamiliar thing will become part of our lives, how it will open a door to new ways of being in the world. In 1979 I had never heard of Fluxus, I didn't know about Cornelius Cardew or the Scratch Orchestra or the Portsmouth Sinfonia, I had no frame of reference for artist Dieter Roth, I hadn't seen Tom Phillips's artwork or his serially editioned book *A Humument*. But these future flashpoints were all there in that quizzical little box, squished up like spring snakes waiting to explode in my brain, triggered by 123 alternately helpful and confusing directives.

The deeper meanings latent in Eno and Schmidt's prompts had to do with a philosophy, or better a praxis. They were gentle challenges to Cartesian logic. I picked out another—"Change instrument roles"—and thought, "Huh, I guess you can do that, maybe play guitar like drums." Finding these clues felt like getting close to working out a Rubik's Cube, seeing how one good choice influences others, with choices and consequences alternating until the solution is clear and the cube is solved. I wouldn't know; I never could. I'm shitty at games like that.

"Don't be afraid of things because they're easy to do," advised one card, while another said: "Don't be afraid to display your talents." To understand those slips of paper as not representing opposites or collapsing into mutual exclusivity but instead as implying a point of resolution between said opposites, or maybe to imagine that the ideas like those can exist simultaneously without needing to be resolved, reading through the cards, I could see remarkably deep into my own future.

I could also see into the future of music. Some consider the more adventurous lineage of seventies rock as belonging to David Bowie. I'd nominate Eno, instead. He showed that it was possible to work counterintuitively, using non sequitur, for example, as part of an indirect method, an actual strategy of obliqueness designed to obtain an enlivened result. And he demonstrated this not just in experimental contexts, like the field of ambient music that he helped invent, but with a string of exciting pop records, four to be exact, each utterly unique and impossible to imitate.

We have a tendency to think of "art rock" as being rock dressed up to seem artistic, hence its pretentious reputation. But Eno's quartet of seventies pop—*Here Come the Warm Jets*, *Taking Tiger Mountain (By Strategy)*, *Another Green World*, and *Before and After*

Science—understood popular music-making to be a fundamentally inquisitive, rather than expressive, process. And although it was not until the second of these records, made a year before *Oblique Strategies* was publicly available, that Eno would directly apply the cards to his composition and recording of songs, the contrarian spirit is there from the start.

I stand by all these LPs as peak examples of smart, innovative, humorous music, spit out in such a burst of concentrated and then expended energy as to insist to others that they, too, could make music this great, as if Eno needed to get his own music out of the way so that the others wouldn't be intimidated. It's a generous and generative gesture, and there are surely musical statements that could never have been formulated and bands that wouldn't have spawned were it not for his example—I am thinking of the group Wire most obviously, though much of the post-punk diaspora fits this description—while in truth only a few of them match the wit and wisdom of Eno's four releases. They're indispensable, but my favorite is the first one to directly use the cards: *Taking Tiger Mountain*.

From the first track, "Burning Airlines Give You So Much More," Eno's handiwork is evident in the nuanced mix, which places one jangly guitar part at a distance, like a quotation of a rhythm guitar, while a slippery pedal-steel part occupies the middle ground along with Robert Fripp's infinite-sustain ray guitar, and Fripp's gapped-interval melody stands out front, a tree frog on the song's windowpane. Every detail is precisely chosen and placed, which sounds more antiseptic than it is—but each track is a whole new world unfolding in a few minutes.

On "The Great Pretender," a damped bass motif on piano and drum machine established an ominous starting place for an unlikely mechanical seduction, a three-chord cycle builds queasiness through repetition and accretion—queered pitch guitar, voice, kettle drum and metallic clank, distorto-guitar, surf guitar, synthesizer set to African night animals, and the line: *Monica sighed / Rolled onto her side / She was so impressed that she just surrendered.* In the end, the crickets have the last word, a full minute of last words, chirping dronefully. One of the most delightful and surprising passages comes in "China My China," as Eno sings, *These poor girls are such fun / They know what God gave them their fingers for,* and then stage-whispers, *To make percussion over solos,* and indeed a sudden chorus of typewriters drums under a rubbery guitar spotlight for Fripp.

Eno sings with uncanny earnestness on "Put a Straw Under Baby," a riotously blasphemous Christmas ditty, replete with barrel organ, that implies animism in the crèche as it name-checks a Family Stone song: *There's a brain in the table / There's a heart in the chair / And they all live in Jesus / It's a family affair.* Robert Wyatt adds an achingly beautiful high vocal, and the Portsmouth Sinphonia, a radical orchestra made up of non-musician musicians, saws its way through a string section.

Listen to "Third Uncle" to understand why *Taking Tiger Mountain* proved to be manna for the post-punks years after. It hurries ahead of itself, Phil Manzanera's frantic rhythm guitar part threatening to divide the instruments into chaotic competitors, ultra-simple four-note guitar solo appealing in all ways, also the poetic structure of the lyrics, a terse registry of things, which might have come right out of the *Oblique Strategies* manual of style:

There are tins
There was pork
There are legs
There are sharks
There was John
There are cliffs
There was mother
There's a poker
There was you
Then there was you

There are scenes
There are blues
There are boots
There are shoes
There are Turks
There are fools
They're in lockers
They're in schools
They're in you
Then there was you.

The form morphs slightly at the end of Eno's text:

Burn my fingers
Burn my toes
Burn my uncle
Burn his books
Burn his shoes
Cook the leather
Put it on me
Does it fit me or you?
It looks tight on you.

The peculiar attitude here, which is cool and distanced but acknowledges and draws on emotionality, feels prescient to me, like Eno could tell what kind of tune-up popular music needed. It's smart and funny, topical and sacrilegious—two of the songs, including "Third Uncle," refer cruelly to a recent Turkish Airlines crash. He had the tools and the skills, even those needed to deskill the whole endeavor, to neutralize its dependency on virtuosity and performance, to rethink making music as more of an essayistic procedure than art of inspiration, an act of the intellect rather than the id. *Taking Tiger Mountain* is, to me, what Sophie Taeuber-Arp might have made if she'd been a thinking person's rock 'n' roller rather than a Dada puppeteer.

...

Eno and Schmidt's most prophetic card had been drawn: "The tape is now the music." It was the dawn of a new era of studio production. At one point, Eno gave an influential lecture titled "The Studio as Compositional Tool," but for him the studio was more than a way of writing music via recording. The challenge to conventional attitudes toward musicality was deeper for Eno, related back to his initial hesitancy at being labeled a musician when he played with Roxy Music. Forget that he could coax anything from a synthesizer, sing with a voice unlike anybody else, play basic keyboards and guitar (he usually referred to it as "snake guitar"), and percussion where needed. All of this was done à la carte, to order, not as part of a musician identity. He had already been working for most of the decade with the studio as his instrument.

The mid-seventies saw the rise of the producer-auteur. Of course, producers had always been there, back to Sun Records and Sam Phillips and earlier, but they were rarely called out explicitly in print. By the time Eno made *Taking Tiger Mountain*, the in-house producers, company men who gave each label its particular sensibility—much the way that the studio system had imparted a particular fingerprint onto films made in each studio—were in fact disappearing. Most often working without a line credit on the records, great producers like Ahmet Ertegun, founder of Atlantic Records, had helped shepherd and shape the career of, for instance, Ray Charles, all the way down to the selection of takes, decisions about material, arrangements, and even writing some of the music. Remember that it was Ertegun who added Neil Young to Crosby, Stills & Nash. These producers were not passive facilitators; they actively participated in the cultivation of their artists and the sound of the music they issued. But this kind of invisibly influential producer was fading out in the heyday of rock's ascendency, as musicians and bands became powerful enough to assert authority over the music they made, often opting to produce themselves. Consider the Led Zeppelin records, all produced—and thoughtfully so—by Jimmy Page.

What arose in the place of the in-house producers were producer-auteurs, people often working independently who were guns-for-hire brought on board to help acts make exceptional and successful records. And they were named. Right there on the back cover. The record producer, in these cases, functions more like a film director, as a proper name that represents a particular approach or aesthetic. Sometimes the record company would hire them, sometimes they were chosen by the musicians, but they were given some degree of decision-making power and brought their own vision, sometimes their own sound, to projects.

Eno produced his first record—a solo effort by Hawkwind's Robert Calvert called *Lucky Leif and the Longships*—along these lines while working on *Taking Tiger Mountain*. He went on to produce all but one of the Talking Heads records in the seventies, debut records by Ultravox! and Devo, *Sinking of the Titanic* by composer Gavin Bryars, the four-band compilation *No New York*, his own collaborations with Fripp, Dieter Mobelius and Hans-Joachim Rodelius, and David Byrne; and of course later he produced records by U2, David Bowie, and James. What you hear Eno bring to many of these productions is not a signature sound, but a mental framework, an inquisitive intelligence, a manner of proceeding meant to bring out the best in the artist. In the end, you get the four finest Talking Heads records, the classic Devo outing, and a No Wave sampler that seems to have left them to do their own thing. I suspect the *No New York* cover concept was his contribution, more than anything a listener would hear. No need to put your stamp on somebody else's music if it's ready to go.

...

The producer-auteur was already part of the Jamaican music firmament long before it became the norm up northward. Starting in the sixties, reggae conflated the studio system with that auteurist notion so that records coming out of Coxsone Dodd's Studio One had a particular sound, Duke Reid's Treasure Isle another, Vincent Chin's Randy's studio yet another. The producer was the visionary, an artist in his own right, not just an engineer or a businessman. Indeed, retrospective surveys of reggae and dub are often assembled according to producer, rather than artist, and many Jamaican producers have the same level of celebrity as the folks they've produced. Or more.

The same year Eno was working on *Taking Tiger Mountain*, a reggae producer named Lee "Scratch" Perry was building a new facility behind his Kingston home. Black Ark Studios opened in 1974, and over the next six years Perry would record one track after another that perfectly exemplify the producer's elevated role, also documenting one of the wildest and most adventurous figures in seventies music. Perry was one of the principle architects of dub, together with King Tubby, and his Black Ark sides are commonly considered to be his crowning achievements. Not long after the space had been equipped and Perry—a genuine scriptomaniac—had scribbled his first of an endless stream of words directly onto the studio's walls, a toasting deejay named Winston Thompson, aka Dr. Alimantado, took the microphone and laid down an unforgettable track with a hilarious name borrowed, no doubt, from a local jerk joint. On "Best Dressed Chicken in Town," working under his pseudonym as "the Upsetter," Perry was the engineer, though when the track, which was first issued as a single, was later compiled by the Greensleeves label, the good Doc was listed as producer. Perhaps it's a technicality, but these are delicate distinctions.

Alimantado talks over Horace Andy's cover of the Bill Withers song "Ain't No Sunshine," starting with organ and fluttering fragments of sped-up vocals, then a truly hysterical screech of the title line and a follow-up: *Don't fly, don't fly, don't fly*. His rhythmic delivery is sometimes put through an echo chamber, two or three voices congregating like a gaggle, the tape speed quickened on one to imitate his opening squeal or turn it into a chipmunk, the echo loop timed to match the loping pace of the bass and drums so that everything is reflected back and forth until Alimantado's final *cock-a-doodle-doo*. It's a song with Perry written all over it, from the hall of mirrors to the hilarious theme.

At Black Ark, the working principle was the same as Eno's: the studio is an instrument. But Scratch didn't need a set of cards to look for new ideas. He wrote his own on the interior of his brain cage. For a genuine loon like him, oblique strategies flowed like a natural mystic through the air.

...

In many ways, reggae was the secret spice of the seventies. It insinuated its way into so much music in so many different ways, and I think it ultimately helped me understand how to listen to romantic songs. Heavily Rastafarian material, with its African dimension, as well as rootsier and more politically outspoken outfits, and of course stranger stuff, like dub and talk-over, were all immediately attractive, but even the lovey-doviest of the great reggae crooners, say Slim Smith or John Holt, struck me as punk Motown. Scruffier than most American soul, made on a budget in little four-track studios, its power came from a more tangible place, producers placing their indelible stamp on the sound, but all of it on a scale of production that didn't seem completely inaccessible to us. And by the time I was intoxicated by the Gladiators' lilting "Sweet So Till," as sensual a song as there is, I'd sipped from the chalice of love. Indeed, against all superficial indicators, reggae's future would become entwined with punk, perhaps for just these reasons. With the studio as its primary instrument, reggae was human-scale music.

Autobahn

Count to ten and say "krautrock."

1) Düsseldorf myth-crushers, hippie reducers, synthetic transducers, and avatars of electronica.
2) First major campaign in my life against the false consciousness of sweat equity, which in music consisted of a preconception that visible exertion produces equivalent value.
3) Two unemotional men making sounds with machines. Clean, logical, workmanlike, mechanical, disinterested, *mechanistisch*, German: no sweat.
4) Crush also the myth that complexity equals worth—the banality of Kraftwerk melodies recalls Satie in inert ingeniousness, little jingles that go nowhere fast, most ironic in a song about driving: *Fahren fahren fahren auf der Autobahn.* Like Satie, furniture music, except furniture covered in vinyl.
5) Equivalent mesmerization of Pong, our first video game, which vied with the family air hockey set for attention. The latter: play of gravity, buoyancy, and velocity, a jazz game requiring finesse and elbow grease, floating puck subject to body English

and nudge nuance, each exchange rapid-fire, thrilling, and thoroughly analog. The former: an electronic war of attrition, little computer ball moving from side to side, rebounding reliably off the top of the screen, all simple angles and predictable vectors, asking who will let their guard down after indefinite volleys, which attention jockey will psyche him- or herself out? Kraftwerk was just as monotonous as Pong. They turned monotony into a positive.

6) Initial forays into synthesizers turned them into music supercomputers, emphasizing their ability to do impossibly complicated things and make spectacular moves unthinkable by acoustic means—hyperbolic glissandi, for instance, leaping from sub-basement tone to piercing ultra-high frequency. Synthesizer was a virtuoso instrument, an automation or extension of manual virtuosity. Minimoogs and ARPs and Buchlas and Prophet-5s: synth players were the keepers of number-crunching axes, liontamers in the rock circus, literally pushing the envelope. Waveform acrobatics were the name of the game.

7) Kraftwerk made no pretense of virtuosity in their use of synth. Rather, they relied on them as dependable repeaters, ostinato generators, strings of sequenced tones recapped verbatim, slowly mutating, perverting the singing voice into a robotic drone, presaging the ATM talkback and the GPS guide.

8) Imagine a version of popular music that undoes many of its basic pleasures. It looks kindly on Muzak. It courts the generic. It mates with minimalism. It rejects individualism.

9) Ralf Hütter and Florian Schneider helped set in motion the rationalization of pop, cooling off its overheated pyrotechnics, foreseeing a coming age of computerized emoticons—not unexpressive, exactly, but with its own peculiar plastiform-industrial-neoconstructivist-binary-videographic connotations. After *Autobahn*, Schneider even tossed his beloved flute. The stripping away of gratuitous sentiment, which had been

so central to our investment in music, was thrilling and brave and new.

10) A new wave—later, the Neue Deutsche Welle—lapped at our feet, tickling our ears in electronic tones, saying: "Put down your guitars and drum sticks, cut your hair, quit contorting, don your uniform, man your sequencer, and oscillate, comrade, oscillate."

Each time you purchase a record, you walk into a brand-new world. Slitting open the plastic wrap, slipping out the LP, opening up the gatefold sleeve or extracting the liner sheet, you break into a miniature mythological realm with its own atmosphere. The effect of the record is not contained just in the music and lyrics, but in a whole cluster of images and sounds, photography and design, patterns and textures, an aggregation of subtle cues that create a consistent psychic space in which the music unfolds. It's like how you subconsciously map the distances and ambience in your home, knowing how many steps cover each room, how high on the wall the light switch is, how dark and what color the wall will be when the light is out, which direction to turn the lock when you're locking a door. The rooms are the space of the action, the given terrain in which things take place. Records have a similar sense of psychic space, mapping out their own mythic domicile.

In Johnny Carson's words, if you buy the premise, you buy the bit.

David Bowie's *Low* is an orange album. So is *Houses of the Holy* by Led Zeppelin. Those colors are more than just ancillary parts of the package; they have become burned into the music itself and are now inseparable from the way it sounds. I would argue that those oranges have *changed* the way the music sounds. I hear the songs and I see bright orange hues. The words of the artist's name and the record's title hang like street signs on the cover, song titles arranged like names on an apartment register, the buzzer number next to them, ready for a ring. Here's your new world, the fantastic universes of *Low* or *Houses of the Holy*, which automatically have more to do with one another because of that clementine color they share. It's so damned close to synesthesia, what I'm talking about, that I can nearly taste the citrusy rind of those records.

...

Van Morrison's *Veedon Fleece* is an outdoor record. It's blue and green dominant, with brown undertones, minty, permeated with the smell of pines and peat, the rolling hills and wind in canine fur on the cover conjuring a specific kind of natural space, a Celtic exteriority, with shrubs and moss and rocks and ruddied cheeks. It's certainly a rural record, but a kind of countryside exotic to me, a very un-American landscape, or translated into the American scene, a northwestern one, with giant redwoods canopied over a gold-rush tent town. Amplifying the record's mythos, one song is called "You Don't Pull No Punches, but You Don't Push the River," conjuring clean air just cold enough to smart when the wind snaps and a waterway that moves at its own pace.

Morrison brought jazz into rock in a particular way. Not as patterned flash and sleek changes like Steely Dan, not as experimentation with form like Frank Zappa, not with long improvisations like the Grateful Dead, but in an easy, rolling, organic manner, a green patch in the reeks of Ireland. Modal jazz, in particular, with its method of hovering and floating in place, fit his agenda magnificently. With a candlelit voice, Morrison built a bridge between modal jazz and nineteenth-century poetry and prose. He mentions Edgar Allan Poe, Henry David Thoreau, and Oscar Wilde in songs that amble along in 3/4 or swing in 6/8, brushes on snare, acoustic guitar, upright or soft electric bass, flute or recorder, piano flourishes. As if they were a band with backup singers or a Bill Graham double bill, he name-checks William Blake and the Eternals with the Sisters of Mercy, on the hunt in an epic quest for said fleece. Morrison extends and distends the lyrics, improvising with them, repeating lines, introducing embellishment to his phrasing by means of melisma, each syllable potentially taken over the hills and back.

Since I first heard it in high school, *Veedon Fleece* has been my favorite of Van Morrison's worlds to inhabit. I also think it's one of the best records of its day, albeit not among the best known. A supremely relaxed and confident set of performances, its lyrics make good on his claim to the mystical inheritance of transcendentalism, poetically rich and dark and beautiful. It's very much music that conjures another epoch, maybe overlaying several epochs, the afore-mentioned nineteenth century stretching back to earlier days of English language literature, even a touch of the bard. But it's tinged too with American soul, in places recalling the way James Brown permuted a line as part of an extemporaneous delivery. Morrison doesn't go for the hard angles and heavy backbeats of funk, rather the airier side of soul, the Jackie Wilsons and Sam Cookes and Smokey Robinsons. He can growl and dig for a gruffer note, too, but when he breaks out up high, he's indeed transcendent.

Although most of my time has been spent with the sublime first side, the whole LP is a wonder, including the two less-cottony tracks, "Bulbs" and "Cul de Sac," light country rockers that were released together as the record's single. One moment on the record transfixes me with its special mojo, however, along with the full cut that follows. The track "Linden Arden Stole the Highlights" witnesses the invention of an American pioneer character, a churchgoing man who is for some unstated reason pursued by a murderous posse.

> *But he found out where they were drinking*
> *Met them face to face outside*
> *Cleaved their heads off with a hatchet*
> *Lord, he was a drinkin' man*

And when someone tried to get above him
He just took the law into his own hands.

In a few short minutes, Morrison composes a portrait of a man of contradictions, a genuine outlaw about to set out on the lam, but a strangely sympathetic guy. The last line lingers, like smoke from a fireworks display.

And he loved the little children like they were his very own
He said: "Someday it may get lonely."
Now he's livin', livin' with a gun.

In the breath between the last words of "Linden Arden" and the first of "Who Was That Masked Man," the song changes and it continues, both at the same time. Morrison moves from his natural range up to an aching falsetto for the duration of the subsequent track, beginning with an incandescent line that directly extends the firearm in the final line of the previous song: *Oh ain't it lonely / When you're living with a gun / Well, you can't slow down / And you can't turn 'round / And you can't trust anyone.* The portrait gets more intimate, looking inside the head of a hunted man, exploring the precariousness of life on the run, its fragility and unreality serving as metaphors for the ambiguities of daily life, the loneliness in one's petty hypocrisies, the lies we tell ourselves to insulate us from the plain chill of the world, the windburn of human existence, all sung with acoustic guitar obbligato. *You can hang suspended from a star / Or wish on a toilet roll / You can just soak up the atmosphere / Like a fish inside a bowl.* Morrison makes a passing reference to the ghost in *Hamlet* en route to an anxious close. *And no matter what they tell you,* he sings, his crystalline voice a straight shot to the heart. *There's good and evil in everyone.*

...

John Cale's *Paris 1919* is an indoor record. Pale walls the color of eggshell, drawing rooms, sitting rooms, parlors, ship cabins, train coaches—the spaces of the record are as divided up as Europe on the dire eve of the record's title. *From here on it's got to be / A simple case of them or me*, sings Cale on "Half Past France." *If they're alive then I am dead / Pray God and eat your daily bread.* The record's people are all as white as its interiors, northern Eurofolk—genteel Brits and French and Germans—sipping tea and deciding the fate of the Continent. It, too, is a literate outing, with its own Shakespeare moment ("Macbeth"), a flash of Cale's Welsh countryman Dylan Thomas, and an entire song dedicated to Graham Greene.

Paris 1919 is, for Cale, a soft record. Compared with his early experimental music—the work with the Velvet Underground or his minimalist viola in the Theatre of Eternal Music with La Monte Young and Tony Conrad, or even the rock records he made for the Island label—it has a tender complexion, sometimes even childlike, rhymey, and singsong. *There's a law for everything,* Cale lullabies on "Hanky Panky Nohow," in a pure church choir tone. *And for elephants that sing / To keep the cows that agriculture won't allow / Hanky panky nohow / Hanky panky nohow.* This wistful image of bovines too wild to be selectively bred is crosscut with a more ominous image of someone engaging in hanky-panky, defying laws of nature or humans or religions or nations, laws of decency and decorum, laws of democracy or socialism or fascism. Cale coos into the crib, and what echoes back at him is the sound of early twentieth-century global angst. Brilliantly produced by Chris Thomas, with majestic arrangements that include guitarist Lowell George of the group Little Feat (like the entire cast, uncredited on the LP jacket) and a symphony orchestra, *Paris 1919* is gentle in appearance, but in fact it's a powder keg.

I recall the first time seeing Cale solo in Providence, Rhode Island, in the early eighties. He played piano and sang songs from across his extensive repertoire, five or so completed without incident. Then he started "Fear Is a Man's Best Friend," from the album *Fear*, recorded a year after *Paris 1919*. Halfway into the lyric, Cale's voice departed from its calm, grew agitated, then angry, then hostile, then ballistic, and finally cataplectic, as he drubbed the keyboard mercilessly and shouted the refrain, hoarse and strangulated and actually genuinely frighteningly out of his mind, like he'd had a seizure or a psychotic breakdown. Like Antonin Artaud on a rough night, or Buddy Rich bad-mouthing his band; like Peter Finch as Howard Beale in *Network* or Faye Dunaway as Joan Crawford in *Mommie Dearest*—Cale went completely off his nut. I saw him perform a few more times and realized that this extreme pressure-explosion drama was part of his routine, but he never seemed to do it in the same place or to the same song, reserving the right to surprise his audience with the sudden, inexplicable appearance of Mr. Edward Hyde.

Paris 1919 is all Dr. Henry Jekyll, but you do feel the lurking presence of malevolence within. Decades later, Cale told a writer that the record was "an example of the nicest ways of saying something ugly." The ugliness concerned the European predicament at the close of the First World War, the rights and ritual and rigid thinking that led to the spawning of the Holocaust, and by analogy, of course, the implications of that polite treachery for contemporary European life circa 1973. It's told from a poetic perspective, beautiful and fragile, and the world he invokes is one of fishbowls, crystal decanters, and pheasant under glass. Even when it departs from the chronological framework on the last track to touch on the film *Sunset Boulevard*, it trembles with a kind of preciousness and persnickety propriety, its warm exterior covering up ice coldness. Cale painfully describes the Gloria Swanson character Norma Desmond, equally referring to the freeze-drying of Western civilization, the ensuing shit show of late twentieth-century culture depicted as a lace doily of whispery manners about to be obliterated in a psychobiddy blowout. *Her schoolhouse mind has windows now / Where handsome creatures come to watch / The anesthetic wearing off / Antarctica starts here.*

Robert Wyatt

Rock Bottom

What would it mean to turn time around?

Gary Hill did it in his 1984 work *Why Do Things Get in a Muddle?* In preparation for the half-hour-long video, Hill taught himself to speak backward, so that he could tape himself and then play the tape in reverse, resulting in a partially intelligible speaking part, a personal and philosophical meditation on messes based on Gregory Bateson's book *Steps to an Ecology of Mind*, in which Bateson explains the idea of entropy to his daughter. Hill coined the term "metalogue" for the piece, defining it as "when a conversation about problems between people mirrors the problems themselves."

Along with Stephen Dixon's traumatic short story "Wife in Reverse," another of my favorite chrono-flip works is the Martin Amis novel *Time's Arrow*, in which events move backward but the narrator interprets them as if they were moving forward. The contours of a love affair as seen from either approach, frontward or in reverse—obliviousness and distance, mounting interest, magnetic captivation, waning interest, distance and obliviousness—are striking and provocative, as is Amis's ultimate revelation of the proximity of the ordinary and the villainous, the way that temporal unidirectionality appears to give those values shape and meaning.

Backward recordings have been used since the dawn of the gram-ophone, when time assumed its material manifestation, or at least a concrete representation. Jean Vigo had turned sound around for a film soundtrack by the early thirties. Bruce Conner made *Break-away* in 1966, a five-minute experimental film that I could watch endlessly, featuring an irresistible young Toni Basil, her jump-cut gyrations then repeated, but in reverse. In the pop era, the Beatles were gatekeepers of time-turnaround. Their *musique concrète* piece "Revolution 9," from *The Beatles*, introduced unsuspecting listen-ers to an extreme use of the reverse tape effects, but earlier in their oeuvre the Fab Four included backward guitar parts on two songs on *Revolver*. The Bardo-like state described in "Tomorrow Never Knows" seems to nicely sum up the logic of time reversal: *Turn off your mind, relax and float downstream.* Or upstream, as the case may be, drifting away from tomorrow rather than toward it. I remember endless searches for backward-masked evidence of Paul's death, mangling a stylus in the process of spinning records the opposite way. The Beatles created a veritable cult of the reverse. On his song "Driving Me Backwards," Brian Eno evokes the uncanny rubato sound of contrary motion without—best I can tell—actually turning anything around. *Turn the beat around . . . turn it upside down*, sang Vicki Sue Robinson in her 1976 disco hit, recalling two of the methods for variation (retrograde and inversion) used by Vien-nese tone-row composers at the fin de siècle. Let's just say there's been ample upstream action in twentieth-century culture.

To return to Hill and Bateson and Bateson's daughter and their basic question: Why do things get messed up? When events are mov-ing forward, inching ever into the future, never mind why, they just do. Stuff breaks down. Fear eats the soul. Rust never sleeps. Things fall apart. You pick them up, put them together, but they fall apart again. It's an automatic do-over. Have no fear—even in the best of times, things will get in a muddle. Just ask Robert Wyatt.

. . .

Turning back time might have meant something special to Wyatt in 1974.

On a June night in 1973, at a party, blind drunk, Wyatt fell from a third-story window and fractured his spine. Earlier in the evening, pre-muddle, he'd beamed to his girlfriend Alfie Benge: "I'm so happy." Wyatt emerged from the hospital seven months later paralyzed from the pelvis down. Not a great prognosis for a drummer. It was a flash point in his life, a personal restart. Two years earlier, he'd been strong-armed out of his own group, the Soft Machine, and now he was without use of his legs and sans band. But he took the opportunity, if you can call it that, to finish working on a solo record, which he committed to memory, as he doesn't write music and had no way to make scratch recordings from his hospital bed. When he emerged, he had both a new record to make and a refreshed way to make it, as a studio project rather than via a band. The working template for this LP would provide him with the methodology he's used on all six of the solo records he's made since.

Rock Bottom is one of the most ambitious and important releases of the seventies. It is also unique. If you need a point of comparison, perhaps Eno's song-based records are best, the quieter passages of the latter ones. Like those records, Wyatt's is genreless, neither fish nor beast—a fitting metaphor for a record marinated in the aquamarine. Later in the year, he appeared playing hand percussion and singing background vocals on *Taking Tiger Mountain (By Strategy)*, adding his warm voice to the disconcerting lyrics of "Put a Straw Under Baby." Like Eno on *Tiger Mountain*, which was co-produced with guitarist Phil Manzanera and involved many walk-on appearances, Wyatt worked with Pink Floyd drummer Nick Mason as producer, building the tracks from the ground up, adding parts, inviting guests, working with a group of musicians the range of whom suggests the restless nature of Wyatt's musical thought. Adventurous jazz musicians, former prog rock bandmates, art rock friends, and spoken-word artists all thickened the proverbial soup.

It was in the space of this record that Wyatt emerged as a great songwriter. His lyrics stretch from dreamy and figurative evocations of a submerged undersea world, a "rocky bottom" of the imagination teeming with activity, to painfully honest descriptions of everyday life. On "Sea Song," his admiring portrait of Alfie Benge as *Partly fish, partly porpoise, partly baby sperm whale,* he poses the question: *Am I yours / Are you mine / To play with?* The poignancy of this would come home as he married her on the same day that *Rock Bottom* was released. But from the surreal fantasy of his idealized mermaid, he moves directly to a more day-to-day observation of Benge, especially ironic given his tragic fall: *When you're drunk you're terrific / When you're drunk I like you mostly late at night / You're quite alright / But I can't understand the different you in the morning / When it's time to play at being human for a while / Please smile.* Wyatt's voice expresses a kind of pure vulnerability when he intones, *can't understand the different you*, a high falsetto that channels Milton Nascimento and Sam Cooke. *Your lunacy fits neatly with my own,* he concludes.

It's hard not to think of the connections to Wyatt's accident on a record called *Rock Bottom*. The phrase connotes the punishing solidity of the earth and the low point of a career—both pertinent at this moment in Wyatt's life. And he'd made a habit of focusing on the specifics of a moment; he'd changed the lyrics of the Soft Machine's "Moon in June" as a surprise when the band appeared for a second time live on the BBC:

I can still remember
The last time we played on Top Gear
And though each little song
Was less than three minutes long
Mike squeezed a solo in . . . somehow
And although we like our longer tunes
It seemed polite to cut them down
To little bits—they might be hits
Who gives a . . . after all?

Tell me how would you feel
In the place of John Peel?
You just can't please
All of the musicians all the time
Playing now is lovely
Here in the BBC
We're free to play almost as long and as loud
As a jazz group, or an orchestra on Radio Three

The world of *Rock Bottom* was even more immediate and intimate, painting Wyatt's relationship with Benge as an open book, disagreements and all. On "Alifib," over the sound of his own breathing and wormy keyboards and Hugh Hopper's upper-register bass, he shares spousal baby talk, the nonsense and half-sense speak that couples unthinkingly adopt as a mark of loving exclusivity and also in the wielding of all sorts of what might now be called microaggressions. *Not nit not / Nit no not / Nit nit / Folly bololey*, he coos cutely. *I can't forsake you / Or forsqueak you*, continuing the aquatic allusions: *Burlybunch, the water mole / Hellyplop and fingerhole*. But in calling his girlfriend *my larder*, perhaps thinking it would arouse her ardor, instead she responded negatively, and her *I'm not your larder* was recorded and dropped into the song at the end of Gary Windo's explosive tenor saxophone solo. The relevance of water, arguably a placental place of rebirth, could also be seen as an alternative to the memory of falling in air, the failure of the gassy atmosphere to buoy him up. *Please don't wait / For the paperweight*, he sings, evincing Newtonian gravity on "A Last Straw." *Err on the good side / Touch us when we collapse / Into the water we'll go / Head over heel / A head behind me / Buried deep in the sand.*

The whole record is as low-key as Benge's delicate graphite drawing on the cover, as full of detail as well. On "Little Red Robin Hood Hit the Road," which features Mike Oldfield's humming harmonized guitar solos, Wyatt gives the second half of the track entirely over to Ivor Cutler. A Scottish poet and one of the true oddball geniuses of

his era, Cutler was known to Brits via his surreal comic radio broadcasts, and as the closer of *Rock Bottom*, he's in character as an angry
immigrant, maybe Pakistani or Jamaican, or maybe as Little Red's
wolf: *I hurt in the head and I hurt in the aching bone / Now I smash
up the telly with the remains of the broken phone.* He boasts about
popping car tires, in cahoots with his pal, a hedgehog, on the highway. Cutler drones harmonium and baritone concertina, abetted by
Fred Frith's viola; Frith would also join Cutler on the poet's great LP
Velvet Donkey the following year, part of a multi-record deal struck
as a result of their performance on *Rock Bottom*. A homegrown surrealist whose work was full of absurdity and insight, "Uncle Ivor"
later went on to compose "Women of the World," a song that should
be a global anthem, with the lyric: *Women of the world, take over /
Because if you don't the world will come to an end / And we haven't
got long.*

The most remarkable cut on Wyatt's incandescent record is the
other "Little Red," a companion track that closes side one. "Little
Red Riding Hood Hit the Road" is among the most daring pieces of
popular music in the seventies, even as it holds to Wyatt's humble
standards. An exultant feature for South African trumpeter Mongezi
Feza, who is overdubbed multiple times, creating a hornet storm of
brass, Wyatt joins for some wordless vocals, one of his trademarks.
The first of these, over a pedal tone, sound like pained gasps, ending as the chords change, brightening and darkening dramatically,
then adding Wyatt's singing voice.

At the halfway point through the song, as he sings, *Oh blimey
mercy me, woe is me oh dear, oh stop it, stop it*, the tracks turn
backward. Literally, the music flips. Only bassist Richard Sinclair
forges forward. It is a kind of transcendent moment, miraculous
in that it continues with the same momentum and doesn't break
but is continuous. Imagine if that continuity were possible here in
this writing, gnitirw siht ni erch elbissop erew ytiunitnoc taht fi
enigamI .suounitnoc si tub kaerb t'nseod dna mutnemom emas eht
htiw seunitnoc ti taht ni suolucarim ,tnemom tnednecsnart fo dnik

a si tI .drawrof segrof rialcniS drahciR tsissab ylnO .spilf cisum eht
,yllaretiL .drawkcab nrut skcart eht *,ti pots ,ti pots ho ,raed ho em*
si eow ,em ycrem yemilb hO" ,sgnis eh sa ,gnos eht hguorht tniop
yawflah eht tA

The degree of difficulty is outrageously high. Wyatt turns time
around and yet keeps it moving forward, not unlike Martin Amis.
He sneaks back into the song forward, adding: *Why did I hurt you /*
I didn't mean to hurt you / But I'll keep trying and I'm sure you will
too. And Cutler gives a little preview of the full story on the companion song, arguing with the hedgehog perhaps at precisely the same
point as on the other side of the record. I wouldn't put it past Wyatt
to have made that calculation, to have meddled with the muddle,
turned the beat around and upside down, placing the two stories at
the same place, thinking about the music on the flip side of the disc.

After all, if you were listening to the other side of the record at
that point, the music would automatically be backward.

On the Beach

An elegy for some words.

I went to the radio interview / But I ended up alone at the microphone.

This is a gut punch. I hear the words and they echo as if in a gaping hole, a pit of melancholy, a cavern of woe. They aren't the saddest or most poignant in Neil Young's oeuvre, or for that matter on this record, or even in this song. That honor is reserved for the lines: *I need a crowd of people / But I can't face them day to day / Though my problems are meaningless / That don't make them go away.* Or the song's opening volley: *The world is turning / I hope it don't turn away.*

But the strength of the radio line is in its obliqueness, an image it depicts of the loneliest broadcast from the standpoint of the abandoned guest. Maybe it was drawn from life, from an experience of being interviewed by someone who abdicated midway. Or maybe it was pure fantasy inspired by the legendary "honey slides" he and his comrades were consuming on the sessions, a heavy distillation of pot essence suspended in a sweet tincture. Dead air is always fearsome. It's a symptom of calamity. When the broadcasting stops, a key lifeline to normalcy is erased. And here the visitor ends up unaccompanied. The internal rhyme gently bobs—*alone . . . microphone*—Young's voice bouncing angrily off the minor guitar chord. A lone high note is fingered, then removed, all as bleak as the crust of the moon.

The way Young sings on "On the Beach"—plaintive stoned hillbilly tremolo, a crackle of resentment or disbelief—his words are nearly too strong and too sad to bear. Like much of the album, there's an implicit reference to an imminent apocalypse, a personal and political betrayal. Young swiped the title from a post-apocalyptic novel by Nevil Shute, which in turn referred to T. S. Eliot's "The Hollow Men," specifically the lines: "In this last of meeting places / We grope together / And avoid speech / Gathered on this beach of the tumid river" and "This is the way the world ends / Not with a bang but a whimper." Both of these appear as epigraphs in Shute's book.

During the seventies, singers and songwriters began to regularly sing about themselves. Many an autobiographical record was waxed. Not simply idealized versions of their love lives, but complex replays of their personal histories, their failings and fuck-ups, travels and travails, innermost secrets and outermost accolades, accountings of friends and foe, and especially reprises of their careers and colleagues. Think of Carly Simon's "You're So Vain," about her tryst with Warren Beatty, or Leonard Cohen's "Chelsea Hotel No. 2," about Janis Joplin, or Van Morrison's "And It Stoned Me," about a childhood friend and a day they went fishing together, or Loretta Lynn's "Coal Miner's Daughter," about growing up in Butcher Holler, Kentucky. John Lennon's "How Do You Sleep?" was a vicious personal attack on Paul McCartney, who retorted with equal distaste on "Let Me Roll It." Derek and the Dominos' "Layla" admitted Eric Clapton's unrequited love for George Harrison's wife. There's Laura Nyro's coming-of-age song "When I Was a Freeport and You Were the Main Drag," and Elton John's whole album *Captain Fantastic and the Brown Dirt Cowboy*, spelling out the rough-and-tumble early days for John and Bernie Taupin. And the song that Joni Mitchell wrote about Neil Young, "The Circle Game."

Some of the songs on *On the Beach* are drawn from life. On the hypnotic "Motion Pictures," Young diagrams the dissolution of his relationship with actress Carrie Snodgress, depicting her circle of Hollywood friends with us/them venom: *Well, all these people, they think they've got it made / But I wouldn't buy, sell, borrow, or trade / Anything I have to be like one of them / I'd rather start all over again.* Though he'd meant for the record's sides to be swapped, which would have put the major-key, self-determined-sounding "Walk On" in the more logical first position of the second side,* Young was convinced to start the album with it, and it's a bold if slightly bracing start, a coming to terms with the venality of others. *I hear some people been talkin' me down / Bring up my name, pass it 'round / They don't mention happy times / They do their thing, I'll do mine.* The pot-smoking reference of "pass it 'round" is a light touch in a song of bitter resignation, a ballad of turncoat friends. *Ooh baby, that's hard to change / I can't tell them how to feel / Some get stoned / Some get strange / But sooner or later it all gets real.* Elsewhere he laments his formative years up in Canada, a special nostalgia for his place on Isabella Street: *Back in the old folky days / The air was magic when we played / The riverboat was rocking in the rain / Midnight was the time for the raid / Oh Isabella, proud Isabella / They tore you down and plowed you under.*

Propelled by the rhythm section of the Band, drummer Levon Helm and bassist Rick Danko, "Revolution Blues" is an unsettling track sung from the first-person perspective of a Charles Manson–like militia leader; Young seems to direct vitriol at his own folk-rock milieu: *Well, I hear that Laurel Canyon is full of famous stars / But I hate them worse than lepers / And I'll kill them in their cars.* Young had met Manson via Beach Boys drummer Dennis Wilson, just before the Manson Family killed Sharon Tate and eight others. With Ben Keith, in a down-home duo of dobro and banjo, "For the

---

* On the other hand, sequenced as it is, *On the Beach* is a rare example of a record that progressively slows down as it moves along, ending with an almost nine-minute dream-like song, "Ambulance Blues," that sounds like it was recorded underwater.

Turnstiles" looks back grouchily at the road to riches, particularly the Darwinian nature of the folk circuit, the "shattered confidence" of young singers: *All the bush league batters / Are left to die on the diamond / In the stands the home crowd scatters / For the turnstiles.*

Young makes reference not only to his own past and present but to then-current events, including a swipe at Patty Hearst and the pettiness of her social critique in "Ambulance Blues" (*So all you critics sit alone / You're no better than me for what you've shown / With your stomach pump and your hook and ladder dreams / We could get together for some scenes*). The most overtly political cut, "Vampire Blues," sets its sights on big oil, *sucking blood from the earth,* and it includes two of the strangest guitar breaks in popular music, the latter testing the bounds of viability, a little fumbling one-note patch (Neil Young's specialty) finally breaking into something Derek Bailey might have played. On the languid, extra-stoned "Ambulance Blues," over a fingerpicking pattern borrowed from Bert Jansch, in tandem with legendary country and bluegrass fiddler Rusty Kershaw, Young includes a fanged depiction of President Nixon: *I never knew a man could tell so many lies / He had a different story for every set of eyes / How can he remember who he's talking to? / 'Cause I know it ain't me and I hope it isn't you.*

...

Four years later, Johnny Rotten would snarl a rhetorical question—of his audience, of his manager, of the era, of himself—from the stage at the end of the Sex Pistol's final performance: "Ever get the feeling you've been *cheated*?" In his own premonitory way, Neil Young pondered the same conundrum on *On the Beach*, not only in the record's withering take on the day's politics, but also in his inquest into the star status he'd achieved after *Harvest* (the single best-selling record of 1972), and even in the record's sound, which was widely criticized for its strange, rough mix, and awkward combination of styles. But Young chose precisely the right mix, the per-

fect collaborators, the honest position, the anti-nostalgic move—
walking out onto the windswept Pacific, Cadillac tail fin poking out
of the sand, evoking some sort of nuclear aftermath. *It's easy to get
buried in the past*, sang Young in his inimitable high lonesome voice,
When you try to make a good thing last.

Sheer Heart Attack

Kimono My House

God save drama glam and all her glitterati, the international heavy metal burlesque show, and please preserve her hubcap diamond-star halo.

As a squeaky pip, pageants were my thing. When I was seven, before my family decamped to Virginia Beach, I used to round up the kids in our Cleveland Heights neighborhood and lead them in a performance of Three Dog Night's "Joy to the World." The mottled array of elementary-age children would wear household linen as capes and robes, younger kids marching in the lead, clanking aluminum pots and pans, older ones trailing behind in close formation, singing harmony in parts: *Jeremiah was a bullfrog / Was a good friend of mine / Never understood a single word he said / But I helped him a-drink his wine / And he always had some mighty fine wine.* Some folks are born to be out front, singing and carrying on, and others are meant to organize behind the scenes, which is where I felt most comfortable, coordinating the activities, selecting a site, and gathering the adults as an audience, to listen to our little shambolic parade.

A decade later, in junior high, friends and I attended midnight showings of *The Rocky Horror Picture Show*. We refrained from

dressing up—I was still less comfortable putting myself in the lime-
light, even if that light was directed into an audience, but I delighted
in throwing popcorn and toilet paper, singing along, and shouting
responses on cue. It was there that my long-standing love of Queen
took on a different set of associations. From the vantage of Tim
Curry, I could see more clearly how the British band's music, and
Freddie Mercury's persona in particular, was rooted in theatricality.
Lots of seventies rock involves stagecraft, but Queen took it beyond
pyrotechnics and costumes, welcoming pageantry into the DNA of
their songs, infusing extravagance into every unfurling frond of
Mercury's fern-like voice.

There was a time in Western music that most pop songs origi-
nated in theater, much of it deriving directly from show tunes, like
those adapted from Tin Pan Alley. The basics of Broadway applied
complications of romance, clever lyrical devices, basic narrative
form (exposition, conflict, resolution), and music with an attendant
implication of formal development (also: exposition, conflict, resolution). Each song should be a compact drama, a tempest in a tea-
cup. And whatever function those compositions had in the logic of a
play, they could be extracted and stand on their own, bearing enough
meaning independent of the plot from which they emerged to speak
on their own to an audience, by means of sheet music, phonograph
record, or radio broadcast.

And on the other hand, there was the blues. Rooted in a songwriting tradition distinct from Tin Pan Alley's, with variation on
stock phrases that didn't necessarily build into or feed off of a continuous storyline, but drew instead from a massive repository of text
fragments ("I woke up this morning . . . ," "Sun's gonna shine . . . ,"
"How long, how long . . ."), endlessly contrasted and modified and
retooled as the singer went along, creating a gestalt built of familiar
but personalized lines, juxtaposed, almost always appearing in the
same lyrical form, AAB, and with a matching harmonic structure,
I-IV-V-I, that repeats until the song is over. Tonic, subdominant,
dominant, tonic—*écouter et répéter*.

You can simplify the difference between Tin Pan Alley and the blues under the banner of one idea: the bridge. The blues, at least as every suburban kid with a guitar learns it, never has a bridge. Or a chorus. No key change, no mounting harmonic tension with a contrasting section, each phase of tension-release executed within the bounds of a single verse. They call it strophic form, from the Greek *strophé*, or "twist, turn about," which relates to the idea of a turnaround, the place where the harmonic structure repeats. Complexity in the blues comes primarily in the delivery, the details of how it's sung, the nuance in how it's played, rather than the structure, which is simple, even if it can be effectively messed with and distorted by means of craziness like thirteen and a half bar lines, weird chord substitutions, and other gizmos. But rarely through contrasting sections or more composite structures.

It's instructive to reduce the rock, soul, and funk worlds, circa 1974, to those who follow the blues path and those who don't. There's no question that it's more complicated than that, but at least you can see how different these two songwriting concepts are, in their embryonic form. Think of James Brown's "Night Train," a bridge-less blues, and then consider a song like "Cold Sweat," in which he made the bridge a dramatic part of the song, posing the eternal question: *Can I take it to the bridge?* The bridge was so central to Brown's image that in 1993 an actual bridge was dedicated to him in Steamboat Springs, Colorado, and it was titled the James Brown Soul Center of the Universe Bridge. I'd like to take it to *that* bridge.

To return to Queen, in their music not only are all the ornamental flourishes dramatic—every hilariously over-the-top mannerism, every stage whisper, every fainting spell, every star-is-born outburst—but the song structures themselves are given over to narrative drama, making a stage for a full cast and crew of thespians. Take "Brighton Rock," where Mercury plays two parts—anticipating the operatic lineup of "Bohemian Rhapsody"—including Jenny (falsetto) and her married lover Jimmy (tenor), and an over-dubbed choir on the chorus. Even Brian May's guitar solo contains a conversation, picked dialogue panned (like Mercury's voices) back and forth from side to side. My friends and I always tittered when Mercury sang of being . . . *so decorously laid 'neath the gay illuminations all along the promenade.* We thought they didn't know what they were saying. But then again it didn't dawn on us that their name was Queen and that they might know what that was all about, too.

In the context of Broadway musicals, there's always the issue of getting from the dialogue into the songs, a task often accomplished through a transitional verse at the outset of the song, setting the narrative premise and softening the shift from speaking to singing. "Tenement Funster," written and sung by drummer Roger Taylor, starts with just such a verse, introducing the character, a hedonistic musician: *My new purple shoes / Been amazing ze people next door / And my rock 'n' roll forty-fives / Been enraging the folks on the lower floor.* Indeed, a number of songs on *Sheer Heart Attack* are portraits, a kind of rogues' gallery—a high-class hooker ("Killer Queen"), an evil agent ("Flick of the Wrist"), a dominatrix ("She Makes Me [Stormtrooper in Stilettoes]"), a madman-gangster ("Stone Cold Crazy"), a gangster-politician ("Bring Back That Leroy Brown"), a gold-digger ("In the Lap of the Gods . . . Revisited"). Nearly all the songs are steeped in theatrical drama, heavy on contrasting sections, suites and medleys and reprises, background vocals that comment on the action like a Greek chorus, sound effects that set a mise-en-scène. Later the band would bring the elements together into a single multi-sectioned song, but on *Sheer Heart Attack* the contrasting elements are mostly played off each other as separable parts. "Bring Back That Leroy Brown" is composed in an Andrew Sisters vein, a sort of kitschy slice of vaudeville or British music hall, bringing to mind the off-kilter comic rock of the Bonzo Dog Doo-Dah Band. Hard rock groups hitting that kind of contrast key were not totally unheard of—consider Aerosmith's cover of Bullmoose Jackson's "Big Ten Inch Record" or the barbershop insert on Van Halen's "I'm the One." In Queen's case, the song refers to Jim Croce's hit song "Bad Bad Leroy Brown," a staple of wide-eyed gawking white America fantasizing over the perilous black side of town.

Here already on their third record, Queen looks into the future, when their songs "We Are the Champions" and "We Will Rock You" would become staples of seemingly every American sporting event. For *Sheer Heart Attack*, Mercury composed a closing track titled "In the Lap of the Gods . . . Revisited," with exactly the same intention: to galvanize the audience into clapping and singing along. It's a quintessential theatrical ploy, audience participation, and I must say it has always been distasteful to me. When I go to see a concert, the folks around me are the last people I want to hear singing, most of the time. But that kind of immersive engagement was as much a feature of the era as yelling "Free Bird" when asking for an encore, a fact evidenced by the development of the karaoke machine, new technology released in Japan at the dawn of the seventies. Queen calculated the impact of the sing-along on the audience, and they were merciless with their earworms, which would end up lodged in our heads evermore.

Let's spend a moment on Brian May. A typical rock guitar solo comes on like a big rectangle mowed into an overgrown field. The guitarist hops onto the field and runs around playing the solo, then jumps back into the brush when finished. You could say that approach simplifies one forged in hard bop jazz during the fifties, where soloists extrapolated at length, one at a time, over cycling chord changes. Queen's guitarist treats soloing more like a sculpted garden, with discrete little clearings for trysts and a labyrinth carved into the hedge. This, I'd say, comes from another point in jazz history, from the time when big bands were king and swing was the rage, when arrangements were complex and solos were secreted into ongoing events rather than treated as epic yarns. May is a master of the fill; he's capable of doing more in less time than nearly anyone, the antithesis of someone like Jerry Garcia or Gregg Allman or any of the twiddle-on guitarists of gratuitousness. In a series of cameos, May can sound like a snarling cat, an air-raid siren, a bowed cello, or Chuck Berry, but most often he plays around with the unique sound he invented, the product of laboratory research so intense it reminds us that when he's not a guitar hero, he's an astrophysicist.

We didn't know the slightest thing about what it really meant, but my friends and I talked a lot at the time about selling out. We speculated on whether this or that artist had sold out, wondering if they were tempted to sell out, if they had become a certifiable sell-out. The Faustian pact was a hearty part of the pop and rock star mythos. Songs like the Dramatics' 1971 hit "Whatcha See Is What-cha Get" appealed to our sense of staying true, not sold out, real. *Some people are made of plastic*, they sang, alternating high and low voices, invoking the ultimate sellout materials. *You know some people are made of wood / Some people have hearts of stone / Some people are up to no good / But, baby, I'm for real / I'm as real as real can get / If what you're looking for is real loving / Then what you see is what you get.*

On "Flick of the Wrist," Queen caricatures the sellout, render-ing it a long con by an evildoing businessman-devil. *Seduce you with his money-make machine / Cross-collateralize (big-time money, money) / Reduce you to a Muzak-fake machine / Then the last good-bye / It's a rip-off.* We wondered about whom they were talking. Was it their British label, EMI, or their American label, Elektra? Their producer or manager? Some other unidentified behind-the-scenes manipulator? Was it even Queen or was Mercury singing about an-other band, perhaps a hypothetical one, about to be ripped off by the industry? Our hyperactive imaginations oversimplified the sellout, but even framed with the thought bubbles and speech balloons of a comic strip, Queen got us thinking about who makes the decisions and what hangs in the balance.

...

In my circles, the word "fey" was always pejorative. But to describe Freddie Mercury and Russell Mael, there is no better term. The way they sing makes me want to wrap myself in a feather boa, to prance and flounce, exaggerating every move, pouting and sucking in a deep breath held at the lips by a pointer finger. *Talent is an asset*, asserts one song by Mael's band Sparks, speaking of hered-ity as if it were accomplished onstage. I know for some even sex is a performance . . . with an audience of one. Mael savors a genetic double entendre: *We are his relatives / That's parenthetical.* Blood may be thicker than water, but the casting couch is a constant condition for Sparks, and, alas, let's be honest, most often the candidate doesn't get the part. *When you turn pro / You'll know / She'll let you know*, go the lyrics on "Amateur Hour." *It's a lot like playing the violin / You cannot start off and be Yehudi Menuhin.* On "In My Family," Mael sings: *Manufacturing many, many me's / Gonna hang myself from my family tree.*

It makes sense for them to be concerned with heredity. Sparks is a brother act. Ron and Russell Mael: an odd couple if ever sibs there were. The singer is a right fancy chicken, with a bush of black plumage, delicate feminine outfits, black hot pants, red gloves with matching scarves, and a falsetto like a ray of light through parted clouds. His brother yins his yang—an accountant with a dark secret, in high-waisted trousers and requisite tie, Ron maintains a tuft of hair beneath his nose, evincing Chaplin or Hitler, Chaplin as Hitler. When they play, he sits nearly motionless at the electric keyboard, his face a sequence of psycho expressions. They're Southern Californians who relocated in 1973 to London to be closer to the eye of the glam storm. Once there, Sparks made a riotously ambitious triptych starting with *Kimono My House*, followed by *Propaganda* and *Indiscreet*, that blended quirky and hilarious lyrics, deft and subtle song structure, and the flash and pose of metal.

Like Queen, who in fact opened for them once in 1972 (and who might have lost May to the Maels that year, when they invited him to join them), Sparks' sound is irrevocably theatrical, a kind of blown-out, amped-up, camped-up cabaret, with a parade of hilarious conceits. One song imagines Romeo pining above after Juliet had betrayed him and lived a long life ("Here in Heaven"). Another song muses over a confusing affair with a non-English-speaking gal: *You mentioned Kant and I was shocked / You know, where I come from none of the girls / Have such foul tongues* ("Hasta Mañana Monsieur"). They remind me of the ragtag freak show in John Cassavetes's *The Killing of a Chinese Bookie*, but on steroids and armed with Gibson Les Pauls and Rickenbacker basses.

Sparks' words are laid into long, complex melodies, sometimes threaded together contrapuntally, as on "Equator," where Russell's voice is overdubbed almost as many times as a normal Freddie Mercury track. With Russell's Gatling gun phrasing—dozens of words crammed into each packed stanza—the lyric sheet was essential. Indeed, lyric sheets were a hotly desired part of my record-buying repertoire; I nervously opened new arrivals, hoping they'd deliver the goods. In the case of Sparks, because they were so baroque and also so literate, and because they were funny enough that we wanted to know every snide and misanthropic phrase, reading the lyric sheet enabled us to put words to the song, in a kind of backassward way, applying what we'd read to what we heard. The brothers' identities seem once again to enter "Falling in Love with Myself Again," a ridiculous waltz that considers the upside of self-adoration: *Similar mother, similar father / Similar dog, cat, and fish / And we'll make the same wish / When the birthday candle's lit.* For everyone who ever dreaded the winter holidays, "Thank God It's Not Christmas" should be a national anthem, with its overdramatic huff. Russell is especially coy here. He sulks, he draws out his *s*'s and convolutes *aaah-bviously* into ostentatious glamour-puss pomp.

The record's hit single is still my favorite. "This Town Ain't Big Enough for Both of Us" casts romance as a gunfight at the OK Corral, a showdown between the singer and his intended. Over power chords and proto-new-wave keyboard, the glam comedians complete the song's title with an answering line that still makes me think of their strange dog and pony show, their yin and yang, their uncanny theater of brotherly shove. *This town ain't big enough for the both of us*, declares Russell, belting it out like he's winding up the big number in a Broadway musical. *And it ain't me who's gonna leave.*

1975

Mothership Connection

Were I doomed to live in isolation with just one record, and I don't mean lolling around on a desert island so much as being jettisoned into outer space, an actual rocket man living out his life up there alone, I think that solitary record would be by Parliament. For four decades straight, I have been listening to *Mothership Connection*, and through all those repetitions it has never grown dim. Even today I continue to hear new sounds in its intricate arrangements, pluck associations out of its web of metaphors and allusions, and find previously dormant pockets of kineticism in its antechambers.

Mothership is the everlasting gobstopper of seventies music.

Here we go 'round the corner into the fourth quarter of the twentieth century. Keep funk alive in '75, our motto told us. Shit lord almighty, funk as we knew it was nowhere near dead, it was just learning to walk, a toddler getting into things with assistance from papa George Clinton. Guitarist James "Blood" Ulmer rightly proclaimed: *Jazz is the teacher, funk is the preacher.* Hallelujah, amen.

...

Once upon a time called now, hollers Clinton on "P-Funk (Wants to Get Funked Up)," assuming his guise as Lollipop Man, alias the

Long-Haired Sucker. For emphasis, a short while later, he adds: *Once upon a time called RIGHT NOW!*

To which "now" does he refer? When is "right now" in the parlance of Parliament? What constitutes the present tense for a Parliamentarian?

It might be the now of the recording, which would place it between March and October 1975. It could be the now of the initial listening, which for many people would be early in 1976, when the band cemented the record's legacy with a gaga lunatic tour. Now could be more general, placing the middle of the seventies into the framework of a fairy tale through its "once upon a time," linguistically converting the landing of their urban spaceship into a contemporary ghetto folktale, as if it was both specifically of its time and outside of history. But with that emphatic "right" affixed to "now," Lollipop Man seems to say that if *Mothership Connection* is going to be a fairy tale, it's got to be a brand-spanking-new one, freshly conceived, a fairy tale for today.

In other words, the myth starts here.

Tap the space brakes. One more possibility: the floating now. By which I mean the now that meanders from now . . . to . . . wait a sec . . . feel it . . . *now*. The immediate present, the ever-shifting end product of imminence that is the subject of all music, traversal of which is the concept opened up by electromagnetic technology. The recording angels of tape and album, alluded to by name in Lolli's selfsame monologue, allow one now to be invoked directly in another, one present tense to take place at a different time altogether. Those funky Afrocentric spacemen from 1975, they're hustling along through time by means of their record album shuttle, stopping off every now and then—no, every now and now—to get played, get laid, get it on, move along.

. . .

P-Funk first landed on my planet in the year we changed the motto to take funk to heaven in '77. *Mothership* was foisted upon me by my record-store mentor Mike, who told me it was necessary to my education. Bringing it home that afternoon coincided with my pal Scooter arriving for his only visit from Philadelphia to my new home in Iowa City. It sat unattended for the first few days he was there, but near the end I suggested we check it out. We'd been mildly stoned most of his stay, got more so in anticipation of the listening session, and when I put the record on, we hit the traditional position, both reclining on my bed, arranged feet to head.

I recall the sensation of that first listen. It was very much like visiting an alien environment, one that I would liken to the first scene in the factory in *Willy Wonka and the Chocolate Factory*, a paradise of pure imagination, with its own space cakes and candy man—hey now, Sir Lollipop Man calls himself *Chocolate colored, freaky, and habit forming!*—in voices that are sometimes sped up to make them sound like Oompa Loompas. Clinton compares the P-Funk spacemobile to William DeVaughn's caddy on "P-Funk (Wants to Get Funked Up)," a reference we caught immediately. *Gangster lean*, Clinton boasts. *Y'all should see my sunroof top*. He threw down a gauntlet at the Doobie Brothers and David Bowie, an explicit challenge that was strange and amazing to us. Musicians didn't usually invoke each other by name, let alone damn one another by faint praise.

On the title track, Clinton informed us, *We are doin' it to you in 3D*, which seemed perfectly descriptive of the unfamiliar multidimensionality of the music. We felt something we couldn't quite make out pulling us into it, an undertow, a riptide of rhythm. And for me it was the layers that knocked me out. Like when the singers change over to a joyful gospel delivery, *Swing down sweet chariot, stop and let me ride*, inviting us to hop on and shuttle onward into the future, the funk girding still there, vamping tirelessly, the horny horns brassful and not bashful, building up their own layer of activity, zigzagging syncopatedly against the main beat. A wicked wiry guitar part joins on "Unfunky UFO," classic funk back-filled by the butt-bump of Bootsy Collins's heat-seeking bass, nevertheless there's superimposition there too, and when we reached the end of side one, we were overstimulated.

"I have never heard anything like that," said Scooter.

"It's symphonic, all those things happening at the same time, like the different sections of an orchestra," I replied, moving to turn the record over. Having my friend there was key to the experience. We'd basically taught each other to listen, mostly by way of rock, but also with soul and funk, which had dominated the radio back in Filth-adelphia.

"Either I'm too baked or it's beyond me. But I'm having trouble keeping it together over here."

"Onward?" I raised the tonearm.

"Oh yeah. Heck yeah. Funk yeah!"

On the second side, a new hero began to emerge: Bernie Worrell, aka the Wizard of Woo. With "Supergroovalisticprosifunkstication," chimes and bells and scrapers and wood blocks complicated the chant *Give the people what they want when they want and they wants it all the time*, meanwhile Worrell's wah sounds and synthesizer squiggles teased our aural canals. I couldn't follow his contribution on the first audition of the first side, but by the time of "Give Up the Funk (Tear the Roof Off the Sucker)," I'd identified the keyboards as the craziest and most exciting element in the stratigraphic sandwich. On the nearly lyric-less season finale, "Night of the Thumpasorus People," Woo counters Georgie's cave baby talk— *Gaga goo ga, gaga goo ga, gaga goo ga ga*—with keyboard noises that can only be called flatulent. Scoots and I snickered as the record tickled us to our scatological core. Once laughing, we were undone.

...

Hop on board the mamacraft and head out from my adolescent bedroom into the future of my past for a few quick stops that directly involve the *Connection*.

As an act of self-provocation, I chose the song "Handcuffs," the record's most conventional moment of R&B, as the first selection on the after-wedding dance tape for my short-lived first marriage. A track celebrating possessiveness, it declares: *If I have to keep you barefoot and pregnant | Oh, to keep you here in my world | (Lay down, girl) lay down and take off-a your shoes / Girl, I'm a-gonna do to you / What it is I've gotta do.* We always loved the irony of a song that wanted to tie you down for your own good, likening marriage to being incarcerated. I think I knew more than I understood.

A few years later, in the early nineties, George Clinton gave me one of the best interviews I've ever conducted, up in Detroit, where between minuscule, medicinal snorts of coke, he told me how his producer Neil Bogart had wanted to title the record *Landing in the Ghetto.* "I said, 'No, no, ghetto is a cool place by now. You're late with that shit! People ready to build up the ghettos and *keep* 'em!'" Understanding the new positive valence of urban life reflected in the box office performance of blaxploitation flicks, he'd opted to turn it on its head, sending Super Fly into outer space rather than restaging an African American *The Day the Earth Stood Still.* They did however use the actual spaceship prop from that 1951 sci-fi classic on the cover of *Mothership Connection.* And soon Clinton would name the first record by Parlet, a Parliament girl-group spin-off, *Invasion of the Booty Snatchers.* The concept was ghetto positivity, not salvation from the ghetto.

My conversation with Clinton formed the basis of a cover story in *Option* magazine, reprinted in my first book, *Extended Play: Sounding Off from John Cage to Dr. Funkenstein,* and it helped me write an essay I'd been contemplating for several years comparing three central musical figures associated with what would soon be called Afrofuturism. "Brothers from Another Planet: The Space Madness of Lee 'Scratch' Perry, Sun Ra, and George Clinton" was the first chapter in the compilation, which also included interviews with all three of them. *Extended Play* was published in 1994, the same year Mark Dery's essay "Black to the Future," which introduced the term Afrofuturism into academic discourse, came to widespread attention via his collection *Flame Wars.* Coincidentally, both books were published by Duke University Press. I didn't know it, but I was setting out in a sketchy form the basic plot of one line of my research for the next couple of decades.

Not long after *Extended Play* came out, I received a call from

Edward George at the Black Audio Film Collective in London. He asked if I would be willing to participate in a film they were shooting, which seemed fun, so in 1995 I took a day-long break from the Vancouver Jazz Festival, a week-long event I was covering for *DownBeat* magazine, and flew to Los Angeles, where I knew little more than that I was to be picked up. A disheveled limo driver held a sign aloft with my name. We walked to his black stretch.

"Strap in. We'll be about three hours en route," he said.

"Where the hell are we going?" I asked, shielding my eyes from the searing sunshine and slipping into the cool black leather of his ride.

"Joshua Tree State Park."

Along the way, he entertained me with stories of his most recent escapades driving for Courtney Love, recounting her shopaholic tendencies and public intoxicatedness, which seemed as foreign to me as the social customs of a little green man with antennae. I watched the landscape change as we headed into the desert, stripping away buildings until the topography was lunar and beautiful.

When we arrived, the Black Audio Film Collective team greeted me. I gave them a copy of the Lee Perry video I'd shot in Switzerland in 1990, to excerpt for use in the film. We found a scenic spot to shoot my interview. By that time, the sun was getting low on the horizon, and after some futzing with lights and finding the proper cactus backdrop, we had about fifteen minutes for Q & A. I thought we were just warming up, but with the heavy desert darkness rolling in, they called it a wrap. I thought, "What a crazy thing to haul me all the way out here for such a brief encounter." But we chatted on the way back into town, this time in the crew's van, and Edward George told me that my essay had been the original inspiration for the film, so they'd felt it was important to have me represented. I was of course flattered.

In 1996 director John Akomfrah's *The Last Angel of History* was released. I recognized the Joshua Tree environment in the stylish, somewhat overwrought film, with its quick-talking, time-traveling narrator. My appearance was, as I'd anticipated, mercurial, but I was honored to be the lone honky amidst such luminary Afrofuturists as *Star Trek*'s Lieutenant Uhuru, Samuel Delaney, Ishmael Reed, Kodwo Eshun, Juan Atkins, and Greg Tate. And, center stage, fresh off the ship, reminding us we all come from outer space, in fact where do you think we are?, it's my main man, Sir Lollipop, alias the Long-Haired Sucker.

...

It's that everlastingness, man. That funk ever after. The *Mothership* tablet is still in my mouth after light-years of travel. I've been sucking on it, biting and chewing a little, but it never does get any smaller.

"The Hustle"

Two groups of children in a gymnasium.
One lined up against the near wall, the other opposite.

The kids face each other.
It's boys here, girls across.

We have been instructed to dress up on this day.
Our teachers are going to show us how to dance.

We are in fifth grade.
Our teachers are in their twenties or early thirties.

In the classroom we do not segregate by gender.
We play and learn together, girls and boys, one group.

Here we are looking across the varnished pine floorboards.
It seems an unbridgeable expanse.

Disco will bring us together.
Step by step.

Our teachers square off.
Teacher Peggy and Teacher Rick.

Someone drops the needle on the single.
Teacher Rick nods his head, smiles at Teacher Peggy, she nodding,
    also smiling.

Nebulous angelic voices coo: *Ooooh, ooh ooh ooh ooh.*
Then less softly, a command: *Do it!*

One footfall at a time, they advance on one another, closing the gap.
Away again, same footsteps, marching in halftime to the piccolo.

One, two, three, step; two, two, three, back.
Turn, two, three, step; four, two, three, step.

Somewhere in the trumpet solo, they clap.
And spin and wheel their hands around, like gathering wool.

And exclaim, in time with Van McCoy: *Do the hustle!*
Then turn to us expectantly.

We are to pair off.
Across the room, I count from left to find my partner.

She looks down.
I look down.

As the strings swell, I step, two, three, four.
In line with the others, she meets me, her dress a flare.

Two formally clad lineups of twelve-year-olds on a collision course.
Averted by the numbers . . . two, three, back.

One boy turns the wrong direction.
Another takes a fifth step forward, mashing her foot.

Soon enough, confidence enters the auditorium.
The little bodies move with pep.

Some of them find the sassiness in the music, its camp.
Their hips flex, their shoulders tilt, the tinkling xylophone
    a subliminal lift.

They point into the air, a punctuation mark.
They chant in time with Teacher Van.

It is all innocent movement.
This dance is pure jubilance, no guilt, no shame, no judgment,
    no failure, no regret.

Almost only
calisthenics.

Four years on, Steve Dahl's Disco Demolition Night brought
    Brownshirts to Comiskey Park.
Hard rockers and headbangers stage a dance-music execution.

Apotheosis of Disco Sucks ideology, a smoking pile of charred
    vinyl.
Drawing lines of straightness and whiteness against an
    insidious subculture.

Musical mob justice.
Torch-bearing townsfolk.

Code gay.
Code black.

Another single:
"Rock Your Baby," by George McCrae.

Another:
"Kung Fu Fighting," by Carl Douglas.

And:
"Get Down Tonight," by KC and the Sunshine Band.

After the kids have been successful awhile, as a reward, the lights
    go out.
A mirrored ball speckles these little people in tiny pricks of light.

At the side, Teacher Peggy and Teacher Rick sit one out.
They watch the whole class move in tandem, the twilight
    of childhood an unidentified presence in the middle-school
    makeshift dance hall.

"Philadelphia Freedom"

There's speculation on the terrace about tonight's entertainment. It's a misty evening in Chicago, in October 2016. Four hundred people have assembled across the river from the Civic Opera House, waiting to be bused to an undisclosed site for a lavish biannual party pitched by Helen Zell for her husband, Sam, in celebration of his birthday. With my wife, Terri, and my art gallery partner, Jim, I'm huddled in conference, trying to decode a smattering of clues as to the identity of tonight's secret performer. Two years prior, we had correctly guessed Fleetwood Mac. Tonight we're stumped. My first intuition tells me it's Elton John, but I'm quickly dispelled of the notion, all the officially dropped hints not quite adding up, and soon we're hearing rumors: Tony Bennett and Lady Gaga or Bette Midler. An architect in the bus seat in front of me wheels around and informs me: "It's definitely Paul McCartney." He points to a motif on one of the T-shirts, a cartoon of someone looking through a periscope. "See, kaleidoscope eyes!"

When we hit the party room, ceiling forty feet high, decorated by artists and artisans from around the city, we decide not to sweat the mystery and instead head for a seafood station, where oysters are being shucked and a sushi chef is carving directly from a huge tuna. Straining not to overindulge, our attention is drawn to action on the other side of the voluminous space, and we pull anchor and head over to check it out. A choreographed routine is just finishing up, live big band and dancers mashing traditional swing with break moves, a mass of attendees shuffling toward the activity, hands overflowing with drinks, plates of savory munchies, and cell phone cameras, in piecemeal arranging themselves into a semicircular audience where one seems like it should be.

A hush falls, lights dim, and a spotlight hits a bedazzled man in a black jacket and round-rimmed, mirrored glasses. We are about twenty feet away as Elton smacks the piano and kicks the celebration off with a new, unfamiliar song. It turns out to be the only one. Everything else he plays in the eighty-minute set is one of his hits. "Saturday Night's Alright for Fighting," "Candle in the Wind," "Daniel," "Crocodile Rock," "Honky Cat," "Bennie and the Jets," "Rocket Man," "Tiny Dancer," "Goodbye Yellow Brick Road," one after another, barely a stop for a sip of water, to bow for the crowd, and to make a periodic campy little pirouette to show off his rhinestone-studded coat, then back to the keyboard. Not many musicians can do that, play nothing but favorites for more than an hour, but Elton could have kept going with lots to spare.

...

I turned eleven in 1974. That year MCA Records issued *Elton John's Greatest Hits*, the first LP I bought with my own cash. Elton was already a star in my sky, my first great musical passion, a celebrity with whom I exchanged my initial pangs of personal identification and for whose music I felt vehement gratitude. I'm not absolutely sure what it was about Elton I was so smitten with—he was a slightly roly-poly, balding guy, in full feather wearing silly glasses, brash outfits, and a goofy grin, part Christopher Robin, part Liberace. I liked that he and lyricist Bernie Taupin were a team, Elton out front, Bernie behind the scenes. And together they made music I loved, some of it nostalgic and dopey, but all of it with undeniable originality. Elton was a character, maybe in a way I enjoyed watching and listening to but didn't feel comfortable embodying. I'd heard that he was going to star in the movie version of *Pinball Wizard*, that he was slated to wear five-foot-tall Doc Martens. That sounded way cool, as did the cavalcade of chart-busting songs on my shiny new record.

The seventies saw the coming of age of the greatest hits package, compilations that were popular with audiences and music industry execs alike. Culling existing tracks from previous releases, they allowed labels to mine their back catalog, selling the same music under different guise to people who might want all the top selections in one convenient place. No additional money was spent on studios or licensing or mastering—just a new sequence of cuts extracted from older records, maybe a few singles that hadn't appeared on an LP, a little set of liner notes casting the career survey in a developmental narrative, a bit of fresh artwork, et voilà: money in the bank. Some bands didn't like to be recontextualized like that. The Rolling Stones unsuccessfully tried to keep *Hot Rocks 1964–1971* and its follow-up volume from hitting the shelves. On the other hand, David Bowie helped shape what was considered canonic in his oeuvre by personally selecting non-hits to leaven the well-known tracks on his huge best-of compilation, *Changesonebowie*. Inclusion on that successful LP made "Ziggy Stardust," "Suffragette City," and "John, I'm Only Dancing" into hits. (I was partial to the last for obvious reasons.) So the greatest hits record wasn't just a review of hit making gone by; it allowed revisiting and revisionism, reviving dormant parts of an artist's production.

A year after Elton's greatest hits album changed my world, introducing me to the thrill of long-playing vinyl, he released a single titled "Philadelphia Freedom." I was living in Flourtown, Pennsylvania, a suburb of Philadelphia. From our vantage, he'd written it specifically for us, inhabitants of the greater region of the birthplace of our democracy, where we were gearing up to fete this country's bicentennial. Honestly, I couldn't imagine that the song meant anything else. And it was on the radio constantly. The disc jockeys seemed to confirm our suspicion. When I listen to it now, I am transposed into the backseat of our Saab, heading down the Schuylkill Expressway into Philly to drop my father off at work, probably on a Saturday, Dad himself manning the jams, raising the volume on the upbeat song. Freedom was all we heard about in the home of the Liberty Bell those days. In another year, we'd be hip deep in *Rocky*, Stallone punching meat and running up the steps of the art museum to an orchestral soundtrack that reminded us a bit of Elton's single. Alex Haley's *Roots* and the ensuing miniseries would soon give us a different take on the rhetoric of American independence, but for the moment we were totally immersed in the Spirit of '76.

The song starts with arranger Gene Page's orchestral fanfare: strings bowing a one-note motif, brass, and fife-and-drummish flute trills, before Elton begins a series of bluesy verses, violins caressing a blues line behind him, the lyrics sidelong and oblique, positive and upbeat. Halfway through the song, a second lead voice echoes Elton in a thrilling falsetto. An electric guitar occasionally pokes its head through the arrangement. *Philadelphia freedom*, the chorus presses, *Shine on me / I love you / Shine the light / Through the eyes of the ones left behind.* I interpreted this as a reference to Elton and Bernie being British, looking at the American bicentennial from their vantage. *From the day that I was born, I've waved the flag,* Elton sang in a patriotic flash, later adding a line that tickled my funny bone, even though it seemed like a metaphorical mess: *I like living easy without family ties / Till the whippoorwill of freedom zapped me right between the eyes.* We had occasional whippoorwill sightings in the park out behind our house, but the creatures were incredibly secretive and brilliantly camouflaged and they'd never struck me as particularly free or like the kind of animal to fly into you by accident. We tried to get bats to do that by throwing pebbles at them at dusk when they flew around the streetlights, but the night birds could see well enough to avoid us completely.

One line really confused us. *Philadelphia freedom took me knee high to a man / Gave me a piece of mama daddy never had*. All the flag waving and optimistic music made sense as a theme song for the country's two hundredth birthday, but this seemed weirdly personal rather than political. And also sexual. And also *hetero*sexual. We understood that Elton was gay, or perhaps bi-, but that *piece of mama* almost seemed like a cock-rock boast about one's own mother. "He's knee high to a man," we thought, "so maybe he's giving someone a blowjob." We could understand that about as easily as a lyric that we thought went: *Don't let your son go down on me*.

This begs a few more mishearings in Elton John songs. It's a whole category in itself, and there are websites devoted to collecting these hilarious homonyms. The best one I genuinely believed in came from "Bennie and the Jets": *She's got electric boobs, a mohair suit, you know I read it in a magazine* . . . Other folks mistook the central line in "Tiny Dancer" as: *Hold me closer, Tony Danza*. But when it was later revealed that the line Taupin had written in "Philadelphia Freedom" was *Gave me peace of mind my daddy never had*, I realized two things: (1) the song wasn't about sex, and (2) I didn't really know what it was about.

Many years later, I discovered that the song was composed in homage to tennis player and outspoken feminist Billie Jean King. Elton and Billie Jean were new friends. Around the time of her celebrated victory over the boorish Bobby Riggs in a match commonly referred to as the "Battle of the Sexes," she asked the singer to record a song for her team, the Philadelphia Freedoms. Theirs remains a special alliance, one that bucked the supposed conventional disconnect between gay men and second-wave feminists. Without addressing tennis explicitly, Bernie and Elton put together the song, conceiving it as a double dedication to the Philly soul sound, which they had long loved. That there was a third layer of significance was, if you believe them, not in their minds. But it certainly helped sell the record, and it lodged it forever in my head as the same moment I first felt a sense of shared Americanness, a pivotal point of collective reconsideration for the young nation, and a triumphant year in the City of Brotherly Love.

One other memory sits incongruously next to these in my head. Same year, my class went downtown into Philadelphia for a field trip. In Chinatown we were introduced to the joys of dim sum; I distinguished myself by applying my god-given prowess with pierogis to another culture's version of the dumpling, eating twice as many as anyone else. As a class, we hiked to our next destination, a museum, if I recall correctly. The boys were out in front, walking fast and jammering like little birds; we all fell silent the moment we arrived at a marquee for a burlesque theater at which was then performing another of the city's treasures: Chesty Morgan. By the time the teachers caught up and caught on, we were glued to the show's surprisingly explicit posters, the stripper's breasts teasing the bounds of morphological variability, testing the limits of our imaginations, and causing me to reflect on the porous threshold between sexy and scary. All I recall from the balance of the day is the crack in the Liberty Bell.

...

My fascination with Elton John only deepened. The album he'd been working on when he took a break to record the single for Billie Jean King, *Captain Fantastic and the Brown Dirt Cowboy*, gave me new material to ponder, new lyrics to decipher and interpret. Inspired by the survey nature of *Greatest Hits*, he and Taupin seemed to be in a retrospective mood, and on the record they narrated their hand-to-mouth early years accompanied by vibraslaps and Gene Page orchestration. I'd bought the ticket and was eager to take the ride; even still, it's a record that has a particular place in my heart. Its big hit, "Someone Saved My Life Tonight," the story of Elton's narrowly averted first engagement to be married, provided me and my friends with all sorts of questions to turn over in our minds. Fifteen years later, I would wish I'd had a wise friend to slap some sense into me that way.

I still ponder my affection for Elton John. I wonder if I hadn't been parentally predisposed to have an interest in things English. For the first few years of my life, my mother dressed me as a posh

British kid. Caps with straps, pinstriped shorts with bright red knee socks and saddle shoes, checked shirts and little tweed blazers, tartan wool overcoats. My first bike was a red three-speed Raleigh, my second a black ten-speed Raleigh. No fluorescent orange Schwinn with banana seat and tail flag for me; mine were classy British ones. I had a leather fringe jacket and a Davy Crockett coonskin hat to remind myself I was American, but my middle name is Christopher, and I think the choice was inspired by the A. A. Milne character of whom Elton indirectly reminded me. One day around the time *Pinball Wizard* was released, my mom and I were at a shoe shop, where I found a pair of purple velvet boots, not exactly platform, but with maybe two-inch heels. After a session of unusual pleading and cajoling, she bought them for me. I thought they were the choicest, most to-the-max kicks I'd ever seen. I wore them one time to school, earned the clever nickname Frankenboots, and then buried them deep in the closet.

A few years later, in a different town, I became addicted to pinball on a Captain Fantastic machine in a little diner near my junior high school. In the illustration on the backsplash, Elton is playing pinball, which made the machine delightfully meta—it meant playing a pinball-machine-themed pinball machine. I heard him play once in the eighties, but from such a distance that he seemed like a flea doing tricks on a dollhouse piano; even so, his glasses were so massive that we could see them clear as day, probably visible from outer space.

Kiss

Alive!

Electric Light Orchestra

Face the Music

The seventies were the double-live decade. Concert recordings spawned a flurry of two-, even three-record sets.

Consider the evidence:

Miles Davis, *Live at Fillmore* (1970); The Grateful Dead, *Grateful Dead* (1971); The Allman Brothers Band, *At Fillmore East* (1971); James Brown, *Sex Machine* (1971); The Band, *Rock of Ages* (1972); James Brown, *Revolution of the Mind* (1971); The Art Ensemble of Chicago, *Live at Mandel Hall* (1972); Deep Purple, *Made in Japan* (1973); Hawkwind, *Space Ritual* (1973); The Beach Boys, *In Concert* (1973); Yes, *Yessongs* (triple album, 1973); David Bowie, *David Live* (1974); Bob Dylan and the Band, *Before the Flood* (1974); Barclay James Harvest, *Live* (1974); Emerson, Lake & Palmer, *Welcome Back My Friends to the Show That Never Ends ~ Ladies and Gentlemen* (triple album, 1974); Kiss, *Alive!* (1975); Miles Davis, *Dark Magus* (1975); Miles Davis, *Agharta* (1975); Blue Öyster Cult, *On Your Feet or on Your Knees* (1975); Led Zeppelin, *The Song Remains the Same* (1976); Bob Seger and the Silver Bullet Band, *Live Bullet* (1976); Rush, *All the World's a Stage* (1976); Lynyrd Skynyrd, *One More from the Road* (1976); Renaissance, *Live at Carnegie Hall* (1976); Horslips, *Live* (1976); Peter Frampton, *Frampton*

Comes Alive! (1976); Miles Davis, *Pangaea* (1976); Paul McCartney and Wings, *Wings Over America* (triple album, 1976); Kiss, *Alive II* (1977); Be Bop Deluxe, *Live! In the Air Age* (1977); Genesis, *Seconds Out* (1977); Jethro Tull, *Bursting Out* (1978); Little Feat, *Waiting for Columbus* (1978); Van der Graaf Generator, *Vital* (1978); Ted Nugent, *Double Live Gonzo!* (1978); Kansas, *Two for the Show* (1978); Thin Lizzy, *Live and Dangerous* (1978); Queen, *Live Killers* (1979).

We had to be taught about live music. How to properly attend a concert. What one should expect from live events, special features one might hope for in them. What might differentiate a concert recording from a studio session. It seems so natural now, like these ideas would all be common sense, but stadium events were a relatively new phenomenon in the seventies, and in order to push the popular music apparatus to the next level, listeners needed guidance. A symbiotic relationship was forged between the studio record production, concert performance, and live recording.

Record labels were eager to help us understand all this. To help us get with the program, so we could see how important concerts were in the global musical ecosystem. And just as greatest hits LPs had served them so well, allowing them to inexpensively compile existing music into an irresistible package, often double- or triple-dipping on fans who had already bought singles and albums with the same music, so too did live records provide them a simple way to record a whole program—not one, but two or three albums worth—of audience-tested songs. They could be made cheaply, recorded quickly, without months of studio time and dozens of engineers to overspend wildly or artist equivocation and hand wringing that might hold up a release and drain money from the system. Also, as live records inevitably contained new versions of songs on other records, they helped sell those LPs too and were in effect promotional materials. Here's the genius: live records were promotional materials that people *bought*. You paid to be sold something, a novel concept at the time.

The logic of the double live already tells us something. It's double, first off. Concert music, this suggests, might take longer than studio music. The musicians are free to stretch out. If inspiration strikes, they'll take liberties, improvise, extrapolate, jam. And there will be visuals to contend with—a stage show, some explosives, lights and what have you, costumes, theater, special guests, all of which will need space to reproduce in the packaging. Who knows how long it might take and what images it will conjure, but one thing's guaranteed, the music industry told us, and that's the fact that live music is going to add some value to the studio version.

...

My friend Scooter and I had not yet been to any concerts, but by 1976 we already had some ideas about what to expect. From Peter Frampton's *Frampton Comes Alive!* we had learned about the extended solo, like the very fine one he plays on "Do You Feel Like I Do," in which we heard him scandalously utter *I wanna fuck you* under cover of talk-box. But the double live that we pored over and which yielded the most to our desperate little minds was Kiss's *Alive!* Between us, Scoots and I had all the studio albums by Kiss, so we compared the canned version of "Strutter," from their eponymous debut, with its live counterpart, likewise the title track and "Parasite," from *Hotter than Hell*, and "She" and "Rock and Roll All Nite," from *Dressed to Kill*. All three of those LPs were advertised in the gatefold of the live record—note: we'd paid to be sold something—alongside four handwritten notes from the band. Ace Frehley's letter is addressed "Dear Earthlings," Peter Criss's "Hi Cat People," Paul Stanley's "My Dear Lovers," and Gene Simmons's "Dear Victims." We're talking total Kiss product synergy. Scooter and I were impressed at the length of solos and the energy of the playing, which was higher than in the studio, but then again studio recording was cleaner and sometimes there seemed to be more than just four instruments playing at once. There were pluses; there were minuses.

Frehley's guitar antics are about as rudimentary and idiotic as you could want if you were into rudiments and idiocy. We were. And somehow their kabuki/glam/clown getups worked for us, as comic book hard rock superhero team, each character with its own overblown traits (look at Simmons's white clogs on the cover of *Dressed to Kill*—a ballsy move, not un-awesome), but also as four archetypes of male mid-seventies identity—the half-girl glamor puss (Frehley), the sexy introvert (Stanley), the cute 'n' cuddly (Criss), and the demonic predator (Simmons). Two years after *Alive!*, Kiss had its own comic book, published as a Marvel Comics special edition; in a freaky stunt, blood drawn from all four members of the group was added to the red ink used to print the comics.

On the back cover of *Alive!*, two Kiss fans, androgynous guys with feathered hair parted in the middle as we did at the time, held a sign with the name of the band and likenesses of its members, crudely drawn. This was clearly meant to represent us, me and Scooter, behind us a massive stadium, every single audience member apparently training attention on the cameraperson. The gatefold to *Alive II* opened to a panorama of the band on a high platform, flames shooting around them, the band's name outlined in lights behind Criss's drum kit, some ritualistic insignia below them, Simmons raising a fist in righteous rocking power, spreading his patented bat wings.

We bought *Alive!* at the same time as we did their next LP, *Destroyer*, which came with an invitation to join the Kiss Army. Of course we enlisted immediately. In that voluntary enrollment, I think we were conscripted into the double-live life.

I attended my first rock concert with my mother. Sha Na Na played vintage fifties rock and doo-wop, always pitched somewhere between nostalgia and parody, with duck's ass hairdos, cuffed jeans, and white T-shirts. I liked the way singer Jon "Bowzer" Bauman growled his way through the low parts, occasionally pushing a short sleeve over his scrawny shoulder and flexing a wimpy bicep. They were funny in a goof-off way, which appealed to my twelve-year-old sensibility. But, to me, it wasn't a real concert, taking place in a revival-like tent miles outside Philadelphia, a far cry from the grand canyon of people I'd seen on the back of *Alive!*

My parents allowed me to go to my first arena concert in 1976: Electric Light Orchestra at the Philadelphia Spectrum. I took my girlfriend Susie Miller. I knew she was my girlfriend because she had accepted a leather bracelet that I'd gotten embossed with her name at a fair. I wore a matching bracelet without my name. In our parlance, we were "going together," which meant that we held hands now and then. And went to concerts together. We never swapped any spit, but we shared a ton of music, listening to Crosby, Stills, Nash & Young, Fleetwood Mac, Foghat, Bad Company, Genesis, and ELO at her house after school. Many sessions were spent with Susie and her older sister Beth. They could have been a good girl/bad girl act. Susie was sweet and light, smiley, blond, curly haired, and generous to a fault; Beth was a smart-ass, sardonic, with straight brown hair, looking for fun and spoiling for trouble in about equal measure. A year later, after I'd moved away (and had subsequently "gone together" with Beth, swapping spittle and a modicum more), Susie sent me a letter recalling ELO fondly, but opining that it couldn't compare to the life-changing Pink Floyd concert we'd seen. This was accurate, but seeing ELO will always be important for having been my introduction to live music. As Foreigner put it: *feels like the very first time*.

We arrived at the Spectrum, two rank beginners, a bit sheepish at the gate, but once in we searched for our seats in the top section, just under the rafters, in the next-to-last row of a stadium that held more than 20,000 people. It was dizzying to look down at the stage. The setting was remarkably like that photo on the Kiss record: wall-to-wall people carpeted the huge room on the main floor, divided up into geometric areas like agricultural fields seen from the sky. The stage was dark and roadies seemed to be scurrying around on it, laying out cables and tuning guitars. Lights flashed on and off for a second, a test. The kick drum pounded a few times, then the snare, and each microphone, one-two, again testing. Then the house lights dimmed, the crowd began to cheer, and we were swept up in the first moments of ELO.

At this point, to our surprise, the arena seemed to be filled with smoke. Pot smoke. It came in a wave, all at once when the place had darkened enough that security couldn't see so clearly. Being up that far, we found ourselves in a dope nimbus. Neither of us had smoked before, but during the hour concert we got mild secondhand highs. From this distance and through the haze, both the audience-generated fog and the smoke machines onstage, we could barely see the band, but they sounded fantastic playing songs we'd come to know on *Face the Music*, a unique mix of rock and pop decorated with classical string music. Their hits "Evil Woman" and "Strange Magic" were crowd-pleasers, and I loved the instrumental track "Fire on High," which CBS Sports had used as theme music, much to our utter amazement. Though we were in a huge venue full of their fans, which should have suggested their status as universal property, somehow ELO were, in our minds, like a secret whispered between only a few lucky people, and a track like that, with no words and therefore no radio airplay, we figured, was even more arcane, so it seemed miraculous that someone at a network television company had discovered it.

Although Jeff Lynne's singing and guitar playing were key to the band's spectral sound, the focal point of the concert was cellist Hugh McDowell. Cello set the band apart, gave them a universe of references that other pop rock bands couldn't make. Onstage it meant there was a soloist who—spike planted firmly in the ground—didn't jump around like all the antic guitarists. As a way of animating him, the lighting crew tacked a little mirror behind his bridge and while he played, they shot lasers at the mirror, fine lines of colored light ricocheting into the crowd. This was just part of an extensive laser show, an unexpected bonus for us first-time arena rockers. Susie and I drank in the rest of the evening, understanding when we left that in the future we should bring lighters for the encore request.

It was an education, but as a card-carrying member of the Kiss Army and a double-live lifer, I knew too that it was but a glimpse of my destiny.

        ...

As a coda, I recall the first club concert I ever saw. It was 1980, I was seventeen, and Captain Beefheart & the Magic Band had just played on *Saturday Night Live*, turning in one of the most electrifying and alien performances I'd ever seen. I'd been playing my copy of *Doc at the Radar Station* to death when I heard that the Cap would play at the Crow's Nest in Iowa City. A purchased ticket firmly in hand, I headed over on the evening of, only to find that they were carding and wouldn't let me in. For the length of the show, I stood at the door to the bar, a forlorn minor, waiting for anyone to enter or exit, relishing the few moments of "Ashtray Heart" or "Hot Head" emitted just before the door swung shut.

Bruce Springsteen

Born to Run

Count to ten and say "heartland rock."

1) Forget the cowbell, it's all about the glockenspiel. Pinpricks of pleasure. Almost inaudible high-frequency sparkles, like sonic fireworks, shadowing the tremolo guitar on three cuts: "Born to Run," "Thunder Road," and "Night." Used as such, the glock engages a technology of bliss as fail-safe as adding highlights to a photograph, almost a cheap effect, but it succeeds in evoking the triumph of home team victory as celebrated by a high school marching band. *Your graduation gown lies in rags at their feet*, the lyrics tell us on "Thunder Road," so leave this crappy place by car for a transcendent time in parts unknown. *All the redemption I can offer, girl / Is beneath this dirty hood / With a chance to make it good somehow / Hey what else can we do now? / Except roll down the window / And let the wind blow back your hair / Well, the night's busting open / These two lanes will take us anywhere.* The glock is in the mix all along, a spark plug igniting air and fuel, permitting the American-built engine to drive the young lovers away from New Jersey.

2) Three small points: (a) Fluid mechanics of working-class Yankee

freedom mythology. *The poets down here don't write nothing at all / They just stand back and let it all be*; (b) Honesty as class heroism. *You ain't a beauty, but, hey, you're alright / Oh, that's alright with me*; (c) A city of angels with dirty faces, a highway their exclusive up, up, and away. *It's a town full of losers / I'm pulling out of here to win.*

3) The flora and fauna of euphoria and melancholia, assessed from the confines of a concrete jungle.

4) Suburban Jersey death trip with Elvis twang, Phil Spectorisms, and an ultra-square tenor saxophonist. Clarence Clemons is the most unswinging horn man, though he possessed a huge sound and seemingly infinite projection. If King Curtis had played with a top-shelf Jersey bar band rather than the Coasters, this would have been his jam.

5) These songs are actually rather close to Broadway show tunes— *West Side Story* for the rock set, with the same vivid narration and unreconstructed romanticism. *Babe, I want to know if love is real*, Springsteen sings on the title track, glockenspiel again exploding with delight, before he moves on to propose dying on the street *in an everlasting kiss.* Could this not be a parody of melodrama? Springsteen's a showman, loves to stage his drama, minus the mellow. *Man, there's an opera out on the Turnpike*, he growls on "Jungleland." *There's a ballet being fought out in the alley.* For the Broadway angle, see especially "Meeting Across the River," his two-character dramatization of a doomed-to-fail Hail Mary drug deal.

6) Springsteen's *runaway American dream* is openly nostalgic and forcefully heterosexual, looking back to the rock 'n' roll fifties and soul sixties, with none of David Bowie and Lou Reed's kinkiness or decadence.

7) On the other hand, which is more decadent: singing love songs about drugged-out transsexual hookers or taking fourteen months and a small fortune to wax your renegade rock record?

8) So with all this music that we loved, all that we adored and

emulated, what did we disdain? Which musicians did we deride? The Boss was one, perhaps first for being called the Boss, but also for a kind of outsider mythos that differed from our own, a macho *Rebel without a Cause* road-hog scene that seemed to have a superiority complex, poised between *American Graffiti* (1973) and *Happy Days* (debuted in 1974), an evangelistic greaser. *Born to Run* is a minor masterpiece. I can see that now. But back then something about it didn't ring true, didn't appeal to my experiences or fantasies, in fact irritated me. Or maybe it was just because I was living in Philadelphia, where everyone went "down the shore" on vacation, and those New Jersey aspirations were just too familiar, too pedestrian. The music that interested me was exotic, and the last thing I wanted in a liberation theology was one scripted by a half-beard tough from only a few zip codes away. Whatever spurred the rejection, Springsteen joined Rod Stewart, Eric Clapton, and Billy Joel in my personal parade of star losers.

9) When Springsteen's drummer, Max Weinberg, helped Phil Collins retool the sonics of the drum kit by means of gated reverb on his drum tracks for "Born in the U.S.A.," totally screwing up the natural acoustics of recorded percussion for the duration of the eighties, I disliked Springsteen even more. Listen to that song, as well as Collins's "In the Air Tonight" and David Bowie's "Let's Dance," for snare and toms treated to the nasty new normal.

10) There's plenty of popular music I liked in the seventies that I now detest, your Foghats and Foreigners, your Lynyrd Skynyrds and Supertramps, your Journey and Jethro Tull, but precious little that I rejected then that I embrace today. *Born to Run* is one such reclamation.

Blood on the Tracks

I like to drive. My family raised me that way. We drove everywhere when I was growing up, including back and forth from the Midwest to the Northeast. I got used to long trips, delighting in the feel of a highway late at night, the lunar glow of Gary, Indiana, with flaming chimneys and factory lights and phosphorescent fetidness, the foul smell of industry a sure sign that we were nearly there as we headed up I-94 on the way into Chicago. Driving came to connote freedom for me, as it did for many Americans in the extended postwar period of prosperity and mobility. I think of my dog Hieronymus, a black Hungarian sheep dog, pushing his snout into the oncoming air at the top of a vented window as we trucked along between school and home. Or my own hand, which I held outside as we drove, sensing the uprush of air as I pressed it up or down to create an airfoil, soaring and dipping depending on the angle at which I held it, the flaps and spoilers of an airplane wing. Those were halcyon days of childhood, and I associated driving with their sense of near euphoria, the bliss of an open road a picturesque metaphor for the future.

My parents never installed fancy sound systems in our cars, just radios, AM ones to start with and eventually FM. Early recollections, for me, include lots of National Public Radio broadcasts during lengthier runs. I heard the SLA shootout, the one in which Patty Hearst got away, which I suppose was my 1974 version of radio theater, completely riveting; around that time Dad began listening to *A Prairie Home Companion*, which was not so much, with Garrison Keillor's insufferable fables of whiteness, cuteness, and insularity. As soon as I was in college, I started making long drives myself. Coordinating the music was half the fun, with cassette tapes strewn around the car and special designer mixes tailored to the trip. Certain stretches of the American highway took on particular significance, especially the magnificent floodplains of upstate New York along I-90, where little river towns are nestled into the breathtaking topography and the rest stops all have bracing vistas. Normally I'm a goal-oriented driver, but when journeying alone from Iowa City to Providence, I would stop to rest at these picnic tables even if rest was unwarranted, just to take in the view.

Summer after my junior year, I made a road trip with my friend Russell Fine. He'd just graduated from Brown, and we packed up his car and drove south to visit his folks and drop the load off in Nashville, where I'd never been.

We all need a pointer dog now and then.

Russell was my pointer dog for country music. Also for Bob Dylan. For a year or so, along with many other important films and jazz and novels that he turned me on to, Russell corrected some stinkin' thinkin' I'd inherited about that down-home genre. I arrived at school saddled with one major—and proudly proclaimed—musical bias, which was against anything country. By the time we left on that trip to Music City, I was a certified fan of George Jones, Lefty Frizzell, Ernest Tubb, Patsy Cline, the Carter Family, the Louvin Brothers, Johnny Cash, early Willie Nelson, and Hank Williams. Bluegrass was beginning to seem like a kind of Appalachian bebop, and I was nibbling hillbilly music, the high lonesome Stanley Brothers, Gid Tanner and the Skillet Lickers, and Dock Boggs, whose warped voice seemed part of a pantheon of croakers and moaners that included Howlin' Wolf, Wanda Jackson, and Joseph Spence.

Traveling to Tennessee, I have a vivid memory of the soundtrack each leg of the way. Russell invited me to take the first crack at the tape deck, and I chose the Minutemen's *Double Nickels on the Dime*, a two-LP set that, even in its title, celebrates the highway—in this case, doing the speed limit on I-10 from L.A. to San Pedro. Each side starts with the sound of one of the band members' automobiles revving the engine. By the time we hit New Haven on I-95, it was Russell's turn, and he selected Dylan's *Blood on the Tracks*. I'd really never been much of a Dylan guy. I played "Blowin' in the Wind" in group guitar classes at age seven, an event perhaps traumatic enough to turn me off to him, ditto my parents' clandestine use of "Lay Lady Lay" as an aphrodisiac. But I knew well enough that he was important so I'd bought and enjoyed *Highway 61 Revisited*, another classic road title. Russell expressed dismay that I didn't know and love *Blood on the Tracks*. He told me to pay attention; we were passing Manhattan as it hit. I was all ears. We drove without speaking, listening as the cassette rounded side one at "You're Gonna Make Me Lonesome When You Go," another quintessential title of onward motion. We turned inland onto I-78 at Newark about the time that "Buckets of Rain" unspooled and the cassette was complete.

When it was over, I pressed rewind, waited for the straining sound as the tape returned to the top and the deck automatically restarted with "Tangled Up in Blue." We had listened to the whole record three times by the time we passed north of Philadelphia, where we turned off for a diner meal. Over cheeseburgers followed by flaky blueberry pie, Russell and I discussed the songs, the incredibly easy way it moved from the unleashed hostility of "Idiot Wind" (vicious, yes, but sporting one of the funniest lines I know in popular music: *They say I shot a man named Gray / And took his wife to Italy / She inherited a million bucks / And when she died it came to me / I can't help it if I'm lucky*) to the caress of "You're Gonna Make Me Lonesome," the session band who had been dismissed because they couldn't keep pace with the singer in the studio, same guys who were so well known for their appearance in the movie *Deliverance*, the "Dueling Banjos" crew, and a group of other musicians not even mentioned on the record sleeve, who were recruited at the last minute to record up in Dylan's neck of the woods, in Minneapolis, finishing the sessions with a different sound than the initial stripped-down versions, organ, piano, mandolin, twelve-string guitar, and spare drums filling out Dylan's songs.

When we got back onto the four-lane blacktop, we agreed to alternate between the Dylan tape and a newly issued cache of Hank Williams demos. Driving straight on through the sixteen-plus-hour trip, we stuck to that plan with a brief detour to listen to one of Dolly Parton's early records around the time we passed by the newly opened Dollywood, in Knoxville. By then my attention was trained on "Shelter from the Storm," aptly timed to a brief downpour, which led us back into "Buckets of Rain," and then jumping to "Jambalaya," "Your Cheatin' Heart," "'Neath a Cold Gray Tomb of Stone," and "There's Nothing as Sweet as My Baby." Russell informed me that the archival Hank Williams recordings we were enjoying had been issued by the Country Music Foundation, which was part of the Country Music Hall of Fame and Museum. "We'll head over there tomorrow, after we've had a good rest," he said.

One the way into Nashville, we observed its skyline, not exactly the one after which Dylan titled his 1969 record *Nashville Skyline*, nor the one immortalized in Robert Altman's 1975 movie *Nashville*, which I had seen with my dad. Instead, a Nashville interrupted by monstrous postmodern architecture, gleaming fractured buildings pretending opulence, a nouveau riche Oz. Once in town, two days sped by, with visits to the museum, where I saw Elvis Presley's gold Cadillac, Gram Parson's pot-leaf Nudie suit, and Johnny Cash's black Manuel jacket. I visited Hatch Show Prints, the shop where all the classic posters were made, whose services I would turn to twenty-five years later, making posters for my art gallery.

We hoofed it over to the Grand Ole Opry for a performance, and then on to Broadway, where Russell took a portrait of me in front of the massive guitar sign at the Ernest Tubb Record Store. It's a me that I recognize as the one I am now, by that point mature enough to listen to *Blood on the Tracks* and make something of it. Those songs would have made no sense to me a decade earlier, when it was first issued with a botched back cover and inexact liner notes, no more so in the fixed version that followed hot on its heels, nor at any point in the decade between then and my Nashville sojourn.

It's not a country record, at least in the sense that *Nashville Skyline* is with its Johnny Cash duet "Girl from the North Country," nor in the manner of that record's direct predecessor, *John Wesley Harding*, on which Dylan started experimenting with country, but instead it infuses a whole ethos of southern music into Dylan's unique poetic and musical worldview. *Blood on the Tracks* stands apart from genre. It brings together several of them, country and rock and folk, only to turn them into Dylan. At once, it is traditional and breaks with tradition. It is a travel record, like Joni Mitchell's *Blue*—by at least one direct report, the very blue he's tangled in— but it's more than just a road trip, more even than the Rolling Thunder Revue, the fifty-seven-date tour ten months later in 1975, documented in a book by Sam Shepard, featuring an unruly troupe that included Mitchell in one concert, consolidating this newly struck music.

Ten plasmatic tracks: intersections that soon become forked roads and inevitably lead to a parting of ways. They're track marks, hard-fought lines scraped into a vinyl LP.

All the people we used to know
They're an illusion to me now
Some are mathematicians
Some are carpenters' wives
Don't know how it all got started
I don't know what they're doin' with their lives
But me, I'm still on the road
Headin' for another joint

We always did feel the same
We just saw it from a different point of view
Tangled up in blue

The past is a highway. I'm feeling the curves and straightaways, getting back to those bygone friends, lost friends, former friends, including ones like Russell who pointed me toward the good shit and steered me away from the just plain shit. Whether we know each other anymore or not, we're a community, an imagined family, a pack of bloodhounds, foxhounds, bulldogs, and English setters united in the end by the fowl we have flushed. You leave the people but keep their quarry. Look at all I have inherited.

I can't help it if I'm lucky.

Patti Smith

Horses

Three Patti Smith scenes:

1—Iowa City, 1979

Primal Patti, for me, came by myself in my bedroom, late at night, headphones on—normal situation. Knowing a tad about her history and status in the punk lineage, I'd read an interview in one of the British music newspapers in which she'd said something about the importance of having masturbated in front of a mirror, that everyone should do it to learn about themselves. Something about the unbridled honesty and literal narcissism of the statement compelled me. I finally ponied up for *Horses*, an LP I'd been circling for ages at the record store, and thus it was the object of my after-hours session. Listening to music in a house of sleeping people has a particular charm—it's not exactly being alone, but it's being left alone, which is different but almost as good when you're sixteen. I might as well have been masturbating in front of the mirror. In fact I tried, but I honestly didn't find myself enough of a turn-on.

Fingering the record cover, I caught some references I'd not expected, along with ones I had, meaning the New York nexus—Velvet Underground's John Cale, who produced it; Television's Tom

Verlaine, who plays guitar on "Break It Up"; photographer Robert Mapplethorpe, who nobody knew at the time. On the last track, something called "Elegie," I noted a cameo and writing credit for Allen Lanier, guitarist with Blue Öyster Cult. I wasn't aware that he and Smith had been lovers, as had Smith and Verlaine, but BÖC was from such a different spot in my rock Rolodex that I found his participation immediately intriguing. Also, here was a punk progenitor kicking off her debut record on a brooding, religious, albeit heretical, note (*Jesus died for somebody's sins, but not mine . . .*), seguing into a version of a Van Morrison song, anathema in my mind to the punk vibe, and adapting reggae on "Redondo Beach," four years ahead of the Clash.

Even having heard "Birdland," with its visionary tale of extraterrestrial bodysnatching recited in Smith's visceral *Sprechstimme*, it was another track, "Land," that made me catch hold of my breath. Smith starts unaccompanied in a soft, conversational, almost conspiratorial tone with her plainspoken New York accent, two identical overdubbed voices twining, spinning a tale, a vivid gay rape-murder fantasy set in a high school, the deed done against a locker, much, I imagined, like the ones at my own educational institution. The song only takes a minute to build from hallway whispers to a convulsive version of the exultant Fats Domino/Wilson Pickett song "Land of a Thousand Dances," dipping back down in dynamic to examine the dead kid *in his sperm casket*, an angelic presence challenging him not to take it lying down, not to let someone else do it, but to get up and kill himself. The track is nearly ten minutes long, and with hallucinatory intensity it snakes between poetry and song, Smith's twin voices coaxing the kid to slit his already dead throat, and to do so, I imagined, with the switchblade I'd spied in drummer Jay Dee Daugherty's hand on the record jacket.

I don't think I've mentioned that the kid's name is Johnny.

The first time I heard Smith say, *The boy looked at Johnny*, alone at the foot of my bed, the silence of the house compounded by headphones that muffled even the gentlest ambient creak and bump, I was overcome with a paranoid sensation that it was me she was talking about.

2—Video Data Bank, Chicago, 1992

Alone again, this time in an archive, watching video art, performance documentation, and artist interviews, ostensibly preparing to teach a core class called 4-D at the School of the Art Institute of Chicago. Up on the shelf, among the Bruce Nauman and Paper Tiger TV quarter-inch tapes, I saw a stray VHS labeled "Patti Smith Interview." It turned out to be a late seventies appearance on a New York local access talk show, black-and-white, with an intelligent host who talked with the extra disheveled, but typically candid and intelligent Smith about, among other things, the baby she gave up for adoption as a teenager. She calls attention to the guard stationed at the back of the studio who had carried her amplifier for her, thanking him, and she's clearly moved by the down-home quality of the show. In a strange segment without the guest, shot from above, the host, reclining on a couch, is interviewed by a psychotherapist, who asks how he feels about having Smith on the show. "Scares me," he says. "She reminds me of my sister. It's like a live grenade rolling around the studio."

Smith performs a piece on the show, voice and guitar, sans band. "What I feel when I'm playing guitar is completely cold and crazy," she intones, but just then her amp fritzes out, she abandons it, and the poem "High on Rebellion" achieves a critical sharpness.

> *The artist preserves himself. Maintains his swagger. Is intoxicated by ritual as well as result. Look at me I am laughing. I am lapping from the hard brown palm of the boxer. I trust my guitar. Therefore we black out together. Therefore I would wade through scum for him and scum is ahead but we just laugh. Ascending with the hollow mountain I am peaking.*

At this point I was acutely aware that I was by myself in a cubicle, a little private room watching an incandescent recitation. And then

on the tape something happens that I've only seen or heard performers do a few times, somewhere on the continuum between charisma and spirit possession, a kind of inhuman intensity takes hold
of Patti Smith, her eyes look outward unblinking, each sending a
line of force through the air as if they are laser beams, as if she's
reading directly to everyone in the little broadcast studio and all the
viewers of the show and now all the viewers of the VHS, myself, for
instance, perhaps everyone on the planet, everyone who has ever
been on the planet, penetrating us to land this final line in each of
our ears, for us personally to hear in our loneliness: *We are kneeling
we are laughing we are radiating at last*, she says, her voice like a
foot stepping into gravel, a torn page of gnostic transcendentalism,
her wall-eyed gaze glowing like Godzilla. *This rebellion is a gas, it's
a gas that we pass.*

3—Park West, Chicago, 2016/17

> *Lipstick on her reefer / Waiting for a match.*
> LAURA NYRO, "Blackpatch"

After thirty-seven years of listening to her music, I finally saw
Patti Smith in concert. It was the day after her seventieth birthday,
and she had recently ratcheted up her celebrity by performing—
poignantly, passionately, with mistakes that made it that much
more genuine—"A Hard Rain's Gonna Fall" as a stand-in for Bob
Dylan at the Nobel Prize ceremonies. At a medium-sized concert
venue in the city of Smith's birth, we were celebrating New Year's
Eve at the end of an annum being bum-kicked on the way out the
door. And in this context, it was not about the solitary listener or
the lone onanist; it was about the crowd, the people together, which
comprises Smith's comfort zone.

In a 1971 BBC documentary called *West Side Stories*, the singer
describes the transition from being in the audience to being in the
spotlight: "Being a spectator, you can never have the powerful feeling you feel onstage. I'm going through that right now. Everybody

goes through it when you go from one to the other. You have to transcend the excitement of waiting for the curtain to open when you're in front of the curtain to the surge of power you feel when people are applauding for you. Man, what a great feeling. I have to admit it's even better than being with a man. It's almost better than that. When people stand up and cheer for you, it's so moving. I guess I'm a real ham."

Smith's band that night included two of the original players from *Horses*, her longest-running musical partner, guitarist Lenny Kaye, and the drummer Jay Dee Daugherty, he of the switchblade. Kaye led an opening set peppered with soul and Television's "See No Evil," but focused on garage rock, the pre-punk music he'd produced in 1972 for a two-LP titled *Nuggets*, working together with Jac Holzman for Holzman's Elektra Records, later the home of the Stooges and MC5. An influence on several generations, *Nuggets* was the first place many of us began to think archaeologically about underground music; Kaye and Holzman dug up such valuable fossils as the Seeds' "Pushin' Too Hard," the 13th Floor Elevators' "You're Gonna Miss Me," Count Five's "Psychotic Reaction," and the Electric Prunes' "I Had Too Much to Dream (Last Night)," the last of which Kaye and company gave a playful reading.

It was all quite affable and fun, even when Patti took the stage and bantered jovially with the crowd. She started with a rousing take on her very first single, "Piss Factory," and the fan favorite "Walking Barefoot," then dedicated Blue Öyster Cult's "Astronomy" to the recently dead Sandy Pearlman.

"Tammy," a cute duet with Kaye, was offered in homage to Debbie Reynolds, and "Father Figure" commemorated George Michael, also just passed. They played the Byrds' arrangement of "Jesus Is Just Alright" and "Because the Night," which she co-wrote with Bruce Springsteen and which bears both their trademarks, a combination of musical identities that once seemed utterly unimaginable. Smith kicked out a nice version of "Break It Up" and a satisfyingly hypnotic "Land," but her manic focus was a little diffused, perhaps by a looming cold she was fighting, and she occasionally lost track of where she was in a song, recalling her recent experience in Stockholm.

At one point in "Ain't It Strange," in fact, she stopped singing, clearly off a bit, and asked bassist Tony Shanahan whether the monitor sound had changed. After a moment, she returned to the microphone with: "Where were we?" And then she told a tale. With the band vamping behind her, Smith began the story of Scheherazade, weaving it in spectacular detail, calling on her early New York days beguiling wealthy guys with made-up stories for spending money, so richly recounted in *Just Kids*, going further back in her personal history to knock on the door of her mother, who she has called "a real hip Scheherazade" and who taught young Patti about fantasy and how to improvise stories. Magically, mesmerizingly, she pulled her impromptu train of thought up to the ongoing song and hitched them together, effectively staving off execution the same way her protagonist had with the king. It was spectacular, a virtuosic turn on a night that was more frivolous than freighted, watching her wend her way from ancient Persia to Vineland, New Jersey, in a few moments of surreal narration.

As the clock wound down, the band played "Gloria" and balloons fell from the ceiling. Basking in the warmth of the crowd, Smith played "Power to the People," bringing her daughter onstage to play keyboards and adding some kid who'd flown from Tokyo to be there for the event on guitar. Kaye toasted the crowd, and Smith seemed reluctant to leave the stage, her people, the surge of power boosting her immune system and sending her endorphins into overdrive, but she gave a parting thought: "This is gonna be a good new year. You all celebrate tonight, have this party, enjoy yourselves, then go home and in a few days sit up and think hard about what's going on. You can't get complacent. If they tell lies, you gotta stand up. If the president tells lies, you gotta hold him accountable. I'm telling you something, it's gonna be a revolution. A revolution of love, motherfuckers!"

Happy New Year, Patti.

1976

"Long Time"

For Joe Brainard

I remember the long, flat, straight road parallel to the beach.
I remember the sweltering heat.
I remember our blue Saab without air.
I remember my sisters on either side, making hand puppets
    on my back.
I remember having to pee.
I remember my sisters having to pee.
I remember the standing traffic, for hours, both directions.
I remember tempers flaring as fellow vacationers watched
    vacation hours snuffed out like the lives of roadkill.
I remember "Long Time."
I remember my father pointing out the difference between
    a hawk and a vulture.
I remember the vultures.
I remember the picnic lunch my mom had packed.
I remember wishing there was something to drink.
I remember "Long Time," again.
I remember the radio announcer.

I remember asking Dad to turn it up but missing the name
     of the band.
I remember thinking that I'll hear the song again before we move.
I remember not moving.
I remember the line for gas that we'd waited in a few weeks
     earlier, also not moving.
I remember that Dad did not let the car idle but kept the radio on.
I remember when he changed the channel, and I begged him to
     turn it back.
I remember "Long Time," again and again.
I remember Cat Stevens and my mother, father, and sisters
     singing along to "Moonshadow."
I remember that on the third pass I understood the structure
     of "Long Time."
I remember the acoustic guitar chords, *chicka-chicka*.
I remember the electric guitar chords, *chicka-chicka*.
I remember the shock of the latter, which were produced in
     a pronounced manner, the song opening a gap out of which
     amplified strumming exploded.
I remember the gumball after a nickel and a turn.
I remember motors starting and the column moving and the
     Massachusetts sand vacation that ensued.
I remember Horseneck Beach.
I remember thinking it was funny we were so close to Boston.
I remember seeing Boston six months later in Iowa City,
     our new home.
I remember sitting at an oblique angle to the stage, row 3,
     to the right.
I remember "Foreplay," the introduction to "Long Time," on
     which Tom Scholz fingered an interminable keyboard solo,
     back to the audience, in a black cape.
I remember the pipe organ being manually raised above him.
I remember reading that it cost them $100,000 and they named
     it Bertha.

I remember that it seemed flimsy, like it was made out of
   cardboard.
I remember the stagehands hoisting it up as we could see all
   too well from our vantage.
I remember snickering with my friend at the ridiculousness.
I remember losing faith.
I remember thinking what's taking such a long time, when
   the hell will they get to "Long Time"?

Rocks

Frustration is the grandmother of invention.

How's that? Well, they say that necessity is the mother of invention, but who's *her* mom? Frustration, I say, is the mother of necessity. The blunt end of not being able to do something, the mounting feeling that an answer is there but not quite available, the *ugh* and *what-tha?*—frustration leads, via necessity, to li'l baby invention.

Aerosmith frustrated me in ways I didn't immediately comprehend. They get less respect than Led Zeppelin, but like their British counterparts, they should be acknowledged as one of the hard rock bands to sneak real music into their posturing. They followed a familiar path: a couple of good but uneven first records in which they figured themselves out, followed by two golden-period masterpieces. *Toys in the Attic* cemented their celebrity; *Rocks* was the artistic coup de grâce. Aerosmith lyrics are not, by the standards of much contemporaneous popular music, particularly obscure, nor does Steven Tyler swallow or mumble or weirdly pronounce them like certain of his peers. But one time singing along with my friend Scooter, trying to get their cool-ass harmonies, I realized that I was fudging some of the words—pockets of the songs that I'd committed to memory in phonetic form, not as meaningful signifiers but as approximate shapes. Using our normal techniques—listening and simultaneously hollering along—did not yield complete stanzas. So that day I decided to try another approach.

Contractions getting closer together, frustration was heading into labor.

I took a pencil and paper and started obsessively listening to the segments on *Rocks* that I couldn't understand, transcribing them as best I could. On "Last Child," I heard that one line starts, *Yes sir, no sir, don't come close to* / *My home sweet home* / *Can't catch no . . .* and then I lost the thread in a staccato jumble of funk strut. Plopping the needle on the same groove over and over, nothing changed for a while. Then, in the drop of a guitar pick, a meaning suddenly opened up, the words. . . *dose of my hot tail poontang sweetheart* / *Sweathog ready to make a silk purse from a J. Paul Getty and his ear . . .* tumbled out, and the puzzle solved itself. I was startled that this mechanical repetition unlocked the song, but it worked. And writing the words down was interesting, even the ones I already recognized. I began to hear *Rocks* differently. This would be the first time I listened analytically to a record, the first time I diagrammed and attempted to interpret it rather than just enjoying it.

OK, to be honest, I couldn't figure out "sweathog." And I didn't know what "poontang" was, though the word was being used frequently in music at the time and I eventually figured it out.

I found those transcriptions recently. Scribbled in a hand that has barely changed in forty years, you can see my struggle in graphite and white. I erased incessantly. There are blank spots with circles around them where I was left baffled by words like "sweathog." And there are heavily underlined parts where the sound and the meaning have mysteriously aligned, sending the correct word or phrase into my cerebrum. *I was the last child* / *Just a punk in the street.* I recall writing "punk" and then beginning to hear about punk rock shortly after, somehow knowing that Aerosmith was not punk, though a song like "Rats in the Cellar," which we knew had some mysterious relationship to "Toys in the Attic," now seems like it might describe the New York Dolls. Listening closely, I heard other things that had only previously appeared in overall impression, like the kinky sound effects on "Back in the Saddle Again"—the horse hooves, cracking whip, and neighing noises—or the nearly subliminal door creak in the organ-like rolled-up guitar chord intro to "Nobody's Fault," just before a bloodthirsty riff takes over.

On that song I had always adored the projectile way the second guitar solo launched from the chorus, but I'd never really heard that it was a song about an earthquake apocalypse, hence the double meaning of "fault," the line *shove it up their Richters*, and Tyler singing of *too many houses on the stilt*.

California showtime
Five o'clock's the news
Everybody's concubine
Was prone to take a snooze
Sorry, you're so sorry
Don't be sorry
Man has known
And now he's blown it
Upside down and hell's the only sound
We did an awful job
And now we're just a little too late

...

Aerosmith was able to bridge hard rock and black funk as if the two were fraternal twins. I wouldn't discern it until I heard their later collaboration with Run DMC, which made such complete musical sense that it retrospectively explained their secret mojo. Maybe it has something to do with drummer Joey Kramer's stint with P-Funk's Bernie Worrell in Chubby and the Turnpikes before Aerosmith formed. Whatever the origin, Tyler's swagger subsumed a kind of street attitude that came back in the music without calling attention to itself, a deep feeling that other supposedly funky rockers rarely captured in their labored shuffles and overeager back-beats. On the lighter "Get the Lead Out," they ask: *Do you like good boogie? / Like the real boogie woogie?* They're talking about the real thing, the uncut stuff, the bomb. They don't mean 38 Special or Bachman-Turner Overdrive or even the bugle boys from Company C; they mean Pinetop Smith and Jimmy Yancey and Albert Ammons. Even if they don't know that's what they mean, that's what they mean. Those 78s, right over there on that jukebox, fire them up and we'll shake a tail feather, honey.

We were of course aware of Aerosmith's mammoth drug use. On *Rocks* they explore both sides of heroin chic, celebrating guitarist Joe Perry's look on "Combination" (*Walkin' on Gucci / Wearin' Yves Saint Laurent / Barely stay on / 'cause I'm so goddamn gaunt*) and warning against the ravages of abuse on "Sick as a Dog" (*Sick as a dog / You'll be sorry / Sick as a dog / You really ain't that young*). It was cartoony abuse, and we found it endlessly amusing.

"Home Tonight" always seemed like a superior counterpart to the wretched Kiss song "Beth," a smoke signal from the road back to the little lady who keeps the home fires burning. But Aerosmith's was a hand-waving power ballad tacked on to the end of a hard-rocking record, designed to douse the flame at the finale of raucous gigs. We only ever listened to it by accident, if we happened to leave the record player on auto return. And it didn't seem to matter that the song's sentimental love-ya-babe/miss-ya-babe smooch was so obviously contradicted by the groupie groping celebrated on "Lick and a Promise." As we imagined it, that hypocrisy was an honest part of the rocker's lifestyle. *He gets his lovin' every night for free / He's out there rockin' like you wouldn't believe / . . . He started thinkin' 'bout the fortune and fame / And the young girls down at his knees / He dug the money but forgot all the names / So he knew just how to appease.*

Words to songs were cryptic and often out of reach, inhabiting a spongy world between language, texture, and attitude, but I'll tell you one thing—it didn't take any transcription for our squad of pubic pinheads to understand what those lines were about. Leering aside, sustained exposure to indecipherable lyrics, I think, was indirectly responsible for my future interest in abstract art and obtuse poetry. Some kids in our neighborhood couldn't get into music until they understood what it was trying to say. I wasn't immediately drawn to the question of interpretation—wonderment over what something was supposed to mean was a lesser feature than experiencing it palpably.

If, in Susan Sontag's famous formulation, interpretation boils down to a duel between hermeneutics and erotics, it's the latter that most reliably held my attention in its sensuous grip.

Bootsy Collins

Stretchin' Out in Bootsy's Rubber Band

Carol was hot to trot.

My mother was the first to notice, which is embarrassing but true. Should have been my call, but I guess my radar was broken. Mom saw Carol in a two-piece at the swim club and then watched her parade around in shoes that laced all the way up to her knees.

"Those shoes are slutty," she said. I'd never heard Mom utter a phrase like that. I didn't know she knew that word.

"What are you talking about?" I protested, turning it over in my head, trying to imagine the shoes she meant.

"They're hooker shoes and you are forbidden to have Carol in your room. Do you understand?"

Now I did. True to form, the first time we were alone in my room, which was about as soon thereafter as I could engineer, Carol immediately locked the door, pushed me down on the bed, and said: "So what are you going to do to me?"

Carol was six months younger than me, which at that age seemed like an eternity. She smelled sort of musky, an overly sweet eau de toilette dueling unsuccessfully with her body's god-given fumes. Without being overweight, she'd never lost her baby fat, so she had a visage that softly staged her piercing eyes and pouty mouth.

Standing before me, in one swift move, like undoing the bow on a Christmas present, she pulled a strap on her pants and they dropped to the floor, leaving her in nothing but her tube top and minuscule bikini bottoms.

It was all I could do not to explode in a suicide belt of wantonness, but my parents were right downstairs, visiting with Carol's mom and stepfather, and I was chicken shit. Plus, something about her forwardness put me off. I was a romantic. A sex-craven romantic, don't get me wrong, but one for whom getting off would be about mutuality, curiosity, and discovery. If not for my folks, I might have tried that sensitive line of reasoning on Carol. But the situation was fraught and I balked, leaping up, raising her drawers, unlocking the door, and ushering her out and down a flight of shag-carpeted stairs.

By the time summer was over, Carol's outlook had changed. Understanding that I was immovable, she ceased her direct onslaught. Instead, whenever we were together, she would mope and pine, which I found unattractive, so I tended to avoid her. One afternoon at the tail end of the season, my family drove to the countrified suburb where her family lived. While the grown-ups hung out inside, we spent the day on a gravel driveway and walking down to a wooden-fenced nexus where some of her cul-de-sac friends congregated to shoot the shit. After a little while, an older girl ambled by, waving and calling us over.

I'd never met Carol's sister. I'm not sure I ever learned her name. Five years our senior, she had a demure presence in marked contrast to that of her sibling, but undercut by an air of authority and insider knowledge. Pushing brown hair off her shoulders and out of her long black eyelashes and training dark irises in my direction, she instantly took my guts in her hands, threatening to yank them out and stomp on them, but doing so painlessly, picking apart my intestines with delicately glossed fingernails and forearms a-frost in soft fuzz. Good god, she was sexy.

I knew a few older girls, the sisters of guys I hung out with. Most of them ignored their brother's friends. All of them acted superior.

And they no doubt were. What could they have in common with pipsqueaks like us? Only one of them was different, my friend's red-haired sister. She helped out babysitting for my sisters when I complained to my folks that having me constantly do so was like indentured servitude. My ulterior motive in filing that complaint, however, came from knowing that she was also a little randy, which I turned to my own devices by convincing her to make a drawing of her lady parts. I kept it in my bedside drawer, and when my mother found it, I "confessed" to having made it myself. I like to think this was a true innovation in adolescent perversity, an advance on the time-worn trope of playing doctor. In any case, it was a cheap thrill, and my buddy's sister seemed to dig it too.

The rest of the time I was too timid to step up in any way when dealing with elder gals. So it took me by storm when Carol's sister addressed me straight on and asked me what I was into. I told her music, of course, and we launched into a conversation about what music could excite a little guy like me. Pink Floyd, I told her. Fleetwood Mac and Genesis. Jethro Tull, Blue Öyster Cult. All the greats, you know, Foghat, Bad Company.

"Far out," she said. Then: "Come with me, I have something to show you."

Carol, who had been hovering drearily, huffed a mighty huff and sulked off with her friends. I trailed along behind her awesome sister, wondering what the fuck. We went inside, and my gutless belly tightened as she motioned toward the stairway.

"C'mon," she said. "I won't bite you."

We headed up to her bedroom, which was sparsely decorated, with gauzy curtains, a futon on the floor, and a stereo setup, also on the ground, with about forty records lined up next to it. She'd be heading to college the following year, and she was already well prepared. I could hear the parents laughing and talking in the living room, and briefly wondered what my mother would think about this arrangement, but I canceled that thought and sat on the purple circular rug in the middle of the space. A hazy light came through the window. Carol's sister went to the albums and pulled one out, handing it to me.

"You don't know this one, do you?"

Here was Bootsy Collins, riding straight at me, his boss hog emerging from a bank of heavenly clouds, star-shaped glasses perched atop his brow, the headstock of his bass peeking over his shoulder. On the back you could see the gear better—the bike a three-wheeler, the bass shaped like a rubberized star. It was the baddest-ass cover I'd ever seen.

"No, I don't," I managed. "You like it?"

"Well, dear, I have to catch up with my boyfriend, but I'll put it on and you see what you think. Make yourself at home."

With that she broke my turned-on heart. Then she turned around and turned me on to something even better. The name is Bootsy, baby. A living cartoon in technicolor. Not the Holy Ghost, the Friendly Ghost. As if knowing that I'd go back to check the rest out, she moved straight to the second side—first track, side two: the money shot. For me, a quick education in the form of "I'd Rather Be with You." She lingered a bit while the hippopotamus bass line broke the silence, a glockenspiel tinkling like starburst on chrome. And then she slipped away just as I felt Bootsy's sealskin voice crooning: *If I can't have you to myself, then life's no fun.* Fun? I guess fun has something to do with it. *You might think I'm trying to be funny, but I'm really serious this time, baby.* His voice was so louche, it was clownish. Fun, sure, but could sex be funny? Come to think of it, what could be funnier? All the convoluted positions and silly utterances seemed, best I could tell, tops in knee-slapping humor. Heck, nakedness alone is a hoot.

This is how I learned to love the slow jam. Barry White was a bit too adult for me, I couldn't quite take him seriously; with his admonitions and pillow whispers, White was *too* serious. Here was a super-slick dude who had discovered that the funny bone was connected to the horny bone, a guy who could get down to bottom-end business better than any bassist alive. *I know I sound strange, but*

*I really mean it / We gonna make it this time, baby / . . . I'm comin'
at you with both hands tied behind my back, baby.* The monologue
at the end was obscene, nearly buried in the fade-out. I played it
repeatedly, straining to make sure I really heard what outlandish
shit Bootsy was saying: *I'm gonna stick my love in your eye, baby /
You can see me coming, baby Just cumming all over you.*

Naturally, I devoured the rest of the record. It was a thoughtful hand-me-down from Carol's big sister, far more gratifying than
letting me cop a feel, and though I never saw her again, I owe her
thanks for extending that generosity toward a love-struck little pup
and for teaching me that laughter and sex go together, gland in
gland.

Zombie

After gassing up, I park and run inside to use the facilities. Bottle of cola and bag of nuts in hand, I walk back into the bright spring day just as she pulls up to the pump. She pushes the nozzle into her tank, circular sunglasses and blond curls adding allure and mystery to her placid face. I crack open the pop and sip it loudly as she leaves the gas flowing and moves to my side of the car to wash her windshield, bending over the hood. When she is done, she opens the passenger door and leaves it ajar, making her way around the teal MG Midget to squeegee the other windows.

I crush the can and toss it into the trash, pocket the nuts, cross over to her car, and get in. She pulls onto the two-lane road. The tape deck plays *T. Rex* at concert hall volume. Marc Bolan sings: *Hey, let's do it like we're friends / Let's do it, do it / Hey, let's do it like we're friends*. She drives very fast. The car can handle it. We pass farm stands and more gas stations, microscopic towns for which she does not slow to thirty-five mph, cows and horses, rings of turkey vultures and a solitary falcon, rusted machinery, cars on blocks, state parks and historical markers, a bridge over a river into another state. We hurl along the rural routes. After a long time, a grove of trees opens into a glade, at which without notice she pulls off onto the gravel shoulder, cutting the engine.

She is first out. I dismount, catch up, a skip in my step. We follow train tracks until they reach a wooden trestle. The day is warming and the cross ties smell of creosote. She leads us across the bridge, which spans a dry creek bed, and when we reach the other side, we are in a small cemetery. We sit together on an old stone bench, covered in lichen, echoing the gravestones. I take the liberty of laying my head in her lap. Her bare legs are surprisingly cool, almost cold. Around the bench it's a riot of bird sounds. I rise and explore the graveyard. One stone arrests me. It has my name, exactly.

And now the excitement of the afternoon is overcast. Everything sexy begins to seem sinister. We walk back along the tracks toward the car. A snake slides down the rocky embankment into the brush, startling us both. I am seized with an unfamiliar impulse to take off after it and kill it with a stick.

Back in the Midget, eeriness hovers like humidity after a shower. She starts the motor but leaves the stick shift in neutral, ejecting *T. Rex* and reaching across my lap into the glove box to retrieve a new cassette. As she leans on my leg, I'm shocked again by the chilliness of her skin. She puts the tape into the deck and in a single motion shifts into gear and tears away from the side of the road, reversing the original trip. We travel the same roads. This time I notice different things. A defunct Dairy Queen, a big leafless tree in an open field, signs advocating political candidates who have lost their elections, a dead deer, three dead raccoons, a crow prying something off the pavement before jumping up into the air, spreading huge wings, and flapping to the side of the road. A hotel with the "O" of the word fallen forward onto its face.

The music starts to play. Two electric guitars Jiffy Pop together, interweaving tones; one of them picks single notes in a funky line, the other fills in with patchy chords. A few rounds like this and then a gradual onslaught of electric bass, a single maraca, trap drums, and tenor saxophone, followed by a whole horn section, big and full, with baritone saxophone and trumpet. It's Fela Kuti, a song from the terrible turning point in his life when his political agitation came back to haunt him. As if acting out the lyrics of the song, the dictatorial Nigerian government sent a thousand soldiers to burn down his commune, the Kalakuta Republic. They beat Fela near death. They decimated his studio and destroyed his tapes. They murdered his mother.

Go and kill, sang Fela to the soldiers of his enemies, speaking from the point of view of their generals, who would soon say exactly that to the soldiers, who in turn would do as told. *Zombie, oh zombie / Zombie, no go go unless you tell 'em to go / Zombie, no go stop unless you tell 'em to stop / Zombie, oh zombie, oh / . . . Go and die!* Fela responded to his attackers by sending his mom's actual coffin, her corpse inside it, to the government with a dedication in the form of the song "Coffin for Head of State." His persona in the song and in life is utterly defiant. He refuses to be crushed, seems even to have been stimulated by the violence, an awful power conjured in him, a priapic uprising, like a character in an epic Indian saga, becoming the song that his enemies sing, his libidinal domain expanding to god-like scale, judging at least by the fact that two years later he married twenty-seven women in homage to the memory of his dear Kalakuta.

We pass a billboard with a half-clothed woman engaged in some activity beyond excitement, and I transpose Fela onto her; in the false promise of her airbrushed skin, I envision him singing his battle song, buff and sweaty and bare-chested, face painted in black-and-white, surrounded by his harem, who are chanting the song's title in trancelike repetition. I try to imagine an army of a thousand soldiers attacking Bosstown, Wisconsin, as we pass its only intersection; I picture the helmeted force torching its shuttered junk store, flushing its 127 citizens into the street, demolishing its two barns, breaking all the Amish furniture, damming up its trout stream.

My pilot seems intent on this song. We have listened to it five times by the time we are back at the gas station. Each iteration has lasted twelve minutes and built to a merciless climax. After the last round, I sit for a moment, wondering at the afternoon before opening the door and pushing myself up out of the bucket seat and onto the asphalt. I start away from her car, tapping my pocket for the keys, noticing that the nuts are still there, but then I turn back and bend down, leaning crossed arms against the door. We have spent three hours together and have not said a word.

She pushes the glasses up her nose to mask her eyes, cracks an indefinite smile, and raises the volume on Fela as the bass resumes and the female choir chants *Zombie, oh, zombie*. Pushing the clutch down, she jams into gear and takes off, pebbles flung from beneath the British machine. As it leaves the station, headed the opposite direction from the one we took, the Midget hits the main road already at cruising speed.

She doesn't even check for oncoming traffic.

1977

Blank Generation

Marquee Moon

In the closing sentences of the memoir *I Dreamed I Was a Very Clean Tramp*, Richard Hell describes bumping into Tom Verlaine at a bookstore. I will leave you to read it for yourself, but the gist is that in this chance encounter with a former bandmate, Hell's hidden affection for the old friend overtakes him, in spite of the deeply hurtful shit that's passed between them. In Verlaine's aged state, Hell recognizes himself and remembers their shared youth, even as he is made uncomfortably aware of his own aging. It's quite a tender scene for an agnostic old school punk rocker to have documented, and it leads him to a final few lines that I continue to return to for their poignancy and wisdom.

I'm thinking about friendships, how they relate to music, how music infuses them with meaning, saves and catches those meanings to be savored later.

Across the table at a sushi restaurant at St. Mark's Place, in his New York neighborhood, Richard is still as handsome as he was forty years ago, eyes sparkling through dark-rimmed glasses, a generous, gentle smile under a formidable nose, scruffy salt-and-pepper facial hair, thick do of wavy locks, vintage chamois shirt. He's filled out now, having kicked the junkie's hollow cheeks and eye sockets.

Other than significant hearing loss, Hell is basically intact, more than can be said for his former comrades in Television, the Heartbreakers, and the Voidoids, some of whom didn't make it out alive, few of whom are in such good shape.

Through a mutual friend, Hell and I have become pals. Casual ones who meet whenever we're in the same town, usually for a meal, just to chat and enjoy each other's company. He's a nimble conversationalist, well read and curious, and we've found we have plenty of common interests, from pulp noir to contemporary art to music. In the background, of course, there's always music. We discuss books we're working on, exhibitions we've seen or oughta see, recent enthusiasms or downers. Plans to do projects together have been hatched, but nothing's come to fruition, and that's not really the nature of our relationship. Better to just leave it what it is, open-ended and undefined.

My first impression of Richard dates back from when I was fifteen. I'd seen the LP *Blank Generation* in a record store, the phrase "You Make Me _____" scrawled on Hell's chest like a tattoo, and read about his big tour with the Clash in the British music tabloids, but my first acquisition was a Radar single of "The Kid with the Replaceable Head." Of all punk's leading men, he was the most fearsome in my mind. They'd given themselves jokey surnames like Rotten, Sensible, Moped, and Strummer, or in one loony move all adopted the same nom-de-tomb, like a punk Three Stooges—the Ramones. But Richard had cut to the chase: Hell. That meant business. I knew from my dealings with heavy metal—you don't call yourself Odin unless you're ready to marshal a procession of the dead through the night sky. Hell's name was a kind of cosmic throwdown. And it scared me.

Like all scary things, it also fascinated. Ignited by the single, I bought the LP. Guitarist Robert Quine funneling solar energy into economical solos, great ideas, and ripping tone. The band extended a distinctly American garage band tradition, also hitting on the Byrds and the Velvet Underground and the Stones, while charting something new and untested. Hell's singing and songwriting were the focal point. His voice bounced around in register, but it was more relaxed than I'd expected from a guy with that name, and it gave him maximum expressive leeway, from lilting to snide. One moment he could sound like a confident man, the next like a sniveling schoolboy.

Though I adored songs like the hilarious and touching "Love Comes in Spurts" and the Voidoids' American gothic cover of Creedence Clearwater Revival's "Walk on the Water," it was the title track, "Blank Generation," that captured my attention. Few lyrics so perfectly rev contradictory energies as this revisionist rockabilly rave, positive and negative polarities rolled into one.

The "blank" in "Blank Generation," to me, functions like a blank slate. Our generation, the post–"me generation" generation, the punk generation, draws a blank, comes up empty, is shit out of luck. But it's also a blank to be filled in. Deprivation that instigates invention. Nihilist optimism. Blank and more blank. Expressive potentiality: blank expression. At the gun range, a target is nothing but a hole waiting to happen—we're shooting blanks.

The phrase transecting Hell's sternum contains a conundrum: You make me . . . *what*? Sick? So happy? Feel like a natural woman? Maybe it just makes him . . . blank? Or is it simply saying, "You *make* me," suggesting that the audience invents the performer? In the song, Hell alternates between singing "blank" and actually leaving it blank. He can take it or leave it each time. I love it when Quine is about to fill in the blank with his lacerating, unearthly solo, and Hell points the way by saying "take it."

. . .

Befriending one of your childhood idols is a funny business. On record, to a replaceable-head kid from Iowa, Hell was unreal, a figment, the straight-up personification of a New York punk ethos. As a person, he's delightfully mortal—vulnerable and funny and skeptical and one of the rare music men I've known who pays equal or more attention to my wife, Terri, when she's around. They're both writers. He is innately respectful of women. Anyway, to me Richard is both an icon and a human being. I have trouble connecting the two, not that I doubt the fact of his having been there and done that, but my perception of him as an artist is somehow predicated on his being out of reach, a fiction, something made up by him on his listeners' behalf. Hell renamed himself for the purpose, after all. That act of reinvention, like Sun Ra's renaming, asserted the precise blankness of contemporary personhood, a delirious revelation of the falsehood of inborn identity. "We came from somewhere here," said Ra, "why not go *somewhere there!*" Hell asked the same question in a punk accent. But somehow at the end of that rock 'n' roll inquisition, there's a guy, the one sitting opposite me over tiger rolls and combination number one.

I met Verlaine once at a party a few years ago. He was by himself, long trench coat and stringy hair, still sporting that gaunt look of yore. I approached him and introduced myself. He asked if I was the Corbett who wrote about Sun Ra. I felt a strange sensation knowing that Tom Verlaine could identify me. It was unthinkable that the musician whose "Marquee Moon" my little high school chamber band played at a rally for the presidential candidate John Anderson—me playing lead on steel string acoustic guitar, my friend Charlie on nylon string rhythm, and our buddy Aaron on cello—that this fellow could possibly know who I was. It was more than an ego boost, though it certainly was that, but it seemed fundamentally wrong, the world turned upside down. Like "Yonki Time" from Verlaine's first solo record, which once spun constantly at the record store where I worked, reminding me of my insanity and sanity. Television's "Little Johnny Jewel," like other "Johnny" songs by Patti Smith and Suicide, was something I secretly considered my own, part of a New York bohemian alter-universe in which I fantasized I had played a pivotal role. The whole LP *Marquee Moon* was in heavy rotation for two years. When *Adventure* came out, I defended it against its many critics, still would.

...

Hell and I discuss Trump, the unsavory shift in the world, dangers that lie ahead, our fears and comforts. I describe my exciting day the day before, spent with drummer Milford Graves, another hero I'm somehow lucky enough to be friends with; I'd been lost in conversation with the master for five hours at a crack in his basement study hall at his home in Jamaica, Queens, and as usual my head was swimming with ideas.

Richard asks me about Milford's history, and I talk about Albert Ayler, the recordings they made together at the end of the sixties, also professing my abiding loyalty to the saxophonist's trio recording *Spiritual Unity*. He says he'd never really gotten into Ayler, though everyone used to talk about him and he wished he had known more about the music. Ayler's incredible, unflagging energy, to me, is a vital link with the original American punk scene. He locates that blankness, the space without anything taken away or written out, an emptiness of unbounded possibility, and he fills it with joy so utter and intense that it seems to spill over into anger or pain or woe. But no, it's joy. It's constructive destructive pleasure. Just a few weeks earlier, on a trip to Cleveland, I'd been to Ayler's grave, and I'd met Jon Goldman, who used to chauffeur the Ayler brothers around and had recorded the legendary concert at La Cave in 1966, and I'd felt that power, the vibration of an infinitely renewable resource, the culling force of regeneration, a preview of the blank generation.

...

A week later, by email:

Happy Valentine's Day to you and Terri!
It was great to see you and talk to you. Listen, I've been meaning to write because later that night I pulled out my Albert Ayler and I played myself *Love Cry* (to get Milford) and then *Spiritual Unity*. I'm glad you got me doing that! It was a strange experience because I was

transported back to about age twenty. I'd forgotten that I listened to him a lot back then, and it came back. I played it while I cooked. I was completely wrong in what I said to you in the restaurant. I loved the action. I loved the world of that music and also the laughs—he's a funny guy. It still always blows my mind the way music is really worlds. You start it up and it remakes or opens up and presents everything. No other medium quite has that particular power the way music does. Thank you for getting me started with him again.

Heart,

Hell

Bäbi

Milford Graves discovered my hypertension. You could say he saved my life, and you'd probably be right. I lay on his exam table in 2007, strapped to an EKG machine, when he broke the news. "So, John," said the drummer, my name processed by his Queens accent. "There's something up with your heart. I think you need to get it checked out. Strange goings-on in there." A few weeks later, my GP confirmed that I had very high blood pressure. Since the onset of adulthood, I'd always been borderline, but this was another ball game. I'm lucky Milford told me.

I was in his basement think tank that day allowing him to record my pulse. He offered to do so as part of the research he's been doing on the music our bodies make. Milford is a certifiable polymath. As a keystone to his ongoing studies in the interconnectedness of everything—which have included not just music, but also traditional medicines, herbalism, acoustics, physics, acupuncture, and martial arts—he's been concentrating on the behavior of the central organ of circulation. "Cardiologists know a lot about the heart," he told me. "But they don't know anything about rhythm. And if they want to really know more than just how the heart is set up, they have to understand how rhythm works." When he was awarded a

Guggenheim fellowship, he used the money to buy EEG and EKG machines; his studio looks more like a computer center than a music room, although his beautifully hand-painted drum kit is always in the mix, as is a bright orange piano that's been in the Jamaica, Queens, house since before he inherited it from his grandmother.

Here's the basic notion as I understand it: each person's heart is shaped slightly differently; all hearts have four chambers, the left and right atria and the left and right ventricles; there are four valves that move the blood from the chambers into the rest of the body, the tricuspid valve, the pulmonary valve, the mitral valve, and the aortic valve; the openings to those valves function as little drumheads, each one making a pitched tone as the blood is pumped through it; the particular sound of the heart depends on the size of those chamber valve holes, which are variable within a range. By recording the heart as it is beating, then slowing it way down but keeping the pitch the same, Milford observed that each person's heart has a signature melody, the sound of the four different notes played in succession. Our bodies are singing to themselves.

Before he even got to my melody, he knew something was amiss. But after he'd told me about it, he went ahead and recorded my heart. About a month later, he sent me a CD with my heart melody.

Milford's research, which is really an extension of his initial work in music starting in the early nineteen sixties, has led him to conclude that people's bodies are constantly working to heal themselves by means of those melodies. Bodies under stress, he's suggested, come up with the melodies that the people need to make themselves well. Hence, in a manner of speaking, if you listen to your heart, the answer to many of your problems is a song you are already singing. The particular resonance of African American song in the recent history of our country is explainable using his concept—think of Billie Holiday or the blues as an example of biofeedback on an organismic level, or even more far-reaching than that, blues bodies and jazz hearts working overtime to heal the suffering of an entire race or a broken nation.

...

Five years earlier, I got a panicky call from Milford at four a.m. We were in Berlin, where, in my capacity as artistic director of the Berlin JazzFest, I had booked him in a duet with saxophonist Peter Brötzmann. He didn't sound so good. "John," he muttered into the receiver. "Uh, something's not right up here." I rolled out of bed, threw on some pants, ran upstairs a couple of floors to his room, where he answered the door ashen and sweaty. After a quick consult with my wife, Terri, we decided to call an ambulance.

All three of us were afraid he was having a heart attack.

The paramedics wheeled him downstairs. Members of the Andrew Hill Group, including Hill himself, who had played earlier that night, were standing in the lobby checking out. Hill's entourage approached me worriedly, inquiring about Milford as he was scooted into the ambulance. I found their concern reassuring, somehow.

After several hours in the emergency room, the doctor gave Milford his assessment—he has the heart of an ox, all vitals are totally fine, but he kinked his neck on the transatlantic flight and then seems to have experienced an anxiety attack. Milford listened and nodded, an ideal patient. We cabbed back to the hotel, relieved. The sun had risen while we were in the hospital. It was a glorious day in Berlin. Milford slept into the early afternoon, and that night he and Peter played a fiery, tensile set. Nobody would ever have known that anything had been up in the well-being of the drummer.

...

If, however, you were indeed going into cardiac arrest, I think you could confidently use *Bäbi* as a defibrillator. Milford's playing from the moment it starts on this extremely rare LP is spectacularly intense. It's a trio with Hugh Glover and Arthur Doyle, saxophonists who blow with unmitigated energy, veritably turning themselves inside out. This is not angry music, nor is it strictly speaking black power music, though it's certainly powerful black music. It is music that has a palpable effect on the listener. It can change your temperature, help with gastrointestinal distress, tune up your nervous system. Milford's been working on using tonal information to stimulate acupuncture needles; *Bäbi* is an earlier version, and rather than using a diaphragm connected to the needle, Milford simply uses our god-given diaphragms, the eardrums.

Imagine all the power necessary to revive a body without a pulse—placing the paddles on the pectorals, no jolt of electricity, instead a blast of "Bi," moving the chi around with life-energy force, invoking a kind of subtle body experience that might breathe life back into a corpse straight through all seven chakras at once, the drumming more immediate and affirming and explosive than almost anything you can imagine, rolling and tumbling with a gravitational pull, an interplanetary impulse, satellite motion, all the sensations of the spheres brought to bear on this our fleshy plane. If that track doesn't get your blood flowing, I'm sorry, you're done for.

...

At the end of the summer 2016, Milford invited me to his seventy-fifth birthday. The group of people gathered in his backyard dojo suggests the breadth of his activities and the esteem in which he is held in diverse fields. Scientists came from Italy and Boston, joining herbalists and traditional medicine specialists, high-level martial arts practitioners, a few tough-looking guys from the neighborhood (sweeties, in fact), musicians including John Zorn, Bill Laswell, and William Parker. Parker played the African harp called *doussin gouni* most of the afternoon, while Milford sat at the tablas. We spent five hours eating, mingling, listening to them play, and enjoying stories and thoughts from the honoree.

At one point, a tall, fit man entered the hall. Milford immediately stood up and called for everyone's attention, introducing Bob Beamon. I recognized his name and asked if he was the Olympian, the one who I'd been hearing about since he broke the long jump record in the 1968 Olympics. And not just by a fraction, but by two feet. My father, who was a very good high school long jumper, had told me about him the day it happened, effusing at the dinner table. "You don't understand, we're talking about *two feet*! That is incredible. It's like he has wings on his shoes." Beamon said yes, that's who he was, and suggested that we take a picture together to show my dad, which I did.

Beamon explained how he knew Milford. "I was living in the 'hood, and even though I'm just five years younger than Milford, and he was only fifteen or sixteen himself, he set a great example for me," he said. "I was heading down the wrong path. Then one day I heard some great Afro-Cuban music coming from one of the apartment buildings. I listened from outside the door and finally mustered the courage to knock. Milford invited me in, and I sat and listened, and the discipline was very inspiring to me. I'm not a musician, but it helped me keep myself out of trouble, definitely." Beamon smiled, removing his red Adidas hat. "You could say he saved my life, and you'd probably be right."

Rumours

The front door is open, but I ring the bell anyway. Beth's voice calls from the hallway to come on in. She's sitting hip deep in a mushy brown couch, part of a living room set that curves around the room and opens onto their kitchen, which looks out onto the backyard. We are in a housing development about a mile from my house, across a big dividing road that makes it seem an even greater distance. The house is a cozy, simple two-story. Opposite Beth, on bookshelves, the stereo is blasting *Fleetwood Mac*, a favorite of ours by the recast and re-formed British blues band that had surprised the world by adding a couple of Americans and making a number-one-selling record. The Yanks were Lindsey Buckingham and his girlfriend Stevie Nicks.

"Where's Suze?" I ask.

"My sister is indisposed," says Beth, tilting her head toward the stairs with a tilt. "She has a little tummy upset. You know she's very sensitive."

"And your parents?"

"Mom's still at work. I don't know where George is, but wherever he is, I bet he's stoned."

Beth sands a crimson fingernail with a file. Her legs are tucked up under her cut-off jeans. No shoes or socks, but a delicate anklet encircles one leg, a deep plum tube top encases her upper torso, and from her neck dangles an amulet on a gold chain. Beth's lids are lightly glazed in opalescent eye shadow. She pats a spot on the couch next to her just as the doorbell rings, and Scooter yells: "Anybody home?"

He joins and we sit in a semicircle in the living room. We all three have identical haircuts, parted in the middle, feathered, medium length, in descending order of thickness from Scooter to Beth to me. Scooter's is coarse and full, Beth's straight and fine, mine even more so. Beth puts her hand behind my head and plays with my hair a little, twisting a lock onto her forefinger.

"I love this record," says Scooter. "But we've listened to it a ton. Can I put something else on?"

"All right, how about *Déjà Vu*?" says Beth, pointing at a small stack of LPs. "Or *Bad Company*?"

"Actually, I brought something." Scooter unzips his backpack and extracts a sealed LP that looks so much like *Fleetwood Mac* that at first I think that's what it is—similar black-and-white photo of two figures on white background, same elaborate font spelling out the band's name.

"I went to the mall," he says. "They'd been out of this more or less since it came out in February, but I managed to get one today. Finally!"

He hands it to Beth, who razors open the plastic wrap with one of her talons. We pass it around, first looks at a future talisman.

"Wow, check out those . . . what are they? Gonads, I guess," she says, pointing at two small globes dangling from Mick Fleetwood's crotch.

"Good eye," I say, flinching as she pretends to smack me.

"Shall we?" says Scooter, removing the other record from the turntable and replacing it with *Rumours*. We are so engrossed with the prospect of new sounds that we barely notice another person in the room, but Susie clears her throat to announce her presence.

"Hi, Susie," I say with a smile. "How you feeling?"

"Perfectly fine, why?" She shoots a glance at her sister.

"Let's listen, but after a quick smoke." Beth pops up off the couch and produces a pack of cigarettes, offering one to any takers. We all decline, Susie snubbing her nose judgmentally.

"So grown-up," she says.

"Suit yourself, more for me," says Beth.

Scooter accompanies her, the side screen door slamming behind them.

"So what did she say?"

"Just that you weren't feeling well, which was why you were upstairs."

"Beth is so manipulative. She's just afraid I'm going to steal you back from her." She gestures at the new arrival. "What's that?"

I hand Susie the record cover.

"Scoots just got it. I hear it's the best record of the year."

"The year's not really that far along yet. Shouldn't we give other records a chance?"

"Right, sure, I guess so." I fidget with the laces of my Converse low-tops, aware that she's no longer wearing the bracelet I had given her when we were going out.

"Looks promising."

Susie's soft, makeup-less features are caught in an afternoon sunbeam. We sit silently waiting for the others to return, the cat stirring from its spot nearby, nestling into her lap. It's an after-school gathering that has become like a club. The four of us, sometimes with another friend or two, sit around their living room for hours at a time, cracking jokes, listening to records, trying to decipher and interpret lyrics. Their mother is sometimes part of it, cooking while we hang out, fencing with the sisters; not so frequently, their stepfather participates. Often we are left alone to do what we want. Which is not much of anything.

When Beth and Scooter return, we drop the needle on *Rumours*. Somehow we all know it's the audition of something we'll turn to many times. We savor it. The cover is passed from person to person. Now and then someone comments, usually after a song. When "Dreams" finishes, I offer: "That's this record's 'Rhiannon.' I think I'm in love with Stevie."

"No shit, Sherlock," says Scooter. "She's hot."

"For sure," says Beth. "Not like I'm a lesbo, but I'd probably take a trip on that train."

The record continues to "Go Your Own Way." We're all looking down, nodding, eyes closed, communing with the song, as Lindsey Buckingham sings: *Tell me why / Everything turned around . . . / If I could / Baby, I'd give you my world.* Beth puts her head on my shoulder then nuzzles into my underarm. I glance up to see Susie looking my direction, then out the window. A knot in the pit of my stomach. *You can go your own way,* they sing during the chorus. I think I hear Susie quietly join: *You can call it another lonely day.*

The side ends with "Songbird," Christine McVie's stripped-down feature.

"That's a beaut," says Beth, a little while after the automatic return has shut off. "Flip it?"   . . .

Three weeks later, we are in a hillside field below a nunnery at three o'clock in the morning. We've all snuck out of our houses to meet at a point roughly equidistant between our neighborhoods, hiding in ditches and behind trees to avoid cops along the way. I'd shimmied down a piece of wood resting against the side of our house, and Scooter met me at the bottom, to receive the alcohol I'd stolen from my parents' liquor cabinet. Our friend Scotty joined us, and we skulked over to the field, where Beth was waiting for us. Susie was a sensible girl and remained fast asleep in her bed.

Beth has a tape of *Rumours* and I brought the portable Sony, packed with D batteries, so we wait for the nunnery dogs to stop barking in the distance and then crank it up. It's a mild early summer night and the sky is clear, a waxing gibbous moon lighting up the landscape. We start the festivities with side two of the record,

Buckingham singing "The Chain" with his gal pals backing him up: *Break the silence / Damn the dark / Damn the light.*

"This song is kind of a downer," says Beth. "Can you fast-forward?"

We do, and just about nail the beginning of "You Make Loving Fun," which fits the desired mood. An inexperienced drinker, I have culled from various liquor bottles, anything from port to vodka to Bailey's, combining them into a diabolical mix. Because our time out here is limited, we decide that the best plan is to guzzle the booze in a standing position, then look up at the sky and spin around. For some reason, this seems like it will not only make us dizzy but will speed up getting drunk. It does both, and we repeat it several times, falling about ourselves in peals of giddy laughter. After several spins, Beth and I fall together and fool around a bit, all lusty tongues and roving hands. In my mind I hear, *Lay me down in the tall grass and let me do my stuff,* but by then the tape is playing the Buckingham-Nicks duet "I Don't Want to Know," crisp twelve-string and hand claps a perky backdrop for warbled mediations on the ambiguities of their relationship.

After a while we all sit, arms on knees. Our buzzes have worn down to a glow. Stevie is singing "Gold Dust Woman," cowbell and slide guitar penetrating the night, her smoky voice locating the knife handle to give it a little twist. *Rulers make bad lovers,* she warns, *you better put your kingdom up for sale.* We have no idea what she means, but it seems like sound advice.

...

We don't have a category for Fleetwood Mac. They contain country, folk, pop, and rock, but they're none of these. Anyway, genre is not so important to us right now. Fleetwood Mac transcends classification to become pure, nameless emotion. Highly produced feelings. Fancy perfumes, not wildflowers. The band etches a pentagram into the sand on one dark track, tendering crystal visions and damning love and lies, offering up a theme song for optimism on another. Electric piano meets acoustic twelve-string; an indelible melody sits atop an inconsolable drone. Songs are alternately full of Appalachian twang and London fog. They span the Atlantic, amalgamating American spunk with English manners. On *Rumours*, the "u" is always there in the title, to remind us they were a British band to begin with.

The record's bedrock is Mick Fleetwood. His drumming can be precise as a metronome, but he adds counterintuitive syncopations that gently thicken the patterns. He attributes these offbeats to his dyslexia, but wherever they come from, they're integral to the record's power. When Nicks hits the word "heartbeat" on "Dreams," Fleetwood pounds a tom-tom, and when she lands on "thunder," he chimes in with a resounding cymbal crash. (No wonder they're in sync—she's in the middle of an affair with him after her breakup with Buckingham.) Those cymbals. Fleetwood smacks them so tenderly you'd think he's in love with them.

···

One evening toward the end of the summer, I am readying myself for moving away, and we gather one last time, Scooter and Beth and me. In a little woodsy area, the three of us make a pallet out of pine needles, this time fortified with beers from Scooter's dad's supply. We have the tape machine but play it quietly. Hearing the music doesn't matter by then, we know the record inside out, and the songs just sort of remind us of themselves.

They've come to symbolize that summer, those parties, afternoons in Beth and Susie's living room, and we've mapped some of our soft-core adolescent version of love-life complexity onto those ultra-fucked-up cocaine-addled superstars. I know now that my image of Beth, which was about to transform from one based in observation to one based on memory alone, would merge forever with Nicks, the gauzy, dangerous one who projected raging confidence but was so deeply insecure. And Susie embodied something of the gentility I heard in Christine McVie's voice, which was bright and clear but also a little sad. Or so I remember thinking.

We watch Beth smoke a couple of cigarettes, finishing the first beers.

"Hey, give me that empty," she says. "Let's play spin the bottle."

She starts and lands on Scooter. I watch as they make out a little, strangely free of jealousy. Now it's my turn, and I, too, land on my friend.

"I love ya, man, but not tonight," I say, and lean over to smooch my girlfriend instead, tasting smoke and hops. For a half an hour, we continue like this, Beth alternately kissing me and him. Then Beth says she's got to go home. I give her a squeeze, and Scooter and I pack up the bottles, toting them across the big hill, one song running through my head: *She broke down and let me in / Made me see where I've been / Been down one time / Been down two times / I'm never going back again.* Scooter helps me shimmy up the plank onto my porch. I look down at him, flash a thumbs-up, slip into the house, and hit the sack.   . . .

I know now that the Spinners had it right when they sang of bowing out gracefully. Only I always heard it as *bow-wow*, not *bow out*, so to me it meant something else.

"Sit and stay," a distant voice commands. "Good boy!"

Sometimes, even when everything is hunky-dory and mouths are but smiles, the stars in the clear sky twinkle and life couldn't get any sweeter, you have to cut and run, hit the highway, no forwarding address, no hope for protraction. And anyway, when your parents tell you you're moving again, you have no choice.

Ted Nugent

Cat Scratch Fever

Three boys are hanging out in the upstairs bedroom of a suburban house. The tallest, whose teeth are braced in silver, is also the
quietest, but it's his room so he's the one who puts on some music.
The next tallest is well-built, his body tanned and toned from the
swim club. The third is compact. His hair is golden and parted in
the middle, and it cascades over his ears to his T-shirt collar.

The needle drops onto Ted Nugent's new record, a current favorite of this triumvirate. The first sound comes from the title track,
built of power chords and bad attitude, lifting the tall one to stand
erect and leave his perch on the unmade bed. Swiveling his head,
he looks one way, looks the other, then starts to walk. His shoulders
slump, his head dips, his feet drag.

He's doing a pimp strut.

He's not sure what a pimp is.

He is thirteen.

The song bursts into action and the trio is on top of it, the short
one leaping atop the mattress, bouncing in rhythm to the thunderous sound pummeling the little speakers. At the guitar solo, all
three lock into air guitar stance, their faces grimace, right hands
dropped low, feigning rapid-fire picking, left hands maniacally
kinetic, matching each note of the solo.

Braces: "Hey, numb nuts, what are you doing?"

The three slacken to a halt like they've run out of battery while the music blares on.

Biceps: "Who do you mean?"

Braces, to Hairdo: "You. You're doing it wrong."

Hairdo: "What are you talking about? I was totally into it!"

Braces: "But you were going the wrong way. When the guitar notes are getting higher, your hand has to move toward you, not away. The way you were going, the notes would be getting *lower.* Nobody goes lower in a guitar solo!"

Biceps: "He's right. You don't go down if the guitar solo is going up. Anybody knows that."

Braces: "Let's go easy on him. Remember his condition."

Biceps: "What condition?"

Braces: "Terminal spaz."

Hairdo: "Dickwads."

The tall one lifts the tonearm and moves it to another track.

"Are you ready for 'Wang Dang Sweet Poontang'?"

"Hit me," says the medium one. "Hit me hard!"

Pantomime begins again as the Nuge starts soloing. Small one, careful not to go the wrong direction, dives into the center down on his knees for all to see.

They don't know what poontang is either.

...

The significance of most of Ted Nugent's significations was lost on me. The headband, the bird feathers dangling from his shirtsleeves, the animal teeth on his necklace, his leather wristbands, his fur boots, the shaggy goatee and muttonchops, the fact that he played a Gibson Byrdland, a hollow-body guitar normally heard in jazz, not hard rock. He was fancy enough that I thought he might have something to do with glam.

Now I see that he was made up as a backwoods Michigan badass. These are the baseball-cap-forward guys in dust-covered pickups with nude-girl mud flaps and gun racks. There are normally lots of guns around because they all shoot animals for pleasure from the safety of a blind. Nugent has a penchant for hunting without ballistics, by means of bow and arrow. Not that he's against firearms. He sits on the board of the NRA. He also runs Kamp for Kids, an outdoors experience where he makes a personal appearance "to present the kids with an upbeat pro-hunting, anti-drug lecture and musical appearance." In the Kamp's PR, all the kids are cradling rifles.

I appreciate the wilderness positivity and Nugent's message of wildlife conservation, and I am also deep under the spell of Michigan's natural beauty, its starkness and hardness, especially in the Upper Peninsula, where Wisconsin cedes territory to its rival state. As for his focus on animals, all good, except I don't see why you have to kill them. Overpopulated deer, for sure. No ethical objection at all. But there's something fundamentally creepy about the connection between the words "thrill" and "hunt," the quest for "adrenaline dump"—his words—in the act of shooting a creature. In any case, this is the least of the creepy. Nugent is outspokenly anti-Islamic, homophobic, and called Barack Obama a "subhuman mongrel." And he has repeatedly made anti-Semitic comments, suggesting on Facebook that Jews are the dark force behind gun control. If so, more power to them.

Heavy rock was sometimes conceived explicitly in terms of war sounds—Jimi Hendrix's "Machine Gun" transforms the Stratocaster into a military sound-effects generator, and Black Sabbath inserted an air-raid siren at the end of "War Pigs" to amplify the song's bleak intensity. Combining the two, Blue Öyster Cult's "ME 262," named for a German staple of the Luftwaffe, substituted civil defense siren sounds for a guitar solo.

When it comes to Nugent, he titled one song "Stormtroopin'," adding the funky apostrophe to his ode to assault troops to give it a jazzy twist. This dumb affectation of biker lingo and Nazi iconography dovetailed thoughtlessly with our adolescent interest in WWII ephemera, though its true pea-brain-ness has revealed itself over time. When I brought the tour brochure home from a Cat Scratch Fever concert in 1977, I delved into it and one turn of phrase jumped out at me. I figured it was the work of some dim-witted promotions person, but now I wonder who described Nugent's guitar soloing as "Ted's holocaust lead." Even then, equipped with an underdeveloped conscience, I knew that comparing the stylings of a guitarist to an act of genocide was abominable.

...

Most of what I want to say about that concert has to do with the opening band.

To set the moral: on his LP *Comedy Minus One*, comedian Albert Brooks tells a story about being the opening act at a gig in Texas. The headliner was Richie Havens. Sometime before Brooks's slot, the audience started chanting "Richie, Richie, Richie!" Brooks mustered his courage and headed toward the stage, but a guy sitting at the edge stopped him.

"Your name Richie?" he said.

"No," replied Brooks.

"They're gonna kill you."

Now to Nugent: at the Philadelphia Spectrum that July evening, a capacity audience of twenty thousand was on hand to hear the Motor City Madman ply his special brand of heavy mania. My best friend Scooter Johns and I were celebrating my imminent departure from Philly, though if we'd managed to catch the performance six months earlier, we'd have been treated to a double bill with Black Sabbath, alas. We'd been fans of the Nuge for a few years, were familiar with the songs from several records, and couldn't wait to hear him rock out.

But first, there was Starz.

I already knew Starz because I'd bought one of their records based strictly on the symmetrical power of their insignia, a proud star form standing tall, wrapped in a circle and trailing stripes like it was wearing them as a cape. Starz had a minor hit that spring with "Cherry Baby," from their record *Violation*, which we liked pretty much. I didn't know it at the time, but they had the same manager as Kiss and their record was produced by Jack Douglas, who had worked on our favorite Aerosmith LPs. Starz figured they were part of the big happy heavy metal family. (We had no idea that they had once been Looking Glass, whose "Brandy (You're a Fine Girl)" was a soft rock smash in 1972. A lyric about a sailor who can't marry a girl because he's too in love with the sea. Good thing we didn't know. We hated that song.)

There was no palpable electricity in the air when the houselights dimmed. For some reason, they didn't bring them all the way down, which made the band come out into a sort of half-lit room, perhaps confusing the crowd. Oblivious to this, Starz was primed and ready to slay. Lost in curls and chest hair, gold chains and double-necked guitars, they swaggered onto the stage, singer Michael Lee Smith twisting the microphone cable around his arm à la Steven Tyler, staggering like a Mick Jagger understudy. There were smoke machines, roving spots, and flash pots, all slightly undermined by the penumbral light.

The audience was unresponsive. Dead. Cries of "How y'all feeling?" went unanswered. The more the band flailed around, the less welcome was their flailing. They were pathetic. Guitars were publicly tortured. The drummer twisted the ends of his ridiculous handlebar mustache. The bassist all but exploded in quarter notes, to no avail. But Starz didn't seem to take it personally. They had a job to do, to give the people the best pop-metal experience of their lives, and they were gonna do it. The most excruciating passages from Spinal Tap might have been cribbed from this concert. The band thought it was positively on fire, and meanwhile the audience was growing openly hostile. It was a full-fledged standoff.

Smith retired to the wings, dragging something huge back onstage—a cock-shaped balloon perhaps twenty feet long. The band soldiered on, thinking, "This is it, we'll get them with our special effects, no worries." With help from his guitarists, the singer placed the huge prosthesis in his crotch, pointing it outward, waving it back and forth mirthfully. Nobody made a noise; there was not one shard of appreciation for their swank waggery. Then, unexpectedly, at a predetermined moment timed to some crescendo in one of the songs, the tip of the balloon exploded, shooting foam all over the first five rows. This time the crowd did respond, but rather than shouts of rapturous excitement, there issued forth a stream of boos so damning that after a short while, the balloon a shred of rubber, Starz left the stage for good.

...

How was Ted Nugent? From the cheap seats, he looked tiny on the big stage, even with his large black guitar and matching wristbands. There was a rash of bomb-potency fireworks being launched into stadium concert audiences at the time. Their terrifying detonation was a constant distraction, and we peered over our shoulders afraid that one M80 would cost us our hearing. We should have wondered the same about the sound coming from the stage, which was beyond loud. We measured a concert's amplitude by how many days it took for the ringing to subside. This time it took five. We had never gone more than three.

The Nuge was suitably wild. He played the songs we wanted, including the three-chord rave "Cat Scratch Fever," what we understood as its logical counterpart, "Dog Eat Dog," the libertarian litany "Free-for-All," "Stranglehold," "Wang Dang Sweet Poontang," and other songs we didn't know, including "Snakeskin Cowboys." That was from his eponymous solo debut, for which we hadn't yet ponied up. His soloing was indulgent in the way we liked, and he made lewd comments between songs, some directed at women in the first rows, who were still drying off from the Starz money shot.

Anticipating encores, we headed from the bleachers down to the floor, occupying a vantage from which we could better gauge Nugent's stage behavior. He struck poses that we duly memorized, shaking his mid-back-length mane of hair in a distinctly ladylike way. He was wearing white tights and was shirtless. Leaning back to the point of falling over, he went down on his knees, then upright he struck poses as if he was sliding into second base, gritting his teeth and pointing the Gibson headstock like he was aiming a shotgun or maybe a crossbow. He flicked guitar picks into the audience at random intervals. I caught one of the black plectra, which had his name engraved in gold on its side.

...

Decades later, en route from Detroit home to Chicago, my friend Jim Dempsey, also a childhood Nugent fan, spent an afternoon at Ted Nugent Adventure Outdoors. I will leave it for you to convince Dempsey to spin the whole story, well worth the effort, but at the end of the visit, Nugent was chatting with Jim and his friends, and he casually dropped the word "nigger" into his spiel. Sensing their discomfort, he leaned in for a conspiratorial whisper: "You know why I can say that word? Because *I'm* a nigger!"

Jim and pals beat a hasty retreat, youthful fantasies dashed, any residual hero worship sputtering like the balloon in Michael Lee Smith's groin. When somebody says something like that, I have no idea what they mean. And I don't want to know what they mean, no matter whether they're Norman Mailer, Patti Smith, a homeless guy on the bus, or Ted "Journey to the Center of Your Mind" Nugent.

When we grow up, what we learn about someone like Nugent we learn about ourselves—how much intolerable crap we had to overlook in order to get our rocks off. One of our cartoonish idols turns out to be OK, another is a sad, scary right-wing lunatic. I had thought he might be glam—little did I know he was a raging homophobe. Ten years earlier, Nugent and Iggy Pop occupied a similar bandwidth of wildness. Who could tell the difference between the psycho and the freak? Not much separated them, but as their fellow Michigander George Clinton once put it, paraphrasing Chesterfield cigarettes, that's a killer millimeter.

The Clash

The seventies were many things. But they were many things divided into two: before and after punk.

We could be talking about the Sex Pistols, with their startling mix of nihilism and power pop. Or the Damned, a superior act with a sense of humor, great songs, and a vampire. Or Stiff Little Fingers, the ballistic Northern Irish band. We might have settled on any of the other big-time OG punk groups. But we haven't. We've chosen the Clash.

I bought *The Clash* on the same day that I did Wire's *Chairs Missing*. BJ's Records was in its first location in a cargo container building on the edge of the outdoor pedestrian mall in downtown Iowa City. BJ's was tiny and packed, neat and well stocked. They obtained new imports early, a few months after they'd been released in the UK. It was September 1978, and the Wire record had just been issued. The Clash LP had been out for a year, but their second was still a few months from hitting the shelves. I'd been reading about them in *New Musical Express*, which I bought from a drugstore around the corner from BJ's. As with the records, *New Musical Express* and *Melody Maker* came my way about two weeks off date. I felt like I was living in London vicariously and in an alternate time frame, experiencing it all remotely, in print, and a little delayed.

I'd been following the Clash. I read reports of their Complete Control tour with Richard Hell and the Voidoids, perused reviews of their first single, "White Riot," and the eventful tour that bore the same name, and scanned write-ups of the full-length LP, all of it tantalizing. None of the record stores in town had managed to bring in the LP, which only heightened its desirability. I remember walking into BJ's and spying it immediately against the back wall, to one side of the rock stacks, in the new releases bin. A jolt hit my brain—the joy button had been pushed—and I grabbed the single copy of *The Clash* fast, as if someone else would rush in and snatch it away. Although I already had *Never Mind the Bollocks* and a few other punk and post-punk pieces in my collection, something about this one seemed mandatory and acute. A secret was about to be revealed, something dating back to a TV news report I'd seen on punk just before we left Philadelphia in 1977.

As a rule, imported records were more expensive than American productions. To my adroit little hands, they felt finer, more elegantly constructed out of better materials, including thinner cardboard, rough on the inside and smooth on the exterior. Domestic LPs seemed chunky in comparison, rough and disposable, like they were made of packing material. The British ones were more like precious small-press poetry books, their seams meeting in ingenious places, their inner sleeves coated in a waxy film that made them slip in and out as if they were made of silicone. Sometimes import inner sleeves even had a thin plastic liner, to protect the vinyl, or they were board stock, slightly lighter weight than the outside cover, and had the lyrics or other messages printed on them. I could imagine the person on the assembly line putting together my copy of *The Clash*. I pretended that while they were carefully folding and gluing, they had the record's purchaser, me specifically, in mind.

Although I listened to punk, I never dressed the part. There were perhaps two or three full-fledged fashion-plate punks in town, one that teased up a stellar Technicolor Mohawk, wore a safety pin in his nose, and moon-stomped around in black Doc Martens. Meanwhile, I looked more like a soft-rock dude, more Eagles than Adverts, with feathered hair and a favorite T-shirt from my first job, "Pulling for Funk's," which referred to detasseling corn (I liked the musical reference to funk, though it was actually the name of the hybrid corn company), and another from my soccer team, the Iowa City Kickers. I guess that was sort of British, but it was also the only sport I really wanted to play.

The members of the Clash were fashionistas. They carefully crafted their image to emit a waft of volatility. In the gritty black-and-white images on the cover, the band marauded, staring unsmiling at the camera, suspects in a lineup; the staged photos were made to seem documentary. I loved the olive green of the cover and the violent orange of the CBS Records inner label. The Clash's music was taut, choppy, just as I'd imagined it might be, and when a track ended, it was so abrupt it caught you off guard. But that explosive power was offset by a premeditated style that you could detect. Great as their music was, they seemed like poseurs.

I was attracted to the political dimension of their lyrics, and all reports suggested that the band was actually cool and supportive and helped out fledgling groups like the Slits. That's a real political stand, quite unusual in the punk world, where respect for others meant you had to care, and caring, for most of them, wasn't cool. In this arena—providing a leg up when they got some traction rather than kicking their colleagues in the face—I gave the Clash points. Nonetheless, something in their mussed-up pretty-boy stance never quite sat right with me. When Joe Strummer sang *I'm so bored with the U.S.A.*—a fascinating sentiment to which I could certainly relate, and a great song—their rockabilly affectations and sleeveless tees seemed to suggest something else, maybe the opposite. I didn't quite trust them.

In spite of being dubious of the Clash, I loved *The Clash*. I think in part because "White Riot" was so unlike anything I knew. It was stiff and brash and totally un-groovy, turning an uptight beat into a positive attribute. With bassist Paul Simonon's popping octaves and drummer Terry Chimes's chugging 2/4, it would make a nice polka.

The Clash made no bones about being white—really, really white, especially in the rhythm department. Musically, they embraced their whiteness, without anything supremacist about it. This set them apart from many Caucasian bands of the day, who in one way or another mooched off black music. I think of Robert Palmer, whose whole shtick was doing covers of soul and R&B songs, or white soulster Boz Scaggs, whose "Lowdown" bubbled with slap bass. The lyrics to "White Riot," written after Strummer and Simonon were involved in the racially charged upheaval at Notting Hill Carnival in 1976, trade musical jealousy for activist jealousy. *Black man got a lot of problems / But they don't mind throwing a brick / White people go to school / Where they teach you how to be thick.* Of course we know that thickness doesn't keep skinheads from throwing bricks. Anyhow the point was made. Their visual aura seemed contrived, but the Clash's glaring admission of whiteness, which was evident in most of their pogo-stick songs, struck me as unusually honest.

I also dug *The Clash* because there was one different song: "Police and Thieves." This track attracted me for a reason that contradicted the other one. The firebug-thug quality of most of the album's songs was one thing, and this song had that too, snarling intensity and working-class bluntness, but it had something else, a dreaminess, perhaps a fantasy of being elsewhere, somewhere relaxed, where singing about corruption was done through a smile. Grin across face, outlaw revolutionary, well stoned. Tucking into all the barricaded streets on the Clash's blue-collar stage set, I found that momentary intimation of dreamtime brilliant. The little falsetto "oh yeah" choir, for one, was an endearing curveball, a delicate touch amid the tough-guy posturing. And there were some dub elements in the song's arrangement, like an echoed-out guitar chord in the early going, sudden reduction to bass alone (executed not by engineering, but by all the bandmates sitting out), and even some gratuitous panning of Strummer's sandpapery voice. It paid homage to reggae, to the ghosts of early mixology, but it retained its integrity as the Clash.

Junior Murvin was unknown to me. His vulnerable high alto filtered Smokey Robinson through a cloud of spliff smoke. When I heard his version of "Police and Thieves," I decided the Clash were horseshit. They'd stolen the best parts from Murvin, tried to make them seem original. The weird scatting, the "oh yeah," which in the Murvin original is delayed a tad and set off in the mix, sounds like little mice singing background, a classic twist added by producer Lee "Scratch" Perry, another deeper humming choir adding more texture in the rich Black Ark recipe. What makes the song tick is the juxtaposition of Murvin's honey-sweet voice and the safety-off sentiment of the words.

> *All the crimes committed day by day*
> *No one tried to stop it in any way*
> *All the peacemakers-turned-war-officers*
> *Hear what I say, hey*
> *Police and thieves in the street (oh yeah)*
> *Fighting the nation with their guns and ammunition*
> *Police and thieves in the street (oh yeah)*
> *Scaring the nation with their guns and ammunition*

I kept listening to the Clash's version even after my bubble had been burst, and gradually I came back to my earlier position, hearing the song for what it was. It was more of its own thing than I'd given it credit for. In fact, the way they'd turned it into their own song grew more exciting the more I listened. The significance of a frontline punk band playing "White Riot" and "Police and Thieves" on the same LP began to sink in. It was a statement of alliance. We don't have to be identical to admire and respect one another, it said.

The knee-jerk frisson created by white acts playing black music had been familiar since the fifties—think of Pat Boone mauling Fats Domino or Elvis Presley softening Arthur "Big Boy" Crudup— and it was already the basis of decades of outright theft and other approaches to economic exploitation. Listening more carefully, I heard that the Clash weren't vainly trying to sound like Junior

Murvin, but seemed to be paying homage: white musicians—pasty doughboy white musicians—inspired by black music. The difference between the two versions was exactly the point, a critical distance that was also a mark of reverence. In that sense, they were not too distant from Led Zeppelin, a comparison I'm sure would have chafed like the dickens. The Clash weren't after a doomed shot at authenticity; theirs was an act of transubstantiation.

As a listener, I must confess to having discovered more than one great black original through a white cover. Some of them are embarrassing. I did know Otis Redding's famous version of "(Sittin' on) The Dock of the Bay" when I heard a British group called Thursdays cover it on a Fast Records compilation called *Earcom* in 1979 (which also featured a yet unknown band called Joy Division). But Soft Cell's take on "Tainted Love"—how could I have missed the wonderful Gloria Jones version? Blondie's "The Tide Is High," originally by the Paragons? The Slits doing Marvin Gaye's "I Heard It Through the Grapevine"? Talking Heads covering Al Green's "Take Me to the River"? Even "Black and White," initially a top-ten hit in the UK by the British reggae band the Greyhound, known to me only as being by Three Dog Night? Then again, race aside, I should mention that I found out about Leonard Bernstein's *West Side Story* via Alice Cooper. The holes in my knowledge could fill Albert Hall—a venue I learned about through the Beatles. Cultural literacy was a game of connect the dots, where ignorance of origins is broadcast time and again.

In the long run, to me *The Clash* is a record about being white, what it means to be white, and what it meant to be white and British in 1977. It's a solid rock 'n' roll record, but it's got little of the poisonous intensity of Johnny Rotten, who would go on to make his own extraordinary kind of bridge to reggae with Public Image Ltd. I'd seen a photograph of Rotten in Jamaica with Big Youth, which was a surprise to a Pistols fan. (More surprising later to discover Rotten was doing A&R work for Richard Branson's Virgin label, which had a newly minted "Front Line" series of reggae records, and that he signed the great Prince Far I, who would subsequently issue the vicious rebuke of Branson titled "Virgin.") PiL's *Metal Box* came packaged in an aluminum film canister. Its three twelve-inch records were 45 rpm, but I didn't realize that at first and listened to them at 33 rpm a few times before figuring it out; the dub infusions were even more hypnotic and mind-expanding when slowed down. Listen to "Poptones"—a horrific ditty about a murder scene, the victim hunched in a car with the radio still playing. This is not music about whiteness or blackness; it's some new sort of confabulation, a place where punks don't just proclaim their respectful difference but throw it all into a pot and put it on simmer.

PiL's post-punk was something new. To my ears, it was more convincing than *Sandinista!* would be, or Big Audio Dynamite. It didn't transcend race, but neither did it reify racial categories. And lots of British musicians in the late seventies had the same notion, bringing together punk and reggae, punk and dub, punk and soul, punk and funk: The Pop Group's "Thief of Fire," A Certain Ratio's "Do the Du (Casse)," The Slits' "In the Beginning There Was Rhythm." In 1979 an influential Southern California band called the Urinals issued their sophomore EP with a song on it titled "I'm White and Middle Class," adding another dimension to the Clash's race confession.

…

Lee Perry heard the Clash's version of "Police and Thieves." He played it for Bob Marley, who responded by recording a song of his own, "Punky Reggae Party," released in 1978 on *Babylon by Bus*. Consider the act of celebratory reciprocity:

> It's a punky reggae party
> And it's alright
> What did you say?
> Rejected by society (do re mi fa)
> Treated with impunity (so la te do)
> Protected by their dignity (do re mi fa)
> I search reality (so la te do)

New wave, new craze
New wave, new wave, new phrase

Now I'm saying the Wailers will be there
The Damned, The Jam, The Clash
Maytals will be there
Doctor Feelgood too, ooh
No boring old farts
No boring old farts
No boring old farts
Will be there

In the long run, what reggae and punk share is not only their respective subcultural affirmations—that they provide a voice for marginalized, subjugated, and disaffected people—but perhaps equally their ability to make those afflictions into a posture, a style, a pose. I remember seeing Black Uhuru in the early eighties; they were five hours late, unapologetic, callous, and their disdain for the overly patient and fawning audience lent a shallow sensibility to their songs of righteousness. That's the same rock star bullshit that always emanated from the Clash, just as it did from the Rolling Stones—something ultimately cashing in on an image of rebelliousness, armchair hardcore, never really putting up or shutting up, just strutting around like the world should kiss their ass, more fashion runway than political rally, a slideshow of sugarcane cutters projected on the walls of an art museum.

David Bowie

Low

Count to ten and say "art rock."

1) Our common method of insult deflection: *I know you are, but what am I?*

2) David Bowie said: *I am a clean slate. I am whatever and whoever I imagine myself to be. I am a chameleon.*

3) Old World chameleons are my favorite lizards. When I was four, my parents gave me one, purchased at the exotic pet shop somewhere in Rhode Island. We induced it to change colors, shining the terrarium lamp on it from above while shading half its body so it turned bicolor lime green and dark brown, then placing a warming light behind a piece of pegboard, which gave it a uniform of spots, like it had chicken pox. The animal's domed eyes were beautiful devices that moved independently like little turrets, one looking forward at me, the other cast down scanning for prey. I watched it hunt—sloth-like motion along a branch, grasping with bifurcated toe, fixing on a mealworm or cricket, growing perfectly still, darting its pink tongue like a spear, retracting the insect into its otherwise stoic mouth. To me, the chameleon was both human and reptilian, capable of emotional expression yet impassive and cold-blooded.

4) Major Tom, Ziggy Stardust, Aladdin Sane, the Thin White Duke, the New Romantic—made-up characters, slippery sexualities, cultural hybrids. From 1974's *Diamond Dogs* until halfway through college, when I saw him on the Let's Dance tour, Bowie was the ever-shifting through line of my youth. We expected him to change, but we depended on him to be there. His affectations were romantic fodder. As vain and narcissistic as Egon Schiele, the artist who melodramatically depicted himself as Saint Sebastian during his brief imprisonment for pedophilia, but less dark than lovelorn Richard Gerstl—who burned all his personal effects including most of his works on paper before the artist watched himself in a mirror stab and hang himself to death— Bowie wouldn't martyr or kill himself, only his characters. He was always on our minds, as éminence grise and figurehead, heroic to glam and punk, the next great ambassador of style and substance from the underground to the general public after the Beatles.

5) The best record of the best period of Bowie's many periods, *Low* is his high point. The first of his Berlin Trilogy, recorded after he'd left L.A. for the bleakness and anonymity of the German metropolis, it finds him uniting with Brian Eno, whose influence is undeniable, continuing the fruitful relationship with rhythm guitarist Carlos Alomar, deploying Iggy Pop, who shouts marvelously on one track, and working with producer Tony Visconti. I think of it as Bowie's J. G. Ballard record, no doubt because of the song "Always Crashing in the Same Car," a reference to the writer's dystopian novel *Crash*, but also because of the synthetic atmosphere in which he seems capable of emotional expression and yet is impassive and cold-blooded.

6) Visconti used an Eventide Harmonizer H910 on the drums, combined with a gate on the snare, souring each thwack, perversely turning Dennis Davis's powerhouse hits into a detuned electronic beat box. The producer famously gushed about the newly marketed effect to Bowie and Eno: "It fucks with the fabric of time!" The drum sound is part of what gives the record its

unique ambience, the future sound of new wave, a reptilian quality that haunted my first trip to Berlin, years later, as if all percussive noises in the city would be pitch-shifted, as if all its residents hid their scales under trench coats, as if their bulbous eyes would be trained on you and looking for prey both at once.

7) Yes, in fact, I do wonder sometimes 'bout sound and vision. Much of the time, truth be told. I remember hearing that lyric and thinking: how pleasant of him to ask, even rhetorically, whether I see and hear things like he does, what a caring gesture, the query posed in harmony with Eno, who delivers another reptilian performance, recalling the title "Sombre Reptiles" from *Another Green World*. Bowie's record presents another gray world: *Pale blinds drawn all day / Nothing to do, nothing to say.*

8) The first side is the pop side. Short tracks with song form and drum drive.

9) Side two is the art side. Nearly wordless dreamscapes floating cloud-like, in spirit close to Eno's duets with Robert Fripp. Withered flowers in cracked pavement, "Warszawa," homage to the people of the Eastern Bloc, a snatch of Polish folk music in ambient aspic. On the final track, "Subterraneans," he used the cut-up technique of William Burroughs and Brion Gysin to assemble a beautiful, cryptic lyric: *Share bride failing star / Care-line / Care-line / Care-line / Care-line riding me / Shirley, Shirley, Shirley, own / Share bride failing star.*

10) Bowie was not just a chameleon because he assumed new identities. He had a saurian presence.

Suicide

Baseline buzz baseline buzz

...

Ay-y-y-y-Y-Y-Y-Y-y-y-y-y! No guitars, no basssssss, no drumsssssss, jusssssssssssst Martin Rev rocking cheesy commercial-grade keyboard and Alan Vega on microphone and an endless chain of variationsssssssss on boomerangingingingingingingng echo. Repetition, rapid diction, incantation, tin can station, *wow-w-w-w-w-w-w-w-w-w!*

...

Throb and hisssss throb and hisssss throb and hisssss throb and
hisssss throb and hisssss throb and hisssss throb and hisssss throb
and hisssss throb and hisssss throb and hisssss throb and hisssss
throb and hisssss throb and hisssss throb and hisssss throb and
hisssss throb and hisssss throb and hisssss throb and hisssss throb
and hisssss throb and hisssss throb and hisssss throb and hisssss
throb and hisssss throb and hisssss throb and hisssss throb and
hisssss throb and hisssss throb and hisssss throb and hisssss throb
and hisssss throb and hisssss throb and hisssss throb and hisssss
throb and hisssss throb and hisssss throb and hisssss throb and
hisssss throb and hisssss throb and hisssss throb and hisssss throb
and hisssss throb and hisssss throb and hisssss throb and hisssss
throb and hisssss throb and hisssss throb and hisssss

...

Mumble, mumble, mumble. *Woo-o-o-o-o-o-o-o-o-o-o-o!* Reduc-
tio ad absurdum rock with roots in the fifties, out-Spectoring Phil,
out-Vincenting Gene. That's why Springsteen covered their "Dream
Baby Dream," drawing out its romantic anthemic qualities—Bruce
and Martin and Alan have greaser instincts, upturned collars, jean
jackets, leather pants. Drum machine preset burble, one or two
chords droning, herk and jerk of words ejaculated over pulsing syn-
thpunk backdrop, a soundscape facial. Mumble, mumble, mumble.
Aaaaaaaaaaaaaay!

Doug and me attentive in my room. I brought *Suicide* home
thinking the red star meant politics and the name and bloodstain
meant metal. Nope-*ope-ope-ope-ope*. New York street music disco
carnage, Giorgio Moroder busted face on pavement, proto-glam with
whisper-scream vocal and keyboard stuck in first gear, revving, so
stripped down and fucked up we couldn't peg it, had no coordinates,
were without a clue. We didn't know these were the first punks to
call it that, little as it had to do with what we thought of as punk,

knowing as little as we did, knowing so little but feeling so much. Their punk was more than thud, crash, and bellow; their punk was smeared with a paste of pure irony; their punk was an aneurysm in rock's basilar artery. *Ghost rider, baby baby baby baby he's telling the truth / America, America is killing its youth*, Vega sings, then sends a *whoop* into the abyss like a pebble down a well. No idea what to make of it. So reduced. So repetitive. So stylish. Dinky li'l organ melody on "Rocket USA," a fill like in the breaks at the ballpark or roller rink, on a doomsday song about 1977. "Johnny"—rolling five-note bass ostinato, fay postures and tuff stances, two voices saying different things at the same time, confusing, generally untrustworthy. The elegant love song "Cheree." And politics of a sort, wrapped up in a song called "Che," less historical lesson than psychotropic intensity of martyrdom: *Said he was a saint / But I know he ain't.*

...

I'm a goin' and a comin' I'm a goin' and a comin'

...

"I like it," I told Doug.

"I don't," he told me.

We put on side two and sat through "Frankie Teardrop," the merciless murder-suicide ballad with hissing accompaniment. I literally jumped when, in narrating the twenty-year-old Frankie's desperate final act, Vega screeches, either reliving the scream of Frankie's six-month-old or his horrified wife as she takes the bullet: *Aaaayyyyyyyyyy!*

"Holy mother of shit," I said. "That's as messed up as Cronenberg's *Rabid*. I think I'm gonna stick to side one."

"I'm gonna avoid it altogether," Doug replied. "Just to be safe."

Joe McPhee

Tenor

Somewhere in the Swiss countryside in September 1976, in a cha-
let belonging to the cellist Michael Overhage, without professional
equipment, direct to cassette tape, Joe McPhee recorded one of the
landmark solo saxophone recitals in the history of creative music.
Swinging a microphone over a rafter, in front of a few friends with
whom he'd just eaten dinner and had a few drinks, including both
his record producers Craig Johnson and Werner X. Uehlinger,
McPhee wended his way across four pieces, three of them simple,
bluesy melodies he'd been working on for an upcoming solo project,
patiently unfurling their contents, opening them up and improvising away from and then back to the tunes, the final piece long and
spacious and without a theme.

In this period, improvising musicians often felt the urge to
expand their instrumentarium, playing all the related instruments
of a family, following the lead of people like Eric Dolphy, Ken McIn-
tyre, and Yusef Lateef; or branching out and embracing anything
they could coax into sound making, like the Art Ensemble of Chicago
did with their tables of so-called little instruments—whizbangs,
scrapers, gongs, slide whistles, electric guitars, and police sirens.
On *Tenor*, McPhee the multi-instrumentalist restricted his instru-

mentation. For an afternoon, the Poughkeepsie-based independent left the pocket trumpet in its case, likewise soprano and alto saxophones, and the valve trombone he'd inherited from Clifford Thornton.

Anthony Braxton had followed the same procedure on a landmark double LP called *For Alto* in 1969, which was something of a gauntlet for reed players in the seventies. McPhee picked it up almost without realizing he was doing it, on a record made by accident, a private performance, somewhere between practicing, rehearsal, and a concert.

On one side of the LP, McPhee weaves his way through "Knox," a lullaby in twelve-bar blues form; the economical "Sweet Dragon," which sprouts cascades of slurring sound like a spider plant; and the elegiac "Good-Bye Tom B," a theme with its own little internal call and response, McPhee feeling around for the bottom of the tenor's deep pool, injecting his voice into the already highly vocal saxophone, like Dewey Redman before him, but chewier, more ductile and melancholic. The title track is a twenty-three-minute exercise in turning oxygen into emotion, an open letter to Albert Ayler, and an almost direct communion with the universe, from the depths of McPhee's thirty-seven-year-old heart.

...

A common conception of the function of music is that it is meant to communicate with others, that it comes from an urge to express so that fellow humans can feel what the musician feels. This impulse is familiar. And no doubt in the main it is true: people make music for each other. We recognize the magnetic way that music calls forth a community. But there's another way to understand musical desire: imagine that it comes from a very private place, not to be in conversation with others but as a means of meditating on one's own situation. To frame it as an act of intimacy is perhaps not enough. It can be hermetic. A way to commune with the walls, to depth sound the ceiling, to feel oneself exhaling and inhaling, to measure existence in terms of what sound it makes, and not to do it for anybody else, but just to do it, alone, without concern for aesthetic quality, communicative value, or popular success. It is no wonder that McPhee was such close friends with experimental composer and musician Pauline Oliveros, whose Deep Listening Band made a habit of this kind of music.

The crudeness of the recording does not dim *Tenor*'s sheer questing authority. In fact it intensifies the record's solitary quality, the feeling of not playing *toward* anyone; McPhee's sound emanates into the atmosphere, more like a radio wave or the silent spirit of trees or the gentle ambience of a brook, not designed to show someone something but also not without a magnificent gravitational force. Reflected in the tarnished gold of his Selmer bell, you can hear the dark interior of the day.

Little Queen

"Remember: Aunt Vi's frozen egg noodles are *the best*!"

Those words, inscribed in the front of my 1978 Heart tour brochure, have always carried a vaguely sexual tinge for me. I think they were an inside joke from my girlfriend, perhaps something ribald, but time has robbed me of that meaning. Ceil Miller, the inscriber, would soon break off our summer-long fling because she did not want a long-distance relationship. As she explained, we were graduating from junior high to high school. I was headed to West High, she to City High. We would have been about two miles apart.

As the summer wrapped, we made the two-hour trek with Ceil's parents to Des Moines for a concert by Heart. They were playing at the Iowa State Fair. It was a beautiful day, the sun beginning to shift its angle, signaling the start of autumn, cornfields finished yielding their crops and turning colors right out of a Grant Wood painting, the smell of pig shit a constant and not unwelcome ambient aroma as we drove due west along I-80. I had a premonition that, as far as Ceil and I were concerned, the end was nigh, so the trip was already a little forlorn, but also strangely titillating, as we covertly held hands in the backseat, avoiding the occasional glance of her father.

At home in Iowa City, where he was chief of police, Ceil's dad had made it clear that although he approved of me, he thought things should proceed at a proper pace with his daughter. Thankfully, he never caught me sneaking her out of their house at midnight to go partying in the dark—I recall the first time she descended from her window to my shoulders and then the ground, pointing up at a bedroom window and whispering: "Shhh, he's right up there . . . and he has a gun!" I fear I might have gone to jail if he'd found us doing any of the other less properly paced things that we did, often outdoors, once at a cemetery.

Hitting the fairgrounds, we shucked Ceil's folks and headed to the livestock pens for a look at the cows and sheep, procuring some much-needed funnel cakes before heading to the concert area. A smaller-than-expected stage in the open air faced a bank of stadium-style bleachers. I had already seen Heart once and would see them twice again, not because I was a superfan, but because the timing was right. The first time, TKO opened for them, and later I'd see them with Walter Egan and then with the Joe Perry Project. I barely remember anything about those supporting acts, but on this occasion Elizabeth Barraclough was the opener, and I remember her well. Working at the record store, I'd gotten a promo copy of Barraclough's eponymous debut, which came out on Bearsville, a label owned by Albert Grossman, the crafty little fella who had assembled Peter, Paul and Mary and managed Bob Dylan, the Band, and Todd Rundgren. I knew and dug Barraclough's music, even though she was obscure. None of my coworkers at the shop shared my admiration. I'd talk her up, but I never sold any of her records.

Poised somewhere between country rock and pub rock, straddling Gram Parsons and Graham Parker, Barraclough's music sometimes interpolated reggae into that mix, as on the topical political "Who Do You Think's the Fool" and "Shepherd's Bush," but the underlying sensibility was blues rooted. Her voice was unvarnished, sometimes ragged, not unlike another Grossman artist, Janis Joplin, but I preferred Barraclough's delivery, her raw effort, and the way songs like

"Covered Up in Aces" managed to be poetic and prosaic at the same time. Way ahead of the curve, presaging Lucinda Williams and other hard-rocking alt-country women, with guest spots by Rundgren on lead guitar and Paul Butterfield on harmonica, *Elizabeth Barraclough* remains a bizarre omission from the digital domain, never having been reissued since it first came out.

Barraclough played a blue Fender Mustang. I found this powerfully and confusingly erotic. Perhaps it would not be too much to say that my adolescent mind had an aptitude for finding anything arousing, lust like water seeking its own level, but guitar-slinging gals were something else. Four decades down pop's highway, it seems strange to say, but at the time leading ladies were extremely unusual in rock. There were plenty of acoustic-guitar-wielding women in folk, but very few in hard rock bands, and electric axes were basically men's instruments. When a girl slung one over her shoulder, a fundamental principle was invoked: anything coded male and then adopted by a woman was automatically exciting, be it button-down shirts and blue jeans or solid-body guitars. I'm sure a Freudian interpretation would be more colorful, after all guitars are incontrovertibly phallic in all details with their necks and machine heads, cords are plugged and unplugged, special fingering is required to play them, and they're regularly eroticized in performance. The guitar-dick interchange was an open secret, and even my notoriously oblivious friends and I had noted the homoeroticism in hard rock guitar-hero worship, which was in most cases exclusively MoMA—man-on-man action.

One of the sisters at the helm of Heart played guitar too. The younger one, Nancy Wilson, was blond and a heavy rocker. Her older sib, Ann, the lead singer, was a demure brunette whose disposition was set on simmer. I always confused them. To me, Nancy didn't seem like a Nancy, much more like an Ann, and Ann was much more Nancy. I didn't have a type—light or dark, skinny or full—so they were equally dazzling to me. Also, they lived in Vancouver, so we assumed they were Canadian. Who knew, maybe up there Anns and

Nancys were swapped? Ann was a dynamo, her voice marvelously pliant, from a light breeze to a hurricane. Nancy donned a solid Fender like Barraclough's when a song needed extra horsepower, but most of the time she played an amplified acoustic guitar made by Ovation.

Ah, the Ovation. Allow me a momentary sidebar on these ubiquitous contraptions. Because of Nancy Wilson, I grew fascinated by them and thought for a bit about buying one. They were appealingly designed, came outfitted with baroque o-holes and a cool dual-tone look melding the delicacy of an acoustic with rock-out-ability of an electric. The Ovation's curved back was made of dark plastic and its front was wooden; when set facedown it had a dichromatic appearance and looked something like a turtle. But when I rested the instrument in my lap, it slid down and off my knees because it was sleek and there was no bottom edge to hold it up. Played with a strap it was equally unwieldy, like holding a shallow meditation bowl against your abdomen. More damning was the feeble, tinny sound. I associate the Ovation guitar with the same compromised moment in audio fidelity when Japanese solid-state electronics began to make middlebrow home stereos sound like a string of empty beer cans.

The Wilsons were self-identified as hard rockers, relishing riffs and getting off on high-test boogie. Even saddled with this uncouth axe, Nancy could put the proverbial hammer down. She'd taken a few cues from Led Zeppelin records and knew the allure of contrasting energies, plucking crystalline contrapuntal lines and mandolin-like trills before jerking forth a strum so forceful it could kick-start a Harley. You can hear the madness to her method on their hit "Crazy on You," a song that unleashed desire in a way that we unripe fumblers never could. Nancy had her fingers on the rip cord of our rapture.

Heart tore the Iowa State Fairgrounds a new earhole, Ann's confident singing muscling its way past the wafting aroma of hay bales and cotton candy. As always, they were dressed as if they were rolling with Robin Hood and his merry gang, if his merry gang had been an amateur ballet troupe—corsets, kerchiefs, petticoats, knee-high leather boots, the boys in the band decked out in kimonos, vests, leotards, and shirts open to their navels. They dug deep into "Magic Man," a silly mama-doesn't-understand-him lyric set to a fairly ingenious dark distorted motif and wailing lead guitar. As Ann and Nancy took their bows, I leaned over to Ceil and assured her that they'd be back for an encore, I knew because they hadn't yet played "Barracuda," and they'd never leave without having satisfied the lighter-waving crowd—funny, since it was only midafternoon and the lighters were invisible beacons in the warm sun. As advertised, Heart returned, the lurking opening chords chugging, burning it to the wick with a singularly vicious and wonderful flip-of-the-bird to sleazy guys and their predatory ways.

The Wilsons remind me of many of the girls I knew then. Their feathered hair and femme image said one thing, but the authority with which they got down gave me something else to think about. I was already listening to Siouxsie Sioux and Patti Smith, soon to hear X-Ray Spex and Kleenex, so the chromosomal mix of rock was broadening, and with it the range of topics and sounds. Heart continued to make solid rocking records, even pushing themselves into fresh places, like on the enduringly excellent *Dog and Butterfly*. But they were standing on the wrong side of a fault line in the midst of a tectonic shift, the one that would separate a new kind of independent music from the megalithic hit-makers of yore. Ten years later, in the hair-band era, they would not seem so triumphant or self-propelled, having been coiffed and coached by a cadre of dipshit industry guys. Still, Ann and Nancy were pioneers. Let's just say that as hard-rocking heterosexual women, their swagger added another layer to the gender cake. They demonstrated convincingly that preening, strutting singers like Robert Plant and Steven Tyler weren't necessarily the hottest ladies in town, no matter how they fussed over their hair and moaned and groaned. I was glad to have seen the Wilsons sashay onstage and kick out the jams four times, none more entrancing than that one afternoon in Iowa's capital city.

After "Barracuda" had headed for deeper waters and Heart blew its final smooch, Ceil and I located her folks back at the funnel cake stand. Out in the parking lot, a Ferris wheel overhead made its eternal rounds; we climbed into the back of the car, enjoying a private tryst, inflamed by images of guitar-toting gals, bellies full of dough, a little powdered sugar still sprinkling our shirts.

On the way home, her dad took a rural route detour to a friend's farm. There, in a little wooden farmhouse, heartland sun casting its rays low on the horizon, we were treated to an additional snack, gilding the gastronomic lily with a serving of truly memorable egg noodles.

Pink Floyd

Animals

A riddle.

What happens to your soul when you love something, I mean love it with every molecule in your makeshift little person, then you cast it aside and laugh at it, embarrassed to have once been so enthralled, only to love it again later?

Do you ever regain karmic credibility? Or have you become unreliable to everyone—the once-loved thing, anyone who might care that you do or do not love it, and yourself, a lover of things in the world?

...

I once mistreated Pink Floyd's *Animals* this way. It had been inestimably dear to me. I had cathected upon it like a leech on a heel. If someone asked me to name my favorite record, I did not hesitate. I learned it note by note, word for word, pored over the cover, on which I etched my name in ballpoint lettering. All the important things in the world seemed contained within that gatefold sleeve, with its cryptic industrial building and flying pig. The smokestacks were a complete mystery to me, but I was as sure of the depth of their psycho-historical resonance as if it had been an image of Stonehenge or the immense statues on Easter Island.

For a thirteen-year-old listener, the LP contained multitudes. Its four tracks were all interrelated—here was a concept album for contemporary times, my very own *Tommy* or *Freak Out!*, even more tightly conceived, with three four-legged species serving as human archetypes: sheep, dogs, and of course pigs. There was mystery and drama and humor and sentimentality and darkness and melancholy and paranoia and angst. A little barbed rewrite of biblical verse, nods to Orwell and *Lord of the Flies*, some contemporary British politics. Exactly what a nerdy young fella looking for some righteousness might love.

Who was born in a house full of pain?
Who was trained not to spit in the fan?
Who was told what to do by the man?
Who was broken by trained personnel?
Who was fitted with collar and chain?
Who was given a pat on the back?
Who was breaking away from the pack?
Who was only a stranger at home?
Who was ground down in the end?
Who was found dead on the phone?
Who was dragged down by the stone?

Then two things happened. I changed and Pink Floyd changed. I went to college, passed the big 2-0, at which point the record began to take on unwanted adolescent connotations. It felt like reading *Catcher in the Rye* on the side while studying Frankfurt School theory. Kid stuff. I hid *Animals* in my collection and started to catalog it differently in my mind. Also, Pink Floyd had released *The Wall*. This, I thought (and still think), was heavy-handed and juvenile. How could the same band have made these two records? It made me reflect upon *Animals* with a jaundiced ear. Perhaps the sociological perspective of the earlier record was just as dopey and obvious as its follow-up in a way that I'd missed. Rather than risk it and stand up for my previous passion, I ditched it.

...

Back when *Animals* was still the hub of my tire, before the betrayal, I engineered seeing Pink Floyd in concert. The band was on its In the Flesh tour, a series of fifty-five European and American performances legendary for its ostentatious stage show. I arrived at the Philadelphia Spectrum with three friends—two of them the Miller sisters, my first and second girlfriends, the other one my best friend Scooter. We were driven to the downtown venue by Scooter's parents, but my own folks were adamant that I call them when we'd found our seats. All of us had sequestered bottles of stolen booze on our person—mine consisted of a container full of rum stuffed in my pants. Carefully siphoned from my parents' nearly disused liquor cabinet into a Wella Balsam bottle, the hooch seemed an important part of the concert experience for us. I'd not expected to be frisked on the way in, but held it together even when mid-pat-down the contraband slipped down my leg, halting at my sneaker. I hobbled past security, quickly repairing to the bathroom to retrieve it, and we pretended to enjoy it even though it tasted like shampoo.

Knowing the size of the Spectrum, I brought binoculars; these were my father's Leica glasses, late forties vintage, very precious, handed down from my grandfather, who had been gifted them by a grateful patient. Having called home to let my folks know that we were seated, I promptly left the binoculars at the pay phone, only to discover them missing moments later, and returning to find them gone. My father was not pleased at all, but he handled the news with restraint when, finding myself empty-handed back at the phone booth, I called him a second time to confess their loss.

As a sound check, Pink Floyd's devious soundmen simulated a jet plane passing about ten feet above the heads of the crowd in a diagonal maneuver only possible with their extremely fancy quadrophonic equipment, placed like bunkers at four stations around the hall. I've heard about the so-called brown note, a frequency that should immediately cause the listener to lose control of their bowels.

It's apocryphal, but this tremendous and unexpected engine sound came as close as anything I've ever experienced, and sent a tremor of shrieks and pale faces through the capacity crowd.

"They should have called that one record *Wish I Could Hear*," said Scooter, cupping his hands to my ear.

As usual, we were primed to see whether the band could re-create their studio album in a live setting. Exact reenactment was a major litmus test for us. To fail at such a task meant the band had relied unfairly on electronic tricks rather than raw skill, the wizardry of knobs, wires, endless takes, and studio sweetening instead of mind-bending musicality. That these two concepts were not antithetical or that achievements in the studio were musical in and of themselves did not occur to us. And neither did another one that makes our preoccupations seem especially idiotic: if we wanted the record reproduced verbatim, why were we at a concert?

On this count, Pink Floyd did not disappoint. They played the record exactly, with precision and nuance, replicating every oink, bark, and baa, each talk-box croak and guitar wail, all the atmospheric Rhodes piano clouds and perfectly measured drumming, so closely hewn to the original that our attention was drawn easily from the music to a gigantic projection above the stage. An animated film was playing on a circular screen and consisted of engrossing surrealistic images, reminding us immediately of Terry Gilliam, timed to the fraction of a second to correspond with the music. A little drunk and nauseated from the soapy liquor, I found the stream-of-consciousness film almost unbearably fantastic. Lizards scampered across the circle and disappeared into fleshy holes only to emerge as phoenixes. The images touched on many of our buttons: geeky, horny, political, umbilical, magical, organic, slick, and psychotropic, like British versions of underground comix.

This cinematic gear had been part of the Pink Floyd presentation since at least their big hit "Money," which they also performed for us, deviating from the conceptually coherent *Animals* show. What were new and unexpected were the inflatables. On the back cover of the LP, a note identified the pig and its maker, which tipped us off to the fact that the porker flying above the Battersea Power Station smokestacks had actually been staged, rather than being a collaged-in graphic. Stark black-and-white photos in the center of the gatefold strengthened that case, but it wasn't until a forty-foot balloon pig was cabled over our heads that I really understood it palpably. A foreign presence, the effigy hung above us, occupying the airspace with an ominous muteness. Think of the way that a beach ball, once launched into a crowd, activates and aggregates the crowd's members, changing them from microscopic particles into a single self-aware organism. Around this time, stadium audiences started doing the wave, which is that concept on a larger scale. Pink Floyd's pig did the same thing, but by casting a paranoia-inducing shadow on the band's listeners, it implied something about their docile and abiding nature, the fact that they'd amassed and headed together into a large place, where they'd been told to sit and wait and pay attention, so that it made us think twice when, on "Sheep," Roger Waters sang: *Meek and obedient you follow the leader / Down well-trodden corridors into the valley of steel.*

The pig was soon joined by a gigantic Cadillac, a refrigerator with pink sausage projectiles emanating from its belly—like a sculptural Peter Saul painting, the closest cousin in inflatable land to the surreal film images—and a man and woman with two rotund children. The balloons bobbed and weaved high above us like a demonic Macy's Thanksgiving parade, their stiff limbs locked, unchanging expressions inflected by the song lyrics. It was a spectacle like I'd never imagined, some sort of Bread and Puppet Theater meets Archigram instant city. I didn't stop to think about how much it cost or how excessive it was or whether its sensational over-the-top production standard was consistent with the anti-corporate message it professed. Those things dawned on me later, but in the moment my friends and I thought we'd gone to Oz and peered behind the Wizard's curtain.

Animals is one of the emblematic records of the nineteen seventies in that it so effortlessly encapsulates the contradictions of the era. In a quick ten-year span, from their debut in 1967 to this record, Pink Floyd went from being abrasive iconoclasts pioneering psychedelic rock inspired by free improvisation and surrealism to being establishment figures in a world of music executives and million-dollar handshakes. The fact that Johnny Rotten wore a Pink Floyd T-shirt with "I hate" inscribed above their name suggested their status amongst the denizens of punk.

Animals was as harsh as it was as a riposte to such dismissal, to show the punk generation that Roger Waters, David Gilmour, Nick Mason, and Richard Wright were down and dirty, independent, and not at all compromised by, for instance, the fact that they'd bought a three-story building to use as a recording studio for the sessions. Understood retrospectively as classic rock dinosaurs that had started out as real innovators, they attempted to manage a balance between those realities, and their extraordinary stage show coalesced both sides of the band's newly established persona, the puffed-up spectacle and the biting social critique. In the long run, it was an untenable identity, but for me, as someone who was beginning to perk up and take note of the aggressive new music in London and New York, I found it fascinating and potent.

That is, until I shunned and banished it from my life.

...

Sitting on a bar stool in what comic artist George Herriman once termed a "refreshery" on New York's Lower East Side in 2016, I heard the acoustic guitar chords of "Pigs on the Wing (Part 1)" for the first time in nearly forty years. Knowing every single peep on the record, I sat quietly, nursed my drink, and listened as the bartender played the whole LP. Strumming my pain, singing my life, killing me softly.

Revisiting *Animals* was surprisingly emotional, like seeing an ex looking particularly fine across the room. There's a somber quality to music from earlier in your life, a song you've lived with, perhaps because it's absorbed so much of your own mental and spiritual energy, sponging it up for later, when you need it again. You freshen its memory and it can be gently squeezed.

1978

Van Halen

There's a fatal misunderstanding in the movie *Whiplash*—the sadistic jazz teacher tortures his student by telling him to play faster. If this were a lifelike jazz conservatory, speed would not be the goal. The objective would be feel. To play with the right kind of swing or groove, to find the pocket, to push or pull the time, the right dynamic—these are the actual subtleties with which jazz masters debase and browbeat their trainees.

Now, if it were a conservatory of hard rock and heavy metal, velocity would be closer to the mark. Speed is not only a valued attribute—it's a value in itself. Me like fast; fast good. Our feeble teenage understanding was that facility was best displayed by playing as quickly as possible, that we could accurately gauge someone's musicianship in notes per minute. If you're a virtuoso, the name of the game is showing it off, so play nimble, man, as quick as humanly possible.

We guitarists believed just such a land speed record had been achieved by Mr. Eddie Van Halen on the debut LP by the group to which he'd given his last name. One brief track flabbergasted us especially: "Eruption." In a demimonde of double entendre, this title loomed large with its trisyllabic phallo-volcanism. The doyen of joyous release, Van Halen delivered the massive cum shot in viscid detail. The piece starts with the band playing a perfunctory intro, then nothing but guitar, bathed in reverb but retaining the intimacy of the live studio recording, so up close and personal that you can hear pick sweep across string like a hummingbird wing fluttering against a leaf, then a whammy bar grabs the bird by its ruby throat and drags it into the abyss. Van Halen has learned from listening to Hendrix how to control dynamics and create dramatic tension, as he does on a little break in action—low hum of Marshall amp awaiting next lightning strike—before reentering with machine gun assault. In the middle of this ultimate passage, the guitarist lets loose a stream of Paganini-like two-hand tapped arpeggios that have become legend in pop metal.

Baroque music lurks in the distant background of some solos on *Van Halen*. Eddie and his brother, drummer Alex, both studied classical piano as kids, and the guitarist brought contrapuntal information into his work with the band, where he maintained a relatively quiet persona, set against singer David Lee Roth's in-your-face tantric yogic strut. Ted Templeman's production is cohesive, with snappy sound and a fast-moving program that rolls from one energy-packed track to another, always featuring Eddie's pizzazzy plectrum and Roth's seamy vocals, which take you innuendo and out the other. A little dash of high school soap opera lends some songs a leering quality, Roth conjuring cheerleader and pedophile alike in one quick trademark squeal. Eddie's guitar wept disingenuously with the protagonist of "Jamie's Cryin'," adding a snarky "boo-hoo" to Jamie's plight, having denied the guy the goods and thereby lost him forever. The cover of "You Really Got Me" milked the Kinks' riff in a rough way that felt like blunt-force trauma, Eddie delighting us with tapping antics and setting-knob dropouts.

Van Halen was almost called Rat Salade in homage to Black Sabbath, and on "Atomic Punk" you can hear how they translate the early seventies British metal into a shinier, more radio-oriented, late seventies American context. Eddie starts with a sandpapery hand-muted scratching, like a mutant itching an open sore. It might be hard rock heresy, but I hear more than a passing resemblance to MC5 in early Van Halen, a kind of polished garage component, much glitzier and slicker, but with enough roughness—Alex's ride cymbal, for instance, can be downright sloppy—to give it protopunk texture. After the fact, of course, so it would be post-protopunk texture.

Van Halen is in no way a generic hard rock record, despite its mondo guitar heroism and cartoony glorification of inflamed male prowess. There are downright strange moments. Take "I'm the One," which kicks off with a wicked intro from Eddie, thumping drumbass interjections, a rumbling boogie, and Roth intoning: *We came here to entertain you / Leaving here we aggravate you / Don't you know it means the same to me.* What masquerades as a simple sex song—*I'm the one, the one you love / C'mon baby, show your love / Hey, give it to me*—turns out to be about Van Halen the band and its adoption of a cocky stance and penchant for lechery. *Look at all these little kids / Takin' care of the music biz / Don't their business take good care of me, honey.* All fine enough and within the pale, but there's a descending Sabbath-esque motif in the song that has a germ of jazz in it, and toward the end the background vocals unexpectedly take over and turn it into a parody of jazzy doo-wop, or less generously barbershop music, hi-hat opening and closing dutifully in the rear.

The lesser-known "Little Dreamer," with its "Come Together" groove (and even a little John Lennon reverbed sigh), has some jazz harmonies secreted away under the terse guitar solos, and Roth shows how versatile his singing is, in spite of all his glammy hamming. He was an outstanding focal point, visually speaking: peals of blond curls, open shirt unveiling mossy pecs, a six-pack, and a garland of gold chains, leaping around like testosterone-overloaded Yiddish man candy. Roth's vocal delivery was a combination of hot and sleazy, or lurid and fervid—I guess you could say it was lurvid. But most important, you can tell from the way he sings that he's not taking it too seriously. We didn't take Van Halen seriously, either, never owned a second record, never really followed them as they moved into pop stardom. They were a lark, a good-time band in a venerable tradition of such outfits, dating back to equally unserious built-to-party ensembles like Foghat and Bad Company, but equipped with their own special sauce, a lurvid singer and a nuclear option by the name of Eddie.

...

At nine a.m., a car horn sounded out front of our house. I had slept late, giving myself just enough time to shower and throw on some jeans and a T-shirt. It was Sunday and the rest of the family was at church, which made the half hour blissful and allowed me to play some loud music, over which I was lucky to hear my friends' signal. It was mid-July 1978, two days before my fifteenth birthday.

This was the era of the jam. Crossing music festival with monster truck rally, jams brought gigantic audiences to huge non-music-specific venues like raceways and football fields. Initiated by the unfortunate Altamont, jams persisted nonetheless. In 1973 the Summer Jam at Watkins Glen, held at a raceway in New York State, attracted 600,000 visitors, breaking records. A year later, the California Jam laid claim to being the loudest musical event in history. In 1974 there were the aptly huge Texxas Jam and Canada Jam, the latter grossing more money than any previous rock presentation in Canada, with over 100,000 attendees. Meanwhile, at a more modest scale, all manner of jam proliferated across the Midwest, whose heartlands were dotted with racetracks and other adaptable arenas.

The Mississippi River Jam was slated to run from "noon 'til dark," so we had plenty of time to drive the hour from Iowa City to Davenport. I climbed into the back of my friend's big sister's station wagon, and we set off for points east, an eight-track blaring Deep Purple, which seemed dated but right. We sped along I-80, the thoroughfare that connected our college town with Des Moines in one direction and the Quad Cities in the other, Chicago looming a couple hours yet farther east. Eastward, as we approached the Mississippi River, the landscape grew less flat; rolling little hills were neatly finished in black topsoil and green corn, already grown hip height. Nearly there, we stopped at a rest area. The elders smoked and I checked my wallet for funds, which I'd procured from lawn mowing, and which turned out to total ten dollars, exactly enough for a ticket to the jam. I leaned against the green hood. Its metal singed my arm. Ten in the morning and already it was blazing hot.

Credit Island was an early Indian trading post, a 420-acre plot of land in the Mississippi River off the coast of Davenport that had been turned into parkland and a golf course and was rented by Celebration Midwest Concerts for the Mississippi River Jam. As we pulled the wagon into the parking area, we could see a line of thousands of people at the gate, and on our way to join the throng, we heard stories about people having been there since last night. There had never been a noteworthy jam in the area, so rockers from a wide swath of the Quad Cities had turned out, 22,000 in all.

Our gang's loyalties were divided in terms of the main attraction. One thing we agreed on: nobody was thrilled that the Atlanta Rhythm Section was on the bill. The ladies were excited about the headliner, the Doobie Brothers, as well as Journey, stocked with hunky guys. I had never cared one way or another about the Doobies, but thought it would be at least interesting to hear them sing hits like "Black Water," "Listen to the Music," "Takin' It to the Streets," and "China Grove," and to hear their agile guitarist Jeff "Skunk" Baxter. Journey's fourth record, *Infinity*, had caught my ear earlier in the year, perhaps because it was produced by Roy Thomas Baker using an approach to layered vocals that was much like the one he used for the classic early Queen records. But Journey was a domesticated cat next to the wild jaguar named Van Halen. Although their LP had only come out in February, I was on to Van Halen before my peers, and having touted *Van Halen*, I was eager to hear what the band could do live.

We paid our entrance and made our way to the bridge that took us onto Credit Island. A guard tore my ticket and said: "There's no in and out. Once you're on the island, you can't leave, so be sure you've got everything you need." Clear enough, I thought. What else would I need? I plunged the sweat-soaked stub into my pocket and joined the others to stake our claim. We found a place about a hundred feet from the stage and, having neglected to bring a blanket, plopped down onto the bare ground. And then we waited. Noon came and passed. Out on the river, people were moored in boats, looking to catch some freebie tunes. People threw Frisbees with MISSISSIPPI RIVER JAM printed on them. It was festive, but by the time the clock turned 1:30, some of the natives were growing restless.

"I hear it's equipment problems," a passerby noted. "Van Halen's and Journey's gear didn't show up until this morning, and they're still setting up."

Finally, half an hour later, David Lee Roth mounted the stage, looking out at the crowd with a cocked head, wiping his forehead with a kimono-clad arm, summoning divine musical forces with the secret passwords: "Hey, Davenport! Are you ready to *rock*?!!!" At which the crowd unleashed hours of pent-up, overheated emotion, giving them a premature standing ovation, at which they tore headlong into "Running with the Devil," Eddie Van Halen wigging out the guitar maniacs in our midst, climbing onto and leaping from the stage scaffolding or from the two-foot-high drum perch, where brother Alex was manning a huge white kit. Roth was sassy and frisky, his hey-there-little-schoolgirl routine already polished to a predatory gleam. Swept by a large fan blowing from the side of the stage, Roth's copious hair billowed back, making us slightly jealous—of the wind, not the mane—but his sleek black leather pants seemed an oppressive accoutrement in the brutal heat. The group played the bulk of their LP, including "Ain't Talkin' 'bout Love" and an impressive "Eruption," evinced from Eddie's customized Frankenstrat, which featured black tape crisscrossing its white body. But the thermometer was pushing 103, and after a half hour of Bikram-hot preening and pole dancing, Van Halen threw in the towel.

At this point, I began to think about all the things I'd forgotten. First, that I was an animal and would require sustenance and hydration, neither of which were available for free and neither of which I'd carried in. There were only a few small patches of shade around the edges of the park, and these were, so to speak, hotly contested. We were in the middle of the grounds, where it was dusty and hard, grass having been beaten down into nothing. I had no hat and neglected to bring sunscreen, so I'd been pulling my shirt into a ball over my head and face like an ill-fitting turban, then periodically putting it back over my shoulders to keep them from enduring immediate second-degree burns. My jeans had kneeholes, so at least they were ventilated, but it was so hot I was tempted to take them off and strip to my underwear, maybe take a dive in the muddy waters of the Mississippi. My modesty had the better of me, so I continued to swelter.

After a short intermission, Atlanta Rhythm Section took the stage. A southern rock band that struck us as Allman Brothers lite, ARS had a soft hit with "So in to You." We were definitely not into them. After determining that their live incarnation wouldn't change my mind, I stopped paying attention to them and went back to being miserably hungry and thirsty, but suddenly someone onstage started screaming, and we could see that one of the huge speakers was on fire. The band ground to a halt, a commotion ensued, extinguishers were wielded, and the musicians were unceremoniously ushered offstage, never to be heard from again. Five minutes and their set was over. Nobody made an announcement. There was another protracted wait while the stage was turned over for the next act. Good fortune had smiled its sizzling hot smile.

Journey's performance, I must admit, is but hazy waves of heat and color in my memory—some gravity-defying hair, precise vocal harmonies, soaring lead guitar. I'm sure I experienced something close to sunstroke, but the next thing I recall with any specificity is the Doobie Brothers, who turned out to be more exciting than I'd expected. By then, the "'til dark" part of the event had come around, the sun had loosened its iron grip, and the temperature was dipping into the nineties.

Collectively, our posse decided to move toward the car in advance of the crowd, and as we did, I remember the Doobies nailing "Jesus Is Just Alright." We stopped and turned mid-retreat and watched them belt it out, not caring about what is said, not caring about what is done, not caring about what is known, not caring about where is gone, their countrified California gospel echoing across the Mississippi like an errant golf ball, teed off and flying, carefree, beyond the confines of Credit Island.

This Year's Model

Declan MacManus got lumped in with the punks. Of course he'd fraternized with the lustiest and crustiest of them, opening for bands like the Damned and the Clash, and he signed with Stiff Records, whose creed—"If it ain't stiff, it ain't worth a fuck"—sure seemed punk to us. Redubbed Elvis Costello, he made his way into the public eye just out of the thick of London's frenzied punk *annus mirabilis*, which stretched from 1976 to 1977. Outfitted with a singularly incisive tongue, Costello wore cuffed jeans, skinny ties, and geek glasses, somewhere between a rockabilly greaser and an accountant, just weird enough to be a card carrier in the no-future brigade.

On the other hand, his verbiage was more stinging than 99.9 percent of the punks. If you listened to the intricacies of his lyrics, you might have detected other input of a pedigree that could have gotten him soundly beaten if anyone at the Electric Circus or the Roxy had been sober enough to decode it. On *My Aim Is True*, most of the songs found him accompanied by Clover, a Gram Parsonsy country band, and his producer of choice was Nick Lowe, an unrepentantly cheery bassist who facetiously titled his own LP *Pure Pop for Now People*. The intro to Costello's "Alison" is almost identical to the intro on Bruce Springsteen's "Tenth Avenue Freeze-Out," from two years earlier. Listen to the guitars: they're nearly twins. Somewhere along the way, I read an interview in which Costello had nice things to say about Joni Mitchell. That sealed it. He was not a punk.

My friend Doug Cannon and I idolized Elvis Costello. I'd gotten ahold of a copy of his debut very early, having read controversial and contradictory reports in *NME* and *Sounds*. Looking back on it, I see that Doug made some sartorial choices based on the singer's example; he already had thick black eyeglass frames, so he came partially pre-equipped, and he added the jeans, white shirt, tie, and a tweed trench coat. Meeting up after a year or so of college, I was jealous to find that he'd hung out with Costello one drunken evening after a concert, when he'd retired to a bar stool and his hero had coincidentally chosen the one next to him. Elvis wasn't a punk, but he wrote about romantic relationships with venomous insight. We adored him for the fact that most of the time he was the snarkiest guy in the room, the uncomfortable one with mysterious superman glasses that could see through all boy-girl horseshit and tell it like it is. It wasn't pretty, didn't reflect well on anyone, least of all the messenger, who sang self-hatred as if it were a lullaby. Nobody was spared the poison pen with which Costello wrote his songs.

...

On a holiday visit to Chicago in 1978, my family spent a few nights with my paternal grandparents. My grandmother served her favorite dessert: rubbery stiff multicolor Jell-O cubes. We ate them in the kitchen, which had a cool circular banquette booth built into a nook, upholstered in light blue vinyl like a diner, above which my grampa had commissioned an artist to depict a trout rising to a fly. Applied à la fresco, the fish puffed out from the wall, remarkably lifelike as it took the bait and met its fate.

On a ledge to one side of the nook sat a little black-and-white TV. Somehow, I'd gotten word that Elvis Costello would be substituting for the Sex Pistols on *Saturday Night Live*, since the Pistols had been denied a visa. That evening I commandeered the kitchen, demanding total silence, as Costello and the Attractions hit the Radio City soundstage to perform two songs. On the second, a few strokes into "Less than Zero," the singer halted his band, apologized, saying that the song they'd prepared would mean what the title said to an American audience, and instead leapt into the rousing up-yours to mainstream media called "Radio Radio." It was a shock I'll never forget, as electrifying and galvanizing as a hot iron branding, and it cauterized my fandom into an indelible E.C. scar. His brash change-up, which was not smiled upon by producer Lorne Michaels, made television real, taking the hints of actual humanity that we so craved—the barely contained tittering of Vicki Lawrence, Harvey Korman, and Tim Conway on *The Carol Burnett Show* as they cracked each other up, or Johnny Carson's encounter with Zsa Zsa Gabor and her Persian kitten Madame Pompadour, where Gabor had invited Carson to pet her pussy and he'd replied, "I will if you get the cat out of the way." Improvised television: it smelled of subversion, rebellion, antidisestablishmentarianism. Maybe Elvis was a punk after all.

A year later, on a similar visit, my grandmother gave me a belated and utterly unprecedented birthday gift. She would drive me into Chicago to that record store I was always carrying on about, Wax Trax, a destination to which I'd never been able to convince my parents to ferry me. At the store I could spend the sensational amount of ninety dollars on anything I wanted. To be clear, my grandmother Corbett did not dole out dough with what you'd call a light touch. She had grown up in a coal-mining family in Pennsylvania, escaped indentured servitude at the helm of eleven siblings by marrying at age sixteen, rapidly divorcing her abusive first husband and locking fates with my grandfather, a successful physician in a doctor dynasty. At birthdays, we normally received a check in the mail for ten dollars. Needless to say, getting almost a full Franklin to waste on vinyl was nigh on orgiastic.

We drove east on North Avenue in Nonie's gigantic Cadillac,

which handled like a cruise ship. It had automatic windows and locks, a novelty at the time. Although she had a driver, today Nonie decided to take the wheel, and I felt the g-force of her heavy foot as we barreled along. We passed through black West Side neighborhoods, where she made a point of clicking the doors locked, telling me about the time that, while she'd been sitting in the driver's seat, thugs had smashed her back window and stolen her purse off the car's voluminous rear seat. I noted that she told me this story from the comfort of a full-length mink coat, not exactly what you'd wear to ward off potential road bandits, but hey, we were on the way to spend some of her fortune on me, so I let it slide.

As we pulled onto Lincoln Avenue and parked in front of the store, Nonie turned up the radio, gave me the cash, and told me she'd wait in the car, that I should take the time I needed. Inside Wax Trax, I gazed around at a venue modeled on the London shops I'd seen in *Melody Maker*. New singles were strung up on a wall in horizontal lines, scalloped like Christmas tree lights, together with rare LPs, some in blazing colors of vinyl. There were items from the New York punk and underground scene, scads of British post-punk, some ska and reggae, but none of the normal stuff that was the mainstay of my regular record haunts. I was in paradise. Before I could start shopping for anything, I ran back to the car, startling my grandmother with a knock on the window, telling her that it might take a little while, and thanking her profusely.

I remember the records that stole my attention. There was a clear-vinyl bootleg of early Buzzcocks that was eighty dollars. I was tempted to blow nearly everything on one object. And they had a copy of the same band's *Spiral Scratch* without Howard Devoto's name on the cover, which meant it was an original first edition. My mind swam in seven-inches by Eater and Nervous Eaters, a Johnny Moped LP, the Vibrators' *Pure Mania*, the debut by Tuff Darts, some Dead Boys specialties, all manner of things I'd read about but couldn't hear. There was also an Elvis Costello rarity that loomed large, held in a glass case at the counter due to its scarcity—

a copy of the legendary 2 Tone release of "The Imposter," which had been withdrawn before it was made available to the public. And then there were the bins of small-label singles, arranged as islands around the room. I had barely made it to them and had already established several possible methods of dispensing with my dollars.

I sidled over to the singles and began working through them alphabetically. Excited by the encyclopedic collection, I determined that I would not blow my wad on a high-ticket item, but would instead amass as many seven-inches as I could. They were mostly picture sleeve imports and cost around three dollars each, which meant that I could buy twenty-five or so. I jumped forward to the Buzzcocks and grabbed all their singles, same for Kleenex, Magazine, and the Monochrome Set, and then made my way to the new arrivals, where I found the Beat's "Tears of a Clown" and glorious music by the Teardrop Explodes and Echo & the Bunnymen, names I had just encountered. I felt like I was part of the scene, not stranded in my time-lagged Iowa isolation booth. Finally, I went back to systematically move through the racks one more time. I'd skipped Elvis Costello, as I already owned all the official singles he'd waxed. There I stopped, discovering three items I'd never seen, all bootlegs. I pulled them into my batch and, realizing that I'd exceeded my limit, asked the guy at the counter to hold my pile while I went out to the running car. I rapped on the window, my grandmother lowered it, I asked for ten more dollars, and without a word, her sunglasses masking any reaction, she raised it back up. Putting three records back, none of them by Costello, I paid, blew the smoke off the end of my pistol, holstered it, and went out to the idling car so my grandmother could drive me back to her house.

Those three bootleg singles helped me understand Elvis and definitively swung the pendulum back from punk to something else. *Honky Tonk Demos* contained six tracks, documented in some tight space with just an acoustic guitar. Certain lyrics, and in a couple of cases whole songs, were familiar. Elvis made a habit of cannibalizing old and unused lines, situating a good turn of phrase in an upgraded context, a method the musician detailed with exquisite detail in *Unfaithful Music and Invisible Ink*, with specific reference to the tracks on this seven-inch. On *Cornered on Plastic*, I found "Cheap Reward," "Really Mystified," and the poignant "Hoover Factory," his working-class ode. And the third single, *Stranger in the House*, contained actual honky-tonk in the form of "Honky Tonkin'/ Honky Tonk Blues," a little Hank Williams medley, as well as the Burt Bacharach/Hal David song "I Just Don't Know What to Do with Myself" and Costello's own "Stranger in the House," written for George Jones.

At a later date, Costello listed some early loves, which included not only Joni Mitchell but also the Beatles and Crosby, Stills, Nash & Young. When I heard that, collated with the country and sophisticated pop on the bootlegs, it confirmed the sense I had that he was trying to be a real songwriter, not a three-chord wonder. He had a unique way of fitting words into a line, drawing out an uncommon rhythm from them. *I don't wanna kiss you / I don't wanna touch.* In one line, the first words of the record, Elvis peeled back the pretext of our leering teenage lust, loosening its grip on our imaginations by means of a novel solvent: self-doubt. The bonehead gurus of relationship philosophy to whom we had previously paid mind— wise men from Robert Plant to David Lee Roth—had taught us that kissing and touching were the name of the game, that sex was about confidence, a short con in which one needed above all to be self-assured. Here comes a bespectacled dork to joust with these learned men, letting us in on the deepest of complexes, the reaction formations of lingering insecurity—diffidence, sarcasm, passive aggressiveness, plotting revenge, licking wounds, whimpering in a corner, lashing out. And Costello imparts his lesson with a wit we'd never encountered. He was letting us in on his personal campaign of vengeance. Each song was a minor apocalypse: boy-girl relations run horribly amok, misunderstandings on the marquee, bonds broken, vows struck. Even successful liaisons were fraught. In "On the Beat" he sang: *There's only one thing wrong with you befriending me / Take it easy, I think you're bending me.* In "You Belong to Me," he was empathetic to her plight: *You act dumb / You say you're so numb / You say you don't come / Under his thumb.*

This Year's Model is an exemplary mix of vicious and vulnerable, the kind of anger hurled in response to being misunderstood. Tracks like "Little Triggers," an exquisite, ineffectual defense mechanism in song form (*Little triggers that you pull with your tongue / Little triggers, I don't want to be hung up, strung up / When you don't call up*)—these plumbed some part of my faulty XY psyche and came uncomfortably close to insight. *No, don't ask me to apologize / I won't ask you to forgive me,* went "Hand in Hand," every attempt at rapprochement a misfire. *Sometimes I think of love as just a tumor / You've got to cut it out,* he sang unrelentingly in "Lipstick Vogue." I wondered if it would come to that, after all Elvis was only nine years older than me; he could be bilious and disaffected, but never crossed all the way into being a total cynic. Was a relationship just a dark passage or mutually assured destruction? On the same song, later, a tiny ray of light: *Sometimes I almost feel / Just like a human being.*

...

The Attractions, Costello's right-hand band, were among the greatest working groups of the era, more than just the songwriter's accompanists, at every turn introducing more to think about, little triggers of their own designed to emphasize the singer's unflinching perspective. I particularly loved Steve Nieve's keyboard choices, including not only piano but antiquated electric keyboards, like Farfisa (although in truth his was a Vox Continental), which he made sound contemporary even as they conjured ? and the Mysterians.

Bruce Thomas proved that a rock bassist could be more than a functionary. Moving around like a funk musician, but not playing funk, he spun melodic lines and made large intervallic leaps, meanwhile covering the fundamentals, anchoring, and driving the tempo. He could insert ornament, sometimes with an under-the-breath flourish, like the snarky little imitation wolf whistle he adds with a brisk up-and-down slide on the string to match Elvis's phrase *Oh, I don't want to lick them* in "On the Beat." Pete Thomas is also magnificent, one of the master fill-makers, inventing new little patterns every juncture. Listen to him for the duration of "Lipstick Vogue," where the drums are in quasi-solo mode much of the time. This rhythm team took one of the decade's most unpleasant habits— the fade-out—and turned it into a special place to plant their most creative ideas. The ends of songs were always full of surprises with Thomas and Thomas in charge.

If one album stands as the totem animal of my late teenagedom, it's *This Year's Model*. Costello's frank evaluation of male motivation gave us a glimpse of our terrifying interior life, the one we hid behind false fronts and assumed attitudes. Frank Zappa had it right: the ugliest part of your body is your mind. *Those disco synthesizers / Those daily tranquilizers / Those body-building prizes / Those bedroom alibis / All this but no surprises for this year's girl*, sang Costello, pitilessly cataloging the emotional penury. Elvis put it to us straight but left a glimmer of hope that from all deceit we might make it out alive. Almost like a human being.

Tales of Captain Black

The front room of Coop Records, the store where I spent most of my
free time and the bulk of my money in 1979, even when I wasn't
working there, was devoted exclusively to cut-out bins. Rows and
rows of vinyl LPs, still shrink-wrapped and brand-new, some portion of their covers violently disfigured, purposely damaged—a tri-
angular wedge of corner cut off, a line band-sawed into the spine,
or a circular hole punched out somewhere on the cardboard sleeve.
This proactive step was taken, my boss Mike Wall told me, by the
record companies, to ensure that the LPs wouldn't be bought as
remainders and then resold at full retail price.

For a few months, Mike had been talking about the end of the
record industry. Prying open a box one day, he pulled out a copy of a
new release on Columbia, Joni Mitchell's *Mingus*. Poising it between
two palms, he shook the LP back and forth, making a little thwack-
ing noise, demonstrating how far it bent.

"These are ridiculous," he said. "They're pressing them thinner
and thinner, like fucking sheets of plastic. There's nothing there.
You could roll it into a tube and snort coke from it." He stuffed the
LP back into its inner sleeve and slipped it into one of the Peaches
crates behind the counter, where we kept store copies for in-house

audition. "RCA used to call it Dynaflex vinyl—what bullshit. It's Dynacrap. They're just trying to save money."

From our position in the middle of the U.S., we were able to sense a spreading panic in the global mainstream music industry. What had started early in the decade as a sharp rise in the sales of recorded music, hitting a peak at nearly a billion in 1978, suddenly appeared to be headed the other direction. The slope of the line on the wonks' graph leveled off and then took a dip in 1979, followed by another modest drop the following year. Every Chicken Little at a major label, accustomed to nothing but rising tides in an era when manufacturing LPs was like printing currency, took one look at 18 percent fewer units sold and cried that the sky was falling.

Disco was in decline. Megalithic rock stars were dimming—drugged, drunk, or damaged. Labels culled the herd, trimming their rosters, making them less diverse and praying for a superstar bail-out, which accounts for the more homogenous and steroidal feel of popular music in the eighties. Soon they would be looking for one Michael Jackson instead of a hundred George McCraes. The end was near, the jig was up, bad shit was going down, and record stores were biting their nails. The industry pointed fingers: cassettes were killing recorded music, encouraging home taping, making music something—God forbid—people could exchange without paying for it; the oil crisis and concomitant rise in the price of petroleum was making vinyl too expensive; labels had raised the price of records too often and too fast, and there was a consumer backlash. We heard these and other explanations. Nobody was exactly sure why it was happening, but big music's house of cards was teetering on the brink of collapse.

...

Meanwhile, boutique labels like producer John Snyder's Artists House were doing just fine. A whole pandemonium of independent and artist-run outfits took off in these years, imprints that didn't make it into the figures being compiled and compared, but the kind of spirited productions that we adored. These small businesses didn't need to sell hundreds of thousands of records to prop up a swollen star system. Their model was one of economy of means and maximum result. Committees of know-nothing middle management didn't second-guess their output. They were fleet and decisive, and they issued whatever felt right.

James "Blood" Ulmer's *Tales of Captain Black* was among the first jazz records I bought. I paid Coop seven dollars, a modest retail price suggested by the label, less my 10 percent employee discount. The guitarist had taken to dropping his last name at the time, often simply being referred to by his nickname, "Blood," but in this case he was also known as Captain Black, the world's first harmolodic superhero—more on harmolodics in a sec. Artists House delivered the music in a generous package, with a gatefold sleeve, heavy card stock with shiny coating, both sides of the gate open with the LP in one and a nicely printed booklet in the other. The eight-page insert contained lead sheets for two of the compositions, drawings and ancillary artwork, a prose résumé describing Ulmer's history, detailed technical information about each microphone used on the recording, and a beautiful diagram titled "James Blood's Harmolodic Guitar Clef." As a mediocre sight-reader accustomed to interpreting guitar tab and box chords, I was dazzled and mystified by this bifurcated graph of notes, like a leftward pointing arrow, which seemed to articulate an arcane methodology behind the music.

The cover and two-panel interior spread feature line drawings by artist Shelby McPherson. Blood gazes back at the viewer on the front cover from under a wide-brimmed hat, calm and penetrating, while inside a comic book image of Captain Black rescues a curvaceous damsel from a filthy, festering city, lifting her from crime and porn and fast food to join three other black women in a spotless, heavenly, Afrofuturistic alter-universe. McPherson's work called to mind Pedro Bell's outrageous designs for Funkadelic, like *One Nation Under a Groove* (1978), *Hardcore Jollies* (1976), *Let's Take It to the Stage* (1975), *Standing on the Verge of Getting It On* (1975), and *Cosmic Slop* (1973). Not to mention *Tales of Kidd Funkadelic*

(1976)—note anything striking in the title? Decoding the signifiers on *Captain Black*, I anticipated something funky. I was right, but it wasn't the funk I expected. It was harmolodic funk.

Snyder called his label Artists House in homage to saxophonist Ornette Coleman's performance loft of the same name, located on the ground floor of 131 Prince Street in New York's SoHo. Coleman was a guiding force for the label, which released two of his LPs, *Body Meta*, featuring an early incarnation of the electric group Prime Time, and *Soapsuds, Soapsuds*, duets with bassist Charlie Haden. I loved the gentle rambling exchange of *Soapsuds, Soapsuds*, as well as its hilarious title, a reference to the TV show *Mary Hartman, Mary Hartman*. The Prime Time LP is a thing of beauty. Guitarist Charles Ellerbie puts down a dirty Bo Diddley rhythm part in step with drummer Ronald Shannon Jackson while Bern Nix overlays pristine melodic lines on a hollow-body electric, echoed by the saxophonist's plaintive calls.

Ulmer's route to the role of Captain Black had taken him from South Carolina to New York City, with residencies in between in Pittsburgh, Columbus, and Detroit. Along the way, by the time of his Artists House outing—his overdue debut as a leader—he'd recorded with organists Hank Marr, Big John Patton, and Larry Young, in a quartet fronted by free jazz drummer Rashied Ali, in a cameo on an LP by saxophonist Joe Henderson, and with Arthur Blythe on the alto saxophonist's brilliant Columbia record *Lenox Avenue Breakdown*, an adventurous jazz outing for the major label.

In the seventies, he'd started studying and working—same thing, in this case—with Coleman, performing in Europe as a member of the jazz pioneer's quartet with bassist Sirone and drummer Billy Higgins, a group that brings together three phases of creative music, drawing Higgins from Ornette's early sixties freebop foursome, Sirone from New York's budding seventies loft scene, and Ulmer from Ornette's proto–Prime Time electric period. It's a shame the brave group never issued an official piece of vinyl.

Ulmer was an Ornette acolyte. He applied harmolodics to his

guitar playing with rigor and ingenuity, not so easy for the notoriously slippery theory. I had an opportunity to ask Ornette about harmolodic theory once in 1987. Of course, the concept has been the topic of much debate, not all of it positive, the gist of which revolves, in some people's minds, around whether there's a concept there at all. I see it as a deeply mutable idea, the definition of which is left deliberately open in order to address whatever comes to bear on its application. You've heard of situational ethics? Harmolodic theory could be situational aesthetics. Maybe that means it's not a concept at all, but a gestalt or a sensibility. Some have said harmolodics is the jabbering of a wack job or the slippery linguistics of a trickster. The way Ornette described it to me did not seem like this, but was basically a call to respect the relative independence of each player. He said that one musician should offer one thing, another should add to it, and another, and so on. I asked him if that was like hocket-style playing, as in West African balafon music, and he said yes, something like that, but all at the same time. It was an expansive definition and made me think about polytonality and multiple rhythmic centers, also about Coleman's insistence on the equal importance of harmony, melody, and rhythm, the search for a way not to subjugate one of these to the others. I've read him giving specific descriptions of harmolodics, even ones that have little to do with what he said to me. Ornette was an improviser, first and foremost, in music and in words. I think he was interested in being generative, not dogmatic. Maybe the answer will be revealed with the eventual posthumous publication of his book *The Harmolodic Theory*, which he started writing at the outset of the seventies. I sincerely hope that happens before the onset of the next ice age.

Ornette contributes his inimitable gliding alto to *Tales of Captain Black*, playing Ulmer's melodies along with the guitarist, whose tone on his Gibson Byrdland is already gruff, scrabbly, and slurred, sometimes with a subtle wah effect, disinterring the blues as he would more pointedly on later records. At other times, single-note runs ring out, pure and resonant. Listening to him at the outset of

"Arena," I knew I loved him. I'd never heard Philadelphian electric bassist Jamaaladeen Tacuma. He was so deeply funky and so wild that I couldn't get my head around what he was doing, his string popping sound on "Revelation March" ransacking and reinventing Larry Graham's "Thank You (Falettinme Be Mice Elf Agin)."

This was heavy music for a first-time jazz listener. It incorporated rock and funk, but seemed to have a different core understanding of those genres than I did. Post-punk helped prime me for Prime Time—I liked the energy of it, the way the musicians worked themselves into little corners of dissonance and freneticism, then uncoiled into more consonant, or at least concerted, actions. What really challenged me on *Tales of Captain Black*, though, was the rhythm. Ornette's son Denardo Coleman is the drummer on the date, and he does something that I still rarely hear—he varies the tempo within a track, speeding up, slowing down, pulling Tacuma with him either way. In my little high school garage bands, we did that too, but never willingly, and always with one of us yelling at the drummer or bassist to keep proper time. Denardo is self-taught. He appeared on records with his father starting at age ten, when they recorded *The Empty Foxhole* as a trio with bassist Charlie Haden. If you want to fathom Haden's loyalty, consider that he stuck with the saxophonist when he transitioned from master drummers like Higgins and Edward Blackwell to Ornette's untutored preteen son.

Ornette knew what he was doing with Denardo, and Ulmer understood what Ornette heard in Denardo and was likewise faithful to his teacher. Denardo's playing on *Tales of Captain Black* is refreshingly free of drum clichés, using simple marching rhythms or singsongy treble time to expand and contract the music, making it feel uncommonly organic. Musicians often talk about a rhythmic sweet spot or "pocket." Denardo is a *pick*pocket, as deft as the Artful Dodger at stealing beats. On my favorite cut, "Moons Shine," the four musicians are each audible on their own and also in constellation. Alto sax joins Blood's guitar as it floats over the top of a skittering rhythm. For a moment you can hear in two time frames at once—a hovering one and a nervous one, the air and the earth below.

...

The plane touches ground and my cell buzzes, a generous offer to meet me at arrivals, gladly accepted. His cool Mercedes purrs as Jamaaladeen Tacuma wends us through the streets of southwest Philadelphia, same neighborhood where he grew up and still resides. Even in casual attire, Tacuma is always dapper. His immaculately groomed beard is frosted white, offset by a jet-black divot of top hair and green-framed glasses, pants cuffed exactly the right distance back up his leg. There are people on the sidewalks, traffic is thick, morning drop-offs at elementary school occasion circus-like maneuvers. A massive, shirtless dude sits on a stoop on this uncommonly warm September morning, the only white person for miles, aside from me.

At the beginning of 1975, still in his teens, back when he was known as Rudy McDaniel, Tacuma joined forces with Ornette Coleman. Forty-two years hence, as we move between row houses in various states of repair and corner stores with hand-painted signs, the bassist narrates his early history—rejecting a full scholarship at a prestigious music school to go on the road with Charles Earland, becoming part of the organist's burning rhythm section, the shock when Earland let him go because he and the drummer were stealing attention from the leader, a rare period of depression followed by the opportunity of a lifetime, touring with Coleman's new electric band after being recommended by Reggie Lucas. A lightbulb illuminates: Lucas, who would later produce Madonna's first album, played guitar with Miles Davis just as the trumpeter's own electric band firmed up. His linking of Tacuma with Ornette offers the most direct link I've heard between the two amplified jazz ensembles, one led by Miles, one by Ornette.

Tacuma and I lived in different Philadelphias. The year he left for Europe to join Coleman and company, I was a twelve-year-old making my first solo Amtrak trip to New York City on a student exchange. Ornette was showing Tacuma about harmolodics, and my host was feeding baby mice to a pet boa. I wonder whose experience was more alien. But now, driving through the streets of this part of town, I'm acutely aware that in the four years my family lived in Philly, we never once came here. It was an area always referred to as dangerous, mostly by people who had never been there.

As the day heats up, street life is bustling. Sections of the neighborhood are poverty struck, with crumbling infrastructure, but other spots are immaculately cared for and brilliantly decorated. We pull up to a corner to park, across the street a bright house painted green and yellow sits opulent as a temple. Around the corner, Tacuma unlocks the door into a building with more subdued exteriors—light blue stucco with black trim. Up a narrow stairway, flanked by spray-painted canvases heavy on fluorescent pinks and greens, we make our way into the Redd Carpet Room, Tacuma's style emporium. It's anything but subdued. Wherever he goes on tour, the bassist looks for exceptional clothes, shoes, bags, colognes, and accessories, and brings them back to his legendary man cave and vintage clothing boutique. *The Rifleman* plays on a TV in a fireplace. A vivid red sofa, slung low to the floor, makes the space's color reference legit. Tacuma's white upright bass is tethered to a swatch of wall also painted bright red.

We talk about the meaning of personal style. Tacuma laments the current lack thereof in creative music: "I came up under Ornette. I remember the first time I went to his loft on Prince Street. Those incredible paintings that are on his records were on the walls. He always wore something sharp and surprising. It was part of the music, for him, how you lived and how you looked." He pauses, then adds: "Even before that, I was listening to Philly soul groups. They were all dressed to kill." On the wall behind him is a poster for Tacuma's 1984 record *Renaissance Man*. He cuts a mean profile in his svelte black tuxedo with side-striped pants and angular lapels.

As an adult, it was not until I met Jim Dempsey, my business partner, that I really thought about my own sense of style, what it meant to project a certain sensibility through how you presented yourself. Before then, I think I'd defaulted to a kind of post-collegiate frump, with oversize button-downs draped like potato sacks over printed T-shirts, unshapely jeans, no belt, inelegant kicks, white tube socks. This dorm-ready get-up made sense for an undergraduate, conveying the correct ruffled insouciance, but when carried over into later life, it was a smidge pathetic. Reclining in the Redd Carpet Room, crossing my wing-tip shoes, I'm grateful to have had Dempsey's guidance.

Tacuma rises, spritzes me with a favorite smell, and suggests we head off to my event. I'm in town reading from a new book, in which there's a short passage on Blood's *Tales of Captain Black*. I show him the part where I mention him. The record is reproduced in color. "Blood's sense of style was intimidating to me," I admit. "Look at that hat on the cover, those incredible comics on the interior. He was named Blood, which was intense enough. If he was Captain Black, you were Lieutenant Brown." Tacuma laughs, peruses the book, and we depart. Later he introduces me to his teenage son, Siraj, one of his ten children. Siraj is wearing a beautifully hand-decorated jacket with a colorful abstract shape on its breast. "I have my own line," Siraj says.

Somehow, as I glance down at Tacuma's *Lost in Space*–themed Gucci shoes, I'm not surprised.

Act I: Cheap Trick, *Heaven Tonight*; The Cars, *The Cars*

Dramatis Personae

RIC OCASEK
  singer and guitarist
RICK NIELSEN
  guitarist and singer

SCENE New York City, September 22, 1978. The Palladium, backstage after a concert

OCASEK Great gig, Rick!

NIELSEN You too, Ric! Outstanding version of "Best Friend's Girl." You had them in the palm of your hand. Speaking of which, I think the Cars are the undisputed masters of the palm-mute guitar. You've taken that technique to a whole new place. And I say that as someone who's used it many times myself.

OCASEK Thanks, much appreciated. You guys were incredible on "California Man." The Move would have been moved. You did Roy Wood's classic song proud.

(Lowers his voice.)

Hey, listen, I'm glad we're alone for a minute. I've got a couple of questions I'd been meaning to ask you. Do you believe in the international power pop conspiracy?

(Nielsen looks around conspiratorially, straightening his bow tie.)

NIELSEN How'd you know about that? I thought we kept it under wraps. You know about the Japanese connection?

OCASEK I've heard you have a double live record in the can that was recorded there, and that the fans went wild like they did for the Beatles. Ring a bell?

NIELSEN You should have been there, it was unreal—after we all hollered, "We're alright" together for a while, a sea of Japanese kids kept chanting, "Cheap Trick! Cheap Trick!" It was particularly surreal to sing a song like "Surrender," with all its twisted South Seas military references. I mean there's a line about a soldier's dick falling off from VD he caught over there.

OCASEK But you're singing about sex work in Indonesia, the Philippines, not Japan.

NIELSEN Granted, but we're also singing a chorus that goes, *Surrender, surrender, but don't give yourself away*, right there in the land that surrendered. And they're eating it up!

OCASEK Hadn't thought of that. Shit, that's crazy. Congratulations on such a massive hit. Number 62 on the Billboard charts is nothing to poke a stick at. I just love the image in that song of old folks fooling around on the couch, smoking dope, and listening to their children's Kiss records. Hilarious. You got your fans to love a song by singing affectionately about their parents—who'da thunk?

NIELSEN You were asking about the conspiracy. What did you want to know?

OCASEK We want in. What does it take?

NIELSEN It's a grassroots secret society, and we're building it from the Midwest outward, though we already have lots of connections worldwide, obviously.

OCASEK Why start in the Midwest?

NIELSEN Look at a map. The U.S. is a horse. Maine is the head, Southern California is the butt, Texas and Florida are the legs. In the Midwest, we're riding high in the saddle; we have to control the knobby stallion, tell it whether to trot or gallop, which direction to go, pull up on the bridle, apply the whip. The conspiracy has a council of elders, chaired by Todd Rundgren, with members including Kevin Godley, Lol Creme, Cyril Jordan, Suzi Quatro, Kim Fowley, Joan Jett, Eric Carmen, and Alex Chilton. Initial applications have come in from some promising new bands that don't even have records out, like Shoes from Zion, Illinois, the Knack from rural Michigan, the Romantics from Detroit, a fella named Dwight Twilley from

Tulsa. And of course there's interest from outside the Midwest, like the Go-Gos, a just-formed girl group in L.A., Greg Kihn from San Francisco, Chris Stamey and the dB's from North Carolina by way of New York, and British bands like Squeeze, the Yachts, the Vapors, the Babys, and the Only Ones. You know their single, "Another Girl Another Planet"? Classical music, in my book!

OCASEK   Naturally, I agree, an immortal song already, and just six months old. Great list of applicants and tremendous advisory group. But, man, have you heard the Babys? They may be pop, but they're weak. Really, what are the criteria for acceptance?

NIELSEN   Well, like you suggest, it's not all about power chords. Those are important, but the presence of an inventive pop melody, you know, the convincing use of a *hook* is key. And for us, power refers not only to hard-rocking guitars—of course I'm all in favor of that, as I have a collection of a couple hundred guitars to choose from—but at least as important is creative song form and something sneaky and possibly subversive in the lyrics or the presentation. Like the way we put the two glam-pusses on the front of the new record and then me and Bun, the two nut-jobs, on the back. It's like an unexpected jolt, and there's plenty of it in the music, too. You guys do that, like on "You're All I've Got Tonight"—by emphasizing the last word, that one move makes it into a one-night-stand plea masquerading as a love song. On the transition between that song and Ben's "Bye Bye Love," you turn the tag ending of your song into the intro of his. Brilliant. Those details push power pop out of the realm of regular radio pop. There's enough sweetness, which is the pure pop side, and the eccentric aspect doesn't ever eclipse the beauty, which would turn it into art pop. You have a lot of keyboards, synthesizers, and Syndrums, but there's plenty of emphasis on hard guitar, and Elliot Easton is really fucking terrific. We haven't reviewed the Babys yet, we're still concentrating on Great Lakes apps, but I'll take what you say into consideration.

OCASEK I know you've heard our record. Don't we belong in the
conspiracy?

(Nielsen gets up and grazes at the snack table, offering Ocasek a stalk
of grapes.)

NIELSEN Yes. And based on tonight's double-bill, I think we can
expedite your membership. But right now, like I say, we're concentrating on the Midwest.

OCASEK Well, just to press a little, you could say that the Cars
were born in Ohio. Ben Orr and I met in Cleveland, and we
played together in Columbus and Ann Arbor before moving to
Boston, where we got together with the rest of the guys.
You've never heard the Milkwood record *How's the Weather?*,
have you?

NIELSEN No.

OCASEK Good thing, it's pretty terrible. But anyway, I went to
Maple Heights High, outside Cleveland, and Ben went to
Valley Forge High, in nearby Parma. He was in a band I liked
called the Grasshoppers. They'd already released two singles
on a local label. I mean the Cars formed in Beantown, no question, but couldn't you grandfather us in?

NIELSEN That's all useful information. OK, so here's the deal, I'll
sponsor your application. If you'll give me a couple copies of
The Cars, I will send them to Todd and the other members of
the council. Amazing that you're a Buckeye!

(He hesitates, chewing on an almond, then sits down next to Ocasek.)
You know, I'm confident enough that you'll be our next induct-
ees that I'm going to give you the secret password, but keep it
between us until you hear from the elders. With the password
you'll be admitted to the annual meeting in Rockford and most
record stores will give you a 25 percent discount, if they're in
on the conspiracy. The password is "halfnelson."

OCASEK Thanks for your faith in us, Rick.

NIELSEN Welcome to the club, Ric.

Act II: Wire, *Chairs Missing*

Dramatis Personae

COLIN NEWMAN
  a singer and guitarist
GRAHAM LEWIS
  a bassist and singer
B. C. GILBERT
  a guitarist
ROBERT GOTOBED
  a drummer
JOHN CORBETT
  a teenager
JEAN-LUC GODARD
  a filmmaker

SCENE Iowa City, late September 1978, late afternoon. John Corbett's bedroom in his parents' white Victorian house on Lee
  Street, the one with the big red front door. Having just finished
  a grilled cheese sandwich, Corbett is lying on his unmade bed,
  headphones on, listening to *Chairs Missing*, intermittently
  dozing. The other characters are lurking spirits, unseen and
  inaudible to Corbett.

NEWMAN This is what we get. We make the most brilliant record
  ever, and our biggest fan is listening to it whilst popping pim-
  ples, procrastinating writing his application essay for university, tossing off, and switching out our masterpiece for a 10cc
  record. Fucking hell.
GILBERT Leave him be. He's an idjut, but he's our idjut.
NEWMAN We deserve better.
GILBERT Sure, probably, but this is America. We've never toured
  here and I don't know what American fans are like. Maybe
  they're all this slack-jawed and half awake.

GOTOBED Let me remind you, we have some right stupid music animals back home in London. Almost everyone misunderstood *Pink Flag*, di'n't they? Thought it was an orthodox punk record.

NEWMAN Not this time. We made sure of that. This one is new wave, but in the sense of the French cinematic new wave, not the B-fucking-52's.

GODARD Messieurs, may I inquire: what is wrong *avec les* B-52's?

LEWIS Rather fluffy and trivial, no? All beehives, surf guitars, rock lobsters. Mark E. Smith called that sort of dross "pop stock." How can anyone take them seriously? They don't even understand irony; they turn it into kitsch.

GODARD And you think your record is closer to my films than to their *petit* single?

GILBERT Respectfully, Mr. Godard, yes, we do.

GODARD Ah, then you don't remember the dance sequence in *Bande à part*. Did you know that the Monochrome Set named a song after one of my movies?

LEWIS We were too busy making our music to pay attention to lesser acts like them.

GODARD It's a good song, *une bonne chanson*. [Sings:] *Alphaville, she sleeps in useless flesh / Alphaville, the rancid, blood-soaked breast / Alphaville, in sunlight and slow death / Don't look now / She's a movie star, she's a little bit touched / Don't look now / She's so wunderbar, all gears, no clutch.*

GOTOBED Better than expected.

LEWIS Colin and I wrote a song called "French Film Blurred" for *Chairs Missing*.

NEWMAN [Sings:] *I suppose that's the disadvantage / Of not speaking a second language.*

GODARD Better than expected.

(Corbett rises from the bed, returns the tonearm from the record, which has finished, takes off the headphones, leaves the stage, returns with a rotary phone, dragging the long cord through his bedroom door, which he shuts. He dials a number.)

CORBETT Hey, man. What you up to? Yeah, I was downtown. No, I went to BJ's, finally got the first Clash album. It's good, but you've gotta hear this Wire record—it's fucking incredible. Might be my favorite new album. Yeah, I'm halfway through, and it's making my big toe stand up in my boot. Nothing like the first. It's edgy and minimal, but really smart, weirdly produced, super British, with some unexpected shit. Like keyboards and synthesizers and tape loops. [Pauses, listens.] Yeah, I guess you could say sometimes it sounds a little like Pink Floyd. Switches back and forth from super-short songs to longer ones, jangly art pop to kinda pretentious and experimental. You gotta hear this one track called "Being Sucked in Again." Right, that's what I thought, but no, it's more like that line from *The Godfather*, you know, just when I thought I was out. . . . No, man, I just got it. You can borrow it when I've had some time with it. Yeah, OK, Doug, see you on the bus tomorrow. Later.

(Corbett hangs up, turns the record over to play the second side, puts the headphones on, climbs back on the bed.)

LEWIS I don't know, guys, he's not totally dim.

NEWMAN Don't be such a panty wipe.

GODARD I think Graham is on to something. He's unformed, what we call in France *un vert*. Not yet ripe. But the bones are there.

NEWMAN You kidding? He's got a Vibrators record in that stack. And not the first one, the second bloody Vibrators record, *V2*. I've seen him listening to it. He likes it! He's a cannibal. We shouldn't let them sell our records to people like him.

GOTOBED Calm down, he's just about to hit "Outdoor Miner." I want to see what he does.

(All five of them gather around Corbett and watch him as he listens to the song. He nods his head, eyes closed, as a gentle smile cracks on his mouth. He rises, goes to the turntable, and repeats the song.)

Ha! He loves it. You're right, Lewis, there's hope for him
after all.

GODARD May I make *une prédiction*?

NEWMAN What are you now, the ghost of Christmas future?

GODARD Based on what we've seen, I believe our little friend will
    discover my films in a few years, not thinking of your record,
    even though it will have predisposed him to the way I con-
    struct and deconstruct *avec le celluloïd*. I think he will also
    enjoy Marker, Snow, and Tarkovsky, and will possibly lose
    his present dalliance *avec mon vieil ami* Monsieur Fellini.

NEWMAN Hold on, what's he doing now? This looks bad.

    (Corbett removes the headphones. Moving to the stereo, he puts
    Chairs Missing back into its cover and pulls Talking Heads,
    More Songs about Buildings and Food from the stack, puts it on,
    assumes the position, and kicks back.)

    Friends, we spoke too soon. *This* is what passes for clever in
    the States. The UK and Ireland have had millennia to per-
    fect clever, we've had Shakespeare and Blake and Milton and
    Chaucer, we've had Keats and Yeats and Eliot and Beckett
    and Raworth, and these American gits spend a couple of centu-
    ries dabbling in the tongue and think they're masters of clever.
    [Pauses a moment.] I think I'll go back to art school.

Act III: *No New York*; Talking Heads, *More Songs about Buildings and Food*

Dramatis Personae

ARTO LINDSAY
　a singer and guitarist

LYDIA LUNCH
　a singer

JAMES CHANCE
　a singer and saxophonist

DAVID BYRNE
　a singer

ALBERT CAMUS
　a philosopher

MRS. PETERSON
　an English teacher

JOHN CORBETT
　a teenager

PAUL, CHARLIE, AARON, ANNE
　classmates

SCENE　Iowa City, early October 1978, morning, West High School, Mrs. Peterson's AP English class, end of trimester, 10 a.m. The musicians and philosopher are all spirits, imperceptible to the teacher and her pupils.

　(Bell rings.)

MRS. PETERSON　OK, class. Today, in lieu of his final paper, John is going to make a presentation titled "Existentialist Music." John?

CORBETT　Thank you, Mrs. Peterson. I have selected some music that seems to me to have something to do with existentialism, as we've been studying it in this class.

AARON　Shostakovich?

PAUL Berg?

CORBETT No, none of that, you nerds. I'm talking about popular music, pop and rock and funk and stuff like that. Things I've been thinking about for the last couple of years. Let's start with something from a new record called *No New York*, which is a compilation of four bands from what they call the No Wave movement. This is the song "Jaded" by the Contortions. Here are a few of the words.

(Cupping the inner sleeve between his hands, pushing it together so that it opens up like an envelope, Corbett reads from the lyric sheet, which is printed on the sleeve's interior, deliberately making it difficult to access.)

I'm jaded, but so in love / Faded, but still want more / My heart, my heart's an open sore and When my pleasure turns to disgust . . . Ill-fated, flesh painted.

(Plays the song on his parents' home stereo, which he has brought into school.)

ANNE That's not even music. By what definition is that musical? He can't sing. And what is that horrible instrument he's torturing—is that a saxophone?

CHANCE I'll take that as a compliment.

LUNCH You would.

CORBETT I'm not here to debate whether it's music or not, but whether it's existentialist music or not.

PAUL Not.

CORBETT Thanks for your prompt reply, Paul. Why do you say that?

PAUL It's bleak. I'll give you that. And I do think it's music. But it's not existentialist just because it's unpleasant. Lots of different things are nasty. Why would *you* say it's existentialist?

CHANCE This should be good.

CAMUS Yes, indeed, I'm on the edge of my seat.

CORBETT The absurdity of it, the fact that the protagonist of the song is "jaded, but still in love." That's paradoxical or at least a willful contradiction, an absurd condition. The proximity of pleasure and disgust seems to me to express the impossibility of meaningful human interaction, key to existentialist philosophy. I don't want to stretch the comparison, but it seems to be an anti-love song, grimy and beaten up, much the way I think of a character in Dostoyevsky. It's slow and grinding, where other Contortions tracks are upbeat, even funky. They cover a James Brown song, for the record, and extract an exact meaning from the lyric *I can't stand myself*. For their singer, James Chance, I don't think it's meant as an inverted negative, like "bad" can mean "good"—I think he really can't stand himself.

CHANCE I'd really like to kick him in the face, even if he's sorta right. But these bumpkins are stranded in Iowa, for Chrissake. We're from the origin of the fucking world, New York City, center cut in the prime rib of life.

LINDSAY Give me a break, James. Half the people on that record are either from St. Petersburg or went to school there. Hardly the hard streets of New York. Ooh, big bad people from bumblefuck Florida!

LUNCH Yeah, man. You know what they say, nowhere = now + here.

CORBETT Let me play another track from this record.

ANNE Oh, yes, by all means, why wouldn't you? It's so delightful.

CORBETT Most of them are short, so I promise it won't be too painful. This is by DNA. It's called "Egomaniac's Kiss."
(Plays the song, which lasts two minutes eleven seconds.)
In particular I like the line: *Less than awful more than naked.* I have no idea what it means, but it sounds great. To me, this song's existential character is more in its vibe than in the lyrics. It's blues with noise guitar. The words are kind of nonsensical. But they're not so far from "Jaded," in a way, since it's the kiss of an egomaniac, you know, like a jaded lover—another paradox. Maybe it all has something to do with the idea that existence precedes essence.

CAMUS That phrase has never said much to me, but this makes me think of something in a stage play by *mon vieil ami* Jean-Paul Sartre. I believe one of the lines postulates that hell is other people.

CHANCE I can relate.

LINDSAY Hell *was* another person. His first name was Richard.

CAMUS It is a lonely feeling, this music, like the uncomfortable thump when you hit a pedestrian. *N'est-ce pas?*

(All the spirits look at him in silence.)

But maybe I have said too much.

CORBETT I have another song that's bleak and unpleasant by a band that takes its name from a book by Albert Camus, but I'll save the Fall for later. Let's stay with New York music, brightening it up a bit. I'm going to play a track from the Talking Heads record *More Songs about Buildings and Food*.

CHARLIE Is it their second record?

CORBETT Yes.

CHARLIE So is it volume two?

CORBETT What do you mean?

CHARLIE Is this the follow-up to *Songs about Buildings and Food*?

CORBETT No.

CHARLIE Was their first record concerned primarily with buildings and food?

CORBETT No. It's a title. Just let me play the song. It's called "Artists Only."

CAMUS These people squabble like *les surréalistes*.

(Corbett plays the song.)

Pretty soon now, I will be bitter
Pretty soon now, will be a quitter
Pretty soon now, I will be bitter
You can't see it 'til it's finished

I don't have to prove that I am creative
I don't have to prove that I am creative

All my pictures are confused
And now I'm going to take me to you

BYRNE Good times.

MRS. PETERSON John, explain how this is existentialist.

CORBETT Well, I think it expresses a sense of anxiety. I hear it in the singer's voice: he's so agitated the way he's talking about bitterness and loathing himself for being a quitter, lashing out and saying he doesn't have to prove anything. But I think it's also a joke about being an artist, how guarded and protective and squirrelly they can be, like they're afraid of showing anybody their work before it's done, as if that would jinx it. Trepidation and anxiety, the impenetrability of language, the stumbling block of interpersonal communication—but from an analytical rather than romantic standpoint—all couched in spastic pop. It's like they're afraid of music.

CHANCE He's almost making me like your gutless songs, David.

BYRNE Thanks. I'll take that as a compliment.

LUNCH You would.

PAUL Isn't there a religious song on this record? And wouldn't that sort of take Talking Heads out of the running for being existentialist?

CORBETT You mean their cover of Al Green's "Take Me to the River." I think it's very different from the original meaning. Like, it's not about baptism. It's about singing about baptism. Instead of gospel, it's sort of a new wave spiritual. The singer, David Byrne, will work on a record called *My Life in the Bush of Ghosts*, together with Brian Eno, who produced *More Songs* and also produced *No New York*. On the Eno/Byrne record, they'll use found recordings of preachers, which is somehow like what I think they're doing on "Take Me to the River." It's not that they're expressing love of God; they're expressing love of a song about loving God. It might not be existential, but it expresses alienation.

BYRNE That's a fine hair to split, but he's gone to the right salon.

CORBETT Now I'm going to play something British, a single by the group the Cure.

CAMUS *Mon dieu*, not that! The song that paraphrases my little novel, *L'Etranger*, which is itself just a parable. You can't paraphrase a parable. That's like diddling a paradiddle. Or summarizing an algorithm. You use an algorithm to *get* a sum, you don't summarize an algorithm. That *petit* book is like an algorithm. Those pretentious twerps turn it into three lines about an Arab in the sand. Monsieur Byrne, I would much prefer to stay with your quirk than that pile of Middle Eastern *merde*.

BYRNE Thank you, sir. I'll pass your encouragement along to the band.

Act IV: XTC, *Go 2*

Dramatis Personae

ANDY PARTRIDGE
   a singer and guitarist
COLIN MOULDING
   a singer and bassist
BARRY ANDREWS
   a keyboardist
TERRY CHAMBERS
   a drummer
JOHN LECKIE
   a producer
JOSEPH KOSUTH
   an artist
JOHN CORBETT
   a teenager
DOUG CANNON
   his friend
ANONYMOUS JOURNALIST #1
   an anonymous journalist
ANONYMOUS JOURNALIST #2
   an anonymous journalist

SCENE London, October 6, 1978, a press conference held by Virgin
   Records in celebration of XTC's new release, *Go 2*. The band
   sits at microphones behind a table, a small group of writers
   in the audience posing questions. The American artist Kosuth
   and teenagers are spirits, imperceptible to the journalists, the
   musicians, and their producer.

LECKIE Hi, everyone. Thanks for being here. We are thrilled to be
   releasing the second LP by XTC. It's called *Go 2*. Barry suggested the title, based on the board game Go, but adding the 2.
   Evidently.

ANONYMOUS JOURNALIST #1 I would like to ask you to put this record in context. Please describe how *Go 2* relates to the records that you will release in the future.

(The band members look at each other quizzically. Partridge addresses the microphone.)

PARTRIDGE Wot?

CORBETT [To Cannon:] You have to admit, that is sort of the main question.

CANNON Yeah, like, who wants to get on a ship that might sink? We have a right to know: Will they make more killer records, assuming this one is great, or will they start to suck?

ANONYMOUS JOURNALIST #1 Will there be many of them? Will they be poppier or more artsy? What will the covers look like?

MOULDING How could we possibly know those things? They are in the future, but we are here now, with a new record, which, by the way, is what we're here to promote.

ANONYMOUS JOURNALIST #2 Hang on now. Let's not get testy. My colleague has asked a reasonable question, which has to do with context. That's our job in the press, to give our audience some kind of context to help them make a judgment. Anyone can offer an opinion. We music journalists must push deeper for the whole story. And why should we settle for records that have already been made? Anyone can listen to those for themselves. We need to know about the records that come after.

MOULDING Have I gone cuckoo crazy? What the hell are you going on about?

ANDREWS Well, Colin, I hate to side with them, but I can say at least one thing about future XTC records, which is that I won't be on them. As of this moment, I am officially going solo.

(Andrews leaves. The band sits silent in disbelief.)

ANONYMOUS JOURNALIST #1 Now we're getting somewhere.

CHAMBERS If anyone's looking at me [they all look at him], I can tell you I'm not going anywhere. At least for the time being, let's say another five years. I suppose that tells you something about the way subsequent XTC records will sound. And we know also that *Go 2* will be the last of the more aggressive records, because Barry was the toughest and most experimental of us. He could have been a jazzer if he'd wanted to. He'll have a tough time of it as a solo act, I think. Anyway, XTC will go more toward pop, but with the clever and quirky details our fans have come to love.

CORBETT Hmm, less aggressive and without those fantastic keyboards, that seems like a bummer to me. I love the Farfisa, the Crumar. Now there'll be nothing but drums and wires.

CANNON More pop, less noise, always good in my world.

ANONYMOUS JOURNALIST #2 What about singles? Will you continue to release them with otherwise unavailable B-sides? And will those be grouped into a B-sides compilation or will they be exclusively for connoisseurs?

LECKIE Ah, um, friends, I meant to tell you all something, but I forgot. Virgin has informed us they're not going to cull a single from *Go 2*.

PARTRIDGE What?! Not one single?

LECKIE No. Not in the UK. They're considering a North American 45 of "Are You Receiving Me?"

PARTRIDGE But we're a pop band. That's what we do—we make singles.

LECKIE Having made *Go+*, a twelve-inch with dub versions of songs from the LP, to be given away with the first 15,000 copies of *Go 2*, I think the label figures it's done all the promoting it's going to do. Not to send good money after bad. Except, of course, for this joyous press conference. There's tea and finger foods on the back table, folks.

MOULDING That's hardly a substitute for a bona fide single, for the love of god. Everyone's doing dub. *Go+* is a loss leader—those 15,000 will sell many more than just themselves, you wait. And these songs are built for airplay. "Meccanik Dancing (Oh We Go!)" is a perfect ironic jab at mindless weekend punters. There's the frantic pogo power of "Buzzcity Talking"

and "Jumping in Gomorrah." I mean, blimey, not everything is as weird as "I Am the Audience" or "Life Is Good in
the Greenhouse"—granted, those would be a real stretch for
deejays. But any of those others could follow up on "Are You
Receiving Me?," which is the album's natural single.

PARTRIDGE   This seems like a clear vote of no confidence.

(He gets up and leaves. Moulding and Chambers hesitate, then after a
minute follow him, exiting one at a time.)

ANONYMOUS JOURNALIST #1   We still haven't heard anything
about the record covers of future XTC records.

LECKIE   Can't you see what's just happened? This is the worst
press event of all time. What do you think I could tell you
about not-yet-made covers? Let's see: there will be pictures of
the band, they will be in funny outfits, there will be abstract
art, the band's name will be subjected to many different treatments, they will break with the black-and-white tradition and
start to use bright colors. I don't bloody know what the records
will bloody look like, but that should give you some plausible
copy.

KOSUTH   I'll say one thing, even though you geezers can't hear me:
you better not use another concept of mine. I'm thinking about
suing your asses. And Hipgnosis, your designers, I'll sue their
tuchuses, too. Pure thievery. If you're going to make a record
cover influenced by my ingenious artworks from ten years ago,
maybe think to change the color scheme or use a typewriter
with a different font. Don't just outright steal the *look* as well
as the *idea*. They'll give me a proper English settlement.

CORBETT   I didn't know it was your idea. I thought it was really
cool. I'd never seen anything like it: a self-referential record,
the motives and strategies of cover design laid bare, openly
detailed right there, on the cover itself. And no mention of anyone named Joseph Kosuth.

KOSUTH   Jesus, did you just fall off a turnip truck? I was still in
art school when I came up with that "art as idea as idea" mon-

key business. Not much older than you, I s'pose. Haven't you read Goffman's *Frame Analysis*? You step outside of one frame and you're in another frame. Step away from the album cover and you're in a meta-album-cover conceptual space. The album cover as idea . . . as idea. It's an echo chamber. I mean, I don't actually own the images that I used—they come from the dictionary, at least the way I did it, with Photostats and the like. But these limey crooks took the way it looks and passed it off as their own, and that, as you'd say, is not cool.

ANONYMOUS JOURNALIST #2 Sorry to be the bearer of bad news, but your snacks have run out.

CANNON What a bloodbath. Remind me never to start a band.

CORBETT Remind me never to deal with artists.

Act V: Devo, *Q: Are We Not Men? A: We Are Devo!*; Pere Ubu, *The Modern Dance*; MX-80 Sound, *Hard Attack*

Dramatis Personae

JOHN CORBETT
    a teenager

DOUG CANNON
    his friend

SCENE Iowa City, October 14, 1978, 10:30 p.m., CST, Doug's bedroom, which is a complete mess, strewn with back issues of *Mad* and *Heavy Metal* magazines, dirty clothes, an unmade bed, and half-eaten snacks. They are watching a small color TV perched on a wooden crate that is full of LPs.

CORBETT This is a momentous day.

CANNON This is a terrible day.

CORBETT I feel anticipation, excitement.

CANNON I feel nothing but dread. Tonight the entire world finds out about our band. Our well-kept secret. Our beloved Devo. Exposed. Given away. Wasted on an undeserving public. The hoi polloi. Crap, this is an awful day.

CORBETT OK, let's not freak out. Maybe there's an upside. Couldn't it be that this will introduce them to a massive audience of appreciative fans, the existence of which will make their record label that much more supportive, which will in turn allow them to do increasingly ambitious projects, make umpteen more records, and explore virtually anything they want?

CANNON Or . . . they will make records of slowly declining interest, novelty having been the most salient part of their mass popularity, and once that's gone, they grow desperate to find something/anything to keep relevant with the kids, finally parodying themselves and submitting to endless soul-sucking reunion tours. Whereas, if they'd stayed underground, their weirdness shared amongst us, the truly Devo-ted, they could have explored to their heart's content and we would have understood, because we have understood them from the start, because we've been there from the start, and now they are fucking betraying us.

CORBETT You are not usually such a purist.

CANNON I know. But these are our boys.

CORBETT I have faith they'll do something so completely deranged, they won't be embraced by the mainstream. Let's give them a chance.

CANNON I hope you're right.

CORBETT Let's imagine some alternative scenarios. Take two other comparable bands, both from our greater midwestern environs, our "boys" as you call them, both signed to reasonably big companies—lest we forget that Devo is on Warner Bros., not a minor label. I'm thinking of the Akron crew's Cleveland brethren, Pere Ubu. We adore David Thomas and his band, have since their first single, "30 Seconds Over Tokyo," and the teenage angst anthem on the B-side, "Final Solution." They are brilliant and incredibly weird, and their debut, *The Modern Dance*, released on Blank Records, which is an imprint of Mercury, contains our newest anti-romantic anthem, "Non-Alignment Pact." And the synthesizer parts, courtesy of someone named Allen Ravenstine, have shown us it's possible to combine non-musical noise with musical noises in a productive way. It's like they recorded in a factory, with all the machines on like someone pressing shirts, pulling a fire alarm, sounding the factory whistle, except it's really just an EML analog synth.

CANNON I love their desolate sound. It reaches back to garage rock days, legitimately by way of Rocket from the Tombs, but places that sound in a deindustrialized rust belt topography of ruinous loss. There is no lyricism to the American version

of Joy Division. No big self-eviscerating romantic gesture.
It's too humble for that, too much grit in the bearings to run
so smoothly. And his voice is just too flipping strange, that
slightly hysterical quaver, like he's perpetually freaked out.

CORBETT So what's happened with them? In the months since
their first LP, Pere Ubu has released another, *Dub Housing*, on a bigger label, Chrysalis. Just heard a promo at the
store, exceptionally great. But what happens now? Do we see
them on *Saturday Night Live*? No. Is that good or bad? I don't
know. Let's imagine a future in which, rather than going for
mass popularity, they retain cult status. Like maybe they
find a small label, maybe a British one. Maybe they experi-
ment with a couple such labels. And in thirty years, there they
are, exactly where they started, except they are known to any
halfway-informed follower of post-punk and new wave and
whatever those kinds of music turn into.

(The two stop talking for a minute to watch a few minutes of *Saturday
Night Live*, sipping on a shared two-liter bottle of Coke. Cannon pulls
a record from the crate under the TV.)

CANNON So there's Devo and there's Pere Ubu. Here's the third
path. Complete obscurity. [Hands record to Corbett.] MX-80
Sound, from Bloomington. Rolls right off the tongue, right?
Detroit, Cleveland, Akron . . . Bloomington. It's a college town
in the Indiana outback, just like ours is here, out in this ocean
of Iowa corn and soybeans. They could be us. You know the
drill: MX-80 Sound makes its first album, *Hard Attack*, for
Island Records, only in Europe, available to their fellow mid-
westerners after a year of hunting, obtainable exclusively as
an expensive import, released to little notice. Except by people
like us. We think it's utterly spectacular, the best of all three.
MX-80 Sound offers the riskiest music, with a vocalist who
sometimes sounds like a lounge singer, an irradiated Frank
Sinatra, some shrapnel of glam and metal lodged in an adventurous Indiana wound. Compare their "PCB's" with Devo's

"Mongoloid" or Pere Ubu's "Street Waves"—their song manages to be hilarious and dystopian in perfect balance.

(Cannon puts the LP on the turntable, plays "PCB's.")

Riding around in my ATV
My wheels got stuck in some PCB's
So I threw the thing into 4WD
But the PCB's were too slippery . . .
Fuckin' PCB's, fuckin' PCB's, fuckin' PCB's, fuckin' PCB's
Fuckin' PCB's, man, in your bread, fish, milk, water!

CORBETT Always takes my breath away, that burst of cursing. I think about it when I'm out tromping around in a cornfield, communing with the pesticides and fertilizers. I'll be vermin-free, but my kids will have three eyes. *Hard Attack* is so dastardly; the whole record sports an unknown emotion, uncompromised by either the mandates of mainstream or the protocols of the underground. Like the song "Facts-Facts," detailing the terror of life in a university town, or "Man on the Move," the album's autobiographical ditty, but one that really puts forward their whole platform as a kind of mantra: *Look out for the roadblock.* We should keep that line in mind for the rest of our goddamn lives.

(Raises the tonearm and finds the track "Man on the Move.")

You know on life's big musical highway
You never know what's gonna come up next
So actually you better look out, hey look out, look out!

Look out for the roadblock.

I'm calling New York and I'm calling L.A.
I'm calling all the big shots from real far away.
I'm saying: You wanna make some money, man?
I got a band that can play.
Give us a call without any delay.

Come on give us a call without any delay.
Oh, why don't you just give us a call?
Or else look out, man.
Look out.
Look out for the roadblock.
Look out for the roadblock of sound.

CANNON And the roadblock is either: to seek a mass audience and struggle to keep your identity, or to stay occult and struggle to keep yourself going. Be seen or stay lean and mean.

CORBETT Nicely encapsulated, Doug. The roadblock of sound. [Looks at the set.] Hey, what's happening?

(Cannon shuts the music off and turns up the sound on the television. Devo's pre-made video for "Jocko Homo," a short film called *The Truth about De-Evolution*, plays in lieu of a band introduction— Booji Boy, Mark Mothersbaugh, as a figure in a cartoonish mask dressed in an orange jumpsuit, runs up the fire escape of an old building the side of which is covered in an enormous mural reading "Shine On America." The building is owned by the father of the Mothersbaugh brothers, and Cannon and Corbett recognize it from the cover of *The Akron Compilation* on Stiff Records, which came equipped with a scratch-and-sniff cover that smelled like rubber. The two fifteen-year-olds sit wide-eyed in front of the little set as they cut to the band live in the *SNL* studio. Devo wears yellow hazmat-like uniforms and square spex that look like safety goggles, moving with the herk and jerk of animatronic figurines.)

CORBETT Oh my fucking god. What just happened? Did they really just do that?

CANNON That was the greatest thing that ever happened on earth.

CORBETT What can all our polite suburban neighbors in their polite little homes be thinking? They watch this show. I think they must think the world has turned upside down. They must fear that those yellow-suited freaks are going to break

into their polite little homes and seduce their poodles and get
their daughters and sons hooked on rat poison. They must be
steadying themselves for the Devo invasion, the mongoloid
insurgence, an uptick in sales of wraparound glasses and goon-
ish face masks. The air raid siren has sounded. Everyone get
under your desk. This is not a test. Everything has changed.
Whatever the future holds for them, I think Devo just stormed
the barriers.

CANNON It's true. This is a staggering day. They drove right
through the roadblock of sound.

1979

Forty-One 45s

A carton of singles circa 1979, acquired the year I turned sixteen, with funds procured by lawn mowing, odd jobbing, cash registering at the record store, and hoarding allowance. Most of the 45s are British, a few from the States or elsewhere, on labels big and small. If the seventies had begun as the decade of the album—album-oriented radio, concept albums, operatic two- and three-LP sets—it ended in little slices that looked like this: pitch-black seven-inch salami discs expressing our taste for lower-denomination vinyl. For us the shift to singles represented growing awareness of musical diversity, a push away from the monolithic megaband toward multifarious music extracted from cultural microclimates, more in sync with the sixties—another high-water period for the single—than the first half of the seventies. These little records no longer necessarily traced an umbilicus back to a mother LP; many of them operated independently, free-floating little spurs or stinging nettles on the pant leg of mainstream music. One thing they did drag over from the dinosaur age of twelve inches, however, was the necessity of visual accompaniment; these are almost all picture-sleeve singles.

One note: In this short list you peer a shallow distance down the post-punk rabbit hole. Every record in this book, no matter its persuasion, comes from a similar warren. Terms like psych, folk, prog, metal, heavy, hard, and deep, each powerfully meaningful to their disciples, at one point or another all mated with one another, creating hyphenate offspring (heavy-psych, psych-metal, heavy-prog, prog-folk) and uncountable litters of obscure artists and bands. Music journalist and editor Pete Frame drew up a phenomenally detailed series of family trees mapping the global interrelationships among musicians. He compiled these into a series of books that suggests that any musician pondered in *Pick Up the Pieces*, from Van Morrison to Teenage Jesus and the Jerks, represents but the outer edge of a burrow down which numerous other musicians have clawed their way.

A Certain Ratio, "All Night Party"
With a name borrowed from Brian Eno, ACR had the gritty mechanical rhythm with miraculous British lack of groove that so fascinated us—unfunky, clod-footed, doom-laden, strafed-garrison disco, direct precursor to industrial dance music. Hollowman vocalizing reminds me of Ian Curtis.

Adam & the Ants, "Cartrouble"
Unusual in that the band released this track re-recorded from their debut LP, *Dirk Wears White Sox*, as a way to satisfy their contract with Do It Records. Not as halting as the music on the uniformly outstanding album, "Cartrouble" is the epitome of post-punk pout. Adam Ant has not yet donned the ridiculous pirate-prince persona, but is already rich in campy fetishistic preening.

Alternative TV, "The Force Is Blind"
Common concept of the proper single: it should be short, catchy, to the point, a promotion for the stage-ready band, primed for a spin on radio or—way back then—jukebox. ATV paid this custom no mind on a seven-inch as dissolute as their second LP, *Vibing Up the Senile Man*. A bleak, beat-less few minutes with psychedelic synthe-

sizer, scraped violin, prominent metallic chimes, and howlings by a singer named Anno, borrowed from an older communal anarchist band called Here and Now. Released as a "memorial single," after ATV was terminated by Mark Perry (aka Mark P., also founder of the early punk fanzine *Sniffin' Glue*). Aimless but right on target, it's a mini manifesto for the DIY movement: *Kiddies playing with their toys* / *"Let's play drummers make a lot of noise"* / *The tape's running and they're doing fine* / *The kids have energy and lots of time.*

Au Pairs, "You"

More four-on-the-floor sing-along than feckless fem-punk, *cum* Raincoats. Lesley Woods's and Jane Munro's monotonal singing would grow increasingly varied and exploratory on later releases like the Birmingham band's glorious LP *Playing with a Different Sex*, but it's already pointedly, explosively feminist and queer-positive.

Bags, "Survive"

The Los Angeles scene only barely cracked our consciousness, but this heavy number crowbarred its way inside. Alice Bag sang, Pat Bag played bass—two women who had met auditioning for the gal band that Kim Fowley planned to start after the Runways ran away from him. Pseudo-jazz hi-hat submits to raucous punk pogo and a sheer cliff of guitar.

Ed Banger, "Kinnel Tommy"

Singles were like tabs of LSD for someone who'd never dropped acid. Sometimes they were so alien and inexplicable that we'd go to inordinate lengths to decipher them. To wit, this Manchester single, by the erstwhile singer for the Nosebleeds—a great band featuring young guitarist Vini Reilly of the Durutti Column—which starts with a spaz-piano outburst and features dabs of dub-influenced keyboard, over which Banger narrates a string of bobbled soccer plays. But the title remained meaningless until I finally heard him berate the poor football player phonetically: *(Fuc)kin' Hell, Tommy!*

The Bizarros, "Lady Doubonette"
Pre-post-punk from 1976 Akron, Ohio, weirdo outpost supreme, four-song 33 rpm EP, wah-guitar solos, creamy organ, fat bass, and the monstrous three-chord anthem "I Bizarro." Some of the stranger American bands leapfrogged over punk, updating surreal tendencies with heavy-psych and garage overtones.

Boys Next Door, "Shivers"
Australian precursor to the Birthday Party, on which the ultra-melodramatic Nick Cave sings: *My baby's so vain she is almost a mirror / And the sound of her name sends a permanent shiver down my spine.* The signal influence of Bryan Ferry stands out, Robert Fripp–like sustained guitar performing filigree stitch-work on the gloomy, gothic ballad. "Shivers" deserves a good remake. Flip side's even better, bonkers helium-stoked vocal harmony, Jim Morrison affectation, and Ping-Pong pan on ripping guitar.

The Buzzcocks, "Orgasm Addict"
A psalm for the palm. I had a little group of friends—just a couple of fellas—who admitted to masturbating. This created a singularly strong bond, a closely held secret that served as a reality check. The Buzzcocks' song further grounded our mutual understanding, confirming that there were other auto-eroticists beyond our craven crew. *Well, you tried it just for once found it all right for kicks / But now you found out that it's a habit that sticks.* I remember reading Patti Smith saying that she preferred masturbating to heavy drugs, an inspiration that gave Pete Shelley's huffing extra oomph.

John Cooper Clarke, "Post-War Glamour Girl"
I'd fallen in love with punk poet JCC on the ten-inch compilation *Short Circuit—Live at the Electric Circus*, where he recited "You Never Get a Nipple in the Daily Express" and "I Married a Monster from Outer Space." Here, as often elsewhere, with layered atmospheric disco-inflected background collage by the Invisible Girls.

Clarke crafted wry, touching verse, which provided richer context for my understanding of the British scene via unforgettable lines like: *Adults only over her pubes / Debutantes they give her dubes / Beatniks visit with saxophones / And the way she eats her Toblerone / Says a post-war glamour girl is never alone.*

Crass, "Reality Asylum"

Singles were the perfect outlet for the fringiest messages of the post-punk diaspora. Crass lived together communally outside Essex. They were prohibited from issuing Penny Rimbaud's blasphemous recitation "Christ's Reality Asylum" on their debut EP on Small Wonder Records, so they started their own label and put it out as a seven-inch instead. In a five-minute tirade, Rimbaud calls Jesus Christ a *sterile, impotent fuck-love prophet of death,* and adds, *you sigh alone in your cock fear, you lie alone in your cunt fear, you cry alone in your woman fear, you die alone in your man fear.* In a suburb across the ocean, what struck us was the fact that Crass lived its ideals and stuck up for the worker-consumer-listener-fan, printing "Pay no more than 45p" right on the cover to keep stores from price-gouging.

The Cravats, *The End*

One of several incredible singles by this eclectic British band, whose lineup included Svoor Naan—here credited as Yehudi Storageheater—on an electrified saxophone, sounding like a primitive analog synth. Like Pere Ubu, the Cravats were too restless to be dogmatic; their sound is infused with jazz and prog elements, including wonderful drumming by Dave Bennett, imaginative song structure, and the upfront sound of big bassist the Shend.

The Cure, "Killing an Arab"

Post-punk was like a bicycle wheel. At the center was a common hub, the starting point, but the bands were all spokes pointing their own direction, and as time went on they moved apart—what you would call divergent evolution if were you studying the development of animal species. The Cure's wan, trebly sound would grow along with singer Robert Smith's hairdo, flowering into early exemplars of goth. This track, with a simple bass line we learned and played endlessly, brought readings from English class directly into our daily lives, adapting Albert Camus's *The Stranger* to Smith's brilliantly whiny vox.

The Dadistics, "Paranoia Perception"

Loving these singles did not guarantee that we'd be able to hear any of the bands live. Our family spent many holidays visiting my aunt Jayne in River Forest, west of Chicago, and often I lost myself in Val's Halla Records, a store in nearby Oak Park, about three blocks up the street from the first apartment my parents rented when I was a newborn. In addition to Val, a thoroughly beneficent record industry wacko with a dog named Halla, I befriended her store manager Mark, who'd been in London in the sacred month of October 1977, attending the concert that became *Live Stiffs Live*, a concert recording stocked with many of my heroes. Hence, Mark had a musical halo in my eyes. He helped me select from the pile of incoming releases, pointing me to the best 2 Tone and pub rock, as well as the weirder post-punk I craved. One of the local groups he recommended was the Dadistics, a rocking pop-punk outfit who'd recorded this splendid little single in Evanston, just north of Chicago. Audrey Stanzler's vocals vie with Fred Endsley's fidgety guitar and David Schutt's electric keyboard. At Val's Halla's annual summer sidewalk sale in 1979, the Dadistics played in front of the store. I bought the single from the band, first time I'd done that.

Echo & the Bunnymen, "The Pictures on My Wall"

Gleaning any definite information about the musicians who made these enigmatic platters was difficult. I bought this single and the Teardrop Explodes' debut on the same day, having read reviews of both in *New Musical Express*, not knowing that Echo & the Bunnymen's Ian McCulloch and Teardrop's Julian Cope had been in a band together earlier in their Liverpudlian past. I was amazed and a bit baffled by the fact that the B-side of both singles was the same, "Read It in Books." It seemed like a Zoo Records conspiracy. This record was hallowed in my home—dark, brooding acoustic fallen-love songs with drum machine. My little sisters, Jennifer and Jill, aged nine and eleven, demanded of their deejay down at the roller-disco rink that he play Echo & the Bunnymen, but he looked at them like they were insane and sent them skating.

"Fatal" Microbes, "Violence Grows"

One thing about the two sides of a single—if you designate an A-side and a B-side, it implies hierarchy. Punks and their progeny were avidly anti-hierarchical, so the question of how to refer to those two playing surfaces was taken seriously and dealt with variously. There were "double-A-side" singles, which just called both sides A. Others called one side A and the other AA, a bit of a dodge. One impishly called the second side B-plus. The ubiquitous Small Wonder label put both titles on the same side of the single, labeling one track "this side" and the other "that side." At the top of what would've been the B-side it just read "that side." I was confused, thinking that it was sending me to the other side yet again, a pleasant paradox in product design. The only release by pubescent post-punks "Fatal" Microbes, with singer Honey Bane, this single contains three inspired songs, especially the second one on "that side," "Cry Baby," which finishes with a kids' taunt: *Cry baby bunting / Daddy's gone a-hunting.*

Patrik Fitzgerald, "Safety-Pin Stuck in My Heart"

With his working-class London accent, Fitzgerald was our resident street poet. Compared too often to Dylan, he was less allusive, vulnerable with a snide side, speaking and singing his quotidian texts, accompanied by acoustic guitar—warm anthems of a tortured outcast seeking same for meaningful conversation and a cup of tea in a drafty flat. Five tracks on a 45-rpm single, the title a veritable love song to the punishments of punk rock: *I don't love you for your graveyard eyes / I don't love you for your shaven thighs / I just love you for that beat beat beat beat beating.*

48 Chairs, "Snap It Around"

Every once in a while something in the DIY world seemed to connect with our earlier musical loves. I could hear a little Yes in this beguiling offering out of Cheshire, released on the Absurd label. The zany female vocals notwithstanding, guitars intertwine like a ball of snakes through chords complex and jazzy. The B-side is a plucky cover of John Cooper Clarke's "Psycle Sluts," with free-blown saxophone and maniacal laughter.

The Freshies, "The Men from Banana Island Whose Stupid Ideas Never Caught on in the Western World as We Know It"

For some bands, the DIY revolution gave outlet to the kind of music they'd been making already. This Manchester group had been around since the early seventies. They were led by Chris Sievey, a loony musician and comedian (on whom the papier-maché-headed character in the film *Frank* was based). The Freshies' shaggy-dog-titled EP, released on Sievey's own Razz imprint, has an extra-quirky take on mainstream pop. The lovely "Children of the World" is a song with hit potential, approached slightly askew, and would have been an interesting Godley & Creme cover.

Gang of Four, "Damaged Goods"

The Fast Product label was arguably post-punk's signature outlet, and Gang of Four's humorless, acerbic militant unsoulful funk was bracing and urgent, especially on the flip's "Love Like Anthrax," which gets an alternative, much more aggressive reading here than on their first LP. With less money on the line, singles were good for that, making an ideal place to toy with the tougher stuff. Without sounding at all dub-like, you can hear the influence of the Jamaican music on Gang of Four's first EP. Bass appears and disappears from the metallic guitar-propelled agit prop rock.

Half Japanese, *Calling All Girls*

Straight out of a suburban Maryland basement. Gleeful amateur lunatic ebullience, deviant high-schoolers name-checking a laundry list of adored heroines including Yoko and Patti. With deliberately dorky drumming and detuned noise guitar, brothers Jad and David Fair manage to cram nine songs into nearly twelve minutes on this 1977 EP, all manner of psycho girl-fear wrapped into bite-sized freak-outs.

The Human League, "Being Boiled"

A dystopian soul song from the synth band with a new wave sound—this creamsicle-colored puppy had me enthralled from its opening electronic ooze. Invoking Buddha and an analog tribe of science-fictional cannibals, "Being Boiled" was sung by Giorgio Moroder collaborator Philip Oakey with a fresh-faced smile, compelling us to dance a robotic dance.

Immune System, "Ambivalence & Spark Plugs"

Infectious new wave by a quintet of alums from the School of the Art Institute of Chicago. As a teenager, long before I taught at the Art Institute, I bought this propulsive single, which featured Jaime Gardiner, a bassist with whom I would have a very short-lived band in the late eighties. I hear a good dose of the B-52's in their light-hearted party vibe, especially the B-side, "Submerged," which has a rockabilly beehive shimmy all its own. Best ever inspirational motto inscribed on the back cover: "Get hot, go crazy."

Kleenex, "Ain't You"

So precious were the first two singles by this Swiss all-female quartet that I bought duplicate copies of them, just because it felt like good juju. Genius cover by Peter Fischli, inside its two sides are equally eruptive with autodidactic enthusiasm and feminist punch. Singer Regula Sing and bassist Klaudia Schiff sometimes deployed nonsense vocals detourned from conventional love songs, the *ee ee* of "Hedi's Head," the flip of "Ain't You." Their faintly incorrect syntax— *Ain't you wanna cut it out*—is demolished by Sing's fierce delivery. *Push it in / Now push it out / Push it out / Now push it in.* Ten years later I met guitarist Marlene Marder in a Zurich record store, and then, twenty-five years after that, painter Albert Oehlen introduced me to Schiff at a gallery opening. I stood awestruck in her presence, though she was humble and very nice and offered me a beer.

Magazine, "Give Me Everything"
With the Buzzcocks, singer Howard Devoto had inaugurated the official era of the self-released single, issuing *Spiral Scratch* on their own New Hormones label at the outset of 1977. Major coup for me, two years later, scoring an original copy without the credit line "With Howard Devoto" printed on the cover, which flagged a less desirable reissue. Devoto's departure and eventual resurfacing split the band like a planaria into two essential groups, the 'cocks, who were in my upper echelon for crafting a brand-new approach to love songs, and Magazine, the Devoto-led vehicle for his singing— imagine a vampire Bryan Ferry—as well as colorful, circus-like music suitable for a Fellini film. You could see the divergent paths representing two gay or bisexual archetypes, the button-downed shorthair and the mascara-wearing camp queen. "Pretentiousness is interesting," Devoto told Jon Savage. "At least you're making an effort. Your ambition has to outstrip your ability at some point."* Magazine's "Give Me Everything" puts an Arabic guitar riff, massive bass thump, and Wakeman-esque synth organ behind totalizing S&M lyrics, sung with lamprey suction and arena-rock echo. The B-side contains a big surprise in the form of Beefheart's "I Love You You Big Dummy."

* Howard Devoto, quoted in Jon Savage, *The England's Dreaming Tapes* (Minneapolis: University of Minnesota Press, 2010), 525.

Manicured Noise, "Faith"

The northern soul scene in Britain, which fetishized American sixties soul and R&B singles much the way we did British post-punk singles, had this fine exponent in Manchester. Steven Walsh's electrocuted vocals and Peter Bannister's tenor sax give the breezy "Faith" its own infectious personality, though Talking Heads certainly come to mind. Memorable cover image of factory workers exercising together, hands in the air like they're dancing. Or surrendering.

Mo-Dettes, "White Mice"

Guitarist Kate Korris provided a link between this all-woman post-punk ensemble and the two preeminent sister groups—she was a member of both the Slits and the Raincoats. This rock-reggae single was total success in our circle, with its satirical soap opera comic strip on the back cover telling the story of "a respectable male groupie." The lyrics turn the tables on the supposed quest for sensitivity. *Don't be stupid, don't be limp / No girl likes to love a wimp.* But the Mo-Dettes take it further, objectifying the guy: *Your arse is tight / And moves alright / Your eyes are big and blue / And if I was a homely girl I'd like to marry you / But I'm naughty, sweet and haughty / Forward with it too / So come and visit / Then kiss it / Like only lovers do.*

The Monochrome Set, "Eine Symphonie des Grauens"

With idiosyncracy and confidence, the Monochrome Set gave us a succession of 45s that didn't end up compiled on an LP, for which we singles collectors loved them. Relative sophisticates, they introduced tidbits of Latin music and jazz into droll ditties like "Apocalypso," "Silicon Carne," and "Ten Don'ts for Honeymooners," starting "Eine Symphonie" with an orchestral tune-up, then stroked *guiro* and a little dervish melody sung by Bid. Didn't know it then, but Bid is Indian by birth—original name Ganesh Seshadri—and the discerning guitarist Lester Square was Canadian. Hardly monochrome, more multicultural, they're responsible for some of the best seven-inch sleeves of the era. After the song is done, a moment of silence, then a hidden track of joker-hysterical laughter—another gotcha for the Set.

Neon, "Don't Eat Bricks"

From county Durham, in northeast England, Neon called what they did "progressive punk"—odd time signatures, challenging tempi, and uncategorizable compositions, like the title track, a spectacular twin guitar feature for Tim Jones and Martin Holder, both veritable post-punk Kenny Burrells, and the B-side, "Hanging Off an O," which suggested they might have been better suited on a double bill with someone like the Bad Brains a few years later. Shame they didn't record more. I never tracked down their first single, "Bottles." Still hunting.

The Pop Group, "Where There's a Will . . ." b/w The Slits, "In the Beginning There Was Rhythm"

Possibly my favorite post-punk release was shared by the two bands. The concept of the split-single suggests camaraderie, a common cause, the repudiation of self-promotion. The Pop Group's broken punk-funk consists of an obese bass line, hand claps, vibraslaps, seventh and ninth guitar chords, Mark Stewart's dubbed-out paranoid squawks, and overheated saxophone recalling Robert McCollough with James Brown. But where the band had issued the condemnatory "We Are All Prostitutes," "Where There's a Will . . ." was a rousing call to arms, positive shot in the arm that we took into the Reagan years and played just to remind ourselves we could.

Public Image Ltd, "Memories"

Jah Wobble's dark dub bass and Richard Dudanski's disco drumming on this post-punk classic propel it to a perfect anticlimax when John Lydon proclaims *the end* but the band keeps chugging and Keith Levene picks more elegant guitar. The version here includes one unexpurgated take of the song, but on the PiL record *Metal Box*, that take is intercut with a much louder take that has a different room sound. Having known the seven-inch "Memories," I was startled listening to *Metal Box* on headphones at two in the morning when the sound abruptly shifted. Later, this collage-editing technique seemed to make sense in relation to the edits in Miles Davis's electric records.

The Saints, "Know Your Product"

From a parallel world of punk down under, Australia's premier band schooled us on the correct use of a horn section, a show-biz wink that tucks Count Basie under its wing and takes off into anti-capitalist snark, updating the Rolling Stones' "(I Can't Get No) Satisfaction" and winning an eternal place for singer Chris Bailey in our safety-pinned hearts.

Scritti Politti, "Skank Bloc Bologna"

Singles pointed to the interests of their makers not only in the music they presented, but in the kinds of information the record packages offered. Green Gartside's band was explicit in its political and theoretical orientation, referring in their name to Italian postmarxist Antonio Gramsci's *Political Writings*. In its liner notes, this seven-inch—which reminded me of Robert Wyatt, another hefty-lefty—detailed every aspect of its means of production, including cost of recording, mastering, labeling, and pressing. An early introduction to the notion of putting apparatus theory into action.

Nigel Simpkins, *X. Enc.*

An unrelenting enigma in its era, this audio collage was "Revolution 9" for the post-punk period. The insistent tape piece "Times Encounter" and its continuation on the flip were constructed by Cally Callomon of the Tea Set, later executor of the Nick Drake Estate, built on fragments of a drum instruction record, and were incorrectly identified by Julian Cope of the Teardrop Explodes as the first record to use sampling. Hilariously bogus bio in the liners says that "Nigel" has gone incognito "to avoid 3 years of lawyer trouble." Of the 1,500 copies that Waldo Records released, mine is number 117. Sounds like a lot, but I've never seen a second one.

Siouxsie and the Banshees, "Mittageisen"

The original version, "Metal Postcard," appeared on Siouxsie's first LP, and when she released a follow-up sung in German, we were delighted. Extending her proto-goth flirtation with Germanic imagery, which must have been a bitter pill for the parents of young Brit punks, the record came with text in medieval font on the verso, the front reprinting a political collage by Dadaist John Heartfield, certainly my first encounter with the artist. The song itself is based around a heavy rock riff that could be by Black Sabbath.

Subway Sect, "Ambition"

Both sides of this little beaut were faves by one of the first groups inspired to band together by the Sex Pistols, transformed within a year and a half to a proto-indie-pop ensemble. Vic Godard's sneering voice bears traces of his love of Johnny Rotten, but the music has a bright tunefulness. With uncredited keyboards and out-of-tempo synth blurps, "Ambition" is thoroughly charming. An LP was planned but sadly never issued.

Swell Maps, "Dresden Style"

The band that sent up the bat signal for doing it yourself, releasing music dating back to the mid-seventies by teenage siblings Epic Soundtracks and Nikki Sudden, together with co-conspirator Jowe Head. You never knew what you'd get with Swell Maps, throbbing punk anthem or free-form freak-out. This single contained both, but everything they did seemed steeped in the in-jokes of home-tapers. I always enjoyed being party to their escapades, even if they were in code.

The Teardrop Explodes, "Sleeping Gas"

I loved the Liverpudlian bloke Julian Cope, whose dreamy, inscrutable lyrics made passing reference to the dreadful TV show *Rafferty* and AAP comic shorts—together, a late seventies pothead's ideal evening. Teardrop's singles, like Echo & the Bunnymen's, were better than their LPs, which made the songs sound more mainstream, like regular rock fodder, not bad but lacking the seven-inch vinyl's vulnerability.

Tin Huey, *Tin Huey*

The essential Akron wack-pack. Ralph Carney's serious saxophone and a clan of crazies merged carnivalesque composing and arranging with post-psyche guitar mania, tipping hat in liner credits to Beefheart, Burroughs, Bukowski, Steely Dan, Roger Chapman, Joe Zawinul, Muhammad Ali, Daevid Allen, and Boston Celtic John Havlicek. Brainy and zany, they're among the groups that kept American music eclectic. Their debut EP has four tracks to help maintain the faith.

X-Ray Spex, "The Day the World Turned Day-Glo"

Let's not forget colored vinyl. My copy of this Action Jackson is bright Day-Glo orange. Poly Styrene was a force, of mixed Somali and British descent, wearing braces, sometimes a turban, peeling the paint off the walls with her lungs. This ditty—X-Ray Spex's chaser to their ultimate feminist punk anthem, "Oh Bondage, Up Yours!"—is a sardonic lament for the plasticization of life. *I drove my polypropylene car / On wheels of sponge / Then pulled into a Wimpy Bar / To have a rubber bun.*

Young Marble Giants, "Final Day"

Where we learn about reduction as a form of composition. Eliminate the inessential. Drain testosterone. Sing at a speaking volume. Leave nothing but the bones of a song. Start with a pop rock band, plop down in the unincorporated area between Little Sister, Kraft-werk, the Who, and the Shaggs, then take away every unneeded gesture. What remains? Minimal mix, drum machine, organ drone, guitar dyad, soft apocalyptic farewell. *And the world lights up / For the final day / We will all be poor / Having had our say.*

Dragnet

It is impossibly difficult writing about things that mean this much
to you. There is always more to say. What you compose will never
adequately account for the music's depth of significance, for how
and why it rocked your world, what miracles are contained in just
a peep of it. To justify your effort, like Borges's one-to-one map of
the territory, every single sound on the entire record would need to
be cataloged, described, and explained, cross-indexed with all the
other music of its time and all the other music made by the same
people across time and all the references the music makes outside
itself, and maybe even all the relevant events in your own life that
assisted in imbuing it with so much electricity. The honorific gesture will fall short. It is doomed. Oh well, let it fall short then. Go
get the music and see if it hits you this way.

It will fail, but here goes:

...

Put the pep back into dyspeptic.

Mark E. Smith, a man so unlikable you have to adore him.
A caustic, occasionally malevolent presence—I've seen MES plunge
his unsuspecting microphone into stage monitors at a random point

in a song, erasing all his band's music with a machete swipe of terrible feedback, just to fuck with them, or to fuck with the audience, or because he was shitfaced, or because he's a seer and that's what the moment called for. He's an extreme character.

Smith's memoir *Renegade* is to post-punk what Charles Mingus's *Beneath the Underdog* is to post-bop. He is his own mythologist and re-fabricator. Nothing that's befallen him has ever been his fault; everyone else is to blame. All his decisions have been sensible, even those made in a blizzard of drink. Like Mingus, Smith's faith in his own rectitude is unshakable, his judgment of others drawn from an all-seeing, infallible eye, which, when equipped with an intelligence that blindingly sharp, is pretty doggone convincing, even when on the face of it something he says is plainly untrue.

A raging ego is not so uncommon in these parts. But Smith is no everyday egomaniac. He is as visionary as he is full of himself. Also, he can be hilarious. But what he does rarely contours itself to an easy flow. He pushes back against his colleagues, against his enemies (real and perceived), against the proper step forward, against the obvious, against the artsy, against the mundane, against people stupider than him, which is almost everyone. He is, using a term he borrows for a song on *Dragnet* from the novelist Luke Rhinehart, a "dice man," always taking chances. Over a Bo Diddley beat, he asks of the Fall, rhetorically: *Where are you people going? / Is this a branch on the tree of show business?* No simple evolutionary steps for MES, he calls it as he sees it: *They say music should be fun / Like reading a story of love / But I wanna read a horror story.* (Indeed, "Flat of Angles," with its slinky acoustic guitar part, tells the horrific tale of a man who kills his wife and gets trapped in precisely such an acute apartment.) Smith insists there's *No time for small moralists*, and ends with a wild-eyed challenge: *I am the dice man / A balls-on-the-line man / Do you take a chance, baby?* Translation: Resist with me, I'll make it worth your time.

...

Our assumption had always been that audio should be impressive. This made us gearheads and stereo snoots. High-volume braggarts. Our aim: booming woofers, crystalline tweeters, molten midrange; components; speakers that hung or twirled or pointed in twelve directions at once; banana-splits stereo separation; muscle-bound amps; many-knobbed preamps with buttons that promised "power," "gain," and "loudness"; remastered recordings pledging that the listener hear every previously inaudible rustle of the performer's clothing.

Then came *Dragnet*. In one album, the Fall funneled all our quadrophonic aspirations down a big black monophonic hole. Or as close as you can get and still have a threadbare version of stereo.

In an interview, Smith complained that the group's first record, *Live at the Witch Trials*, had been too clear, too well recorded, that it just sounded too good. I remember finding his remarks genuinely confounding. Wasn't that the idea, that recordings should be as clear as possible? That a record should have . . . *fidelity*.

With *Dragnet*, one of the originary lo-fi recordings, Smith—a former professional tarot reader and wholehearted believer in other dimensions, time travel, and psychic phenomena—casts a spell on the last year of the seventies. *Life is short and full of thought*, Smith sings in "Before the Moon Falls," a song that sets up the band as *Private detectives onward back from a musical pilgrimage*. He intones, *I use the power, I use the power* as an incantation. *And I will forever end this reign of terror / Before the moon falls*. Using thought-power, a tool he insists few other people in his field deploy, he paraphrases William Blake, explaining the necessity for self-determination, rather than being trapped by commercial music:

I must create a new regime or live by another man's
Before the moon falls, before the moon falls
I must create a new scheme, get out of others' hands
Before the moon falls, before the moon falls
I could use some pure criminals

And get my hands on some royalties
Before the moon falls, before the moon falls

And with one simple variation, he implicates himself, warning the band against getting caught up in its own buzz: *Before the Fall swoons / Before the Fall swoons.*

...

In *Renegade*, Smith parses his intentions:

> When I founded the group it wasn't about me trying to get my picture in some paper or magazine or other—like it is with a lot of bands nowadays—it was because of sounds; of wanting to make something; combining primitive music with intelligent lyrics.

The most "primitive" music on *Dragnet* is "Spectre vs. Rector." You can hear Smith singing to a previously recorded version of the song, replete with a submerged layer of his own vocals, muddy beyond intelligibility. On "Muzorewi's Daughter," an obscure reference to an African prime minister, a sort of war whoop, Smith clenches his vocal cords to screech the end of some lines, unpleasant pig squeals on a track that sounds like it was recorded in a cistern. The whole record has a raw rockabilly feel, channeling recordings made in the fifties by myriad amateurs inspired by Gene Vincent or Jerry Lee Lewis, the more off-the-wall side of the genre. Nasal electric guitars, thumping tom-toms, indelicate cymbal crashes, a trademark drum pattern that rolls its way down the tuned heads. Smith expends part of the record on baring fangs at the music press, lampooning them critiquing him. *I don't sing / I just shout / All on one note*, goes "Your Heart Out," after which he says, monotonically: *Sing sing sing sing / Sing sing sing sing.* In the jabbing "Printhead," he excoriates misunderstanding journalists he's duped: *We laughed with them / When it was take-the-piss time / I'm no egghead / But I'm an ex-worker man / W.C. hero, friend / And not "water closet"!*

Smith's class status was real, and in the place of punk's sup-posed alignment of vitriol and populism, so often a disappointing ruse, he conjured what he called the "prole art threat," a working-man's sarcastic poetics. So if it initially seems petty for him to worry about something as trivial as getting bad or idiotic reviews, I think it's actually part of his program to keep it real, to address the actualities of his life, which include the music business. A select crew of independent label punk songs—I would include the Buzz-cocks' "Boredom," Alternative Television's "Love Lies Limp," and the Fall's earlier cut "Repetition" (*The three R's: repetition, repetition, repetition*)—paid attention to the quotidian, in contrast with major label punk's more grandiloquent aspirations—the Sex Pistols' "An-archy in the U.K.," the Clash's "Complete Control," X-Ray Spex's "Oh Bondage, Up Yours!"

What's more, Smith refused to dress the part. Put an image of him next to concurrent images of the Clash or the Pistols. Mick and Joe and Johnny and Sid look positively foppish in comparison. Mark E. resembled us: pockmarked and sleep deprived, hollow and pale, a regular stiff.

...

Back to Smith's humor, the savage sarcasm, the ambivalent address (*Why are you laughing at or with this song?* he poses on "Choc-Stock"), the comedic routine in "Your Heart Out," which goes:

> *Now here's a joke to cheer you up*
> *In old times no surgeons*
> *Just magicians and dungeons*
> *There they take (your heart out)*
> *With a sharp knife*
> *It wasn't fake (your heart out)*
> *They had no anesthetic*
> *That joke's pathetic.*

A pathetic joke that has made me chuckle for forty years.

...

Phantoms of post-industrial Manchester have haunted the Fall's music. They're the feature attraction of the first two songs on *Dragnet*. "A Figure Walks" is an eerie, threatening ditty describing a monstrous-mysterious shadow as: *Eyes of brown, watery / Nails of pointed yellow / Hands of black carpet / It's a quick trip to ice house*. But the program kicks off on a less ominous foot, imagining the "Psykick Dance Hall," a place where music occurs telepathically. The song starts with a spoken invocation: *Is there anybody there?!* Over an unsteady disco beat, Smith describes a club where *They have no records / They know your questions about no words / Just bumble-stumble to the waves / Twitching out to the waves*. His comment about the words is, again, a response to critics of his cryptic or hard-to-hear lyrics. And then he brings it back to himself, his enduring legacy, one of the Fall's most reliable topics: *When I am dead and gone / My vibrations will live on / In vibes on vinyl through the years / People will dance to my waves*.

"Rock 'n' Roll High School"

All along, we had assumed that complexity was a positive. Maybe *the* positive. To say something was more complex was the same as saying it was better. That there were bad things that were very complex was hard to imagine, likewise that some of them had as their only exemplary characteristic their complexity. Music with difficult time signatures, long and convoluted melodies, unfamiliar harmonies, lack of repetition, velocity, and virtuosity—those were the criteria. Learning about music meant learning why something you'd thought was complex really wasn't and finding things that really were. Growing into maturity, we figured, meant giving up the simple bumpkin pleasures. It meant embracing the intricate and hard to understand.

Had I followed this train to its final station, I might have wound up listening to nothing but the so-called New Complexity bunch, composers who have been making music loosely described as such since the nineteen eighties: Brian Ferneyhough, Michael Finnissy, Richard Barrett, and the like. I do in fact like some of their music, Barrett's in particular, and I have spent much of my adult life attending to freely improvised music, which can, but doesn't always, have its own special kind of complexity. The challenge of music that's complex remains on my plate, but it's there alongside other vittles, some of which are about as complex as a well-chewed wad of gum—tasteless but impossible to spit out.

I began gnawing on the Ramones rather late in the game. They defined a new simplicity. The music was direct and blunt. There were no solos. It was all barre chords and duple meter. Sonically, they were as compressed as you could get away with, everything louder than everything else. The lyrics were repetitive, monosyllabic, punchy, each one an anthem, sometimes sung dulcetly with nary a snarl, otherwise chanted in monotone, songs about pinheads, lobotomies and sniffing glue. Any assault—against brain cells, girlfriends—came cheerfully with a psycho grin. Cretin count off: *one, two, three, four,* then *four, five, six, seven*. Harmony vocals recalling the Beach Boys, girl groups. Sometimes there was a tambourine. It had a fifties vibe, American rock 'n' roll straight up, but with the razor-sharp sound of distorted guitar from an earlier epoch of garage bands. "Good Vibrations" gone bad. The Count Five as a comic strip. A super-fucked version of the Trashmen's "Surfin' Bird." *Ramones* was impeccable. So were the slicker-sounding *Leave Home* and the return-to-the-street *Rocket to Russia*. Tight, concise, lean. They were essential, but I missed them first go 'round.

I dove into punk rock Brit-first. In a reversal of history's actual march, most of the American music came afterward for me. The NY punk sensibility was too identifiable, the Converse and leather jackets overly familiar. Having listened to the Fall, I found the Ramones' sock-hop affectations a little corny. I was a bit slow on the irony uptake, so that dimension was lost on me. In any case, I was asleep at the wheel for the first three Ramones records. More fool me.

By the time I came on board, we were already at *Road to Ruin*. Pretty good, not bad, but not nearly as essential as its precursors. At least it had "I Wanna Be Sedated." Drummer Tommy Ramone was gone, replaced by Marky. I already knew Marky. When he was still Marc Bell, Marky Ramone played drums in Dust, a Neanderthal hard rock/heavy metal trio that put out a couple of unsuccessful records in the early seventies. I still enjoy "Suicide" from *Hard Attack* for Kenny Aaronson's mondo stupid bass solo but also for Bell's impatient tom-tom triplets. For most Ramones fans, knowing that Marc became Marky is a disposable piece of trivia. I'm embarrassed to say that it's the first thing I think of when listening to the Ramones. He was in the Voidoids, too, after a stint with Wayne County and the Backstreet Boys. That's a less embarrassing history to be aware of, but honestly it's not the first thing that comes to mind. Instead of any of these New York street urchins, I remember *Hard Attack*, a record cover showing three Vikings, leg muscles rippling, fighting with swords and battle-axes on a snow-capped mountaintop.

...

Growing up in a college town has its advantages for a local high school kid. Iowa City's cultural life catered to the University of Iowa, so my friends and I got to enjoy some sophisticated perks, from bookstores and record shops to concerts and lectures. Our town was big enough to get into a little trouble, dumb-shit trouble, but not jail-time trouble. Not scarred-for-life trouble. We had no cults promising magic carpet rides—our minor vices included sex and drugs, not sects and rugs. After I left, my sisters told me about a heroin epidemic. I'm sure there was some of that, but I never encountered it. That was big-time dumb-shit stuff.

U of I's film society had a rich and up-to-date program. In one week, I went to see *Eraserhead* and *Rock 'n' Roll High School*. The Ramones soundtrack on the latter made an impression, pressing the band into my memory, their cavalier performances in Roger Corman's film a slack turn-on and the dopiness of the title song's conceit an update to my long-lost affair with Alice Cooper. For me, it solidified an impression that the Ramones were cartoon characters. I found it hard to take the music too seriously, so when people like Lester Bangs exaggerated their importance I tended to lean in the direction of Greil Marcus, who called them "one of the most overrated bands in the world" in a review of the film. Neither writer was precisely on the money, but anyway the Ramones' real significance seemed to have been a particular presence at a particular time in a particular place, what their snide attitude and curt songs suggested to musicians in New York in 1976.

In Iowa City in 1979, I recall that evening at the cinema because of a strange event. My friends Doug and John and I went together, drinking heartily first, then ending up in the folding chairs with a small cache of girls previously unknown in our circles. None of us was a Casanova, but Doug was particularly artless with the ladies, so when he and a blond gal began to whisper to each other quite literally behind my back, I refrained from making a fuss and let them do their thing. This arrangement reminded me uncomfortably of car trips with my sisters, who liked to monkey around on my neck and shoulders when I occupied the middle seat, play that could grow tiresome with the miles. After a stretch, it seemed strangely quiet back there, with me hunched forward and minding my own business, holding it together in solidarity with my buddy in spite of the awkward position. I turned my head to find Doug and his friend clenched in a full-on make-out session, sucking face with pickled tongue relish, all but undressing each other. Like I'd just found myself in a leech-infested creek, I wriggled free and planted myself on the far side of John, who'd nodded off from drink and the dullness of the movie and promptly fell out of his seat and into the aisle. Then we were asked to leave.

There you go: dumb-shit trouble. Our specialty. The Ramones might have been proud.

Do It Yourself

From the edge of the stage between songs, John Lydon glared at one particular member of the audience. The British singer's spiky hair was backlit, and from one of the spikes a long drizzle of phlegm dangled perilously. "How *old* are you?" he asked in a withering tone. The guy—decked out in leather, torn jeans, a neat little Mohawk, and a goatee edged in gray—hocked up another of dozens of bilious streams of lumpy loogies he had aimed directly at Lydon, whom he surely wished he could still call Rotten, and replied: "Thirty-eight." Without flinching or missing a beat, Lydon took one in the face and spat back: "Don't you have anything *better* to do?"

Punk was a youngster's sport. A famous punk motto, itself built on the hippie maxim not to trust anyone over thirty, had it that one should never trust a hippie. The point is: anything old is bad. Or pathetic, especially if it doesn't realize it's old, which was Lydon's point. Matter of fact, popular music in the seventies skewed toward the youthful, probably it always does. Youth are, in my father's favorite formulation, smarter than a rock but dumber than a tree, and there are many nuances of the best music of their time—whenever that may be—that are simply lost on them. Wisdom comes when it comes, not according to a calendar, so the fact that Lydon was ten years younger than his assailant that night in 1984 doesn't mean he was that much less enlightened.

...

Well, they say time loves a hero, sang Lowell George. *But only time will tell / If he's real, he's a legend from heaven / If he ain't, he was sent here from hell.* With a lyric the significance of which I didn't understand when I heard it, this Little Feat song was like many of them in that respect. I think it's about getting older and more courageous. Time loves a hero. It also loves a good song.

One of the things about songs is that you grow up around them. Like a tree that slowly envelops a fence post, the music is always there, and bit by bit you accommodate yourself to it, take it in; if you're lucky and attentive, you begin to understand it more, what it means in general and what it means to you. The songs are there, unyielding as metal. They fling their words at you over the years, repeating them, sitting tight until you understand. Maybe you never will. No matter, music is patient. It waits for us to grow up. The song is not in a hurry. It's got nothing but time. Heck, it's made of time.

Ian Dury was already an older bloke when he contributed the punk-era anthem "Sex & Drugs & Rock & Roll." In 1977, when Stiff Records issued his debut *New Boots and Panties!!*, Dury was thirty-five and had already been through at least two former lives, one as an artist—not a bad Pop painter in the mode of Peter Blake, with whom he'd studied at the Royal Academy of Art—and another as the singer in Kilburn and the High Roads, a London pub rock band of some note with a well-received record called *Handsome*. He'd been an art teacher, had already written his first song in 1970. And he'd lived most of his life with a disability resulting from childhood polio. Rather than shy away from it in performance, Dury emphasized his nonconformity—indeed, in the lineup of the Kilburn and the High Roads, he assembled a provocatively wild range of physical sizes and types, and his drummer, David Newton-Rohoman, used crutches, as did he. The travails of Dury's body became a recurring theme in songs like "Crippled with Nerves," where he sings: *Could have touched her, could have told her | The weight is on my shoulder, sadness the purpose it serves | The day turns to grey, the pain has its way | I'll die 'cos I'm crippled with nerves.*

Dury assembled a new band, the Blockheads, for a legendary and debaucherous tour known as 5 Stiffs Live, arranged by his new record label in the year of his first solo record. Although he wasn't really a punk—too old, too experienced, too funny, too open—he'd become indelibly associated with the movement. Indeed, from my vantage in Iowa City, where I saw his picture in every week's issue of *NME*, he struck me as an essential member of the punk squad, perhaps its elder statesman. A song like "Plaistow Patricia" seemed implicit confirmation of Dury's punk status, with its shouted opening: *Arseholes, bastards, fucking cunts and pricks | Aerosol the bricks | A lawless brat from a council flat, oh, oh | A little bit of this and a little bit of that, oh, oh | Dirty tricks.* It wasn't until years later that I really listened to the rest of the song, which turns out to be a tragic portrait of a hooker and drug addict, more social realism than anarchist situationism.

The song that gave the band its name, "Blockheads," is a riotous but loving catalog of misfits . . . *with blotched and lagered skin | Blockheads with food particles in their teeth, what a horrible state they're in | They've got womanly breasts under pale mauve vests, shoes like dead pig's noses* . . . [a reference to Dury's own orthopedic kicks] . . . *cornflake packet jacket, catalogue trousers, a mouth what never closes.* "Blockheads" continues with a stage whisper—*How would you like one puffing and blowing in your earhole | Or pissing in your swimming pool?*—and ends by implicating the audience: *Why bother at all about Blockheads, why should you care what they do? | 'Cos after all is said and done, you're all Blockheads too. NME* ran an annual All-British Blockhead Competition for a few years. My friends and I were jealous—sure that, had we not been Americans, we could have been contenders.

We felt the punk affinities, but then again there were things about the record that were clearly not punk, like synthesizers, well-played saxophones, and slick guitar solos, and also beautiful slower songs such as "I'm Partial to Your Abracadabra," "Clevor Trever," and "Wake Up and Make Love with Me," or the affectionate tribute "Sweet Gene Vincent," dedicated to one of Dury's rockabilly idols. On "If I Was with a Woman," he diagrams with pinpoint accuracy the paranoid wellsprings of misogyny:

> If I was with a woman, I'd never ask her questions
> But if she did not want me to I would
> If I was with a woman, I'd offer my indifference
> And make quite sure she never understood
> If I was with a woman, I'd threaten to unload her
> Every time she asked me to explain
> If I was with a woman, she'd have to learn to cherish
> The purity and depth of my disdain
> Look at them laughing, look at them laughing, look at them laughing
> Laughing, laughing

Nasty swatch of honest self-assessment there, but the pivotal word that betrays underlying insecurity is "if." There was a level of maturity and sophistication to these songs, even if they were intoned in a Cockney accent and loaded with tantalizingly obscure slang—words like "palone," impossible to translate from the occult gay British dialect called Polari—and double entendre that we could perceive but not fully appreciate. We loved *New Boots and Panties!!* for its crude humor, but richer mysteries lingered in the can before we started to dig them out. A song about a morning erection made more sense to me out of the gate than one about taking the piss out of someone by pretending to be stupid.

When I bought *Do It Yourself*, I knew immediately I had been wrong about the punk thing, as wrong as I had been about Elvis Costello. It's a record that followed Dury's greatest chart action, "Hit Me with Your Rhythm Stick," a single that soared at the end of 1978 to become number one. I still recall the day the LP arrived at the record store where I worked, three copies, each one packaged in a cover with a different pattern. Bolstered by the success of Dury's first record, Stiff ponied up for an elaborate design that printed text on some thirty different varieties of Crown wallpaper, making each copy feel that much more special in a DIY way. It's flawed, but I think *Do It Yourself* is one of the unsung LPs of the late seventies. There are disco and soul elements that weren't there before, cheeky and funny, enriched with snazzy harmonies, snatches of Caribbean music and lounge jazz, egged on by ever-chipper hi-hat. Dury was apparently less than thrilled with the results, but it contains terrific songs like "Sink My Boats," "This Is What We Find," and the nutting "Waiting for Your Taxi," on which the same stanza, *Waiting for your taxi / Which taxi never comes / Waiting for your taxi*, is repeated sevenfold, followed in each instance by a lengthy stretch of near silence.

One song on *Do It Yourself* has been an ongoing source of discovery for me over the course of nearly forty years, ringing in my ears, resounding in my head, and sprouting new significance as I've grown older. "Inbetweenies" is not Dury's most comfortable vocal performance, but its awkward quality offsets the song's slightly unctuous pretense. The protagonist is an aging man whose frailties are complemented by his partners, male and female, as they slip from concupiscence into companionship. A single line, which I'd always heard literally, finally made sense one day. En route to the rhyme *Do lift the heart of my morale / To know that we are pals*, he warbles, rudely: *Through channels that were once canals*. One morning, listening to the record, the meaning just jumped on me. What a fucking line. What an image. Vivid, offensive, brilliant— Dury was describing his partners' slackening orifices. I should have known, of course, because so many of the songs deal with sex and desire and anger and impotence. *Shake your booty when your back is bent*, Dury sings in another verse, the cunning linguist venerating doggie doings. *Put your feelings where my mouth just went*. But then his fears come out and beat back the prurient pleasure: *As serious as things do seem / At least you put me on the team / And friends do rule supreme.*

As serious as things do seem, I grow longer in tooth, shorter in stature, weaker and dimmer and more set in my ways, morning wood a pleasant surprise rather than a nagging nuisance, sleep a cherished necessity. In this phase of life, I return to Dury's wise words, which I'm still busy figuring out: *In the mirror, when I'm debonair / My reactions are my own affair / A body likes to be near the bone / Oh, Nancy, Leslie, Jack, and Joan / I die when I'm alone, palone.*

Reggatta de Blanc

Pretenders

Is there a more precipitous fall from greatness than that of the Police? They went from being one of the most electrifying bands of the era, the reggae-infused pop act with a golden lead vocalist and stripped-down trio sound, to being vacuous and vainglorious. Their tumble is instructive, however, because even though theirs was arguably the worst, it was by no means unique.

Think of Rod Stewart plummeting from gritty greatness on "Every Picture Tells a Story" to mind-destroying disco dreck on "Do You Think I'm Sexy?" Or Heart, who became a hair band in the eighties and jettisoned whatever made them so beloved. Rush recorded some ridiculous, giddy music before becoming untenably pretentious. Genesis lost its first singer and its way. Adam and the Ants made a stupendous debut with smart lyrics and challenging music, but their follow-ups were dime store. The Boomtown Rats, Chicago, the Cure, Paul McCartney, Lionel Ritchie, Linda Ronstadt, Paul Simon, ZZ Top—all folks who should have quit in the seventies while they were ahead.

OK, so let's do our best to forget "De Do Do Do, De Da Da Da," "Every Breath You Take," all Sting's solo records, the unspeakable things he asked respectable jazz musicians to do, and go back to the scene of the crime before the chalk lines were drawn. I recall the exact day I got the Police's debut, *Outlandos d'Amour*. It was my grandfather's seventieth birthday. My aunt and uncle pitched a party at their apartment in Chicago's Lincoln Park. I used the record to shield myself from the festivities, which were boring and went on forever, by locking myself in the library and playing the record repeatedly at low volume. My eight- and ten-year-old sisters huddled with me mostly, and they seemed to respond to the music as well. They were important testers for me, though I probably wouldn't have admitted it then.

I squinted my ears to hear the Police clearly. On *Outlandos* I felt the rush of something unfamiliar. The record cover bore certain new wave signifiers, but the music had more of a pop rock sound, merged on most tracks with a convincing take on reggae. Unlike many post-punk and new wave bands, this threesome had a singer who could really sing, with an impressive range, emotion to spare, and inventive phrasing. I listened to "Roxanne" twenty times that night, digging the way Sting's voice ached. I couldn't wait to get it home so I could crank it up.

When the Police's follow-up hit the shelves eleven months later, I might have been the first Iowan to buy it. *Reggatta de Blanc* made good on the pop rock and reggae quotients, subtracting a little of the rougher rock from its predecessor. But it was the relationship between pop rock and reggae that was so fascinating. There's inherent frisson in the contrast of rock and reggae—you can hear later bands like Bad Brains and Blind Idiot God exploring their fruitful juxtaposition. The Police didn't keep the two genres as alternating-but-separate parts of their portfolio, the way those bands would, nor did they make a smoothie out of them the way Paul Simon had on "Mother and Child Reunion." They didn't subsume reggae into a rock costume like Eric Clapton had with "I Shot the Sheriff." Instead they found a new way for the two genres to operate in the same song.

This wouldn't be possible if not for Stewart Copeland's versatility. He's one of the few drummers in rock who seems to understand

that reggae drumming involves a multitude of different patterns—
much like rock itself does—that they're all distinctive rhythms, or
what Jamaican drummers call riddims, and that each riddim connotes something specific. Drummer Hamid Drake once walked me
through some of them, riddims particular to dub, ones designed for
talk-over, ones for lover's rock, and of course ska and rock-steady
with their telltale tempi and signature moves. Even within dub,
every drummer had his own sound. Producers and drummers in
Jamaica colluded to concoct personalized drum timbres by baffling
the snare drum with gaffer's tape, trying out special techniques like
playing the cymbals close to the nut, and miking the kit in unusual
ways. Producer Bunny Lee and drummer Carlton "Santa" Davis,
for instance, innovated their so-called flying cymbal sound, which
was a Jamaican response to early disco hi-hat like that found on
records by MFSB.

On "Message in a Bottle," a chugging 4/4 rhythm with Andy
Summers's aggressive picked arpeggios leads right up to the title
line, at which point the drums thin out into a sparse dub pattern,
Sting's prominent bass leaping out; the tempo is the same, but it's
magically shifted gears from rock to reggae. The wordless "Reggatta
de Blanc," which lays out their stylistic blend in a purposefully awkward Franglais phrase referring to "white reggae" (but also conjuring a fleet of boats), reverses the process. It begins with Copeland's
skittering reggae rim shots and pulsing bass drum, building to a
rock crescendo.

Summers first signals the reggae component on "Walking on the
Moon." His sustained, slightly flanged chords and chopped hits on
the second and fourth beat are classic reggae guitar parts; Sting
leaves holes in his bass line, creating springy tension under the buoyant drums, but the chorus acquires a pop feel, never quite jettison-
ing its reggae-ness, but heading a direction no reggae song would.
With its simple lyric, high falsetto, echoed-out drums, funky Nassau
bass, and swooshing guitar part, "The Bed's Too Big without You"
was a super hit in my house. There are basically no solos on these

songs, just overall shifts in density following the dub logic of thinning out and thickening up a mix. "Bring on the Night" once again lashes together pop and reggae, Sting's multi-tracked voice and an incredible hook endorsing one of my favorite high-school-era themes: nocturnalism.

Reggatta de Blanc is a better record, a summation of multiple streams of thought at the end of the seventies, but if pressed I might still choose their first, which has more edge and is a tad less slickly produced. There's often nothing for a band to lose when they make the first outing, so they can go for broke; the results might be imperfect, but they have an urgency that refuses to be denied.

...

It was unpleasantly warm at one o'clock on a July afternoon in an industrial park in Rosemont, a western suburb of Chicago. I was working in my uncle's factory making flash tubes, the kind that blink at the tips of airplane wings at night. The factory floor was dusty and smelled like chemicals, as always. Rows of Polish immigrants used propane torches to shape finished piecework; elsewhere more skilled workers blew long tubes of glass into twisty Dr. Seuss shapes. I'd been doing one thing all day for four days straight. Extracting a thin wire from a pile, I carefully threaded a glass bead onto it, slid the base of the wire into a slot in a device that positioned the glass-wire combo in the convergent flames of two gas burners long enough for them to turn orange, melt, and bond with the metal, simultaneously removing one of the cooling glass-wire combos from the machine, placing it on a stack of finished ones, and loading up another to be sent around the mulberry bush. The work was tedious. Tedious! But just meticulous enough that I couldn't space out entirely. Only one thing kept me from falling down into a heap of bent wires and broken beads and burned fingers: music.

It was the summer of 1980. For the duration of my tenure at Amglo that season, I listened to the radio station WXRT. It was the end of one of the most creative periods in music radio history. Free-form still maintained a slim presence outside the realm of college radio, and disc jockeys still had input into what they played. Although 93-XRT certainly had a playlist, it was current and exciting and turned me on to things I'd only read about. And jocks like Johnny Mars, Terri Hemmert, and a new guy named Frank E. Lee, might do something weird and interesting. I remember one day when the new wave–oriented station was suddenly playing a Chopin prelude. All the Poles looked over at me and smiled, then stopped smiling when the jockey followed up directly with the Sex Pistols' "Anarchy in the U.K." The transition gave me a jolt and made me think about the segregation of genres, how it was like musical nationalism.

WXRT championed a new record that summer that is, in my book, the closing bell on the seventies. Recorded in 1979, but technically released a week into the new decade, *Pretenders* had many of the same qualities I so admired in the Police, including a less frequent nod to reggae, but their music was so ferocious that it damn near leapt out of the little transistor radio, and the singer sang with a combination purr, sigh, and shout that gave me gooseflesh. It was rough-and-tumble and sassy and sexy and smart and funny and didn't take shit from anyone. Like Andy Summers, guitarist James Honeyman-Scott was deft with treatments (flange, envelope-follower, stuff like that) and simply hit it as hard as anyone I'd heard, taking short solos that were incredibly cogent. In my book, the Pretenders in that era have proven as durable as Teflon.

Pretenders is as perfectly produced an LP as they come. Chrissie Hynde explodes out of the gate with "Precious," condensing her own success story and narrow escape from a biker gang and drug mayhem in Ohio into a few hot lines, including: *But Howard the Duck and Mr. Stress both stayed | "Trapped in a world that they never made" | But not me, baby, I'm too precious | I had to fuck off.* (Note that the duck she means is the alien Marvel Comics character unable to leave earth, with the tag line "trapped in a world he never made," and Mr. Stress was a blues musician and onetime boss of Hynde's who stayed in Cleveland.)

Hynde's secret weapons include ingenious vocal overdubs; odd time signatures; street toughness boiled down to a voluble sneer; big vibrato and coy sweetness; startling sexual frankness. For the full combo, just listen to "Up the Neck" and the passage:

> Lust turns to anger
> A kiss to a slug
> Something was sticky on your shag rug
> Look at the tile
> I remember the way he groaned
> And moved with an animal skill
> I rubbed my face in the sweat that ran down his chest
> It was all very run of the mill
> But I noticed his scent started to change somehow
> His face went berserk
> And the veins bulged on his brow.

She follows this by saying to him, *Baby . . . oh, sweetheart*, an angelic, cooing high voice dubbed atop her tomboy alto, exactly signaling the split consciousness seduction/repulsion of the song. Similarly, whenever "Tattooed Love Boys" came on the radio, I had to turn it down. The line *I shot my mouth off and you showed me what that hole was for* seemed like it might jump the language barrier and embarrass me and my fellow flash-tube makers.

From a sheer rocking standpoint, the record's masterpiece is "The Wait." Hynde works her sexy contempt into a lather, and meanwhile she contributes a crunchy, nearly feeding-back guitar part, huffing and puffing over its metallic knockout. We recognized those muted upstrokes from reggae, and while this song has nothing else to do with Jamaican music, it borrows a brisk little *chicka chicka* from ska. "Private Life," on the other hand, is reggae straight up, Hynde channeling what she learned in the dub-friendly environs of punk London, where she'd fled from her own hellish midwestern private life dramas. *You've been lying to someone and now me . . . stop*, sing the boys in her band behind her, reversed roles speaking loud and clear about who, in this new day and age, is in charge.

Although I adored *Pretenders* and its successor, *Pretenders II*, I never had much more than the sketchiest background information about Hynde. Reading her memoir, *Reckless*, was a shock and revelation, for the banal torture of her Akron years, but also for the eloquent way she exposed the muddled motivations that could drive a Middle American kid to look longingly at London. In her case, the leap over the big pond provided an escape, a way out of being abused and ending up a waste product or a counterculture casualty. For me, twelve years her junior and not blessed with her talent or charisma, the British music scene was a fantasy and projection, a place with a depth of history and upfront class structure, unlike our shallow and furtive country, such that I could imagine the freedom to be myself.

I watched the London music scene from afar, but she went and lived it, assuming a place of importance as a reluctant (and genuinely reckless) music journalist, a participant in SEX, Vivienne Westwood and Malcolm McLaren's haute punk boutique on King's Road, and finally as a singer, songwriter, and bandleader. Hers is the story of a near miss, a flame-out narrowly averted multiple times, lucky stars aligning improbably, all the death traps and lottery hits that define the seventies as a time of green grass and high tides and tumbling dice and speedball and any other appropriately oxymoronic mix of metaphors.

Here she comes, poster child for the decade, arriving in our ears just a few days after it's over.

"Rapper's Delight"

Count to ten and say "rap." (Nine preliminaries and one postliminary.)

1) 1970, The Last Poets, "Jones Comin Down." Sugarhill did not come from nowhere. The Last Poets were the *original* original gangsters. From the streets of Harlem to the record store, they brought the dirty dozens—barrelhouse braggadocio, an insidious algebra of need strung out on lyrical rhythms and internal rhymes, shooting up the raps, Afro-consciousness and self-righteousness and ghetto politics rolled up and stashed in a baggie or pressed onto vinyl jet-black plastic.

2) 1971, Sly and the Family Stone, "Do You Know What?" How do you get to the texture of early hip-hop? Dig the sly way Sly slipped drum machine into crucial tracks from *There's a Riot Goin' On*, alongside all the other manually handled instruments, a burble of faux percussing in radical anticipation of rap's embrace of the inorganic, the inexhaustible, the electronic, the looped.

3) 1972, Van Dyke Parks, "G-Man Hoover." On *Discover America*, oddball arranger-genius Parks helped many mainstream rock

fans discover Trinidad and Tobago. The calypso concept of one-upmanship, gleeful Carnival jousts between Lord Invader, Lord Kitchener, Attila the Hun, Roaring Lion, the master Wilmouth Houdini, or the lesser-known Sir Lancelot, who, with Gerald Clark and his Calypso Orchestra, in 1937 first sang: *Rat-tat-tat, tat / Rat-tat-tat, tat / Rat-tat-tat, tat / Rat-tat-tat G-Man Hoover.* You don't get to rap without a stop in the Caribbean.

4) 1973, I-Roy, "Leggo Beast." In the epic battle royal of boasting-toasting, deejays I-Roy and Prince Jazzbo staged a war of words against a backdrop whipped up by producer Bunny Lee, their Jamaican sound clash unanimously called in favor of Mr. Roy, who smacked Jazzbo when he was already down by recalling a beating the latter had previously received from promoter Trevor "Leggo Beast" Douglas, inflicted as retaliation for stealing lyrics from yet another major talk-over figure, Big Youth. The dozens continue.

5) 1975, Parliament, "Chocolate City." George Clinton, as usual ages ahead of others, just funnin', he says, but adding content to the texture, telling it like it is, rapping of Washington, DC, and its "vanilla suburbs," warning that they're "gainin' on ya," saying: *Uh, what's happening, C.C.? / They still call it the White House / But that's a temporary condition, too / Can you dig it, C.C.? / . . . Ah, blood to blood / Ah, players to ladies / The last percentage count was eighty / You don't need the bullet when you got the ballot / Are you up for the downstroke, C.C.? / Chocolate City / Are you with me out there?*

6) 1976, Hamilton Bohannon, "Zulu." Hypnotic beat, hard as nails, gangway between the Meters' chicken scratch and Chic's incessant chordal guitar—mechanical repetition, near-subliminal tone hums like a tuning fork. Bohannon is the ultimate disco-funk minimalist, each of his instrumentals buzzing like a rap backing track waiting for its rappers.

7) 1977, John Cooper Clarke, "Psycle Sluts (Parts 1 & 2)." Britain's post-punk poet laureate, rapping fast and furious in his

working-class accent, describing the motorcycle mamas of his native thoroughfares. *No cash / A passion for trash / The tough Madonna whose Cro-Magnon face and crab nebular curves haunt the highways of the UK / Whose harsh credo captures the collective libido like lariats / Their lips pushed in a neon-arc of dodgems / Delightfully disciplined / Dumb but deluxe / Deliciously, deliciously deranged.*

8) 1978, Kraftwerk, "The Model." Call it an issue of optics—by now we're getting used to seeing musicians with barely anything in front of them doing almost nothing, whether it's a blunt synthesizer and a few finger wiggles or a set of turntables and some elbow action. The German band released this celebration of superficiality as a single in 1978, but the translated version waited three years to make it to the top of the UK charts.

9) 1979, Chic, "Good Times." The literal source. Sampling will help keep the actual sound of the seventies alive in the music of subsequent generations. All hail Mr. Nile Rodgers and Mr. Bernard Edwards and the rest of Les Freaks for donating their tune to Grandmaster Flash and Sugarhill and Queen. Times would be markedly less good if not for thee.

10) 1987, Public Enemy, "You're Gonna Get Yours." Contains a sample of Captain Sky's "Super Sporm," the source of a segment of "Rapper's Delight" in which Big Bank Hank promises Lois Lane his "super sperm" instead of Superman's "little worm." With Schoolly D's *Saturday Night!*, PE's *Yo! Bum Rush the Show* was my schooling in rap, introduced to me by classmate Sasha Frere-Jones in the year of its release. Until then, rap had been a vague idea while I explored other frontiers like free improvisation and sound poetry. I languished nearly a decade behind the new art form's many urgent developments.

The Pop Group

Y

The Slits

Cut

Two record covers with muddied figures. Two sets of defiant poses, one a threesome of British women, the other a phalanx of New Guinea warriors. What's to differentiate the slathered topless Slits or the Pop Group's sunbaked Asaro Mudmen from Woodstock's bare-chested guys and gals, who, caught in a downpour one of those fateful days in 1969, as a headline in New York's *Sunday News* put it, became "Hippies Mired in a Sea of Mud"? How do you get from the flower children to the post-punks? What exactly changed in that ten-year gap?

Nothing. And everything. The utopian milieu of hippiedom had largely gone dormant during the mid-seventies, estivated like a lungfish buried deep in the mud. That naive, fragile sensibility, crushed by the normalizing weight of the world, reemerged with a new crop of beatniks—smelly and critical and turned-the-fuck-on. The corporatization of music hadn't killed it. It just sent music's minions underground. Into the mud.

As I neared high school's grand finale, I felt myself drawn into this new bohemianism, with an awakened sense of my world and its limitations as well as other worlds and their creative potential. In London there seemed to be like-minded folks, kindred spirits, also looking offshore, intrigued by something exotic. Anthropology began to intrigue me. I asked questions in social studies class. I looked for records of traditional music from non-Western cultures. My pleasure-seeking impulses were complicated by a new host of considerations. Political ideals. Sexual freedom. Intellectual thirst. Responsibility, or lack thereof.

The Slits were my peers. When she joined the band, singer Ari Up was fourteen, a year older than me. She was a certified wild child and, holy smokes, did she have a set of pipes. With a funny operatic vibrato, Up would worry a note, ululating like her vocal cords had been ring modulated, or she might shriek like a murder victim, as on "Shoplifting." With Tessa Pollitt on bass and edgy texturalist Viv Albertine on guitar, the German-born singer helped the Slits stake out a safe place for women in the post-punk pandemonium, offering the granola crunch of the ladies of Laurel Canyon but adopting a less lovey-dovey stance than their hippie harbingers—harder, more assertive, and definitively done with cock-rock bullshit.

My girlfriend and I explored bohemianism in a joyful summer of expanded horizons, then long-distance when she left for college my senior year, and so on with slowly decelerating enthusiasm through the first two years of my college life. We listened to Oregon, read Adrienne Rich, allowed ourselves to get precious and pretentious and sometimes real, revisited folk and rock from earlier in the decade, Joni Mitchell and Neil Young and Annette Peacock and Bruce Cockburn.

On a whim that first summer—which smells like honeysuckle, chlorine, and sweat in my olfactory memory—we attended an anthropology conference at University of Iowa's student union, where we found deep academia fascinating but Martian. One of the succulent issues on the docket had to do with the politics of ethnographic field methods; I'd examine this topic in ethnomusicology and anthropology courses as an undergrad, growing dissatisfied with the us/them quality of the field. But that summer the totemic mud made perfect sense. Ours was an atavistic camp-out, a back-to-nature fandango. When we weren't sequestered in one of our bedrooms, connecting the dots in a secret solar system, we spent nights rolling around in a tent at a park outside city limits, spinning mother-earth myths, transforming hormones into a spark of resistance that we believed would save the planet.

Both *Cut* and *Y* appeal to an image of otherness as a kind of resource or wellspring, a classic deformity of modernist primitivism and social anthropology. Yes, that image is fraught, maybe even damnable, but it wears its heart on its sleeve and is so earnest in its idealism that it's hard to condemn. I still love both these records. When I listen to them, they rekindle the latent bohemian in me, the one that doesn't shower, grows his hair long, plays guitar in the park, kicks a hacky sack around with some chums, snorts at people in suits or uniforms, thinks he knows better, longs for new experience, and scrapes a message into the sidewalk with the burnt end of a stick. OK, I never much cared for hacky sack, but all the rest.

Senior year in high school, three friends and I plotted and executed an act of vandalism. A nearby municipal water tower was commonly used for competitive tagging between our school, West High, and the crosstown rival City High, slogans emblazoned either in our colors, yellow and green, or theirs, red and white. Late one night, we climbed the 150-foot tower, schlepping cans of black and orange paint, with which we covered the existing "West Is Best" in a borrowed phrase that seemed to sum up the end of our high school experience: "The Horror, The Horror." Snooty little dorks, we added a literal footnote to the graffiti. During class the next day, another English teacher popped his head into our class and said snidely to Mrs. Peterson: "What's it like up there, Nancy?"

...

It's no coincidence that *Y* and *Cut* seem so closely related. The two bands had already shared a seven-inch single, and the Pop Group's drummer Bruce Smith has a speaking role on the track "Love und Romance," so the cross-talk was literal as well as spiritual. A few years later, with the New Age Steppers, Ari Up would record Mark Stewart's "High Ideals and Crazy Dreams," beating the Pop Group singer to his own song. Both records were produced by Dennis "Blackbeard" Bovell, a dub scientist integral to the post-punk scene. Bovell shaped the sound of the LPs, but intelligently he avoided making them into conventional dub outings, instead building on the strengths of each group.

In the case of the Slits, who were reggae-positive enough to include Budgie, a drummer who happened to be a man (*sacre bleu!*), in the sessions, Bovell added sound effects and keyboards, layered Up's voice just so, and refrained from echoing everything into oblivion, instead obtaining a suitable balance of the gals' explosive energy and Budgie's sympathetic snap, crackle, and pop. *Cut* is one of post-punk's genius strokes, a record that at once expresses the vehemence and the jollity of a pro-sex bi-curious anti-patriarchal feminism. *Typical girls are sensitive*, sang Up on the best-known song, reciting a litany of stereotypes. *Typical girls are emotional / Typical girls are cruel and bewitching / She's a femme fatale / Typical girls stand by their man / Typical girls are really swell / Typical girls learn how to act shocked / Typical girls don't rebel / Who invented the typical girl?*

The Pop Group presented Bovell with a different challenge. A politically supercharged band armed with apocalyptic visions, conspiracy theories, and Nietzschean aphorisms, they were post-punks who fancied themselves jazz and funk musicians. That could be a recipe for dire and forgettable music, but in fact their crumbling structures and lunatic screed gave the dub master fresh material, and with the fellas he applied a heavier hand on the mixing console, echoing out, doubling, or miniaturizing Stewart's crazed outbursts and, without reducing their essential shatteredness, assembling and giving contour to the scratchy string, squealing horn, smacked or caressed piano, surreptitious spy-movie guitar theme, and sporadically concentrated rhythm section.

Setting out *Y*'s basic sound, the kick-off cut is a rave in the mode of its free-funk predecessors "She Is Beyond Good and Evil" and "We

Are All Prostitutes," both inflammatory singles. "Thief of Fire" casts Prometheus in the role of Godfather of Soul, stealing solar energy from Simon Underwood's thumb-popping bass and guitarist John Waddington's jangled seventh chords, every groovy fastball offset by a perilous wind-up, dark bumps and mistreated reeds cogitating over a snare roll, until the funk backbeat brings light. Like getting down and dirty in a mud puddle, the Pop Group's shoplifted spark is something every lapsed bohème and ex-utopian should experience again.

...

The Greyhound pulled into the station, which was just a driveway transecting a downtown street corner, across from Iowa City's recreation center, where my girlfriend and I had celebrated her high school graduation a few months earlier. Now, at five in the morning, I was headed twelve hours away to join her somewhere called Appleton, Wisconsin, for the weekend. I hoisted my duffel bag onto my shoulder, the corner of T. C. McLuhan's *Touch the Earth: A Self-Portrait of Indian Existence* poking me in the back. The other book in the bag was *Soul of Wood*, written by Jakov Lind, who had succeeded in passing for a non-Jew inside Nazi Germany. Two years later, I would meet Lind by chance at a party for Günter Grass in New York. But that was a lifetime away.

I helped an older white woman load her luggage onto the bus and we sat together. It was early in the fall of 1980, I'd been following the presidential election closely, and I'd had it up to my earholes with patriotic jingoism. Ronald Reagan seemed to me an utter tool, and I was certain he could not win against Carter, whom I liked. Reagan was a celebrity, not a public servant, never mind that he'd already been governor of California. He was stiff and phony, gave sound-bite answers, and he'd been a snitch for McCarthy. Who could trust him to be president with a bogus slogan like "Let's Make America Great Again"?

Honestly, I didn't know anything about party politics. I watched the RNC broadcast and was generally disgusted. They were all just suits. My new heroes were called punks, but these politicians were the real punks. Those days, along with the Slits and the Pop Group, I was listening to the Dead Boys' "Sonic Reducer," which indeed reduced it all to a fine point, or a dull one. Anyway, theirs was a point I could feel.

It was during the trip-long conversation with my bus-mate on that journey up to Lawrence University that I think I articulated my first independent political observation. After formalities, and a long stretch just looking out the window at hills covered in autumnal effluvia of corn and soybeans, I asked her if she'd ever thought about how our nation was founded on a bunch of lies. I remember that she was patient and asked me to explain.

"We're supposed to be patriotic, waving flags and congratulating ourselves, especially in the midst of this awful election business, but this country has committed two genocides," I said. "White Europeans first decimated the native people and then brought in Africans as slaves to build and maintain the new country."

"Sure, but none of us personally did that," she countered. "That was a long time ago. Nobody's got slaves now."

"We're supposed to be proud of our past. How can we be proud of that? They glossed over it in my history books. And we carve faces on the side of a mountain and salute every time the national anthem is played."

After a long silence, she said: "I think we have to move on. You can't live burdened with someone else's guilt."

I brooded like a know-it-all kid. "Our mass hypocrisy," I thought. "She just doesn't understand." We slept and ate at a rest stop and talked about other things and napped and did it all again and finally reached Appleton as the sun was going down. As we were offloading, she turned to me and thanked me for sitting with her.

"That was a thoughtful conversation," she said. "I appreciate what you said, and I'll keep thinking about it. You're a conscientious person. Keep that with you. But don't let what you've realized make you bitter. You're a sweet guy. I'd hate to think that those nasty people in the past would turn you into a curmudgeon."

"Lola"

When my sister Jill was five, her teachers informed her that girls were not allowed to play on the soccer team. She accosted me, dressed as I was for a game in my shorts and cleats, later that afternoon: "You boys get everything you want just because you have a penis!"

How astute a social critic she had been would dawn on me only slowly over the years, but it's a position around which she based much of her identity. I remember when she announced that she was a lesbian—something that I, in a spasm of callousness and lack of sympathy, felt sure was designed simply to piss off our mother, retribution aimed at the woman who had dressed her baby in frills and referred to Jill as her "pink bundle." But rather quickly it became evident that Jill was being truthful and her sexuality had already been, for her, a matter of fact for a long time, at least since she'd gotten the hots for my copy of the Ohio Players' *Honey*, which seems to have been quite informative. She developed a love of David Bowie and a blazing obsession with Prince; she altered her name, adding a suffix to make it Jillian, the first step in a personal makeover that would gradually distance her from the little girl our mom had tried to project.

Leap forward to 2014. My sister-in-law Effie, who unlike me is an avid Facebook user, texted: "Hey, John, how do you feel about your sister transitioning?" So it was that I found out secondhand via social media that my sister Jillian would be my brother Jack. I immediately sent him a congratulatory text to signal my approval, as if someone who had seen through the smokescreen of gender at five years old needed anything of the sort.

About a month later, on a trip to New York, I met up with Jack at a coffee shop on Fourteenth Street. I think the last time I'd seen him as relaxed and comfortable in his skin was when, as a little girl, he'd traveled with a good friend and her family to Brazil. Since then, there was almost always a little rage simmering under the surface that would sometimes boil over in outbursts, even when Jillian had founded a successful business and things were otherwise hunky. We reconnected, as we always do, over music, and I saw the twinkle in his eye, an ease and lack of tension, a joyful demeanor. I'd always felt that gender identity, like most of our personal characteristics, was profoundly malleable, that it was basically subject only to choice and that there was nothing fixed about it. Sitting there sipping an espresso, I was forced to radically rethink this concept. My own sibling, I could see plainly, had a soul that had been planted in the wrong body. Jack had been chafing inside that uncomfortable edifice. His big change, ironically, taught me that some things don't change; those indelible parts of one's self settle in with age, sharpen, and become that much clearer.

And then I thought about all the feminist post-punk we'd listened to before I left for college, when Jack and I and our sister Jennifer, two years younger than Jack, had enjoyed bedroom auditions. The Slits were a major hit with their cover of Marvin Gaye's "I Heard It Through the Grapevine," also Kleenex and the Mo-Dettes, Lora Logic, Lori and the Chameleons, Martha and the Muffins, the Plasmatics, X-Ray Spex, Penetration, Siouxsie and the Banshees, even Kate Bush and later bands like Scrawl. Jack and Jennifer had introduced me to plenty of music when we were growing up, still do today, our ongoing exchange an important part of our family bond during holiday visits.

The Raincoats enjoyed a place of honor in our mutual pantheon. Their single "Adventures Close to Home" brought working-class British social critique to the feminist table, and we loved their second LP *Odyshape*, more experimental in outlook with Robert Wyatt on drums. But our absolute favorite was their cover of the Kinks' "Lola." Ana da Silva sang unchanged lyrics, and the perfect song performed a swift gender switch that complicated everything, making good on the gender-bending promise of the original, setting loose violin, voice, guitar, bass, and drums to frolic in a newfound land where girls were already boys and boys already girls, all the promise of glam and glitter was fully realized, and Do It Yourself meant Do It to Yourself. It's a concept that L.A.'s Suburban Lawns amplified a year into the eighties in their song "Janitor": *Who's your mother? / Who's your father? / I guess everything's irrelative.* We were fascinated with clones and test-tube babies, things that make our prior notions of genetic relation indeed "irrelative."

Feminist post-punk was important for a gal who would one day be a guy. That this would seem quizzical—the relationship between having been a proud lesbian and becoming an equally proud FTM trans person married to a woman—no doubt shows the limited imagination of this straight writer. But I'd stopped thinking of my sibling as being hetero so long ago that, more than anything, that's what surprises me.

The music I listened to in the seventies shaped my understanding of gender and sexuality. Cock-rock and filthy funk probably put some caveman ideas in my head—Jimmy Castor lampooned those notions in his hit single "Troglodyte," which featured just such a paleo dude relaxing at home, listening to his "steer-eo," grunting, *Gotta find a woman, gotta find a woman*, discovering Bertha Butt of the Butt sisters, grabbing her by the hair, said cave-gal calling out in aggressive submission or passive aggression, *I'll sock it to ya, Daddy*, our caveman replying in a rumbling baritone: *Right on!* Good fun and too stupid to be strenuously objected to, but also secretly the same sermon being preached by loads of less self-parodying songs.

Nonetheless, in the face of the dominant troglodytic hokum,

there were all the contradictions of the era to fog up that mirror, from the leering urban myths that circulated in our suburban hornet's nests to our adulation of cross-dressing heavy metal beauties of unstated orientation like Rob Halford of Judas Priest, a queer man whose image I pinned to the wall next to posters of Farrah Fawcett and Jessica Lange. And Scorpions, whose super-aggressive "He's a Woman, She's a Man" toyed with transgender fascination in 1977. And of course Queen, David Bowie, Lou Reed, and other glam- and glitterbugs, and even mainstream hard rockers like Roger Daltrey and Robert Plant. I adored them all, of course, and libidinal sparks certainly shot off in my youthful trousers, but I really only felt the urge to pair with women. Same as Jack. How you present yourself to the world, how you understand your own drives, or with whom you actually sleep—that complex ball of information must be a little bit nurture and a little bit nature. Did I personally ever fantasize about becoming female? Once, as a cooch-mad boy, I imagined being a girl so that I could play with my pussy anytime I wanted; a moment later I realized this would make it impossible to jerk off. I'm not sure that qualifies.

I am proud of Jack first for having figured it out and then for having acted upon his insight. The music of the seventies may have teed us up for an exploration of our actual inner selves. Maybe it helped some of us repress or sublimate anything uncomfortable and deny who we really were. As it turned out, Jack delved into his inner self and is the better man for it.

1980

Warm Leatherette

The past does not influence me; I influence it.
WILLEM DE KOONING

Present is an arrogant tense. It prefers to imagine other tenses in its own likeness.

In light of that, let's remember that seventies music is more than just music made in the seventies. More than a fixed repository of sounds and sentiments, it's a fluid category, continuously being revoked and reinvented by a bossy present. From the day the decade ended, it was open season on what the seventies meant. Its legacy has been anxiously contested, debates formed about which music made during the ten-year span would be remembered and which would be buried in the construction of a new improved version of *the* seventies. Seventies music is pliant—like my childhood, part experience and part invention. As our present shifts so, too, will the music of our past, and in the future seventies music will be different again. Hell's bells, it was something else already by 1980.

...

Grace Jones pulled right up to the bumper, jostled the wires in the back of the machine, and spelled out another possible seventies.

With *Warm Leatherette*, released just five months out, in the first spring of the new decade, she plucked a few plums from the earlier era's fruit basket. It's the record that found Jones coming fully into her own after a string of serviceable disco releases. It would have been unimaginable even five years earlier.

Warm Leatherette is the first eighties album of seventies music.

First of all, consider the Jones image: a model-thin, muscular, square-shouldered, flat-chested, high-cheekboned, box-Afroed, androgynous black woman with the hots for haute couture, a slightly robotic vibe, possibly cyborg, and a death-ray stare that projected icicles from her irises. Can you think of a seventies record cover that's anyhow comparable, an LP with that particular kind of confrontational image glaring at you? The direct challenge, the crossed arms, the dramatic lighting, the unbreakable gaze, an invitation or a dare—go ahead, try to define me, try to pin me down, just try to stare back at me, you record owner from another era, you think you know me, fuck off back to your hut, this is the fresh beat and all your wanky rock, jangly folk, sloppy punk, and stinky funk, they're things of the past. Now we do differently. Aerodynamically. We do as I say. You must be enslaved. As Sly and Robbie prefer, we tighten up. However they want it, that's how I want it, and that's how it's done. They might choose to fine-tune the reggae feel on the Pretenders' almost contemporaneous "Private Life" or overhaul Roxy Music's "Love Is the Drug," tempering Bryan Ferry's drama, intensifying it with a clipped Jamaican accent and cold, post-Nico diction. It's Sly's and Robbie's world now; it's Jones's world now. Try to stop them. Chronological translation is their prerogative.

Oh, one more thing about the cover photo: Jones was pregnant.

The open confrontation is the big new thing. She's the embodiment of an unforeseen racial and gender complexity, an empowerment zone for ambiguous identity, her disco days having built a huge gay following, her black butch-girl-disciplinarian aura a kink that looks ahead to the queering of the future, inviting her listeners to think beyond binaries, giving birth to a new multiplicitous subjectivity, one in which the submerged agendas of seventies music, our familiar contradictions, our dearly held phobias and fascinations, come to the surface in the guise of Prince, Michael Jackson, Madonna. Jones gives precision to mumbling Tom Petty's "Breakdown," Petty having contributed an extra verse for her to personalize her version. She reaches back to cover a late sixties crossover hit for Smokey Robinson, "The Hunter Gets Captured by the Game," showing the Motown concept in a post–new wave light, as an Afropunk appropriation of *The Big Chill* generation.

Although some of this is reggae, it's not your parents' reggae. It's not even the Sly and Robbie of the seventies, when they comprised the core of the Revolutionaries. Here they're the Compass Point All Stars, house band for Chris Blackwell's Bahamian studio; their sound is now more compressed, explosive, and slick. It's turbocharged. On the title track, Wally Badarou's keyboards bubble like molten plastic, guitarist Mikey Chung detonating power chords, sending shards across the room, Robbie Shakespeare's astonishingly heavy bass locked in with Sly Dunbar's vacuum-packed drums. The song was originally recorded a couple of years earlier by an electronic band called the Normal, with lyrics inspired by J. G. Ballard's *Crash*. Daniel Miller, the composer of "Warm Leatherette," put it out as the B-side from what was intended as a one-off single on his vanity label called Mute Records, future home of eighties synth stalwarts including Depeche Mode, Yazoo, and Erasure.

And there you are, off into something entirely un-seventies. On the Jones record, you still hear echoes of the previous era, but its new sound declares something different, as will come to pass, that we should hear those songs of a few years earlier according to that new sound, recognizing them in our memories as part of the popular subconscious, but assimilating the music as if that whole organ had been processed, tidied up, buffed and varnished and fed through a computer, only to come out in a brand-spanking-new form, as an S&M dominatrix with a flat top and a porcelain glow.

Welcome to the eighties. If you lived here you'd be home by now.

Acknowledgments

Thanks:

To my readers and advisors: Matthew Goulish, John Sparagana, Jim Dempsey, David Grubbs, Josiah McElheny, Jimmy Wright, Jack Corbett, Mats Gustafsson, Adam Sonderberg, Alex Houston, Katie Kahn, Lin Hixson, and J. C. Gabel.

To Lee Froehlich and Lewis Lapham, for assigning me to write the Sun Ra chapter, which appeared in a different form in *Lapham's Quarterly* (Fall 2017).

To Mickle Maher, David Isaacson, and Diana Slickman of Theater Oobleck, for performing select chapters at the Hopleaf.

To Mark Epstein and Arlene Shechet, for a push in the right direction.

To my agent, Anne Edelstein, for being the right direction.

To my editors: Susan Bielstein, for her guidance and judicious use of the scalpel, and Erin DeWitt, for her allegiance to detail.

To Mark E. Smith, there's a grave somewhere only partly filled.

To Scooter Johns, without whom.

To my better half, Terri Kapsalis, for surviving the seventies, twice.

Index

Above Average Black Band (AABB),
194
Abraham, Alton, 156, 158, 159
"Absolutely Sweet Marie" (Dylan), 189
AC/DC, 11, 80
Adam & the Ants, 420, 451
Adventure (Television), 310
"Adventures Close to Home" (Rain-
coats), 469
Aerosmith, 237, 290–94, 329
African Rhythm and African Sensibility
(Chernoff), 9
"Ain't It Strange" (P. Smith), 284
"Ain't No Sunshine" (Withers), 211–12
"Ain't You" (Kleenex), 427–28
Akkerman, Jan, 123–24
Akomfrah, John, 250–51
Aladdin Sane (Bowie), 102, 341
Albert Ayler Trio, 311
Alice in Wonderland (Carroll), 83
"Alifib" (Wyatt), 226
"Alison" (Costello), 373–74
Alive! (Kiss), 263–67
Alive II (Kiss), 264, 266
Allman Brothers, 124, 263, 238
"All Night Party" (A Certain Ratio), 420
"Alone with Just a Memory of You"
(Sun Ra), 153–54
Altamont, 179
Alternative TV, 420–21, 439
Altman, Robert, 188, 276
"Always Crashing in the Same Car"
(Bowie-Eno), 341
Amarcord Nino Rota (Willner), 142,
144, 148
"Amateur Hour" (Sparks), 240
"Ambition" (Subway Sect), 432
"Ambivalence & Spark Plugs" (Immune
System), 427
"Ambulance Blues" (Young), 231–32
"Anarchy in the U.K." (Sex Pistols),
439, 455
Anderson, Ian, 10
Anderson, Jon, 114, 117–18
Anderson, Wes, 137–39

Andrade, Oswald de, 168–69
Andrews, Barry, 406–10
"And You and I" (Yes), 117
"Andy's Chest" (Reed), 97, 100
Animals (Pink Floyd), 356–62
Another Green World (Eno), 205–6, 342
Araçá Azul (Veloso), 168–69
Archway Studios, 133, 135
"Are You Receiving Me?" (XTC), 408–9
Arista Freedom, 132, 134
Armchair Boogie (Michael Hurley &
Pals), 64–68
Arneson, Robert, 202–3
Art Ensemble of Chicago, 50–56, 87,
133, 263, 347
Artists House, 382–84
"Artists Only" (Talking Heads), 403–4
Atlanta Rhythm Section, 369, 371
Atlantic Records, 143, 209
"Atomic Punk" (Van Halen), 366–67
Attractions, the, 375, 379–80
Au Pairs, 421
Autobahn (Kraftwerk), 213–14
Average White Band, 193–96; *AWB*, 195
Ayler, Albert, 1, 49, 54–55, 311, 348

B-52's, 397, 427
Bäbi (Graves), 315–17
"Babies Makin' Babies" (Sly and the
Family Stone), 184
Babylon by Bus (Marley), 338–39
"Baby Needs a New Pair of Snakeskin
Boots (A Pop Operetta)" (Rund-
gren), 149
Babys, 394
Bacharach, Burt, 189, 378
Back in Black/"Back in Black" (AC/DC),
11, 80
"Back in the Saddle Again" (Aero-
smith), 292
Back Stabbers/"Back Stabbers"
(O'Jays), 127–29
Bad Brains, 452
Bad Company, 142, 297, 368
Badfinger, 141–42

Bags, 421
Bailey, Clayton, 202–3
Bailey, Derek, 86–90, 232
Baker, Roy Thomas, 369
Ballard, J. G., 341, 475
Balliett, Whitney, 131
Band, the, 190, 231, 263, 351
Banger, Ed, 421
Bangs, Lester, 125, 443
Barraclough, Elizabeth, 351–53
"Barracuda" (Heart), 354
Barry, Robert, 156, 157
Bass, Fontella, 50–54, 56, 133–34
Bauman, Jon "Bowzer," 266–67
Beach Boys, the, 59, 263, 442
Beamon, Bob, 316–17
Beatles, the, 19, 59, 141–42, 167, 202–
    3, 223, 378; *The Beatles* (White
    Album), 19, 202
Beatty, Warren, 188, 230
"The Bed's Too Big without You"
    (Police), 453
Before and After Science (Eno), 205–6
"Before the Moon Falls" (Fall), 436–37
"Being Boiled" (Human League), 427
Bell, Mark, 442–43
Bell, Pedro, 383
"Bellerin' Plain" (Captain Beefheart),
    37, 40
Benge, Alfie, 224–26
"Bennie and the Jets" (John), 257, 260
Bernstein, Steven, 148–50
"Best Dressed Chicken in Town" (Dr.
    Alimantado), 211
"Be Thankful for What You've Got"
    (DeVaughn), 197–99
Bizarros, the, 422
"Black and White" (Greyhound): cover
    by Three Dog Night, 337
Black Ark Studios, 211–12, 336
Black Artists Group (BAG), 131–32
Black Audio Film Collective, 250
"Blackpatch" (Nero), 282
Black Sabbath, 33–35, 327–28, 366–
    67, 432
"Black to the Future" (Dery), 249
Black Uhuru, 339
Blake, William, 83, 436–37

Bland, Ed, 52–53
Blank Generation/"Blank Generation"
    (Richard Hell and the Voidoids),
    308–11
Bley, Carla, 145–47, 149
"Blockheads" (Ian Dury & the Block-
    heads), 447
Blonde on Blonde (Dylan), 189
Blondie, 148, 337
Blood on the Tracks (Dylan), 275–78
Blue/"Blue" (Mitchell), 59–63, 277
Blue Navigator (Hurley), 69
Blue Öyster Cult, 263, 280, 283, 297,
    327
Bohannon, Hamilton, 459
Bolan, Marc, 300
Bonham, John, 173, 175
"Boots" (Residents), 203
"Born in the U.S.A." (Springsteen), 272
Born to Run/"Born to Run" (Spring-
    steen), 270–72
Boston, 124, 287–89
Boston, Mark "Rockette Morton," 41, 43
Bovell, Dennis "Blackbeard," 464
Bowie, David, 64, 102–5, 111, 137, 205,
    210, 216–17, 247, 258, 263, 271–72,
    340–42, 467, 470
Bowie, Lester, 50, 55–56
Bowie-Eno Berlin Trilogy, 64, 216–17,
    340–42
Boys Next Door, 422
"Brand New Key" (Melanie), 97–98, 107
"Brandy (You're a Fine Girl)" (Looking
    Glass), 329
Branson, Richard, 337–38
Braxton, Anthony, 348
Breakaway (Conner), 223
"Break It Up" (P. Smith), 279–80, 283
Breuker, Willem, 89–90
"Brighton Rock" (Queen), 236–37
"Bring Back That Leroy Brown"
    (Queen), 237
"Bring on the Night" (Police), 454
Brooks, Albert, 328
Brown, James, 25–32, 55, 175, 194,
    218, 236, 263, 430
Brown, Yamma, 30
Bruce, Lenny, 143

Bryars, Gavin, 89–90, 210
Buckingham, Lindsey, 318, 322–23
Budgie, 80, 464
"The Buggy Boogie Woogie" (Captain
    Beefheart), 39
"Burning Airlines Give You So Much
    More" (Eno), 206
Buzzcocks, the, 376–77, 422, 428, 439
"Bye Bye Love" (Cars), 394
Byrd, Bobby, 27–28, 31
Byrne, David, 210, 400–405

Cale, John, 219–21, 279
Calling All Girls (Half Japanese), 427
Call Me (Green), 163–64
Callomon, Cally, 431–32
Camus, Albert, 400–405, 424
Captain Beefheart & the Magic Band,
    36–44, 64, 201–2, 269, 433
Captain Fantastic and the Brown Dirt
    Cowboy (John), 230, 261
Captain Slaughterboard Drops Anchor
    (Peake), 83
Caradec, François, 86
Carlin, George, 10–11, 45, 115
Carroll, Lewis, 81–83, 85
Cars, the, 392–95; The Cars, 392–95
"Cartrouble" (Adam & the Ants), 420
The Case of the 3 Sided Dream in Audio
    Color (Kirk), 144–45
Cash, Johnny, 274, 276–77
Castor, Jimmy, 469–70
Cat Scratch Fever/"Cat Scratch Fever"
    (Nugent), 328, 330
Cave, Nick, 48, 144, 422
A Certain Ratio, 338, 420
"The Chain" (Fleetwood Mac), 322
Chairs Missing (Wire), 332, 396–99
Chambers, Terry, 406–10
Chance, James, 47–48, 400–405
"Change of the Guard" (Steely Dan), 7
Changesonebowie (Bowie), 258
Charles, Ray, 163, 209
"Che" (Suicide), 345
Cheap Trick, 392–95
"Chelsea Hotel No. 2" (Cohen), 230
Cherry Vanilla, 104
Chess Records, 50, 52, 133–34

Chic, 460
"Children of the World" (Freshies), 426
Chin, Vincent, 210–11
"China My China" (Eno), 207
"Chocolate City" (Parliament), 459
"Choc-Stock" (Fall), 439
"Choose Life, Not Death" (Sun Ra), 153
"Christiani Eddy" (Breuker), 89–90
"Christ's Reality Asylum" (Crass), 423
Chubby and the Turnpikes, 292
"The Circle Game" (Mitchell), 230
"Circumstances" (Captain Beefheart), 38
Clapton, Eric, 230, 272, 452
Clarke, John Cooper, 426, 459–60
Clash, the, 280, 308, 332–39, 373, 439;
    The Clash, 333–39
Clear Spot (Captain Beefheart), 36, 38
Clemons, Clarence, 271
Cliff, Jimmy, 22
Clinton, George, 9–10, 32, 77, 199,
    245–51, 331, 459. See also Parlia-
    ment
Close to the Edge/"Close to the Edge"
    (Yes), 115–20
"The Clouds Are Full of Wine (Not
    Whiskey or Rye)" (Captain Beef-
    heart), 38, 40
"Coal Miner's Daughter" (Lynn), 230
Cochran, William "Bugs," 157–58
"Coconut" (Nilsson), 73
"Coffin for Head of State" (Fela and
    Afrika '70), 302
Cohen, Leonard, 144, 188, 230
"Cold Sweat" (Brown), 236
Cold Sweat: My Father James Brown
    and Me (Y. Brown), 30
Coleman, Denardo, 386–87
Coleman, Ornette, 41, 49, 132, 181,
    384–88
Collectus Interruptus (Dr. Demento),
    142
Collins, Bootsy, 27, 31, 247, 295–99
Collins, Phil, 81, 272
Coltrane, John, 1, 123, 189
"Combination" (Aerosmith), 293
"Come Together" (Beatles), 367
Compass Point All Stars, 475
Coney, John, 159

Conner, Bruce, 223
Contortions, the, 401–2
Cooke, Sam, 9, 189, 218, 225
'Coon Bid'ness (Hemphill), 134
Cooper, Alice, 108–12, 337, 443
Cope, Julian, 425, 431–32, 433
Copeland, Stewart, 452–53
Corbett, Mitchell, 110–11
Corman, Roger, 443
Cornelius, Don, 129, 194, 195
Cornered on Plastic (Costello), 378
Costa, Gal, 167–70
Costello, Elvis (Declan MacManus), 80, 373–80, 448
County, Wayne, 104
"Covered Up in Aces" (Barraclough), 352
Crash (Ballard), 341, 475
Crass, 423
Cravats, the, 423
"Crazy on You" (Heart), 353
Criminal Record (Wakeman), 115–16
"Crippled with Nerves" (Kilburn and the High Roads), 447
Criss, Peter, 265–66
Croce, Jim, 237–38
Crosby, David, 7
Crosby, Stills, Nash & Young, 209, 378
"The Crunge" (Led Zeppelin), 174–76
"Cry Baby" ("Fatal" Microbes), 425
The Cry of Jazz (Bland), 52–53
Cuevas, Manuel, 187
Cure, the, 423–24, 451
Curry, Tim, 234
Cuscuna, Michael, 132
Cut (Slits), 463–66
Cutler, Ivor, 83, 226–28

Dadistics, the, 424
Dahl, Steve: Disco Demolition Night, 254
"Damaged Goods" (Gang of Four), 426–27
Damned, the, 332, 373
"Dancing Days" (Led Zeppelin), 177
Darling, Candy, 101
da Silva, Ana, 469
Daugherty, Jay Dee, 280, 283
David, Hal, 189, 378

Davies, Ray, 17
Davis, Dennis, 341–42
Davis, Miles, 32, 131, 179, 263–64, 387, 431
"The Day the World Turned Day-Glo" (X-Ray Spex), 433
Dayton, Jonathan, 137
Dean, Roger, 80, 116
Deep Listening Band, 349
Dempsey, Jim, 388–89
Derek and the Dominos, "Layla," 124, 230
Dery, Mark: "Black to the Future," 249
Destroyer (Kiss), 266
DeVaughn, William, 197–99
Devo, 111, 201, 210, 411–16
Devoto, Howard, 376, 428
DeZurik Sisters, 123
Dirk Wears White Sox (Adam and the Ants), 420
Discover America (Van Dyke Parks), 458–59
Dixon, Stephen: "Wife in Reverse," 222
DNA (band), 402–3
Doc at the Radar Station (Captain Beefheart), 36, 269
"Doctor Dark" (Captain Beefheart), 41
Dodd, Coxsone, 210
Dog and Butterfly (Heart), 354
"Dog Eat Dog" (Nugent), 330
Dogon A.D./"Dogon A.D." (Hemphill), 132–35
Do It Yourself (Ian Dury & the Block-heads), 448–50
"Don't Eat Bricks" (Neon), 430
Doobie Brothers, 247, 369, 371–72
Dorn, Joel, 143, 144
double-live records, 263–64
Double Nickels on the Dime (Minute-men), 275
Douglas, Jack, 329
Douglas, Trevor "Leggo Beast," 459
Dowd, Tom, 145
Doyle, Arthur, 315–16
"Do You Believe" (Lewis), 75–76
"Do You Feel Like I Do" (Frampton), 265
"Do You Know What?" (Sly and the Family Stone), 458

"Do You Think I'm Sexy" (Stewart), 451
Dragnet (Fall), 436–40
Drake, Hamid, 453
Drake, Nick, 136–39
Dr. Alimantado (Winston Thompson), 211–12
Dramatics, 239
Dr. Demento, 142
"Dream Baby Dream" (Suicide), 344
"Dreams" (Fleetwood Mac), 321, 323
"Dresden Style" (Swell Maps), 432
Dressed to Kill (Kiss), 265–66
"Driving Me Backwards" (Eno), 223
Drumbo, 38, 43
Drury, Ian, 446–50
Dub Housing (Pere Ubu), 413
Dury, Ian, 445–50
Dust, 442–43
"D'yer Maker" (Led Zeppelin), 174, 175–76
Dylan, Bob, 1, 149, 170, 188–89, 263, 274–78, 282, 351

Eagles, 116, 124, 190
Earth, Wind & Fire, 80
Echo & the Bunnymen, 377, 424–25, 433
ECM label, 87–88
Edgar Winter Group, 121–24; Edgar Winter's White Trash, 121–22
"Egomaniac's Kiss" (DNA), 402–3
"Eine Symphonie des Grauens" (Monochrome Set), 429–30
Electric Light Orchestra (ELO), 267–69
Electro-Harmonix, 109
"Elegie" (P. Smith), 280
Elizabeth Barraclough (Barraclough), 351–52
Elton John's Greatest Hits (John), 257–58, 261
Elvis Costello and the Attractions, 375, 379–80
The Empty Foxhole (Coleman), 384, 386
The End (Cravats), 423
"English Nobleman" (Hurley), 67–68
Eno, Brian, 64, 204–12, 223–24, 341–42, 404–5, 420
"Equator" (Sparks), 241
Ertegun, Ahmet, 143, 209

"Eruption" (Van Halen), 365–66, 370
Escalator Over the Hill (Bley), 145–47, 149
"Every Picture Tells a Story" (Stewart), 451
Extended Play (Corbett), 249

Face the Music (Electric Light Orchestra), 267–69
"Facts-Facts" (MX-80 Sound), 414
Fagen, Donald, 148–50
Fair, David, 427
Fair, Jad, 427
Fairbrother-Roe, David, 116
"Faith" (Manicured Noise), 429
Fall, the, 10, 435–40, 442
"Falling in Love with Myself Again" (Sparks), 241
"Family Affair" (Sly and the Family Stone), 180
Family Stone. *See* Sly and the Family Stone
Farfisa, 379, 408
Fast Product label, 426–27
"Fatal" Microbes, 425
Favors, Malachi, 51, 55
Fear (Cale), 220–21
"Fear Is a Man's Best Friend" (Cale), 220–21
Fela and Afrika '70, 300–303
Ferrone, Steve, 195
Ferry, Bryan, 422, 474
"Final Day" (Young Marble Giants), 433–34
Fish Out of Water (Squire), 116
Fitzgerald, Patrik, 425–26
Flame Wars (Dery), 249
"Flash Gordon's Ape" (Captain Beefheart), 41–42, 43
"Flat of Angles" (Fall), 436
Fleetwood, Mick, 5, 318, 323
Fleetwood Mac, 256, 297, 318–24; *Fleetwood Mac*, 318–19
"Flick of the Wrist" (Queen), 237, 239
Flowers, Herbie, 73, 101, 105
Flying Burrito Brothers, 187, 189–90
Focus, 121, 123–24
Foghat, 92, 272, 297, 368
Folkways label, 65

For Alto (Braxton), 348
"The Force Is Blind" (Alternative TV), 420–21
"Foreplay" (Boston), 288
"For the Turnstiles" (Young), 231–32
48 Chairs, 426
"The Fountain of Salmacis" (Genesis), 85
Fowley, Kim, 393, 421
Foxtrot (Genesis), 81, 83, 85
Fragile (Yes), 115, 116
Frame, Pete, 420
Frampton, Peter, 263–65; *Frampton Comes Alive!*, 263–65
"Frankenstein" (Edgar Winter Group), 121–22
"Frankie Teardrop" (Suicide), 345–46
Franklin, Aretha, 55, 163, 190
Freeman Brothers, 157
Frehley, Ace, 265–66
French, John "Drumbo," 43
"French Film Blurred" (Wire), 397
Fresh (Sly and the Family Stone), 178–84
Freshies, the, 426
Fripp, Robert, 206, 210, 342, 422
Frith, Fred, 84, 227
"From the Morning" (Drake), 138–39
Fun House (Stooges), 45–49; "Fun House," 49
Funkadelic, 9–10, 383–84
fusion, 8–11

Gabriel, Peter, 81, 83, 85
Gang of Four, 426–27
Gardiner, Jaime, 427
Gartside, Green, 431
Gaye, Marvin, 164–65, 179, 337, 468
Genesis, 80–85, 264, 297, 451
George, Edward, 250
George, Lowell, 220, 446
Gerald Clark and his Calypso Orchestra, 459
Gerstl, Richard, 341
"Get the Best of Me" (Michael Hurley & Pals), 67
"Get the Lead Out" (Aerosmith), 293
"Get Up (I Feel Like Being a) Sex Machine" (Brown), 25–32

Gil, Gilberto, 169
Gilbert, Bruce, 396–99
The Gilded Palace of Sin (Flying Burrito Brothers), 187
Gilmore, John, 49, 157, 158
Gismonti, Egberto, 87–88
"Give Me Everything" (Magazine), 428
Gladiators, 212
"G-Man Hoover" (Van Dyke Parks), 458–59
Go+ (XTC), 408–9
Go 2 (XTC), 406–10
Godard, Jean-Luc, 396–99
Godard, Vic, 432
Go-Gos, 394
"Gold Dust Woman" (Fleetwood Mac), 322
Goldman, Jon, 311
"Good-Bye Tom B" (McPhee), 348
"Good Times" (Chic), 460
Gordy, Berry, 22
Gorrie, Alan, 195
Gotobed, Robert, 396–99
"Go Your Own Way" (Fleetwood Mac), 321
GP (Parsons), 190–91
Graham, Larry, 117, 180, 183
Grateful Dead, 112–13, 217, 263; *Grateful Dead*, 263
Graves, Milford, 311, 313–17
"The Great Pretender" (Eno), 206–7
Green, Al, 150, 162–64, 337, 404–5
Grievous Angels (Parsons), 190–92
Grossman, Albert, 149, 351

Hackett, Steve, 84
Haden, Charlie, 145, 146, 384, 386
Haines, Paul, 145–47
Hair of the Dog (Nazareth), 79–80, 116
Half Japanese, 427
Halford, Rob, 470
"Half Past France" (Cale), 220
"Hallelujah Day" (Jackson 5), 22
"Handcuffs" (Parliament), 248–49
"Hand in Hand" (Costello), 379
"Hand of Doom" (Black Sabbath), 34
Handsome (Kilburn and the High Roads), 446

"Hanging Off an O" (Neon), 430
"Hanky Panky Nohow" (Cale), 220
Hard Attack (Dust), 443; *Hard Attack* (MX-80 Sound), 413–15
"The Hard Blues" (Hemphill), 134–35
"A Hard Rain's Gonna Fall" (Dylan), 282
Harkleroad, Bill "Zoot Horn Rollo," 37, 38, 43
"Harold the Barrel" (Genesis), 85
Harris, Emmylou, 190–92
Harry, Debbie, 144, 148
Harvest (Young), 232–33
"Hasta Mañana Monsieur" (Sparks), 240–41
Havens, Richie, 22, 328
"Have You Been Making Out O.K." (Green), 164
Head, Jowe, 432
Heart, 350–55, 451
Heartfield, John, 432
"Heart Love" (Ayler), 54–55
Heaven Tonight (Cheap Trick), 392–95
"Hedi's Head" (Kleenex), 428
Hell, Richard, 307–12, 333, 403
"Hello It's Me" (Rundgren), 149–50
Hemphill, Julius, 131–35, 134
Hendrix, Jimi, 1, 327, 366
Here Come the Warm Jets (Eno), 205–6
"Here in Heaven" (Sparks), 240
"Heroin" (Velvet Underground), 35
"He's a Woman, She's a Man" (Scorpions), 470
Hi-Fi Snock Uptown (Hurley), 65
Higgins, Billy, 384
"High Ideals and Crazy Dreams" (New Age Steppers), 464
"High on Rebellion" (P. Smith), 281–82
hi-hat, 25–26, 28
Hill, Andrew, 158, 315
Hill, Gary, 222–23
Hill, George Roy, 189
"Hit Me with Your Rhythm Stick" (Dury), 448–49
"Hocus Pocus" (Focus), 123–24
Hoekstra, Dave, 155–56
Holzman, Jac, 283
"Home Tonight" (Aerosmith), 293

Honeyman-Scott, James, 455
Honky Tonk Demos (Costello), 377–78
"Honky Tonk Women" (Rolling Stones), 190
Horses (P. Smith), 279–84
"Hotel California" (Eagles), 124
Hot Rocks 1964–1971 (Rolling Stones), 258
Houses of the Holy (Led Zeppelin), 172–77, 216–17
"How Do You Sleep?" (Lennon), 230
Howe, Steve, 114, 116–17, 120
Howlin' Wolf, 40, 133
How's the Weather? (Milkwood), 395
Human League, the, 427
Hunter, Meredith, 179
Hurley, Michael, 64–71
"The Hustle" (McCoy), 252–55
Hütter, Ralf, 214–15
Hynde, Chrissie, 48, 455–57
Hynie, Tomi Rae, 30

Ian Dury & the Blockheads, 445–50
"I Bizarro" (Bizarros), 422
"I Can't Stand Myself" (Brown), 30
Ice Cream for Crow (Captain Beefheart), 36
The Idiot (Iggy Pop), 47, 64
"Idiot Wind" (Dylan), 275
"I Don't Know (Satisfaction)" (Sly and the Family Stone), 181
"I Don't Want to Know" (Fleetwood Mac), 322
"I'd Rather Be with You" (Collins), 298–99
I Dreamed I Was a Very Clean Tramp (Hell), 307
"If It Were Left Up to Me" (Sly and the Family Stone), 183–84
"If I Was with a Woman" (Ian Dury & the Blockheads), 448
If Only I Could Remember My Name (Crosby), 7
"If You Want Me to Stay" (Sly and the Family Stone), 182–83
Iggy Pop, 45–49, 64, 103, 106, 331, 341
Iguanas, 45

"I Heard It Through the Grapevine" (Gaye): cover by the Slits, 337, 468

"I Love You, You Big Dummy" (Captain Beefheart), 42, 428

"I'm Eighteen" (Cooper), 108

Immune System, 427

"I'm So Free" (Reed), 105

"I'm the One" (Van Halen), 237, 367

"I'm White and Middle Class" (Urinals), 338

"Inbetweenies" (Ian Dury & the Blockheads), 449–50

Índia (Costa), 167–70

"Infant Tango" (Residents), 203

Infinity (Journey), 369

"In My Hour of Darkness" (Parsons and Harris), 191

"In the Air Tonight" (Collins), 272

"In the Beginning There Was Rhythm" (Slits), 338, 438

"In the Lap of the Gods . . . Revisited" (Queen), 237–38

"In Time" (Sly and the Family Stone), 181

Invasion of the Booty Snatchers (Parlet), 249

Iommi, Tony, 34

"Iron Man" (Black Sabbath), 34

I-Roy, 459

"I Shot the Sheriff" (Clapton), 452

"It's After the End of the World, Don't You Know That Yet?" (Sun Ra), 153

"I Wanna Find a Woman That'll Hold My Big Toe Till I Have to Go" (Captain Beefheart), 39

"I Want to Be Sedated" (Ramones), 442–43

Jackson, Michael, 4, 31, 475

Jackson 5, 22, 130

"Jaded" (Contortions), 401–2

Jagger, Mick, 47, 92–93, 179

James Brown and the J.B.'s, 28–32

"Janitor" (Suburban Lawns), 469

"Japan in a Dishpan" (Captain Beefheart), 42

Jarman, Joseph, 53, 55–56

Jarrett, Keith, 87

Jazz in Silhouette (Sun Ra), 159

"Jesus Is Just Alright" (Byrds): cover by the Doobie Brothers, 372; cover by Patti Smith, 283

Jethro Tull, 10, 264, 272, 297

"Jocko Homo" (Devo), 414

"Jocko's Lament" (Michael Hurley & Pals), 68, 71

John, Elton, 112–13, 128, 230, 256–62

"John, I'm Only Dancing" (Bowie), 258

"Johnny" (Suicide), 345

John Wesley Harding (Dylan), 277

Jones, Elvin, 144, 189

Jones, George, 163, 274, 378

Jones, Gloria, 337

Jones, Grace, 473–75

Jones, Uriel, 165

"Jones Comin Down" (Last Poets), 458

Joplin, Janis, 1, 230, 351

Jordan, Stanley, 84

Journey, 200–201, 272, 369, 371

Joy Division, 337, 413

"Joy to the World" (Three Dog Night), 234

Juba (West African dance), 23–24

Judas Priest, 470

"Julia/Moreno" (Veloso), 169

"Jumping in Gomorrah" (XTC), 409

"Jump into the Fire" (Nilsson), 73

"Jungleland" (Springsteen), 271

Just Kids (P. Smith), 284

Kansas, 200–201, 264

Kaufman, Phil, 187

Kaye, Lenny, 283–84

KC and the Sunshine Band, 254

Keith, Ben, 231–32

Kemp, Lindsay, 104

"The Key" (Mitchell), 53

Khan, Nusrat Fateh Ali, 164

"The Kid with the Replaceable Head" (Richard Hell and the Voidoids), 308

Kilburn and the High Roads, 446–47

"Killer Queen" (Queen), 237

"Killing an Arab" (Cure), 423–24

Kimono My House (Sparks), 240–41

King, Billie Jean, 260–61

King, Martin Luther, Jr., 1, 22
King Crimson, 42, 87, 115
Kinks, the, 4–5, 10, 15–18, 59, 172, 469
"Kinnel Tommy" (Banger), 421
Kirk, Rahsaan Roland, 144–45
Kiss, 111, 116, 263–67, 293, 329
Kleenex, 354, 377, 427–28, 468
"Know Your Product" (Saints), 431
"Knox" (McPhee), 348
Korris, Kate, 429
Kosuth, Joseph, 406–10
Kraftwerk, 213–15, 434, 460
Kristofferson, Kris, 188
Kuti, Fela, 300–303

"Lady Doubonette" (Bizarros), 422
Lady Gaga, 147, 256
"Land" (P. Smith), 280, 283
"Land of a Thousand Dances" (Domino/
   Pickett): cover by Patti Smith, 280
The Last Angel of History (Akomfrah),
   250–51
"Last Child" (Aerosmith), 291
Last Poets, the, 458
"A Last Straw" (Wyatt), 226
"The Last Time I Saw Richard" (Mitch-
   ell), 61
"Las Vegas" (Parsons and Harris), 191
"Layla" (Derek and the Dominos), 124,
   230
"Lay Lady Lay" (Dylan), 1, 275
Leckie, John, 406–10
Led Zeppelin, 10, 116, 142, 171–77,
   209, 216–17, 263, 290, 337, 353
Lee, Bunny, 453, 459
"Leggo Beast" (I-Roy), 459
Lennon, John, 47, 230, 367
Les Stances à Sophie (Art Ensemble of
   Chicago), 50–56
"Less than Zero" (Costello), 375
"Let Me Roll It" (McCartney), 230
L'Étranger (Camus), 405, 424
"Let's Dance" (Bowie), 272
Let's Get It On (Gaye), 164–65
Let the Buyer Beware (Bruce), 143
"Let Us Now Praise Famous Death
   Dwarves" (Bangs), 125
Lewis, Graham, 396–99

Lewis, Webster, 75–77
"Lick and a Promise" (Aerosmith), 293
Lick My Decals Off, Baby (Captain
   Beefheart), 36–44
"Light Green Fellow" (Michael Hurley
   & Pals), 67
"Linden Arden Stole the Highlights"
   (Morrison), 218–19
Lindsay, Arto, 400–405
Lipstick Traces (Marcus), 42
"Lipstick Vogue" (Costello), 379, 380
Lithman, Phil "Snakefinger," 201, 203
"Little Dreamer" (Van Halen), 367
Little Feat, 192, 220, 264, 446
"Little Green" (Mitchell), 60–61
"Little Johnny Jewel" (Television), 310
Little Queen (Heart), 350–55
"Little Red Robin Hood Hit the Road,"
   226–28
Little Sister, 183, 434
"Little Triggers" (Costello), 379
Live at Club 7 (Lewis), 75–77
Live at Mandel Hall (Art Ensemble of
   Chicago), 52, 263
Live at the Witch Trials (Fall), 437
Live in Seattle (Coltrane), 189
"Life Is Good in the Greenhouse"
   (XTC), 409
Live Stiffs Live, 424
"Lola" (Kinks), 4–5, 15–18, 469
"Lola" (Raincoats), 4–5, 469–70
"Long Time" (Boston), 287–89
Looking Glass, 329
Love Cry (Albert Ayler Trio), 311
"Love Like Anthrax" (Gang of Four),
   426–27
Love Power Peace (Brown), 31
"Love Train" (O'Jays), 128, 129
"Love und Romance" (Slits), 463
Low (Bowie-Eno), 216–17, 340–42
Lowe, Nick, 373
Ludlam, Charles, 104
"Lullaby" (Wainwright), 61
Lunch, Lydia, 400–405
Lust for Life (Iggy Pop), 47, 64
Luttenbacher, Hal, 53
Lydon, John, 430–31, 445–46. See also
   Rotten, Johnny

Lynn, Loretta, 230
Lynne, Jeff, 268

"Machine Gun" (Hendrix), 327
Mackay, Steve, 49
MacManus, Declan. *See* Costello, Elvis
Mael, Ron, 240
Mael, Russell, 239–41
Maestro Rhythm King, 181
Magazine, 377, 428
"Magic Man" (Heart), 354
Mahavishnu Orchestra, 42, 118
Mallard, 44
Manicured Noise, 429
"Man on the Move" (MX-80 Sound), 414–15
Manson Family, 3, 231–32
Mantler, Karen, 145
Mantler, Michael, 145–46
Manzanera, Phil, 224
Marcus, Greil, 42, 443
Marder, Marlene, 428
Marimba, Ed, 37, 40
Marley, Bob, 338–39
Marquee Moon (Television), 308
"Mashed Potatoes (Part 1)/Mashed Potatoes (Part 2)" (Lewis), 76–77
Mason, Nick, 224, 361
May, Brian, 143, 236–39
Mayfield, Curtis, 77, 199
MC5, 49, 283, 367
McCartney, Paul, 73, 230, 264, 451
McClennan, Tommy, 38
McCoy, Van, 252–55
McGarrigle, Kate, 62
McIntosh, Robbie, 195
McLaren, Malcolm, 6, 457
McPhee, Joe, 347–49
McPherson, Shelby, 383
McVie, Christine, 321, 323
Mead, Taylor, 104
Meat Joy (Schneeman), 46
"Meccanik Dancing (Oh We Go!)" (XTC), 408
"Meeting Across the River" (Springsteen), 271
Meet the Residents (Residents), 202–3
Melanie, 97–98, 107

Meltzer, Richard, 125
"Memories" (Public Image Ltd), 430–31
"The Men from Banana Island Whose Stupid Ideas Never Caught on in the Western World as We Know It" (Freshies), 426
Mengelberg, Misha, 89
Mercury, Freddie, 235–39
"Message in a Bottle" (Police), 453
Metal Box (Public Image Ltd), 338, 431
"Metal Postcard" (Siouxsie and the Banshees), 432
Meters, the, 194
Michael Hurley & Pals, 64–71
Milkwood, 395
Miller, Daniel, 475
Mingus (Mitchell), 381
Mingus, Charles, 144, 148, 436
Minutemen, 86, 275
Mitchell, Joni, 59–63, 230, 277, 374, 381, 462
Mitchell, Roscoe, 53, 55–56
"Mittageisen" (Siouxsie and the Banshees), 432
Mizrahi, Moshé, 53
"The Model" (Kraftwerk), 460
The Modern Dance (Pere Ubu), 412–13
Mo-Dettes, 429, 468
"Money" (Pink Floyd), 359
Monks, the, 47, 61
Monochrome Set, the, 377, 429–30
"The Moonbeam Song" (Nilsson), 73–74
"Moon in June" (Wyatt), 225–26
"Moons Shine" (Ulmer), 386–87
Moreno + 2, 169–70
More Songs about Buildings and Food (Talking Heads), 399, 403–5
Moroder, Giorgio, 344, 427
Morris, Desmond, 83, 85
Morrison, Van, 216–19, 230, 280
Morton, Rockette, 41, 43
"(Sometimes I Feel Like a) Motherless Child" (Havens), 22
Mothersbaugh, Mark "Booji Boy," 414
Mothership Connection (Parliament), 245–51
"Motion Pictures" (Young), 231

Moulding, Colin, 406–10
"Move On Up" (Mayfield), 77
Moye, Don, 52–54
Muir, Jamie, 87
Munro, Jane, 421
Murvin, Junior, 336–37
"The Musical Box" (Genesis), 83–85
Music Improvisation Company (MIC),
    The Music Improvisation Company,
    87–88
Music Typewriter (Moreno + 2), 169–70
"Muzorewi's Daughter" (Fall), 438
MX-80 Sound, 413–15
My Aim Is True (Costello), 373
"My Best Friend's Girl" (Cars), 392–95
My Life in the Bush of Ghosts (Eno-
    Byrne), 210, 404–5

Naan, Svoor, 423
Nashville Skyline (Dylan), 276–77
Nazareth, 79–80, 116
Neon, 430
"N-Er-Gee (Crisis Blues)," 203
"Never Get Enough" (Brown), 31
Never Mind the Bollocks (Sex Pistols),
    42, 333
New Age Steppers, 464
New Boots and Panties!! (Drury), 446,
    448–49
Newman, Jim, 159, 396–99
New Yardbirds, 172
New York Dolls, 106, 111, 292
Nicks, Stevie, 5, 318, 322–23
Nielsen, Rick, 392–95
Night Music, 144, 150
"Night of the Thumpasorus People"
    (Parliament), 248
"Night Train" (Brown), 236
Nilssen-Love, Paal, 75
Nilsson, Harry, 72–74; Nilsson
    Schmilsson (Nilsson), 72–74
"Non-Alignment Pact" (Pere Ubu), 412
No New York (Eno), 210, 401, 404
"No Quarter" (Led Zeppelin), 174–75
Nugent, Ted, 264, 325–31
Nuggets (Kaye and Holzman), 283
Nursery Cryme (Genesis), 80–85
Nyro, Laura, 230, 282

Oblique Strategies (Eno-Schmidt),
    204–7
Ocasek, Ric, 392–95
"The Ocean" (Led Zeppelin), 173–76
Oehlen, Albert, 428
O Guesa Errante (Sousândrade), 168
"Oh Bondage, Up Yours!" (X-Ray Spex),
    433, 439
O'Jays, the, 126–30
Olias of Sunhillow (Anderson), 116
Oliveros, Pauline, 349
"One Rose That I Mean" (Captain Beef-
    heart), 37, 43
"$1000 Wedding" (Parsons and Harris),
    191
On the Beach/"On the Beach" (Young),
    229–33
"On the Beat" (Costello), 378–79, 380
"Open Up" (Michael Hurley & Pals),
    65–66
Orr, Ben, 394–95
Osbourne, Ozzy, 34
"Outdoor Miner" (Wire), 398–99
Outlandos d'Amour (Police), 452–54

Page, Gene, 259, 261
Page, Jimmy, 10, 88, 116, 172–77, 209
Palmer, Earl, 189
Palmer, Robert, 335
Panter, Gary, 202–3
"Paranoia Perception" (Dadistics), 424
Paranoid/"Paranoid" (Black Sabbath),
    33–35
Paris 1919 (Cale), 219–21
Parker, Evan, 87, 89
Parker, Maceo, 30–31
Parker, William, 316
Parks, Van Dyke, 458–59
Parlet, 249
Parliament, 9–10, 116, 245–51, 459
Parliament-Funkadelic, 179
Parsons, Gram, 187–92, 276, 351
Partch, Harry, 201–2
Parton, Dolly, 192, 276
Partridge, Andy, 406–10
Patrick, Pat, 145, 160
Paul Butterfield Blues Band, 52, 133
"PCB's" (MX-80 Sound), 413–14

Peake, Mervyn: *Captain Slaughter-board Drops Anchor*, 83
Peckinpah, Sam, 188–89
"Peon" (Captain Beefheart), 37, 44
People in Sorrow (Art Ensemble of Chicago), 54
Pere Ubu, 201, 412–14, 423
"Perfect Day" (Reed), 105
Perry, Joe, 293
Perry, Lee "Scratch," 211–12, 250, 336, 338
Perry, Mark, 421
"Petrified Forest" (Captain Beefheart), 39
Petty, Tom. *See* Tom Petty and the Heartbreakers
"P-Funk (Wants to Get Funked Up)" (Parliament), 245–47
"Philadelphia Freedom" (John), 128, 258–61
"Pick Up the Pieces One by One" (Average White Band), 194–96
"The Pictures on My Wall" (Echo & the Bunnymen), 424–25
"Pigs on the Wing (Part 1)" (Pink Floyd), 361
Pinball Wizard (John), 258, 262
Pink Flag (Wire), 397
Pink Floyd, 297, 356–62
Pink Moon/"Pink Moon" (Drake), 137–38
"Plaistow Patricia" (Ian Dury & the Blockheads), 447
"Planet Queen" (T. Rex), 147–48
Plant, Robert, 10, 116, 176, 354, 378, 470
Playing with a Different Sex (Au Pairs), 421
"Play That Funky Music White Boy" (Wild Cherry), 194
"Please, Please, Please" (Brown), 28
Police, the, 451–55
"Police and Thieves" (Clash), 335–37, 338
"Police and Thieves" (Murvin), 336–37
Political Writings (Gramsci), 431
Pollitt, Tessa, 462
Poly Styrene, 433
Pop, Iggy. *See* Iggy Pop

Pop Group, the, 338, 430, 461–66
"Poptones" (Public Image Ltd), 338
"Post-War Glamour Girl" (Clarke), 422–23
"Power to the People" (P. Smith), 284
"Precious" (Pretenders), 455–56
Presley, Elvis, 9, 46, 276, 336
Preston, Don, 146–47
Pretenders, the, 455–57, 474; *Pretenders II* (Pretenders), 457
Prime Time, 384, 386
Prince, 467, 475
Prince Far I, 338
Prince Jazzbo, 459
"Printhead" (Fall), 438
"Private Life" (Pretenders), 456–57, 474
Propaganda (Sparks), 240
"Proverbes I, II, III" (Art Ensemble of Chicago), 53–54
"Psycle Sluts (Parts 1 & 2)" (Clarke), 422–23, 426
"Psykick Dance Hall" (Fall), 440
Public Enemy, 460
Public Image Ltd (PiL), 337–38, 430–31
"Punky Reggae Party" (Marley), 338–39
Purdie, Bernard "Pretty," 55
"Put a Straw Under Baby" (Eno), 207, 224

Q: Are We Not Men? A: We Are Devo! (Devo), 411–12
"Que, Sera, Sera" (Sly and the Family Stone), 181
Queen, 106, 124, 142, 234–39, 264, 369, 460, 470
Quine, Robert, 308–9

Ra, Sun. *See* Sun Ra
"Radio Radio" (Costello), 375
Raincoats, the, 4–5, 421, 429, 469–70
"Raindrops Keep Falling on My Head" (Bacharach and David), 4, 189
Ramone, Marky, 442–43
Ramone, Tommy, 442
Ramones, 441–44
"Rapper's Delight" (Sugarhill Gang), 460

"Rats in the Cellar" (Aerosmith), 291–92

Ray, Danny, 28

"Read It in Books" (Echo and Teardrop), 425

"Reality Asylum" (Crass), 423

Reckless (Hynde), 457

Redbone, 194

"Red Ravagers Reel" (Michael Hurley & Pals), 66

Reed, Lou, 97–105, 125, 271, 470

Reggatta de Blanc/"Regatta de Blanc" (Police), 452–54

Reid, Duke, 210

Remaily, Robin, 66

Renegade (P. Smith), 436–40

"Repetition" (Fall), 439

"Rescue Me" (Bass), 50, 133

Residents, the, 200–203

"Return of the Grievous Angel" (Parsons), 191–92

Rev, Martin, 343–44

"Revelation March" (Ulmer), 386

"Revolution 9" (Beatles), 202, 223

"Revolution Blues" (Young), 231–32

Richard Hell and the Voidoids, 307–12, 333, 443

Rimbaud, Penny, 423

Rizzo, Frank (mayor), 130

Road to Ruin (Ramones), 442–43

Robinson, Vicki Sue, 223

"Rock and Roll, Hoochie Koo" (Derringer), 121

Rock Bottom (Wyatt), 224–28

"Rock 'n' Roll High School" (Ramones), 443–44

Rocks (Aerosmith), 290–94

"Rock with You" (Jackson), 4

Rodgers, Jimmie, 9

Rodgers, Nile, 460

Roeg, Nicolas, 183

Rolling Stones, 45, 91–94, 116, 172, 179, 190, 258, 308, 339, 431

Rolling Thunder Revue, 277

Ronstadt, Linda, 145, 146, 190, 451

Roth, David Lee, 366–67, 370, 378

Rotten, Johnny, 42, 47, 232, 337, 361, 432

Rotters, the, 5

"Roundabout" (Yes), 118

"Rufus Is a Tit Man" (Wainwright), 62

Rumours (Fleetwood Mac), 319–24

Rundgren, Todd, 147–50, 351–52, 393

Run DMC, 292

Rutles, the, 203

"Safety-Pin Stuck in My Heart" (Fitzgerald), 425–26

Sain, Oliver, 133–35

Saints, the, 431

Santa Dog (Residents), 201

Saturday Night! (Schoolly D), 460

Saturday Night Live, 143–44, 269, 374–75, 413, 414

Savage, Jon, 428

Schiele, Egon, 341

Schiff, Klaudia, 428

Schmidt, Peter, 204–9

Schneeman, Carolee, 46

Schneider, Florian, 214–15

Schoolly D, 460

School's Out/"School's Out" (Cooper), 108–10

Scorpions, 470

Scorsese, Martin, 183

Scott, Bon, 11

Scritti Politti, 431

"Sea Song" (Wyatt), 225

Seshadri, Ganesh "Bid," 429

"Sex & Drugs & Rock & Roll" (Drury), 446

Sex Machine (Brown), 263

Sex Pistols, 232, 332–33, 374–75, 432, 439, 455

"Shake Your Ashes" (Cherry Vanilla), 104

Sha Na Na, 266–67

Shankar, Ravi, 141–42

"Sheep" (Pink Floyd), 360

Sheer Heart Attack (Queen), 237–39

"She Is Beyond Good and Evil" (Pop Group), 464–65

"She Makes Me (Stormtrooper in Stilettoes)" (Queen), 237

Shepp, Archie, 54–55

"Shivers" (Boys Next Door), 422

Short Circuit—Live at the Electric Circus (Clarke), 422–23
"Sick as a Dog" (Aerosmith), 293
Sievey, Chris, 426
Simmons, Gene, 265–66
Simon, Carly, 230
Simon, Paul, 19, 451, 452
Simon & Garfunkel, 19
Simonon, Paul, 334–35
Simpkins, Nigel, 431–32
Sing, Regula, 428
"Sit on My Face Stevie Nicks" (Rotters), 5
"(Sittin' on) The Dock of the Bay" (Redding): cover by Thursdays, 337
"Skank Bloc Bologna" (Scritti Politti), 431
"Sleeping Gas" (Teardrop Explodes), 433
Slits, the, 334, 337–38, 429, 461–66, 468
Sly and Robbie, 474–75
Sly and the Family Stone, 178–84, 194, 207, 458
Small Wonder label, 87, 423, 425
Smith, Mark E., 10, 48, 397, 436–40
Smith, Michael Lee, 329–30, 331
Smith, Patti, 279–84, 310, 354, 422
Smith, Robert, 424
"The Smithsonian Institute Blues" (Captain Beefheart), 39
Snakefinger (Phil Lithman), 201, 203
"Snap It Around" (48 Chairs), 426
Snyder, John, 382–84
Soft Machine, 225
Solo Guitar (Bailey), 89–90
Something / Anything? (Rundgren), 149–50
Soul Train, 128–29, 194, 195
Soundtracks, Epic, 432
Sousândrade, 168
"Space Age Couple" (Captain Beefheart), 39
Space Is the Place/"Space Is the Place" (Sun Ra), 150, 153, 159–61
Sparks, 239–41
"Spectre vs. Rector" (Fall), 438
Spiral Scratch (Buzzcocks), 376, 428
Spiritual Unity (Albert Ayler Trio), 311

Springsteen, Bruce, 270–72, 283, 344, 374
Square, Lester, 429
Squire, Chris, 114, 116–17
"The Squirrel and the Ricketty-Racketty Bridge" (Bryars), 89–90
Stanley, Paul, 265–66
Starks, John "Jabo," 25–28
Starr, Edwin, 19–24
Starz, 328–30
Steely Dan, 7, 55, 124, 148, 217, 433
Steigman, Steven, 124
Stevens, Cat, 137, 288
Stewart, Mark, 430, 464
Stewart, Rod, 272, 451
Sticky Fingers (Rolling Stones), 91–94
Stiff Records, 373, 415, 446
Sting, 451–54
Stone, Sylvester. *See* Sly and the Family Stone
"Stone Cold Crazy" (Queen), 237
Stooges, the, 45–49, 179
"Stormtroopin'" (Nugent), 327–28
Stranger in the House/"Stranger in the House" (Costello), 378
Stretchin' Out in Bootsy's Rubber Band (Collins), 298–99
Strummer, Joe, 334–35
"The Studio as Compositional Tool" (Eno), 209
Studio One, 210
"Submerged" (Immune System), 427
"Subterraneans" (Bowie-Eno), 342
Suburban Lawns, 469
Subway Sect, 432
Sudden, Nikki, 432
"Sugar Cane Fields Forever" (Veloso), 168
Sugarhill Gang, 460
Suicide, 310, 343–46; *Suicide* (Suicide), 343–46
"Suicide" (Dust), 443
Summers, Andy, 453, 455
Sun Ra, 52–53, 145, 150–61, 202, 310
Sun Ra's Arkestra, 49, 154, 157–58
"Super Bad" (Brown), 30
"Supergroovalisticprosifunkstication" (Parliament), 248
"Super Sporm" (Captain Sky), 460

Supertramp, 200–201, 272
"Surrender" (Cheap Trick), 393
"Survive" (Bags), 421
"Sweedeedee" (Michael Hurley &
    Pals), 68
Sweet, 106
"Sweet Dragon" (McPhee), 348
"Sweet So Till" (Gladiators), 212
Swell Maps, 432
Szwed, John: *Space Is the Place: The
    Lives and Times of Sun Ra*, 159,
    160

Tacuma, Jamaaladeen (Rudy McDan-
    iel), 386, 387–89
"Tainted Love" (Jones): cover by Soft
    Cell, 337
"Take Me to the River" (Green): cover
    by Talking Heads, 337, 404–5
Taking Tiger Mountain (By Strategy)
    (Eno), 205–9, 224
Tales of Captain Black (Ulmer), 383–89
Talking Heads, 210, 337, 399–405, 429
"Tammy" (P. Smith), 283
"Tangled Up in Blue" (Dylan), 275, 277
"Tattooed Love Boys" (Pretenders), 456
Taub, Andy, 150
Taupin, Bernie, 230, 257–60
Taylor, Roger, 143, 237
Teardrop Explodes, the, 424–25, 433
Television, 283, 308
Templeman, Ted, 366
Temptations, the, 22, 179
"Tenement Funster" (Queen), 237
Tenor (McPhee), 347–49
"Thank God It's Not Christmas"
    (Sparks), 241
"Thank You (Falettinme Be Mice Elf
    Agin)" (Graham), 386
"Theme Amour Universal" (Art En-
    semble of Chicago), 53
"Theme de Celine" (Art Ensemble of
    Chicago), 53
"Theme de Yoyo" (Art Ensemble of Chi-
    cago), 50–52, 54–56
"Theme Libre" (Art Ensemble of Chi-
    cago), 54
There's a Riot Goin' On (Sly and the
    Family Stone), 178–82, 458

"These Boots Are Made for Walkin'"
    (Sinatra), 203
"Thief of Fire" (Pop Group), 338, 465
"Third Uncle" (Eno), 207–8
"30 Seconds Over Tokyo" (Pere Ubu),
    412
"This Town Ain't Big Enough for Both
    of Us" (Sparks), 241
This Year's Model (Costello), 379, 380
Thomas, B. J., 4, 189
Thomas, Bruce, 379–80
Thomas, Chris, 220
Thomas, David, 412
Thomas, Pete, 380
Thompson, Hunter S., 121, 143
Thompson, Linda, 190
Thompson, Richard, 190
Thompson, Winston (Dr. Alimantado),
    211
Three Dog Night, 234, 337
"Thunder Road" (Springsteen), 270
"The Tide Is High" (Paragons): cover by
    Blondie, 337
"Times Encounter" (Simpkins), 431–32
Tin Huey, 433
"Tiny Dancer" (John), 257, 260
Titus, Libby, 149–50
"Tomorrow Never Knows" (Beatles),
    223
Tom Petty and the Heartbreakers, 141,
    195, 308, 475
Tormato (Yes), 114–15
"Torn and Frayed" (Rolling Stones), 190
Toys in the Attic (Aerosmith), 290–91
Transformer (Reed), 100–105
T. Rex, 103, 144, 147–50, 300–301;
    T. Rex (T. Rex), 301
A Trick of the Tail (Genesis), 81–82
Tripp, Art "Ed Marimba," 37, 40
"Troglodyte" (Castor), 469–70
"Troubled Waters" (Michael Hurley &
    Pals), 68
Trout Mask Replica (Captain Beef-
    heart), 36, 41, 43, 201
The Truth about De-Evolution (Devo),
    415–16
2 Tone label, 377, 424
Tyler, Steven, 290–93, 329, 354
Tyson, June, 160

Uehlinger, Werner X., 347
Ulmer, James "Blood," 245, 383–89
"Unfunky UFO" (Parliament), 247
Up, Ari, 462, 464
"Up, Up and Away" (5th Dimension),
    19, 20
"Up the Neck" (Pretenders), 456

"Vampire Blues" (Young), 232
Van der Graaf Generator, 81, 264
Van Halen, Alex, 366–67, 370
Van Halen, Eddie, 10, 84, 237, 365–72
Van Halen, *Van Halen*, 365–72
van Leer, Thijs, 123–24
Van Vliet, Don, 36, 41, 43–44
"Variations Sur un Theme de Mon-
    teverdi (I, II, III)" (Art Ensemble of
    Chicago), 53
Veedon Fleece (Morrison), 217–19
Vega, Alan, 343–46
Veloso, Caetano, 9, 168–70
Veloso, Moreno, 169–70
Velvet Donkey (Cutler), 83, 227–28
Velvet Underground, 35, 220, 279, 308
Verlaine, Tom, 279–80, 307, 310
Vibing Up the Senile Man (Alternative
    TV), 420–21
Vibrators, 376, 398
Vincent, Gene, 438, 448
"Violence Grows" ("Fatal" Microbes),
    425
Virgin Records, 337–38, 406, 408
Visconti, Tony, 341–42
V2 (Vibrators), 398

Wainwright, Loudon, III, 61–62
"The Wait" (Pretenders), 456
"Waiting for Your Taxi" (Ian Dury & the
    Blockheads), 449
Wakeman, Rick, 114–18, 172
"Walking on the Moon" (Police), 453
"Walk on the Wild Side" (Reed), 101, 103
The Wall (Pink Floyd), 357
"War" (Starr), 19–24
Ward, Bill, 34
Warhol, Andy, 105; Warhol's Factory,
    101
Warm Leatherette (Jones), 473–75

"Warm Leatherette" (Miller), 475
"War Pigs" (Black Sabbath), 34, 327
"Warszawa" (Bowie-Eno), 342
Waters, Roger, 360, 361
Watkins, Judd, 76
Watson, Doc, 8–9
"We Are the Champions" (Queen), 238
Weatherhole (Hurley), 65
Webster Lewis and the Post-Pop Space-
    Rock Be-Bop Gospel Tabernacle
    Chorus and Orchestra BABY!,
    75–77
Wechter, Julius, 37
Weinberg, Max, 272
"Werewolf" (Michael Hurley & Pals),
    66–67, 69
West Side Stories (documentary),
    282–83
"We Will Rock You" (Queen), 238
"Whatcha See Is Whatcha Get" (Dra-
    matics), 239
"Whatever Happened to Us" (Wain-
    wright), 61–62
What's Going On (Gaye), 179
"Where There's a Will . . ." (Pop Group),
    430
White, Alan, 114
White, Barry, 75, 298
White, Clarence, 191
White Album (*The Beatles*), 19, 202
Whitehead, Paul, 83–84, 85
"White Lightning" (Jones), 163
"White Mice" (Mo-Dettes), 429
"White Riot" (Clash), 333–37
Whitney, Marva, 30–31
Why Do Things Get in a Muddle? (Hill),
    222–23
"Wife in Reverse" (Dixon), 222
Wild Cherry, 9, 194
"Wild Horses": Gram Parsons, 190;
    Rolling Stones, 190
Williams, Hank, 163, 274, 276, 378
Willner, Hal, 142–50
Wilson, Ann, 352–55
Wilson, Nancy, 352–55
Winter, Edgar, 121–25
Winter, Johnny, 121
Wire, 332, 396–99

"Without You" (Badfinger): cover by
    Harry Nilsson, 73
Wobble, Jah, 430–31
"Woe-Is-Uh-Me-Bop" (Captain Beef-
    heart), 40
Wolff, James, 150
Wonder, Stevie, 75, 166
Woodlawn, Holly, 101
Woods, Lesley, 421
Worrell, Bernie "Wizard of Woo," 248,
    292
Wright, Jimmy, 99–107
Wurlitzer, Rudolph, 188
Wyatt, Robert, 222–28, 431, 469

X. Enc. (Simpkins), 431–32
X-Ray Spex, 354, 433, 439, 468
XTC, 406–10

Y (Pop Group), 463–66
Yes, 80, 114–20, 263
Yo! Bum Rush the Show (Public
    Enemy), 460
"Yonki Time" (Verlaine), 310
"You" (Au Pairs), 421
"You Are the Sunshine of My Life"
    (Wonder), 166

"You Belong to Me" (Costello), 379
"You Don't Pull No Punches, but You
    Don't Push the River" (Morrison),
    217
"You Got to Have a Job (You Don't
    Work, You Don't Eat)" (Whitney),
    30–31
Young, Jesse Colin, 64–65, 66
Young, Neil, 189, 209, 229–33, 462
Youngbloods, 64–65
Young Marble Giants, 433–34
"You're All I've Got Tonight" (Cars), 394
"You Really Got Me" (Kinks): cover by
    Van Halen, 10, 366
"You're Gonna Get Yours" (Public
    Enemy), 460
"You're So Vain" (Simon), 230
"Your Heart Out" (Fall), 438, 439

Zappa, Frank, 41, 64–65, 147, 217, 380
"Ziggy Stardust" (Bowie), 258, 341
Zombie (Fela and Afrika '70), 301–3
Zoot Horn Rollo, 37, 38, 43
"Zulu" (Bohannon), 459
ZZ Top, 92, 451